Eco-Urbanism and the South East Asian City

Shireen Jahn Kassim
Noor Hanita Abdul Majid
Dzulkifli Abdul Razak
Editors

Eco-Urbanism and the South East Asian City

Climate, Urban-Architectural Form
and Heritage

Editors
Shireen Jahn Kassim
Architecture and Enviroment
International Islamic University Malaysia
Kuala Lumpur, Malaysia

Noor Hanita Abdul Majid
Kulliyyah of Archi & Environ Design
International Islamic Univ Malaysia
Selangor, Malaysia

Dzulkifli Abdul Razak
Rector's Office
International Islamic University Malaysia
Kuala Lumpur, Malaysia

ISBN 978-981-19-1636-6   ISBN 978-981-19-1637-3   (eBook)
https://doi.org/10.1007/978-981-19-1637-3

This Palgrave Macmillan imprint is published by the registered company Springer Nature Singapore Pte Ltd.
The registered company address is: 152 Beach Road, #21-01/04 Gateway East, Singapore 189721, Singapore

Preface

In South East Asia, past urban-architectural traditions—highly influenced by both local and external factors and working as palimpsest—were written by a range of global and local scholars. In the past, it is the architectural dimension and perspective that had been linked to lessons from heritage, the vernacular, the indigenous archetypes and climate. There is a chasm in terms of what constitutes underlying patterns in urban design, identity and planning. This book attempts to condense such multi-field urbanist perspectives in terms of rerouting it back to heritage and climate of place and thus can potentially be the starting point of a discourse that would continue for many decades to come.

While these fields are not normally linked to 'eco -urbanism'—which is a recent discourse, trending frameworks and theorisation of how modern urbanism can be reconciled with sustainability and ecology—the layered urbanism of South East Asian urban history contains a past which is infused with references to the local natural ecosystem and the natural environments. Thus, this demands a relook into the past and a reframing of past investigations by local scholars. Uncovering a triadic discourse traversing planning, urban design and the visual arts, this book attempts to overcome historical gaps in knowledge and based on delineating archetypes and common patterns, it becomes clear how, across centuries, urban-architectural forms have worked with the topographic, aquatic and geomorphic nature of the South East Asian archipelago, rather than against it. Perhaps to its nature as a dispersed archipelago of land and sea, with densed jungles teeming with life, its urban heritage and local forms had become infused with references to the nature and climate. The nature of historic urban communities in the region itself, filled with cities and communities straddling the littoral, the riverine and the coastal, that is, between 'land, sea, mountains and thick forest' have bred a consciousness in the populations and its planners, builders and artisans, in such a way that nature and ecology have become embedded and littered onto its urban heritage, that is, urbanism, from the macro to the micro.

Urban design and urban settlement have become the centre of the discourse in architectural history and theory of the region for many decades. The book does not present new archaeo-urban historical discoveries or findings, but rather summates and observes overall character and perspectives, thus balancing the past academic and scholarship skewing towards the Western-based ideas and viewpoints, with insufficient and sporadic instances of looking back into tradition as a solution to contemporary problems. Theories and pattern of cities must suggest pathways that are regional if not local, based on local phenomena, and it is high time to look for a local narrative that surrounds the region amongst the increasing urban theories around the world. From that point of view this book addresses a widely forgotten or under-represented episode of the history of human settlement and includes the Malay world or the 'Nusantara'. Compiling individual authors' work under key themes and references to climate and urban architectural form and connecting the past to the contemporary, the book intends towards a contribution in this field of theory and practice. By realigning a focus on planning, urban design and visual history, aside from architecture, there is a range of narratives. These can be seen as complementing and extending from prior scholarship revolving more on the historic process of colonisation and pre-colonisation. The book thus intends to question what is borrowed, authentic and reconstituted as identity through time and space. The significant contribution is aimed by addressing the problem from different levels both vertically (Macro to Micro) and laterally (Tradition, Theory and Practice) and making accessible and summating those from the local scholars who share the same worldview. The chapters are organised keeping this idea of layers in its history and different levels of investigation.

The question of how cities and towns can capitalise on their indige-nous and cultural resources and legacies, to activate a more sustainable future, brings forward a two-fold conundrum, how can such agendas reconcile with developments and how can its regional histories be lever-aged to achieve the rising ecological concerns in urban design and archi-tecture. The rise of eco-urbanist trends and praxis as a way of planning and designing brings forth the need to rethink urban design, planning and architecture place-identity to respond to the local concerns in urban design and architecture, including the need to consider the city as a whole and its significance in historic urban landscapes of communities. In this book, cultural-historical process and heritage of cities are seen as path-ways and tropes towards achieving ecological urban planning and urban design—including architecture—where climatic considerations, which are intrinsic in the historical urban structure and heritages forms, must contribute to the sustainability and identity of the cities.

Ecological urbanism or eco-urbanism is a rising movement which draws from elements of ecology to inspire an urbanism that is more socially inclusive and sensitive to the environment. South East Asia is positioned to shed light on its eco-urbanist ethos found in its pre-colonial forms, from which the 'vernacular' has been recognised for its bioclimatic credential, yet whose planning and urban design have merely said to be 'informal' and 'organic' without further elucidation and discourse. Yet not only architecture but urban forms have, in many cases, local biocli-matic integrity and recall age-old principles of climate. Unfortunately, these have been forgotten and altered drastically in the rush to embrace modern interventions and influences. The book argues that to return to a study of indigenous archetypes in urbanism is an embrace of a sustainable urbanism, an approach that must privilege the city as culture and climatic form. Its cultural (including design) implications remain largely unex-plored, and one must be able to negotiate a difficult path between ecosys-tem and urbanity. Pre-colonial urban patterns in South East Asia, which resonate traits of eco-urbanism, have been typically branded as 'formless' and 'unplanned'. Its characteristics, traits, structures, forms and adapta-tions that arise from aspects such as topography and climate broadly align with ecosystems found in the natural world. As the world becomes increasingly urban, that is, 70 per cent of the world's growing population projected to reach 9.8 billion people by the middle of this century, a theoretical foundation to design and build cities must meet these challenges while enhancing the human experience of urban life. The ecology (including topography, vegetation and water) must align increasingly with the anthropogenic—that is, made by humans (including buildings, infrastructure and culture).

South East Asian cities are crucial as they mostly lie within the littoral and the tropically and heavily forested regions of the world. Their urban patterns and urban sites have evolved through an adjacency and awareness of water, earth and flora, through centuries of 'layering' and within its histories. Thus, the triadic thrust of the chapters revolves around urban design topics, and the authors have tried their best to link or weave into the discussion towards the significance of these heritage patterns which recall past climatic intuitive and wisdoms to contemporary concerns and agendas. In doing so, the aim is to shine light on the undeniable links that the histories of these past forms and patterns of cities and structures with the local ecology and climatic conditions. By doing this, there is a renewed emphasis on the intangible—whether 'macro' to 'micro'. In relation to the field of historic landscape approach which is seen as part of the cultural processes of the local people, yet the discussions do embrace macro-wide findings including cultural, natural, tangible and intangible, before these proceed to the 'micro', that is, more visual and experiential aspects of the physical morphology of cities and the image of the city will underpin the fundamental concept of this region, a series of layers of eco-urbanist histories through time that link past, present and future as in the construct of its cultural landscape. The flow of the book begins with presenting and compiling key mappings of urban morphologies, followed by architectural typologies, and ends with themes in symbolic items and iconography, which culturally define and geographically differentiate the identity of the region. Each theme is then linked to relevance to present eco-urbanist concerns and frameworks, combining ethos such as compactness, climate, diversity, landscape, climatic design and ecology.

This book leverages upon the resources of a wide range of earlier studies and research on the morphological, the architectural and the artisanal. These narratives reveal the 'eco-urbanist' nuances and leanings which constitute part of the tangible and intangible attributes of place. The effort is not merely to share historical findings but to identify patterns which, in the littoral history of the South East Asian region, are often a palimpsest that have been diffused, even erased, through time. To contribute to a more locally rooted emerging theory of localised urban design and place-making, a discourse on the formations, configurational and formal character of the nature-based themes in these sites must be consolidated and reconceptualised in the pursuit of striking the optimal balance between 'man' and 'nature, where living beings as both animal, vegetation lived in balanced equipoise with man.

The structuring of chapters according to macro and micro themes begins with macro scale issues, such as urban planning and design. The structure re-enacts a discourse to combine the past efforts to reconstruct morphologies, typologies archetypes, images, and intersperses, these findings with learned principles, patterns and praxis that constitute to identified 'ethos', to ensure a continuous discourse in theory from macro to micro. Part I looks at topics related to urban planning and morphological relevance, as these chapters condense findings and discourses that characterise the 'pre-colonial' in terms of morphological layering of urban centres. Archaeological, social and archival sources are part of the process to suggest themes and theories before extensive external influences and pressures are exerted endlessly on the historical forms and processes. This includes the historic forces related to colonisation which conflates with rapid urbanisation, thus complicating the city as layers or as palimpsests, as urban-architectural forms have been 'sedimented' or layered upon.

Part II, which focuses on architecture and space the interplay between form, material and construction are seen as essential 'forces' which have shaped local forms of space and planning. Space is seen as an identity tool and the archetypes which differentiate tropical Asia whether macro or micro space, urban or architectural space, are discussed.

Part III then focuses on visual forms including symbolisms and ornamental patterns and argues that these patterns are crucial as they inherently imbue the physical with the consciousness, value-sets, beliefs and emotive dimension of the locality. The link with formal findings in Part I and Part II is discussed. In some chapters, the authors try their best to link or weave into the conclusions generic link with identity and eco-urbanism agendas. The macro-wide findings including cultural, natural, tangible and intangible and proceed to the 'micro', which offers broader, more visual and experiential aspects of urban design.

Each theme is linked to relevance to present eco-urbanist concerns and frameworks yet inflected towards the ecological and the climatic. Though these sometimes referred to as the 'vernacular' or ruralised, the book goes beyond this field to argue that the themes are part of a distinctive urban framework that embodies the wide praxis of 'eco-urbanism' which is less assertive and gentler to the environment. The editors concur that there is a difference in the scale of past and present cities, yet there are lessons learnt that can guide present policies and practices. Thus, there is a weaving of these mindsets into theoretical discourses that can create complexity and room for debate. Thus, the aim is a historical-cultural evolutionary type discourse but one laced and intertwined with contemporary yet relevant eco-urbanist concerns, including climatic design, currently raging in current debates and writings.

In Chapter 1, the authors Shireen Jahn Kassim, and Kamariah Kamaruddin refer to the 'eco–mandalic' as underlying patterns which refer to the four-square cardinal directional alignment of cities resonating with daily and annual sun paths, however, later are inflected with other influences. Seen in the reconstructions of the urban cores mainly from the Nusantara corpus, through mapping of urban cores, and the aim is to reconcile, by a delineation of what constitutes the local urbanism and the traditional city axial or directional precepts under these contexts. An understanding of the layering of cities or historic findings and past research on forms is essential in laying the base for proceeding arguments. It connects certain mapping results on the residual influences of climatic forces. Chapter 2 focuses on the river, where Illyani Ibrahim, Kamariah Kamaruddin and Nyimas Umi focus on the interactions between the river, the related urban fabric and its climatic effects as they delve into the morphologies of traditional cities, whose urban grain alignment and orientation of urban settlements can be read not only as functional and economic, but as climatic, showing the simultaneous impact and influence of the convergence of rivers, onto wind-driven, ventilative and cooling potentials of the river and canals as cooling mechanisms. In Chap. 3, the journey of identifying nodes and datums in urban design begins with Nurhaya Baniyamin, Mazarina Zain and Shireen Jahn Kassim's characterisation of 'mounds' to include mountains and hills as critical panoramic datums and avatars, and its geomorphological significance represents an identity and marker in the urban landscape. Not only do they stand out in the archipelagic 'land and sea' consciousness, but their profiled forms slowly resonate into local symbolisms. In Chap. 4, Nor Zalina Harun presents landscape as a critical historic identity conceptualisation of the Nusantara city in which the notion of the garden is crucial to city form and highlights how the curated garden in Asia is seen as a resistance to the jungle, as a hindrance to encroaching dangers. These gardens are seen not only as manicured forms, but in their productive capacity and as tangible heritage. In Chap. 5, Shireen Jahn Kassim retraces the local definition and the genealogy of the *Alun Alun*, as she muses over past attempts to link the local *padang* with the colonial and external archetypes. It suggests that, locally, there is a particular nuanced morphological form and character of the *alun alun* which evolve from the local roots of the constant celebration of the garden and from an intuitive fragmentation that affords breathability. Thus, the cross-cultural reading of its genesis and evolution is beset by multiple rhizomic influences that had added to confusions as to the genesis of its form. In Chap. 6, Illyani Ibrahim shifts again the discussion to the character of compactness in the local urban core and argues that the eco-urbanist compactness is an intrinsic character of pre-colonial cities. The notion of intimacy and nearness has also explained about relation between man and thing. The nearness can be used to describe the social and culture of such people in the particular place. In Chap. 7, Noorhanita Abdul Majid highlights the interesting junctures between the fauna and the traditional city, focusing on the Malay Archipelago's (the Nusantara) historical traditions replete with mentions and incidences featuring local fauna and varied species of animals. Animals, whatever significance or function to man, have been part of a city's ecological identity, pattern and growth. The South East Asian traditional city carries an almost sacred resonance in terms of being sites or 'sanctuaries' that had celebrated animals. The ecology of such cities was intertwined with the very nature of their spatial boundaries featuring animals' involvement in the planning of streets and orientation of layouts of buildings, which accommodated the routes and whose dimensions made way for animals used for transport.

The architectural discourse and themes of the book open in Part II, with Chap. 8 'The Sacred Charge and Center', in which Shireen Jahn Kassim and Mansor Ibrahim attempt to weave the macro and the micro, the regional and local, notion of the sacred centre that is reverberated in both the macro and micro scale of urbanism in the Malay Archipelago. The centre is seen not only in one location but as core of regions and geography. The idea of the sacred is then filtered down to architecture and is characterised as pillared spaces. The notions of the centre, the pillared dimensions of space and place, evolved into the notions of the sacred centre. The centre was a social and spatial conjoining of power and hierarchy. Thus, this brings to Chap. 9, in which Noorhanita Abdul Majid further extends this idea into differentiated 'punctured pavilions' which is argued as critical to urban identity of cities. She brings to the fore how the idea of the tropical city must be a pavilion-based and thus a 'punctured' one. The chapter highlights varied forms of tropical pavilion which is a common evolving form, its function and variations. It traces this historic archetype not only as transitional space with defining architectonic elements such as varied pillars-column bracket systems. In Chap. 10, Norwina Mohd Nawawi and Shaiful Nadzri Samsuddin focus fully on architecture and pose that the house has, forms a powerful archetype across type and the critical vernacular interpretations of the house vernacular as archetype could even be translated into praxis in tropical urban design ideations arising from essences of climatic elements. In Chap. 11, Azizi Bahauddin sheds light on a different spatial tradition of residential space in 'Matriarchy and Space. In the case of the linear Minangkabau 'Architectural' Planning and Layout', which is both climatic and sustainable in terms of space. Matriarchy is not a construct based on the gendered division of power, but a principle manifested in space and architectural layout, which is based on gendered divisions in the sociocultural patterns and cosmological orders. Deeply rooted in cultural affinities, the Minangkabau is linked to an analysis that arises from its matrilineality, matrilineal authority and the people's understanding of designing architecture that is in harmony with nature.

In Chap. 12, Tengku Anis and Nurhaya Baniyamin argue that a wide range of portico types are found in aristocratic structures and arise from varied internal zoning of functions and spaces. They assert that all public spaces are spatially 'Bioclimatic Thresholds' which can be classified into a large corpus of public space extracted from different sites and eras. This series of conceptualisations of tropicalised porticoes, walkways and promenades with different projections of open spaces on the ground floor is culturally inflected vision of the climatic 'tropical verandah'. There are variants of hybridity (timber-masonry character) which combine the 'heavy' and the 'light', that is, pointing to differences in stereotomy (earth-bound) plinths, differences in positioning and width of tropical recesses and walkways with 'shade' interspersed with opaque elements. In Chap. 13, Siti Norzaini and Harlina Shariff discuss the tropical character of the Nusantara mosque focusing on the shadowed nature of its daylit spaces, a result of its traditional tiered roof forms. It highlights that natural shadowed light, with the reflections from these tiered forms, causes a certain pattern of shade and light, which is particular to the region's traditional typology. In Chap. 14, Elias Salleh, Kamariah Kamaruddin and Shireen Jahn Kassim further suggest how such local models and templates can mutate into tropical models of 'encultured' streetscapes for the city and under denser conditions, facadescapes and walkways which can potentially become 'socio-cultural' activators of economic activities via a range of urban scape strategies as resources of urban design. In Chap. 15, 'Marking the Perimeter: Southeast Asian Gateways' by Noorhanita Abdul Majid, Shireen Jahn Kassim Shamsul Bahrin Buyong and Juliana Abu Bakar highlight an important symbol in the local public realm where the gateways and bridges have marked entrances into specific zones. These reflect a unique and individual morphology and form. In general, the gateway somehow condenses the history of a society in a time frame that flashes back to its initiation into a civilisation from a structured society.

Part III begins with Chap. 16, 'Ecologic Patterns and the Regalia: Tropical Symbolisms in the City' in which Tengku Anis, Puteri Mayang and Shireen Jahn Kassim present a reading of architectural language and embellishments by using Semper's four principles of architecture. It forwards an idea and argument of how the notion of the hearth can be translated into the tropical Southeast Asian context. Chapter 17, by Ismail Jasmani, Zumahiran Kamaruddin and Shireen Jahn Kassim, summarises the whole range of embellishments and surface 'pattern resources' with eco-urbanist underlying forms reflecting 'land and sea' or 'air, ecology and water are seen in artisanal products whose motifs range from patterns of leaves, stems, tendrils and motifs of birds and animals abstracted and stylised into patterns of built form such as woodcarving, roof spires, decorative eaves, moulded staircases and ventilative panels. In Chap. 18, Agung and Muhd Qies suggest forms that can localise typography by looking at historical forms and present streetscapes and community practices, which focus on Indonesia. Throughout the book, there is a reference to previous studies (by others and by the authors) focusing on the efforts of re-estimation of the original layer and to reconstruct arguably how such local identifications can be differentiated from the historic forms due to the process of colonisation. In Chap. 19, Dzulkifli Abdul Razak closes the book by summating and posing ruminations of the South East Asian city as drawing from its histories to strategically advise its potential towards net zero carbon impact at macro levels in terms of urban form, space and architecture. A real-life example is seen in the Sejahtera Complex in South Korea, where such sustainability values are realised and maintained in the micro level of daily cycles and lifestyles of the users, occupants and practitioners of the Sejahtera Complex.

The historical research that went into preparation of the book was a strenuous and challenging one. Many of the cases in the South East Asian region, and the Nusantara or the larger Malay world in particular, have totally and completely disappeared. Thus, the attempts of reconstructing and 'resurrecting' remains complicated by the constant questioning of what is borrowed, authentic and original as identity through time and space. The editors and authors attempt to depart and steer away from nostalgic reminiscing and ruminations. Instead, the aim is to capture the essences and the underlying principles and raise questions about gaps or histories untold. We concede that whether derived from 'local' forms or hybridised forms, all these forms share a common root. These locally rooted urban-architectural narratives are crucial, and it is hoped that the discourse on broad theory, philosophical and value propositions will be continued by others, and further frameworks of thought and practice must be re-centred, re-structured and reconstituted with local ethos and reworked into interpretations to counter the widespread Western-centric concepts and thought processes.

As we conclude this book, the world is still in the grip of the covid pandemic—Malaysia and Indonesia are still in midst of daily numbers of new infections. Yet to shine a light at the end of a tunnel, one continually sees how humanity organises itself locally and globally and reaches out to further inform the future, through the histories, heritage and climatic integrities of its original urban and built environments which must again be re-instated and refreshed in terms of their deep connections with the natural world. To go forward is to look to the past and to gain from the once-empathic relationship between man and nature.

Kuala Lumpur, Malaysia   Shireen Jahn Kassim
Selangor, Malaysia   Noorhanita Abdul
Kuala Lumpur, Malaysia   Dzulkifli Abdul Razak
August 2021

Acknowledgements

The journey of this book is a precious one, and the author-editors would like to convey their deep and lasting gratitude to all the academic contributors and researchers who have been so crucial to the development and completion of this book. They have contributed not only their writings but also their thoughts, energy and time in attending the regular research discourses, meetings and discussions. In the midst of a worldwide pandemic, the workhours naturally included hours of emailing and texting, thus the journey was a new one for all, in adjusting and adapting to the new conditions of online work throughout the COVID-19 pandemic.

The constant challenge of interlinking insights, discoveries and scholarship from a wide and diverse expertise arising from historical, archaeological, urban, architectural, climatic and heritage fields into an integrated approach to heritage urbanism has made the book a unique intersection of scholars and practitioners, researchers and their assistants who had worked the long hours, including reconstructing and modelling, collating and verifying historical information, extracting and summarizing from old documents, travelogues, historical references, cartographic sources, maps and drawings. These had proven a challenge not only to the researchers but most of all to the authors and writers, as they must then condense the historical into the theoretical and sieve the essences from the masses of information. We give tribute to the postgraduate students and to research assistants who had to trace back sources and compile all citations.

We begin with a special thank you from our colleagues from across the Straits and Java sea, namely, Agung Zainal M. Raden, who in his capacity as managing editor of the *Journal of Cultural Syndrome*, As University of Indraprasta, PGRI Jakatra, had given space for discussion and writing and who later contributed to the key area of urban typography mapping, thus allowing thoughts between what had been the historically unified parts of the Nusantara—particularly from Malaysia and Indonesia—to merge. Thank you to our colleagues contributors from Indonesia, primarily Dr Umi Kalsom from University of Raden Fatah, Palembang Sumatera, who had organized a visit to ISTAC, IIUM and shared their research in the short symposium on the history of Palembang and the riverine communities. Somehow it was a group of diverse academics who had managed to create a healthy discourse and which could sustain the vitality and spirits in the midst of the clouded gloom of a pandemic. From a mixture of varied expertise and diverse fields of expertise grew the weaving between history, heritage and urban theory and design, and what we hoped as multi-disciplinary findings captured with reviews and discourses with architectural and urban practitioners—who later gave further focus to capture the key findings relevant to reinstate and reconcile theory with practice. It is the ongoing appreciation and creative discourses with practitioners that constantly fueled the consolidation of historical and critical frameworks and narratives.

A special thanks to Prof. Datuk Dr Alias Abdullah, who in his capacity of the head of a transdisciplinary research group between urban planning, architecture, arts and engineering, had afforded space for the researchers, editors and authors to engage in active and historically challenging discussions. Thank you to the support of MOHE which gave the needed support to the earlier site surveys and visits. We are in great debt and gratitude in particular abundance to Museum Tuanku Fauziah and Gallery (MGTF) USM, who under the excellent leadership of its past director, En Zolkarnian Hassan, had organized and supported key exhibitions, with its associated conferences, symposiums and meetings, in order to afford opportunity for all researchers to meet and compare findings.

A special thank you note to Professor Kenneth Frampton (Columbia University, New York) who gave weight to the findings through introducing the frameworks of architectural theory in the discourse in regional urban design during the editor's sabbatical placement. Professor Frampton gave that needed leap from information-rich archaeo-historical studies to practical insights which were relevant to architectural and urban-related field and its theoretical constructs. Our thanks and gratitude to Professor Dato Seri Salleh Yaapar (Universiti Sains Malaysia), Professor Dr Ken Yeang, Professor Yahya Ahmad (Universiti Malaya) and Professor Othman Bakar of ISTAC, IIUM, who all had afforded opportunity to discuss history, theory, architecture and urban design during symposiums, book launches, seminars and intellectual discourses. Professor Othman Bakar in his leadership in IIUM gave space to use of the facilities of ISTAC and had generously facilitated and held those key symposiums on Asian urbanism, with speakers from Singapore, Indonesia and other nations in the region.

A special thanks to Professor Dr Ahmad Murad Merican who is an academician who stand atop of the field and shed light on the rich, syncretic and multivariate nature of South East Asian and Malay-Nusantara urbanism, a budding field still straddling philosophy, geography, anthropology, history, literature, conservation and heritage urban-architecture studies. A special thanks to members of the industry, particularly, the founders and senior directors of GDP architects Sdn Bhd, Kamil Merican, Kamal Latiff and Syed Sobri, who welcomed the researches in a sharing of industry-academic presentations and inputs and for their enthusiasm in inviting academic discussion into their busy practice and creating opportunities for debates and discourses based on the historical mappings and studies. Last but not least, a depth of thanks to Professor Emeritus Dr Elias Salleh, who in his capacity as the head of the Heritage Living Lab research cluster unit at IIUM, had organized and facilitated the presentations to industry and practitioners. The generation of new ideas to further development of thought in the critical field of urbanism and architecture would not be possible without the senior practitioners who had shared their long experiences and insights into architecture, tropical urbanism, urban design and to those who believed in the intrinsic sustainable value of the modern vernacular, and these included Ar.

Azzaidy Abdullah, Ar. Surea Mamat, Ar. Serina Hijjas and Ar. Dr Norwina Mohd Nawawi.

No scholarship can be possible with the constant support of dedicated librarian and without the constant support of the IIUM library resources; our deepest thanks to, namely, the architecture liaison librarian Norbaya Muda, who had constantly searched and provided the much-needed references and articles without fail, without whom this book would not have been possible. Last but not least, a deep thanks to assistant project manager in sustainable design and artist-architect, Muhammad Wafiy Harith, without whom many of the ideas could not be visualized. A deep thanks to project manager in EAG's design atelier and sustainability group and a postgraduate alumni of IIUM, Mustafa Kamal Bashar, who has the ability to bridge between climate and history and whose insight provided impetus to the needed milestone in consolidating history to theory. Thanks to the ever-present editorial assistants Samayro Saif, Nur Sabrina Kamal, and modeller Zakwan Zakur, without their constant support, this compilation would not be possible.

Finally, an endless thanks and gratitude to our families, who bore with us to the end, especially in bearing with the workloads from home due to the occasional pandemic-related lockdown state.

July 2022   Shireen Jahn Kassim
                                    Noor Hanita Abdul Majid
                                     Dzulkifli Abdul Razak

Contents

Notes on Contributors

Noor Hanita Abdul Majid is formerly an associate professor at KAED International Islamic University Malaysia (IIUM). She taught South East Asian architecture and vernacular studies in undergraduate architecture studies and was responsible for coordinating heritage visits and measurement surveys for several years. Her doctorate was focused on bioclimatic comfort in tropical plazas, and her recent funded research sought to combine both climatic performance and heritage. Her PhD work focused on outdoor thermal comfort studies of urban plazas adjacent to tall buildings, but her most recent research is geared towards bridging environmental science in architecture to culture, heritage, and vernacular buildings. During her academic days as an associate professor at IIUM and University of Nizwa, Oman, she was involved in teaching and research on passive and sustainable architecture, culture, human behaviour, and heritage buildings. Designing academic curricula and reviews were part of her work locally and abroad. She has experience in international consultancy and was involved in developing the Malaysian Standards in Energy Efficiency and Renewable Energy for Residential Buildings published by the Department of Standards Malaysia. She is committed to writing with integrity and a dedication to areas related to architecture, heritage, and culture, focusing on the context of South East Asia.

Siti Norzaini Zainal Abidin is a senior lecturer at the School of Architecture and Building Design, Taylor's University. She previously led the Master of Design Management programme at First City University College. Her contribution on the paper 'Strategic Daylight Visualization for the Green Building Process: Integrating Optimization into An Airport Terminal Design with Skylights' garnered her the Best Paper, PhD Student award for ConVR in December 2016 at Regal Kowloon, Hong Kong, organised by The Hong Kong University of Science and Technology. Her research interests include passive design in green building, integrated design process, design management, built environment, sustainable living, energy and architecture, daylighting in airport design, and green building.

Juliana Aida Abu Bakar is an associate professor at Universiti Utara Malaysia and present deputy dean. She has been involved in research projects such as the digital reconstruction of heritage vernacular and Kuala Kedah Fort for the Kedah Museum. She was responsible for designing and developing three-dimensional models and surroundings, adding interactivity and a portal for easy access by museum visitors. She is also involved in Mobile Augmented Reality for cultural heritage sites where she carries out adaptive multimodal interaction design for enhancing tourists' experience.

Azizi Bahauddin was trained as an architect and worked in the architectural field for 7 years before embarking on an academic career 22 years ago. He is a lecturer and a professor in Interior Architecture at the School of Housing, Building & Planning, USM, from 1999 to the present. His main research areas are in design and culture, specifically on exhibition design/interior design; art and design, especially cultural issues in ethnography and phenomenology; and in architectural and cultural heritage. His main passion is investigating how cultural values influence the built environment, especially in embellishments, details, space planning, and the customs, rituals, and philosophy that are associated with architecture. He has over 200 publications to his name, with over 110 titles reviewed under high-impact-factor journals revolving around design and culture in connection with architecture. He is now studying the traditional architecture of the South East Asia region by looking into cultural influences that govern the way the architecture in the region was shaped.

His studies have looked at traditional houses in Malaysia and Indonesia with cultural influences and mosque architecture relating to Sufism. Current areas of research include the 'sense of place', "sacred places', and cultural influences that govern the way architecture is shaped. Specific topics include the Rumah Gajah Menyusu of Kedah, Rumah Melaka, Rumah Adat Minangkabau in western Sumatera, Rumah Tradisional Negeri Sembilan, Rumah Baba-Nyonya of Melaka and Penang, Rumah Panjang Rungus of Sabah, the courtyard house of Jordan, Masjid Agung Banten, traditional Malay spas, Rumah Panjang Tinggi Melanau, Feng Shui philosophy in traditional Chinese architecture, the Hokkien clan, and mosque architecture relating to Sufism.

Puteri Mayang Bahjah Zaharin is a senior lecturer in the Centre of Studies for Architecture, Faculty of Architecture, Planning and Surveying, Universiti Teknologi MARA (UiTM). She joined UiTM in 2016 after 11 years in industry. She was involved in mixed-housing and high-rise development projects during her professional career. She obtained her Professional Architect qualification in 2009 and is a Registered Architect under the Board of Architects Malaysia and a Corporate Member of Pertubuhan Akitek Malaysia. She was appointed Course Coordinator for the Bachelor of Science (Hons) Architecture programme from 2019 to 2021 and is currently teaching in the Master of Architecture programme in high-rise development and planning principles and practices. Puteri Mayang Bahjah Zaharin has supervised more than 15 Master of Architecture Design Thesis and Master by Research students. She is actively engaged in coordinating and supervising students in international and local architecture competitions. Her students have won several awards, such as the Student Gold Prize at ARCASIA Awards for Architecture in 2018, held in Japan, and the PAM-ZSR Architecture Prize 2019. She was elected as an editorial board member of the Association of Malaysian Environment-Behavior Researchers in 2020. Her paper 'The Implementation of Active Design for Technology-Driven Activities in Malaysia' was awarded Best Paper in the 8th AMER International Conference on Quality of Life in 2020. Her area of interest is in international development and planning, with a focus on sustainable development.

Nurhaya Baniyamin (B.Env.Design Studies, B. Architecture(hons), MA Art and Design, PhD in Built Environment) is an assistant professor at the Department of Applied Arts and Architecture, Kulliyyah of Architecture and Environmental Design (KAED), International Islamic University Malaysia (IIUM). She teaches undergraduate courses on interior design, Islamic geometric patterns, project management and exhibition, art history, heritage studies, and computer visualization. Her doctoral work focused on experiential learning, and she presently writes on cultural heritage in design and sustainability in traditional arts and crafts. She is principal and co-researcher in IIUM research projects related to arts heritage and architecture. A member of Malaysian Institute of Interior Designers (MIID), she presently advises on public projects on the integration of both sustainability and cultural identity in interior environments.

Nor Zalina Harun is presently an associate professor at Universiti Kebangsaan Malaysia (UKM). She completed her Diploma in Architecture and earned a Bachelor's degree in Landscape Architecture at Universiti Teknologi Malaysia in 2000. In 2011, she earned her a Doctor of Philosophy in Architecture from the same university. From 2001 until 2017, she served as a lecturer and, for several years, head of the department and research director at the Department of Landscape Architecture, Kulliyyah of Architecture and Environmental Design, International Islamic University Malaysia. She presently leads a focus group of the UKM Heritage and Civil Society Research Cluster. Apart from heritage conservation, her research focuses on community, settlement morphology studies, and urban landscape development. To date, she has led over 15 research projects and consultancies with more than 100 publications that include 80 peer-reviewed papers. Her works are funded by the Selangor Housing and Property Board, the Ministry of Higher Education, the Institute of National Valuation, Kedah State Museum Board, the Institute of Darul Ridzuan, and Think City. In addition to her profound interest in research and education, she was appointed project leader for the development of communal space for low-cost strata houses in Selangor, served as an advisor for the Tok Janggut Community Gallery Development in Tumpat, Kelantan, and has continuously been invited as a speaker and facilitator for government institutions and related non-governmental organisations.

Illyani Ibrahim is an assistant professor in International Islamic University Malaysia. She is a registered Corporate Member of Institution of Geospatial and Remote Sensing Society (IGRSM), member of the Royal Institution of Surveyors Malaysia (RISM), and an associate member of the Malaysia Institute of Planners (MIP). Her recent research interest has focused on the application of Geographical Information System (GIS) and remote sensing in environmental analysis and cultural conservation of heritage.

Mansor Ibrahim is a professor and professional planner (TPr) at the International Islamic University Malaysia (IIUM). He was a former dean at the Kulliyyah of Architecture and Environmental Design. Before joining IIUM in 2001, he was a deputy dean (research and publication) and head of department at the University Technology Malaysia. Prior to obtaining his PhD (Land Resources) and Master's in Urban and Regional Planning (MURP) from the University of Wisconsin-Madison, USA (1982–1986), he studied at the Universiti Kebangsaan Malaysia (1st batch 1970–1974), DPU-UCL, London (1980), and University of Auckland, New Zealand (1975–1977). His research and consulting experiences in related areas cover over 300 topics, and he has presented more than 200 conference papers and co-authored over 200 books, book chapters, and manuscripts. He has served as editor for various local and international journals related to the built environment. Amongst others, he has been editor-in-chief for the *Planning Malaysia Journal* of the Malaysian Institute of Planners since 2011, *Design Ideals Journal*, Kulliyyah of Architecture and Environmental Design, IIUM, and editor for Habitat International. He has been affiliated with various professional bodies, local and international, as a member and officeholder such as vice president and council member of the Malaysian Institute of Planners since 2000, affiliate member of New Zealand Planning Institute since 1977, member of the International Association for Impact Assessment, member of the United Nations Environment Programme, International Environmental Technical Center (Osaka, Japan), member of the EIA/EHIA Network (World Health Organization), member of the board of town planners, Registered EIA Consultant (DOE l 00036), Registered EIA Consultant (NREB, S'wak), Registered SIA Malaysia, member of Malaysian Nature Society, and member of the International Council of Museums (ICOM).

Shireen Jahn Kassim is currently the Director of EAG Consulting SDN BHD, a multidisciplinary consulting firm in sustainable design, engineering, and heritage services. Formerly an associate professor based at the Faculty of Architecture and Environmental Design (KAED), International Islamic University Malaysia, she taught subjects in architecture and building technology in the Applied Arts and Design programme. In recent years, she headed the architecture and arts research cluster under a transdisciplinary grant (TRGS) aimed at connecting Asian Nusantara heritage resources with urbanism practitioners and policy. She acted as lead advisor to develop sustainable standards (MyCrest) for Malaysian public buildings administered by the Construction Industry Board Malaysia (CIDB) and Jabatan Kerjaraya (JKR). She founded the research cluster EAVR at International Islamic University Malaysia (www.eavr.wordpress), which sought to combine experts in the fields of computing, sustainability, and heritage in Malaysia. She led a series of exhibitions promoting heritage architecture and urbanism. She currently serves as chief editor for the journal *Cultural Syndrome* based in Universiti Indrapasta PGRI, Jakarta, focusing on regional Asian-based heritage and the visual arts, and sits on the editorial board of the *International Journal of Sustainable Built Environment* published by Elsevier and GORD, Doha, Qatar. She is editorial member of the *Journal of World Architecture* (Sydney) and *Journal of Architecture and Design Review* in Singapore. In recent years, she led a series of research-based exhibitions on Malay artisanal traditions, partially funded by Thinkcity (a subsidiary of Khazanah), and 'the Resilience of Tradition-from origin to contemporary) by MGTF, USM. She annually supports student training and participation in Gallery Weekend Kuala Lumpur, an international multicultural marquee event to promote local talents and resources in the visual arts in Malaysia. She has published more than 50 papers and several books on architectural critical theory, heritage, green architecture, and critical regionalism.

Ismail Jasmani is an academic fellow in the Applied Arts and Design (AAD) Department at the Kulliyyah of Architecture and Environmental Design (KAED), International Islamic University Malaysia (IIUM), a built environment and art school. Previously, he practiced as an interior design consultant for 20 years. As an academic advisor, he assisted AAD students at national and international levels, such as Malaysia International Furniture Fair, Terengganu International Furniture Fair, and Street Furniture Design under MBSA and organized university-level exhibitions. He acted as external examiner at Lim KoK Wing University from 2011 to 2012, University Technology Mara (2012), and Geomatica University College from 2013 to the present.

Nyimas Umi Kalsum was born in Palembang on 15 July 1975. Her passion for manuscripts started during her undergraduate studies in Arabic language and literature in 2000 at Raden Fatah State Islamic University. She continued her studies in the master's programme in philology at the Faculty of Cultural Science of the University of Indonesia in 2004. In 2016, she completed her doctorate in Islamic Civilization at Raden Fatah State Islamic University, Palembang. In 2016, she was selected to conduct doctoral research in Germany with support from the Project Implementing Unit of Raden Fatah State Islamic University, Palembang. Some of her published works in recent years include the book *Muzawaroh Palembang* (2021), *Genealogy and Tawasul/Naskah Silsilah dan Tawasul* (2021), '*Manassa*'Spreading the Love for Manuscript in South Sumatra/*Menyebarkan Virus Cinta Naskah di Sumatera Selatan* (2021), an anthology of works on Islamic culture and intellectualism in Palembang during Palembang Darussalam Sultanate and Dutch Colonial Era/*Bunga Rampai Sejarah Kebudayaan dan Intelektualisme Islam di Palembang pada Masa Kesultanan Palembang Darussalam dan Kolonial Belanda* (book, 2021), a *translation of Ma'din Al Asrar fi Manhaj al Abrar* (2019), *The Function of Rivers in the Development of Islamic Civilization in Palembang: From the Sultanate to the Dutch East Indies Era/Peran Sungai dalam Perkembangan Peradaban Islam di Palembang: Dari Masa Kesultanan sampai Hindia- Belanda* (2019), *A Portrait of the Religious Practices of Nineteenth Century Palembang Society in Sufi Manuscripts/Potret Praktik Keberagamaan Masyarakat Palembang Abad ke-19 dalam Naskah Tasawuf* (2019), *The Philosophical Transformation of the*

Scientific Paradigm (2019), *Integration of Knowledge in the Quran/Integrasi Ilmu dalam al Quran* (2018), *Manuscript Comparison between Tuhfah ar-Ragibin Syekh Abd Somad al Falimbani and Syekh Arsyad al Banjari (Philological Studies and Content Analysis,* 2017), *Manuscript and Culture/Aksara Naskah dan Budaya* (2017), *Mi'raj by M.Qosim bin Hasan Nasib: Text Editing and Content Analysis* (2018), and *Beratib* (collective zikir) *Culture in Palembang Now and Then/Budaya Beratib Palembang Dulu dan Kini* (2016).

Kamariah Kamaruddin is an architect, a health facility planner, and urban development consultant embarking on a soft technology path, healthy environment, and strategy of sustainable urban policy for cultural and material landscapes. She has contributed to, designed, and advised on multiple projects and master plans across Klang Valley and Malaysia. She was involved in shaping the urban policy framework for the Physical Architectural Design Guidelines for Cyberjaya (2005), incorporating gradual thematic images and ambience and the Urban Design Guidelines for Pasir Mas, Kelantan (2012), incorporating Malay and Islamic heritage and sustainable design requirements. She is currently pursuing her doctorate in sustainability and heritage urbanism in the Nusantara at International Islamic University Malaysia.

Zumahiran Kamaruddin is a senior lecturer at The Department of Applied Arts and Design, IIUM and served as its Head of Department until 2014. Her PhD focused on the intricacies of Malay woodcarving of the East Coast States and currently she is specialising in conservation and supervising PhD and Masters candidates in similar areas, including Islamic Design and Craftsmanship.

Norwina Mohd Nawawi is a professional architect, with over 19 years of experience in Public Works Department Malaysia since 1979, specialising in healthcare facility planning and architecture prior to joining International Islamic University Malaysia (IIUM) as academic staff in 1998. A Fellow of the Malaysian Institute of Architects (PAM) and a member of Badan Warisan Malaysia (Heritage of Malaysia Trust), she also serves on the scientific committee on heritage with ICOMOS on energy and sustainability, cultural routes, analysis & restoration of structures of architectural heritage and places of religion and ritual. In International Islamic University Malaysia, Norwina teaches in the professional programme of architecture, which includes professional practice, healthcare architecture, and history and theory in architecture, focusing on Islamic architecture and East Asian and South East Asian architecture. As coordinator for the Islamic Architectural Heritage Research Unit (ISArcH) at the Kulliyyah of Architecture and Environmental Design (KAED), International Islamic University Malaysia (IIUM). In addition, Norwina was involved in bridging the gap between different worldviews of history and heritage through symposia and international conferences. She is also the author or co-author of several books and articles that discuss the remnants and shreds of evidence of the endangered Malay world and Islamic resurgence through diverse perspectives garnered through research, discussions, and supervision of theses and heritage studies courses in the programme.

Tengku Anis Qarihah Raja Abdul Kadir is currently a lecturer in the Architecture degree programme at the Centre of Architecture Studies, UITM (Universiti Teknologi MARA). Before her academic career, she practiced as a design architect at one of Malaysia's premier firms, Kumpulan Senireka Malaysia. Amongst others, she was involved with facade design of the New National Palace of Malaysia. She is presently pursuing her Doctorate in the Classification of Aristocratic Architecture in the Malay region. She has published more than 15 papers and posters.

Muhammad Iqbal Qeis is the head of Centre for Design and Visual Communications Study, Universitas Indraprasta PGRI. An assistant professor with a passion for Nintendo game skills, Qeis had previously been appointed communication officer for the Habibie Center Indonesia before launching his career as an academic. Awarded his Bachelor of Design from Institut Teknologi Bandung in 2009 and Master of Arts in European Study from Universitas Indonesia in 2012, his past and present research have focused on the field of design and visual communications, design and media, semiotics, visual language, and visual culture.

Agung Zainal Muttakin Raden began his career as a lecturer in 2013, teaching typography in the Department of Visual Communication

Design, Faculty of Language and Art, Universitas Indraprasta PGRI, Jakarta. He graduated from UNIKOM Bandung with a Bachelor of Design degree in 2012 and got his Master of Design degree in 2014 from Universitas Trisakti Jakarta. He is currently a doctoral candidate at Indonesia Institute of Art, Surakarta. Hi areas of interest include graphic design, visual communication design, typography, visual culture, arts and cultures, and vernacular.

Dzulkifli Abdul Razak is currently the Rector of the International Islamic University Malaysia. He was the Vice Chancellor of USM from 2000–2011. He is the immediate past president of the International Association of Universities, a Paris-based UNESCO-affiliated organisation. Dzul was the first Asian recipient of the prestigious 2017 Gilbert Medal. He is a Fellow of the Academy of Sciences Malaysia (FASc), World Academy of Art and Science (FWAAS), and the World Academy of Islamic Management (FWAIM). From February 2021, Dzul serves as an Expert for the Futures of Higher Education Project at UNESCO's Institute for Higher Education (IESALC) based in Caracas.

Elias Bin Salleh served in various academic capacities in local public and private universities/university colleges since 1973: in Universiti Teknologi Malaysia (UTM 1973–1999) as professor, in Universiti Utara Malaysia (UUM 1999–2003) as a deputy vice-chancellor, in Universiti Putra Malaysia (UPM 2003–2011) as professor, in Universiti Kebangsaan Malaysia (UKM 2012–2016) as a principal research fellow at Solar Energy Research Institute (SERI), and in the Department of Architecture, Kulliyyah of Architecture and Environmental Design, International Islamic University Malaysia (IIUM), 2016–2020), as a professor. Currently he is the Vice-Chancellor/Chief Executive of Genovasi University College. He was a member of the Council of Accreditation and Architectural Education Malaysia (CAAEM) of Lembaga Akitek Malaysia and a member of the MQA Assessment Panel. He served as an external examiner/assessor or member of the board of studies for architectural programmes in various public/private universities. He successfully supervised many local and foreign doctoral and master's degree students. He once practiced architecture as a director in Akitek Jaya Sdn Bhd from 1978 to 1990. In 2019 he and a fellow architect founded Vis

Arch Architect Sdn Bhd. In 2008 he was involved in founding the Malaysia Green Building Council (MGBC) and was a board member of Greenbuildingindex Sdn Bhd (GSB) (2013–2015). He was an Independent Non-Executive Director in GPRO Technologies Bhd (an ACE listed Company) from 2004 to 2011. He was on the board of directors of MARA-owned Malaysia Design Development Centre Sdn Bhd (DDEC) from 2011 to 2020. He was made Professor Emeritus by UTM in 2013 and honoured with the inaugural Architectural Education Award in 2015 by Lembaga Arkitek Malaysia (LAM).

Saiful Nadzri Bin Shamsudin M.Arch (urban design) Glasgow School of Art, Scotland, is a practicing architect. Having graduated with a B.Sc (HBP) University Sains Malaysia, he is currently Director of SNor Interior Design with 10 years' experience, with Atsa Architects Sdn Bhd and, prior to that, with Jurubena Bertiga International Sdn Bhd.

Harlina Md Sharif holds a PhD in Art and Archaeology from the School of Oriental and African Studies (SOAS), University of London (2013), with her research focusing on the morphology and idiomatic expressions of mosques in Island South East Asia. Her early education was in architecture, and she earned her Master's in Design Science, majoring in Computers in Design, at the University of Sydney, Australia. In addition, she earned a Diploma in Islamic Jurisprudence (Syari'ah) from al-Quds University College in Jordan. She is currently an assistant professor and the Coordinator of Conservation majoring in the Department of Applied Arts & Design at the Kulliyyah of Architecture and Environmental Design in International Islamic University Malaysia (IIUM). Her research interests are in the areas of the impact of cultural exchanges and maritime networks on traditional Malay-Islamic design and heritage, as well as the application of digital technologies in the visualization and documentation of cultural heritage.

Mazarina Binti Md Zain worked with an architecture firm and landscape architecture firm for 2 years before beginning his career at Politeknik Sultan Idris Shah in the Architecture Programme from 2012 to the present. She was head of the architecture programme from 2018 until 2021 and was involved in restructuring the programme and developing a new curriculum and syllabus for the Diploma of Architecture, Politeknik Malaysia. Her teaching experience is in architecture design, landscape design, measured drawings, 3D modelling, building technology, and working drawing. Currently a doctoral candidate in the Philosophy of the Built Environment at Islamic International University Malaysia, she focuses on mixed reality in the Malay heritage world. She completed her degree in Housing Building and Planning (majoring in Architecture) in 2008 and Master of Landscape Architecture in 2010 at University Sains Malaysia, Pulau Pinang.

Syamsul Bahrin Zaibon currently is an associate professor of multimedia at the School of Creative Industry Management & Performing Arts, Universiti Utara Malaysia (UUM), and teaches various courses in the areas of creative industry and interactive media. He holds a Bachelor's degree in Information Technology from UUM, a MSc in Multimedia & Internet Computing from Loughborough University, and a PhD in Multimedia from UUM. His research interests are diverse and cover digital heritage, multimedia and mobile applications, web design and development, game-based learning, comics for learning, and edutainment. He has a number of research outputs and publications in these areas and has presented papers at national and international conferences.

List of Figures

List of Tables

Introduction

The aim of this introduction is to outline key theoretical frameworks and operational definitions which form the basis and armature of discussions within the ensuing chapters. The Southeast Asian tropics, including the Malay Archipelago region, is known as one of the regions where large traces of past settlements and cities had thrived, yet disappeared; thus, any study on the patterns of these pre-colonial and indigenous cities or urban centres will uncover the traces of pre-existing layers.

The Nusantara refers to a series of landmasses spread sporadically in the South China Sea, whose regional histories and evolution are largely linked to the seaborne trade routes between China and India. They were historically created when sea levels rose in the last ice age (Bowring, 2018) and as he observed, within which:

> there is an erosion of a sense of self. 'Due to its sea-water nature, its cities grew along the littoral.

The underlying thread of eco-urbanism is seen as an approach to inserting the man-made into the 'natural'. Historically, these are also related to religion and spirituality. The focus will be on what is presently discussed by scholars and practitioners and recognised as 'eco-urbanist', such as planning and designing with a departure and focus on topography, climate, and ecology. Whitehand and Kai Gu (2007) observe a problem of regional fields of historic cultural landscape practised worldwide and affecting policy-making bodies from supranational organisations to local governments is the poorly developed awareness of cities as mosaics of interrelated interrelatedness forms. Awareness of the existence of historic cities and general features is insufficient; one must delve deeper into layers and unearth palimpsest to broaden one's understanding of how they fit together is critical. Historical awareness is interlinked with eco-urbanist perspectives, particularly concerning the climate. Leite and Justo (2017) highlight the broad and particular tenet of eco-urbanism, highlighting their understanding of forms of 'typo-morphology' and climate-related factors:

> *The typo-morphological studies have assumed since the mid-twentieth century an important role in understanding the dynamics of the urban fabric. They reveal their physical and spatial structure based on de-tailed classification by types of the elements that shape its urban form open spaces, buildings, or streets.* (Moudon, 1998)

A sub-region of Asia, Southeast Asia refers to the insular and peninsular regions generally geographically south of China, east of India and inhabiting the geographical plate known as the Sunda Plate. The equator cuts through the region, thus making mainland Southeast Asia, historically known as Indochina, and Maritime Southeast, historically known as the Nusantara, or the Malay Archipelago or Alam Melayu. Wheatley (1966) describes the two main ways why there is the historical significance of the region:

> *Throughout the millennia of prehistoric time, it had served as a gigantic causeway over which a succession of cultures had diffused imperceptibly from the mainland of Asia towards the archipelago, the Southwest Pacific and Australasia.*

The fabric of the traditional urban core was primarily affected as key structures—which traditionally constitute the palace and the mosque—were impacted. Traditionally they were located extremely close to each other—bordering rivers as trading routes—and were urban cores with accretions of trading stalls, structures and associated aristocratic structures nearby.

Kota Melaka, for example, was a Malay-Nusantara royal zone, which is both a city and a state at the same time. It grew from a maritime Southeast Asian city-state that strategically was located midpoint between 'the turn of two monsoonal winds' and at the mouth of a sizeable navigational river and deltaic plain, allowing ships to navigate and berth easily. The hill became a natural defensive tool, and the 'royal' site, which was bordered by orchards and a large field, grew into a dense community represented by royal enclaves, other public structures including mosques and artisanal and commercial neighbourhoods, and on the opposite side of the river was the multicultural commercial area. And with regard to the Peninsular:

> The peninsula was situated almost exactly half-way between the great civilisations of India and China, and as maritime trade developed, it became unavoidable coastline for Mariners sailing east or west....

Thus, what separates nations with individual borders was historically a single unit, as Andaya (2010) describes as the 'sea of Malayu', a single continuum where 'lands' were seen as barriers in an oceanic continuum. Historians, in general, have emphasised the maritime connectivity of Southeast Asia due to pre-colonial functions and workings as a single cultural and economic unit. Thus, Alam Melayu historically comprised South Thailand, East and West Malaysia, Sumatra, Indonesia's Java, and Borneo islands, Sulawesi and Maluku islands, and the southern Philippines. It was an inherited network of Srivijaya, which later became identified due to the advent of Islam. As the region converted to Islam, there was still a continuation, conflation, and inclusion of Islamic beliefs such as the non-inclusion of animal imagery. Foreign elements were slowly adopted like osmosis throughout time but continuously synthesised with local thoughts and elements. Wolters (1999, p. 27) describes socio-political patterns as:

> a federation of kingdoms or vassalized polity defined by or under a loose centric formation, or overlapping mandala, made up of tributary polities; without being a territorially defined state.

The littoral zone in Southeast Asia represents the zone of the nearshore which can be the part of a sea, lake, or river close to the shore. In coastal environments, the littoral zone extends from the high-water mark, rarely inundated, to shoreline areas that are permanently submerged. The adjacency of water gives several distinctive characteristics to architecture and urban design in the littoral regions. In the tropical region, the dense forms of littoral cities are also due to the dense tropical hinterland, which is challenging to develop and sustain, thus; in many aspects, these urban architectural forms are dense and compact forms of development that do not sprawl or encroach into the forest, hence respect their hinterland. Their location implies that their urban fabric can benefit from the climatic cooling through the nearness and availability of water and, with judicious planning, provide enhanced comfort conditions in the outdoors and public spaces and support a greater variety of plant and animal life.

A Definition of Urban-Architectural Form

The term 'urban-architectural form' is used instead of 'urban design' due to the evolution of the term 'urban design' itself. Urban design is rooted in the more temperate climatic context of Western countries. Thus, urban design typically denotes urban 'outdoor' elements such as plazas, parks, urban landscapes, and generally open-air structures that can be enjoyed in temperate and colder regions. However, what constitutes urban design? Urban design describes the physical features that define the character or image of a community, public space, and public monuments, and thus in a modern context, the urban core, the neighbourhood, community, township, or the city. The eventual character of an urban centre must be read as a whole; hence urban design is the accretion or accumulation of various elements horizontally laid out or 'vertically shaped'—at different scales—that impinge upon the memory and visual and sensory perceptions of visitors, tourists, urban dwellers, and city users. This, consequently, affects the relationship between the people and the dynamics between built forms and the natural environment. The built environment includes monuments, buildings, and pathways, and the natural environment includes features such as mountains, river and sea views, coastlines, shorelines, roof profiles, facades modulations, and shapes—all of which must be eventually incorporated into the urban design experience in an interrelated comprehensive and thus framework. Citywide urban design recommendations are vital to ensure that the built environment contributes the qualities that essentially differentiate a place or a city. Elements of urban design range from elements that are generally macro such as planning and layout to micro such as ornamentation and surface modulation as these are basic elements that constitute imagery and identity of a place, that is, that range from the smaller scale to the larger scale, from the experience of the streetscape to the context of a whole tangible and intangible conglomeration of elements that typically make up a city.

Eco-urbanism

Eco-urbanism, derived from the term that denotes a rising movement or the ideation of ecological urbanism, is a new approach to cities. Mostafavi et al. (2017) from Harvard School of Design assert as a critical theory and design praxis from the twenty-first century onwards:

> *the premise of Ecological Urbanism is that an ecological approach is urgently needed both as a remedial device for the contemporary city and an organizing principle for new cities.*

In her seminal book *Ecological Urbanism: The Nature of the City*, Hagan (2014) highlights:

> *The role of such an approach in urbanism particularly in redefining, urban design and architecture in an era of climate change, urbanization and ecology. Initially, the ecological narrative and its 'embryonic modes of practice' must be fused with "the narratives of urbanism and its older, deeply embedded modes of practice".*

The term ecological is used instead of 'green' or 'sustainable' due to the implication of architectural and volumetric, which is not two dimensional. Rather than prescriptive, it captures a framework related to architecture and space rather than focusing on ecological constituents.

Thus, the term 'eco-system' here refers to what is defined by Ken Yeang in his PhD thesis 'a system consisting of "biological and physical" constituents'. The biological is concerned with 'plants and animals and physical is concerned with an empirical character such as 'climate and edaphic features' which sees 'the site as a living and functioning system'. Thus, local archetypes are part of the solution as the tropical region has evolved 'culturally' or localised elements that are climatically and ecologically aligned in a typological and conceptual way.

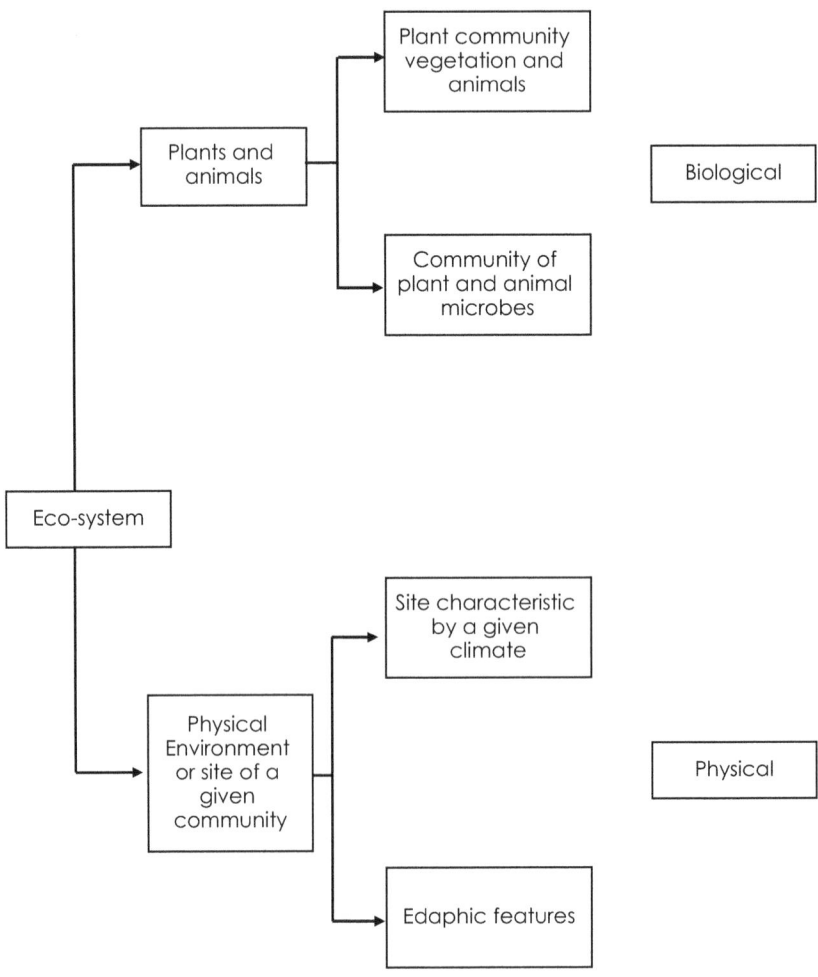

Fig. 1 The breakdown of the eco-system into its 'physical' and 'biological' constituents (Yeang, 1982)

Definition of a City

Wheatley (1961), in his historical-geographical discussions of Southeast Asia, again points to the debates of the word city, which suggests an open-ended definition. He also suggests a kind of differentiation and evolution from village to city. He indicates a 'tipping point' in terms of:

the smaller of these settlements can still have been little more than villages but others such as Langkasuka and Kedah had long since assumed function of true cities, with commercial relations extending far beyond the peninsula the organization of administrative subdivisions, and the collection of a tax testify to the sizeable extent of the territorial bases of these city states. the theocratic element is strong in all these city states.

Miksic (2018) has reinforced that 'a polythetic functional definition of urbanization recognizes two distinct forms of the city: orthogenetic and heterogenetic'. He defines 'heterogenetic' cities as where:

Trade and industry were often concentrated in the same location. Many of these maritime centres grew at a rapid speed along the littoral; and perceived as disorderly, dense and organic, located either at confluences of two rivers or at the mouth of large rivers.

Miksic (2018) also observed that several classic Southeast Asian languages had no word for 'city'. Complex settlement patterns did exist, but these languages employed different factors in classifying settlements. Defining the word, '*nagara*' in Sanskrit carries two meanings. Munoz (2006) implies the presence of a palace, a *pura* or *puri*, both come from the Vedic word *puri*, meaning 'rampart' or 'fort'. With reference to Java, Stutterheim defined the walled palace complex as a *puri* and referred to the inner palace where the ruler lived. The word *nagara* is defined in most Sanskrit-English dictionaries as 'town'. Yet the word *pura* or *puri* evolved into many local variants. The *nagara* in fourteenth-century Java meant a walled palace complex and its immediate surroundings as in Cambodia. In Java in the early Islamic period, the word *nagara* was used to refer to the royal residence, and those surrounded by lands were called *negara agung*. A fourteenth-century Javanese court text suggests that this was a criterion for defining a *nagara*:

> *What is called the nagara? All where one can go out (of his compound) without passing through paddy fields.*

In Indonesia, a fourteenth-century poem about the capital of Majapahit, *nagara* referred to compounds of the ruler or other nobles, usually walled, and others where relatives and high officials lived. People who lived in the *nagara* of Majapahit included artisans, possibly wage-earners independent of patrons, thus forming a kind of floating population. *Nagara* is contrasted with *desa* or *pradesa*, meaning a non-urban district and with *thani*, peasants' cultivated land or rural settlement.

Many of these maritime centres grew at a rapid speed along the littoral. Royal power, defensive structures, housing and community of foreign traders, a concentration of local artisans, and religious or ceremonial centres were variables which could combine in different ways and in different sequences to make up these cities. By forwarding the terms the orthogenetic and heterogenetic, two forms of cities are defined in which orthogenetic cities refer to the early urban centres conceived by Wheatley (1961):

> *They usually have large monuments but little evidence of dense populations or a wide range of economic activity. These sites seem to have been ceremonial and administrative centres. The economies of such societies seem to have been administered by the central governments.*

While the region itself is characterised by typically hot and humid conditions with high temperatures and humidity all year round, the wind patterns are particularly important in the microclimate, as air movement plays a crucial role in relieving heat and discomfort through evaporative cooling. The critical character of its geography and location is how it lies amid the seasonal nature of wind circulation over the Indian and China Seas.

Climate and Wind Movements

Climatic conditions near the equatorial belt display no clear dry season, while northern and southern regions display a clear dry and monsoon season. The term monsoon itself has its origin in the Arabic word '*mausim*', which means season. Traditionally, seamen used this word to describe the seasonal switch of winds and air conditions, and for centuries, it has been used to describe a system of alternating winds over the Indian Ocean and the Arabian Sea which blow from the north-east for six months and from the south-west for the remaining six months. In general, the shift in the seasonal wind is about 120°, mainly caused by the differential heating of land and ocean. Traders and travellers capitalise on the rhythmic change of winds, and it is this rhythm and change that allows the port cities along the littoral to be a temporary sojourn for many while waiting for the wind to change.

Wheatley (1966) summates:

> *This dependence of communication and trade on the rhythm of the wind seasons while the Strait of Malacca, sheltered from both monsoons, was navigable at all seasons of the year.*

Concerning Malaya, he observes:

> *Their unequal incidence on east and west of the Peninsula. The eastern littoral is exposed to the full force of Northeast monsoon....*

Bowring (2020) observed a character of climate that is encountered in most of the region:

> *Equatorial zones generally lack strong monsoon winds as they are at the intersection...of northern and southern hemisphere wind systems.*

Under hot, humid conditions, thermal comfort is achieved through the reduction of convective and radiative exchanges and the effect of wind in enhancing evaporative impact as one of the basic physical and biological needs of human beings. The human body temperature must be maintained at a constant 37±5 °C regardless of the prevailing ambient condition. Air movement is particularly crucial to keep thermal conditions in buildings within acceptable limits and maintain maximum human productivity and performance, particularly in outdoor spaces. The indoor thermal environment is similarly affected by the local climate, and air movement through the building is critical and necessary to decrease indoor discomfort due to heat gain conditions in a tropical climate. Any indoor thermal environment is much affected by environmental factors such as air temperature, air movement, humidity, and radiation. In the warm and humid climate, external air movement crucially assists in controlling the indoor environment.

Thermal Comfort Definition in the Urban Tropics

The air temperature and relative humidity are important factors determining the comfort level in a hot and humid region. The tropical climate has averages of t high air temperature at an average of 28 Celsius with an average of 80% of relative humidity. The hot air and high relative humidity are typically only elevated by increased air movement and evolve a daily life cycle of the quickening pace of activities in the early morning, late evening and nights for there is a drop in air temperature, which reflects the thermal condition of the space air movement, on the other hand, has benefited in the condition where the relative humidity is more than 70% and should be continued for a period of time rather than just a gust. Higher air velocity compared to and specified by the existing standards effectively provides comfort indoors. Studies involving human thermal comfort in urban or suburban microenvironments have adopted the energy balance approach (e.g., Clarke & Bach, 1971; Morgan & Baskett, 1974; Terjung & Louie, 1974; Burt, 1982; Brown & Gillespie, 1986; Jendritzky & Nubler, 1987). Among the many comfort indices, Gagge's SET (Standard Effective Temperature), which is a refinement of his earlier version ET* (Effective Temperature) and Fanger's PMV (Predicted Mean Vote) used in conjunction with PPD (Predicted Percentage of Dissatisfied), successfully integrates all the environmental variables. In outdoor situations, environmental indices based on available climatic data have been used by many investigators, particularly those dealing with human biometeorological classification of climate. The most common approach is to relate the air temperature to humidity, as in Thom's temperature-humidity Index (THI, originally called Discomfort Index, DI). Although most of the indices used in these circumstances do not include radiation and ventilation, they give an excellent first approximation prevailing in the different regions.

However, the first empirical index to be developed was the ET (Effective Temperature), defined as the temperature of a still, saturated atmosphere, which in the absence of radiation would produce the same effect as the atmosphere in question. This index is translated into a nomogram for quick assessment of ET as a function of DBT, WBT and air velocity. Radiation effects are accounted for if DBT is replaced by GT (Globe Temperature), in which case the index is known as CET (Corrected Effective Temperature). Thermal comfort studies were conducted in Singapore by C. G. Webb (1960), resulting in the 'Singapore Index' and later the 'Equatorial Comfort Index' (ECT). The latter was re-examined by Lim and Rao (1977) in a study that also involved Fanger's Predicted Mean Vote (PMV) index. It was found that there was generally good agreement between Webb's scale of comfort level categories to that of PMV. Besides proposing 25 °C to replace the original neutral temperature of 26 °C, it was also concluded that the use of Fanger's comfort meter was to be recommended for general use in assessing a given environment's comfort.

Heritage: The Tangible and Intangible

The broad term heritage is related to architecture and typically encompasses the tangible and intangible. However, the simultaneous reference to the term ecology and heritage also refers to the recent inclusion of landscape and natural elements in UNESCO recommendation on the Historic Urban Landscape (HUL recommendation), which was accepted in 2011 and was the first instrument developed to propose an integrated approach that would place development and conservation of urban heritage on the same plane (UNESCO 2011). The tropical region remains a region significant and precious due to the intensity of its climate, the rapid destruction of its structures and artefacts, and its increasingly extinct flora and fauna species, thus to tropicalised and localised heritage scope remains crucial. It includes the landscape concept, which is:

Natural and cultural heritage in urban areas and in the countryside in areas recognised as being of outstanding beauty as well as everyday areas. Thus, to promote the protection, management, and planning of the landscape 'as an essential component of peoples' surroundings, an expression of the diversity of their heritage, and a foundation of their identity. (Ripp & Rodwell, 2015)

This new discourse made possible, and at the same time, became a response to existing divides between the conservation of cultural heritage and urban planning. In the following years, the UN 2030 Sustainable Development Agenda in its Target 11.4 highlighted the importance of safeguarding natural and cultural heritage for safe, inclusive, and resilient cities. The sustainable agenda provides tools for making urban heritage a resource for urban development. Its broader urban context is to include the site's topography, geomorphology, hydrology and natural features, its built environment, both historic and contemporary, its infrastructures above and below ground, its open spaces and gardens, its land-use patterns and spatial organisation, perceptions and visual relationships, and all other elements of the urban structure. It also includes social and cultural practices and values and the intangible dimensions of heritage related to diversity and identity.

References

Andaya, L. Y. (2010). *Leaves of the same tree—Trade and ethnicity in the Straits of Malacca.* NUS Press.

Bowring, P. (2018). *Empire of the winds: The global role of Asia's Great Archipelago.* Bloomsbury Publishing.

Cheshmehzangi, A., Flynn, A., Tan-Mullins, M., Xie, L., Deng, W., Mangi, E., & Chen, W. (2021). From eco-urbanism to eco-fusion: An augmented multi-scalar framework in sustainable urbanism. *Sustainability, 13*(4), 2373.

Hagan, S. (2014). *Ecological urbanism: The nature of the city.* Routledge.

Leite, J., & Justo, R. (2016, June). Typo-morphology: From research to architectural education. In *Architectural research addressing societal challenges, proceedings of the EAAE ARCC 10th International Conference, Lisbon, Portugal* (pp. 15–18). CRC Press.

Lim, P. B., & Rao, K. R. (1977). Environmental control of buildings. *Journal of Singapore National Academy of Sciences, 6,* 72–89.

Miksic, J., & Goh, G. Y. (2016). *Ancient South East Asia.* Routledge—World of Archaeology. Publisher.

Mostafavi, M., & Doherty, G. (2016). *Ecological urbanism* (M. Mostafavi, & G. Doherty, Eds.). Co-published by Harvard University Graduate School of Design. Integral Lars Müller.

Moudon, A. V. (1998). The changing morphology of suburban neighborhoods. In *Typological process and design theory* (pp. 141–157). Agha khan Program for Islamic Architecture.

Munoz, P. M. (2006). *Early kingdoms of the Indonesian Archipelago and the Malay Peninsula.* Didier Millet, Csi.

Olgyay, V. (1963). *Design with climate: Bioclimatic approach to architectural regionalism.* Princeton University Press.

Ripp, M., & Rodwell, D. (2015). The geography of urban heritage. *The Historic Environment: Policy & Practice, 6*(3), 240–276.

Sabri Zain. (2010). Sejarah Melayu: A History of Malay Peninsula—The Malays. http://www.sabrizain.org/malaya/malays

Spirn, A. W. (2014). Ecological urbanism: A framework for the design of resilient cities. In *The ecological design and planning reader* (pp. 557–571). Island Press.

Steele, J. (1999). Ecological Architecture. In J. Steele (Ed.), *Architecture today.* Phaidon Press.

Stutterheim, W. F., & Goris, R. (1948). *De kraton van Majapahit.* M. Nijhoff.

Vuksanovic, D. (2000). Vernacular architecture: A paradigm for sustainable buildings. In S. Roaf, M. Sala, & A. Bairstow, *Sustainable buildings for the 21st century: Teaching issues, tools and methodologies for sustainability* (Proceedings of TIA 2000: Third international conference, Somerville College, Oxford, Sunday 9 July–Wednesday 12 July 2000). TIA on behalf of the European Commission Directorate General XVII for Energy and Transport.

Whitehand, J. W., & Gu, K. (2007). Urban conservation in China: Historical development, current practice and morphological approach. *The Town Planning Review, 78,* 643–670.

Wolters, O. (1962). Paul Wheatley: The Golden Khersonese: Studies in the historical geography of the Malay Peninsula before A.D. 1500. (Malayan Historical Studies.) xxxiii, 388 pp., front. Kuala Lumpur: University of Malaya Press, 1961. (Distributed by Oxford University Press. 45s.). *Bulletin of the School of Oriental and African Studies, 25*(3), 638–639. https://doi.org/10.1017/S0041977X00069822

Yeang, K. (1982). *A theoretical framework for ecological considerations in the design and planning of the built environment.* PhD thesis, University of Cambridge.

Part I

1

Eco-Inflections of the 'Mandalic' City-Form: Morphologies of the Pre-Colonial Urban Cores

Shireen Jahn Kassim and Kamariah Kamaruddin

Introduction

The recognition of morphological layers in the evolving dynamic histories of South East Asian urban centres is crucial in understanding the original indigenous layer of the city, and from this, to further understand the changes in the configurations of historic urban cores over large spans of time. The legibility of a city must be understood against the evolution of its history, and its morphology which, in South East Asia, includes layers overlaid by changes brought about by colonial impacts and the colonial era. There must be a continuous identification and recognition of urban morphological layers in the evolving dynamic patterns of historical changes, including changes in the configurations of urban elements over time. The continuous changes in urban spaces and configurations in heritage cities remain a crucial factor in the understanding on the underlying identity and landscape of South East Asia. The role of urban analysis

S. Jahn Kassim (✉) • K. Kamaruddin
International Islamic University Malaysia, Jalan Gombak, Malaysia

S. Jahn Kassim et al. (eds.), *Eco-Urbanism and the South East Asian City*,
https://doi.org/10.1007/978-981-19-1637-3_1

3

in itself is to support urban design for urban restoration, reuse, and regeneration. Most important is the layered nature of any historic traditional centre which will be identified in the future as a cultural and historic area yet which must confront a future where its original environment is constantly physically degraded by the impact of the urban development that follows eras of modernisation. Thus Han and Beisi (2016) suggest that understanding the traditional morphology is crucial because "the changing social structure in different historical periods is reflected in the transformation of both urban morphology and building typology in Southeast Asian cities and their buildings'. Only by studying the spatial character in terms of both the macro- and micro- levels can the underlying identities of these cities be deduced and aspects of sustainable development be identified, including dimensions such as inclusiveness and cohesion among co-existing cultures, which must be considered along with the physical elements.

The South East Asian historical trajectory in terms of the morphology of cities follows an evolution from 'agragrian' to littoral. Historically, ethnographers have categorised settlements or civilisations before the thirteenth century as 'inland' or 'nagara-based', and it is only after the thirteenth century that many urban centres emerged as 'coastal' or the *pesisir*. While inland civilisations are characterised by ordered and monumental remains, mainly masonry urban cores, with settlements spread across a large inland area around a strong and ordered centre, 'coastal' civilisations have often been described as 'ungridded' and 'disordered'. There is an existing challenge to describe and classify these. The urban cores of *negeri* (or maritime)-based settlements, which evolved following the gradual disappearance of the *nagara* ceremonial centres and civilisations by the thirteenth to fourteenth centuries, have tended to be described as disorderly, dense, and organic, located on coastal areas and at the confluences of large rivers.

The littoral zone or nearshore is the part of a sea or river that is close to the shore. In coastal environments, the littoral zone generally extends from the high-water mark, which is rarely inundated, to shoreline areas that are permanently submerged. The adjacency of water gives a number of distinctive characteristics to planning, morphology, architectural profiles, structures, and urban design which reflect a gradation of forms in terms of adjacency to water. Due to their compact and littoral siting, they are sufficiently dense to be defined as 'urban' and thus represent the density, increased walkability, and urbane life style defined as being part of 'cities'. They are increasingly of interest due to the need for resilience amidst climate change and the need for both resource and energy conservation, due to, amongst other things, the nature of bioclimatic amelioration including facilitating the induced urban 'breathability' or increase wind flow across buildings and urban structures or blocks in historic core areas. The essentially historical 'organic' character and fragmented urban form in the historic layer, in fact, lends itself to increased ventilation and heat loss in urban spaces due to the nearness and availability of water, which enables buildings and urban spaces despite higher densities, as the proxomity to water and greenery can benefit from a cooler atmosphere and bring about enhanced comfort conditions in the outdoors and public spaces. These are also known to support a greater variety of plant and animal life. Historically, these littoral sites grew rapidly and densely. They additionally grew with the sudden surge of economic activity in the region as trade routes diverted and concentrated along the rivers or coasts as these came to be relied upon as safe passages of trade. This includes 'original' or 'hybrid' cultural patterns, as well as those urban elements that reoccur across cities and sites, with associated climatic features and alignments. Han and Beisi (2016) highlight how the understanding of the traditional morphology is crucial: *"The changing social structure in different historical periods is reflected in the transformation of both urban morphology and building typology in Southeast Asian port cities and their buildings."* The urban cores are particularly crucial, as Gospodini asserts: *Historical urban cores representing long lived survivors from the past constitute counter-structures to the ephemerality of fashions, products, values,* etc., *that according to Dietvorst and Ashworth is rooted in the growing of events in time (acceleration of history) characterizing the era of new modernity.*

'Inflections' of Morphological Form

In mathematics, an inflection point is the point at which the curvature of a function begins to change. An inflected form thus, suggests a pattern that represents a moment when a profile or the coordinates of an original form morph into distinct changes. Both architecture and urban forms can be characterised as 'inflections' as they constitute evolvements or shape movements across space and time—in the context of typo-morphological changes as a result of contextual, sociocultural pressures and forces that exert itself from cultural, temporal and environmental conditions which evolve with time. Both imply that an inflection point is a turning point; and which 'inflect' morphologies or 'shape' due to any dramatic change. In architecture, Frampton promoted that architects exert localisation strategies onto particular parts of a building such as a facade, a window, a roof or an opening in order to regionalise architectural forms to their contextual fit—including climatic fit—and which he argues, as a kind of:

> …*place-conscious poetic—a form of filtration compounded out of an interaction between culture and nature, between art and light. A constant 'regional inflection' of the form arises directly from the fact that in certain climates the glazed aperture is advanced, while in others it is recessed behind the masonry façade.*

Schumacher (1971) suggests that under historically densed urban conditions, a certain degree of contextualism arises from (the dynamics) of a kind of deformation related to architecture and urbanism. Karl Kropf refers to 'inflection' as 'changes to the urban tissue morphologies as a result of external factors'. Jahn Kassim (2002) characterises regionalist tendencies of certain Asian architects as their signatures or their predispositions in evoking their culture through formal strategies such as 'inflecting', 'twisting', or 'fragmenting' their space-form or overall volumetric forms and spaces, and refer to 'organic inflections' as a modern process in the localising of highrise forms and spaces, from the western conception of a homogenous 'glass' box.

South East Asian Urban Core: From 'Mandalic' to 'Maritime'

Historically, in South East Asian urbanist studies, other than religious connotations, the *mandala* refers to a four quarter or cardinal-directional urban conception or predispositiion of ancient planners in conceptualising a city as these reflect their intention to control the unpredictability of nature and climatic forces. Thus the predominant pattern of planning in the urban core or centres, found mainly during the tenth to thirteenth centuries, were related to a mimicry or simulation of the path of the sun and seasons across daily and annual passages of time. It was these patterns which reflect both socio-political conditions which gave rise to polities called the *negara*—meaning (in Sanskrit) all that, pertains to urban sophistication dominance of urbanised civilisations'. These cities are located primarily astride mountain ranges and highlands and at times, are found further inland, namely the city of Angkor and Pagan, on the mainland and, to some extent, the city of Majapahit in Java. Labelled as galactic polities or *mandala*, in the archipelago, they had no marked physical boundaries but reflect a type of established vernacular civilisation whose collective identity was made possible by one or more compact centres of wet rice cultivation. On another note, *mandala* also refers to the heightening of the centre and the fragmenting of the periphery—a character of these historic centers or past urban cities. In the context of South East Asia, Bowring usefully summarises:

> '*The concept of mandala was a set of dependent—relationships in which rulers maintain their autonomy—within a common interest framework.*'

In short, *mandala* refers to the intensity towards the centre and the fragmentation or diffusion at the periphery.

Thus, although the *mandala* is described as 'associated with the ceremonial' in these *nagara* cities such as Angkor and Majapahit, it was an actual reflection and link to an urban core form representing a range. Miksic (2009) describes cosmological thought in Indonesia—which to some extent is seen in the remnants of Majapahit—as based on an 'axis' and 'four corners of the world'. Tambiah (2013) describes the concept of *mandala* as:

> *"Composed of two elements—a core (manda) and a container or enclosing element (la), or complex of satellites arranged around a center"* and more specifically *"elementary geometric designs are the five-unit (quinary) and nine-unit samples. The first consists of four units deployed around a central one, and the second is composed of a center, four places in the major cardinal positions, and four more placed in between at the lesser cardinal points."*

As the *nagara* (in the 9th to 13th centuries) cities and civilisations receded, historians are not in agreement about the common patterns of the *negeri*-based cities or littoral maritime cities. While *nagara* centres had reflected, to varying extents, a predisposition towards cardinal-based constructs, the influence of the *negeri* seem much less distinctive. Miksic (2018) labels these centres—which are linked to the term 'negeri' as opposed to 'negara'—as heterogenetic—as they did not easily or directly reflect any common or shared basic cardinal-based forms, as they grew and evolved along the littoral region—near the sea or river coasts of the region. These cities—of varying scales and sizes—are associated with the term *negeri* (or maritime)-based settlements which had followed the gradual disappearance of the *nagara* ceremonial centres and civilisations. They tended to be located at coastlines, estuaries, and junctions of trade routes, either at confluences of two rivers or at the mouth of large rivers. This chapter argues that by the advent of Islam, the residual of the *mandala* could still be seen with two evolving changes: (1) an ecological inflection to the natural topography and elements and (2) an axial adjustment to the Islamic direction of the *Qiblah*.[1] The word 'mandalic' here is used—rather than *mandala*—so as to represent 'having the character' of the *mandala*, rather than denoting a conscious intention in terms of mandala-based formal planning. It reflects the intentions of the ancients arising from their cosmological outlooks, within which mankind is always attempting to commune with, and even control, nature and its forces which includes the

---

[1] Qiblah or 'qiblat' is the direction towards Mecca which can be Eastern or Western, according to one's location on Earth and which represented the obligatory orientation of Islamic worship.

rising and setting of planetary bodies, and the edges of the universe defined by the horizon line. Thus the *mandala* here is linked to the persistent need to align with such forces, a tradition found in all cultures, from China to India and to South East Asia. It is argued that this represented a residual basis of ancient belief which had eventually been inflected towards certain manifestations in heritage city form along side its associated architectural monuments; which in turn had affected the ecological—topographical, environmental, and climatic—conditions of place, in particular, the climatic nature of these tropical maritime sites. As these cities and their planning forms changes within the subregion of Nusantara, the nature of the four-cardinal universe and the axiality of the urban centre were appropriated for city planning, had also change and later became adapted with the advent of Islam.

It is mentioned again that the word 'mandalic' is used here, so as to represent the character of the *mandala,* without claiming the conscious intention of past planners and builders. The residual of such 'mandalic' forms inflecting with the character of the *mandala* is also found in local idioms and cosmographies, particularly in the 'four-corner local cosmography' of Nusantara traditions that reverberates in the traditions of the populations. In Malay Nusantara terms, for example the phrase *alam empat penjuru* (four corner universe) is a local cosmography that is used in house-building and site orientations. Miksic (2009) similarly suggests that Majapahit's Trowulan city was based on a diffused and localised concept of 'the *mandala*', i.e. a circular square's centricness and axiality, which is linked to Java's traditional cosmological references to Mount Meru and the local conception of the four corners of the world, rather than any specific religious conscious aims or intentions.

In Malay Nusantara thought and traditions, traditional site initiation processes involve the notion of *alam empat penjuru* or four-corner universe as a part of a broad tradition which reflected a kind of negotiation of the self and the forces within the environment and with the universe in traditional thought. This is seen as a necessary step in negotiating one's position in the life-world, of existing with these forces and yet protecting one's life and property. Such forms of cosmography and the life-world are also suggested by Wheatley in his seminal book *The Golden Chersonese* within which, "The pivot of the four quarters" repeats itself in his inaugural lectures on the same interpretive notion and perspective: "*In these religions which held that human order was brought into being at the creation of the world there was a pervasive tendency to dramatize the cosmogony by constructing on earth a reduced version of the cosmos, usually in the form of a state capital. In other words, reality was achieved through the imitation of a celestial archetype by giving material expression to that parallelism between macrocosmos and microcosmos without which there could be no prosperity in the world of men*". Thus, a cardinal-concentric place-conception is seen as a necessary part of the life and time; when one must align with the forces of nature—rather than work against them— and thus, as civilisation grows, and in a large city context, the sacred seat of the ruler retains this intention and the seat celebrates the primacy of its location as the centre. This is seen as the center, from which extends other axial components of the city and community, while the rest of the settlement orbits around it. Physically, the 'mandalic' form also means that the centre of residence and administration is compact, (from the era of Srivijaya), initially known as the kedatuan—a royal precinct—a symbolically sacred 'sanctuary' that denotes the notion of a sanctuary in the centre.

Thus Malay-Nusantara centres and later cities, had evolved a form of spatial planning which can be argued as the residual of both a 'mandalic' structure. With the advent of Islam, these were adjusted but not erased altogether. In addition, such changes which historically reflected the advent of Islam, saw in essence, the city form gradually becoming adjusted again to both the topography and climatic characteristics of the littoral, which was associated with the coast and riverbanks, but which later, the advent of colonisation had disrupted and fragmented. Munoz (2006) observes how the Malays built cities but were never drawn to irrevocably alter their landscape, including their topographical and ecological context. Munoz further described: 'the Malay cities…*which reflected a layout which generally mirrored the structure of the state, consisting of a pattern of concentric circles with a strong centre, surrounded by rings, social stratification corresponding to certain spatial distance from the central point of the city, which was the source of power.*' Cakaric (2010) observes a similar eco-urbanist ethos and principle in the evolvements of the planning and in 'reading' the irregularities of these maritime cities of the past:

Linear or non-linear presence of water within a city directly determines the form of the relevant city, or more precisely, it determines a recognizable geometric appearance of the physical structures. In this manner, it gives a specific particularity to authentic urban identity by means of numerous expressions of individual and collective morphological units, combined within a synthesis as an urban landscape with the presence of a certain forms of water.

The 'eco-urbanist' praxis of in the region is similarly observed and suggested by Munoz: "*Usually, the rulers avoided altering the original landscape, instead they simply adapted their urban layout to pre-existing geographical features.* Widodo (2018) also suggests that South East Asian littoral cities, with their apparent irregularities and lack of common form, hinder a characterisation of their configurations. Generally, Jacobs highlights that in looking at the past order of cities, one tends to look for the 'regular' and 'regimented' order and, thus, at times, overlook certain more 'organic' patterns as chaos. She says: "*To see complex systems of functional order as order, and not as chaos, takes understanding. Once they are understood as systems of order, they actually look different. These areas of vitality need to have their remarkable functional order clarified whatever is done to clarify this order, this intricate life, has to be done mainly by tactics of emphasis and suggestions.*"

By extracting key configurations from past archives, maps and cartographic sources, supplemented with descriptions by travelers and reports, key abstractions of urban morphologies can be reconstructed. This includes original siting of key structures and original landscape. One can compare the different (2) urban elements and (3) architecture and urban core patterns, which seem to constitute of similar key element, and compactness, however merely configured in variegated ways. Then by comparing such essences in the pre-colonial centres' reconstruction in terms of estimated morphology and landscape, including (1) Melaka, (2) Aceh, (3) Banten, (4) Kuala Terengganu, and (5) Alor Setar, one can observe how the local form and diasporic urban configuration can both be argued as 'indigenous' because they occur before the drastic changes during colonialism, although they may include changes due to those influences. The results are summarised in Figs. 1.1, 1.2, 1.3, 1.4, and 1.5. Each represent a simplification of key elements of urban form i.e. the:

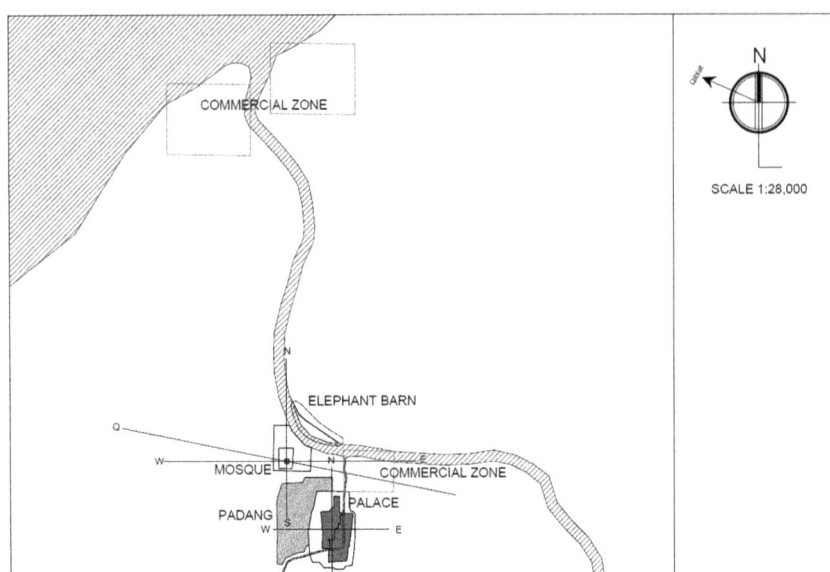

Fig. 1.1 A simplified morphology showing key elements of Aceh city, sixteenth century

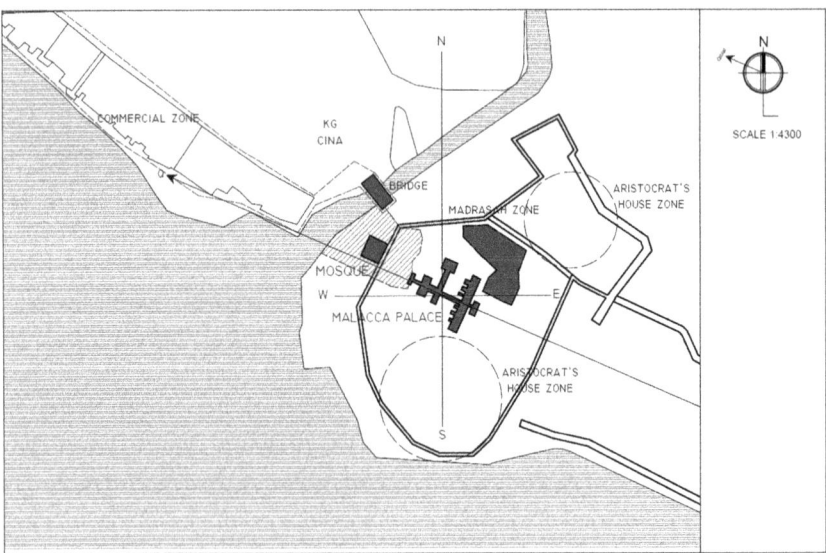

Fig. 1.2 Urban configuration of Kota, Melaka before 1511

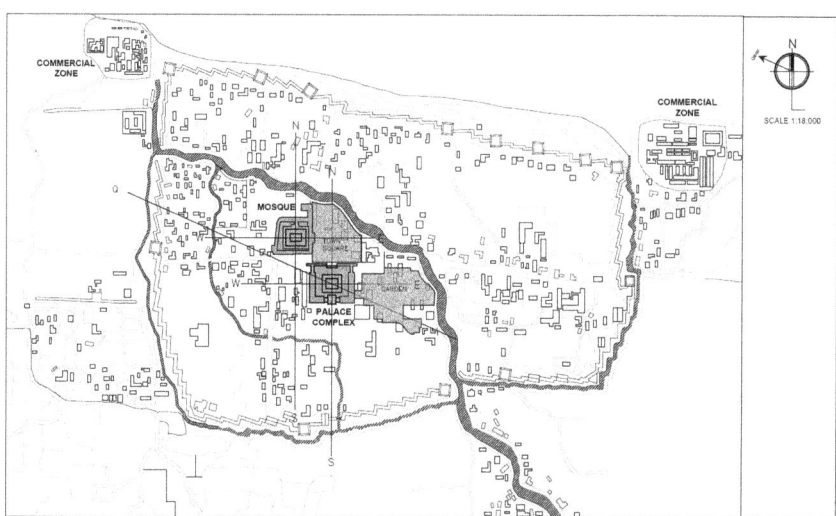

Fig. 1.3 Key urban configuration of Banten city in 1600s. (Adapted from map of Banten)

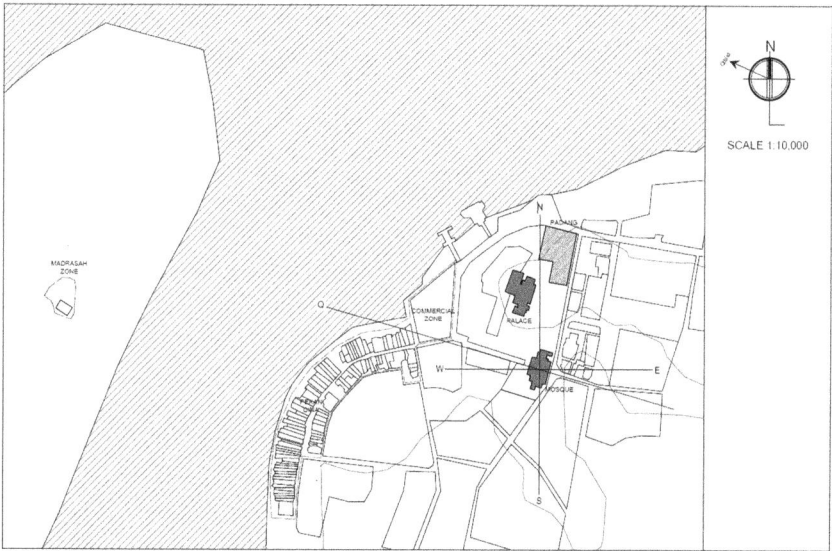

Fig. 1.4 Estimated urban configuration of Kuala Terengganu in 1800s

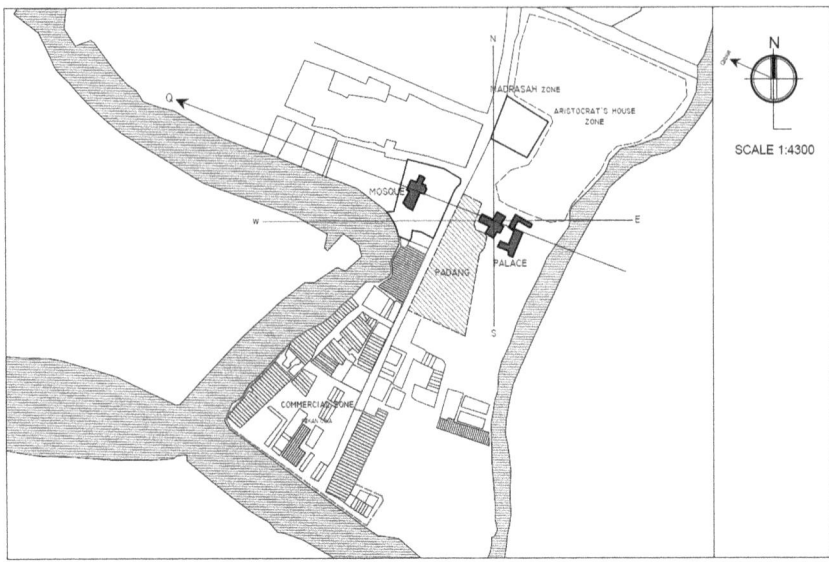

Fig. 1.5 Estimated pre-colonial urban configuration of Alor Setar, Kedah, in 1800s

1. River estuary morphological patterns and evolvements of an urbanism that grew with natural topographic and terrain elements rather than against it;
2. Different combinations of administrative, political, residential, and economic zones;
3. The existence of a diasporic community seen as the guest communities of the sultanate and within their protection;
4. A historical public space growing from the water courses which represent the historical and sociospiritual core of the city. These are further compared with other cities, such as Alor Setar, Pontianak, and Kota Bahru; and
5. In each case, a diasporic community, notably the Chinese community, as part of the city's evolution.

The following are case study cities which represent what is termed a pre-colonial urban core form—a layer beyond the colonial before extreme changes were wrought upon it. What is common in these cities or quasi-cities is the presence of an urban society which is defined by a complex organised society and a substantial population, including diasporic communities. They exude urban characteristics such as substantial population density, political and economic functions, variations in land use, social enclaves, and clear centre and peripheral districts, reflecting a form of hierarchical polity and administration. The following summarises the findings of the original urban configuration before colonial modern development.

Jahn Kassim et al. discusses the climatic character of these historic urban core forms, with these pre-colonial Malay-Nusantara evolving cities as those reflecting a more fragmented yet more breathable configuration or planning arrangement of the centre. Originally evolving from the principle of the *kedatuan*, they seem to be structures arranged amidst an open landscape, and in the absence of large enclosures or overtly encircling predominant city walls, yet they are compact, with spaces continuously enclosed by greenery and large trees. Before the advent of colonial influence, these can be seen as 'royal' sanctuaries, in which natural elements such as gardens and climatic strategies are distinctive in creating an environment of heightened tropical comfort, bordered by an open green field and then a dense peripheral transition zone of commerce and administrative 'centre'. The boundary between the interior and outside of the sanctuary is at times denoted by the *gerbang* gateway with specific treatment marking its entrance (Wiryomartono, 2012) (this will be discussed in Chap. 15). These centres had evolved essentially from a localised cosmology based on the underlying view of the universe as a natural phenomenon which is virtually a manifestation with mythical and metaphysical overtones. With the coming of Islam, these conceptions and patterns were still there, and as observed by Zumahiran in the field of ornamentation, '*Islam came to adjust and not bring revolutionary changes to patterns …*'. Thus, similar configurations were inflected towards a more rational metaphysical cosmology and on religious monotheism (Wiryomartono, 2012). The centre or *kedatuan*—the royal precinct (Milner, 2011) and symbolically the 'sanctuary'—still denote the notion of centre. For example, Tambiah (2013) described a similar planning character of heritage cities in Thailand and Cambodia: '*The most central of these concepts is mandala (Thai: monthon), standing for an arrangement of a center and its surrounding satellites and employed in multiple contexts to describe, for example, the structure of a pantheon of gods; the deployment spatially of a capital region and its provinces; the arrangement socially of a ruler, princes, nobles, and their respective retinues; and the devolution of graduated power on a scale of decreasing autonomies … which represents the radial mapping of an administrative system of departments and their subdivisions, as well as the constitution of successively expanding circles of leaders and followers or factions.'*

Historical Backgrounds

To further link the generic and variant urban forms, one can observe the reconstruction of fifteenth century Melaka (Fig. 1.6). Researchers have commented on how these cities, beginning with Melaka, were quintessential examples of a locally evolved city of the Nusantara tropics. Melaka initially grew due to its strategic location along the Straits of Melaka, striding a wide navigable river. It became known as the 'Venice of Asia' by Portuguese travellers. Originally, it represented a Malay royal, maritime

Fig. 1.6 Evolution of Melaka city from original pattern of Melaka, showing attempts at reconstruction by Jahn Kassim and Kamariah (2018) and Wiryomartono (2012)

South East Asian city which was strategically located midway between 'the turn of two monsoonal winds' and at the mouth of a large navigational river and deltaic plain, allowing ships to easily navigate and berth in the Melakan Straits. The hill became the 'royal' site which was bordered by orchards and a large field and then a dense community represented by royal enclaves, followed by other structures, including mosques and artisan neighbourhoods (Fig. 1.6), while on the opposite side of the river was the commercial area. The open green area represented direct administrative apparatus and support structures under the monarch in the era of medieval maritime cities or river-based cities which grew at the confluence of rivers. Over time, the historic core forms evolved into a more structured, more axial mophological character and which had 'residuals' of the original forms.

Kuala Terengganu was a similar estuary-based city, evolving as a result of higher-impact monsoons from the South China Sea, so its pre-colonial morphology represents an evolution from its topography due to a combination of hill, the river estuary facing the sea, and river concourses and locations which bear the brunt of the South China Sea flooding regime, monsoonal gusts, and storms. A significant topographical factor for the evolvements of the estuary town or city is geographical, evident in the curved coastal profile that stretches from Kampung Cina to Pasar Payang, influencing the urban pattern of Kuala Terengganu as a concentric ribbon generating inwards towards the more recent part of the town. Thus, the palatial zone and public space naturally grew on the leeward side of the hill, while the commercial including diasporic community grew deeper into the riverside. For many years, Terengganu was an important littoral state where the earliest sites of Islamic communities lived side by side with diasporic settlements. It became a centre of religious learning in the peninsula and region. Terengganu's position at the north-eastern part of the peninsula made it one of the entry points, from earlier communities of Chinese traders who plied their trade between southern China cities and the Malay Archipelago. The location of the royal quarters was originally at the foot of Bukit Puteri. Its location and vista were also dictated by the land mass high point—Bukit Puteri—where a small hill shadows the palatial 'city' compound from a sea approach, which can be considered a defensive strategy during times of conflict in its early history.

From this the Kuala Terengganu became a town centre known for its Islamic learning centres, marked also by a distinctive Chinese diaspora. This is highlighted by the discovery of Terengganu coins that bear the name of Sultan Zainal Abidin, dating back to 1708. Prior to this, the Istana Maziah, the palatial core, was built as a self-containing Malay town with the mosque and market built within walking distance of each other to serve the daily needs of the community.

The 46-year-old Pasar Payang was originally a maze of about 200 stalls, densely packed, selling native crafts and products unique to the region. The mosque or masjid was located on a site of prominence bridging the area between the palace and the kampong. The clustering of kampung houses with the particularities of Malay settlements based on a compound centricity recall the close relations/kinship aspect of Malay-Islamic culture's emphasis on familial relationship.

In Banten, West Java, a sixteenth-century city, thrived after the downfall of Melaka in the fifteenth century, with the traders and maritime activities diverted to West Java. Contemporaneous to Melaka, its urban form is especially unique due to a river which courses through the city and separates it into two zones. Reid describes the nature of the Malay-Java city which reflects the nature of Malay cities closer to the influence of Majapahit civilisation, which was a fusion of *mandala* form and organic city form in the Malay-maritime world. Its northern section contained the remains of the residential compounds of the elite. There is a mosque facing a Javanese *alun alun*, a typical layout of Javanese cities. The compound of Shah Bandar or the harbour master was located on the eastern side of the *alun alun*. The Kraton of Surosowan, as well as the Great Mosque of Banten, is located in this area. Its form reflects the generalities in urban form and topography as observed by Reid:

In maritime Southeast Asia, the tradition was quite different. River sites and valleys were preferred to hilltops, and the whole concept of defence was of a quite different nature. Frequently the palace area itself, the kraton, was surrounded by a wall, but as Van Goens said after describing the palace of the Javanese king, Mataram is beyond this a completely open place, which bases its strength on the number of villages around it.

Mapping and modelling unearthed key and recurring characteristics and principles seen as not only characterising a particular kind of city but a configuration where urban life evolved along the main river where craftsmen created and sold products. This region represented a public highway, then, where most economic activities took place on boats and which had produced an 'accretion' pattern in the morphology of the floating market community.

Sixteenth-century Aceh was a city and morphology impacted by the necessity of its royal centre or *dalam* to be further inland. Ibrahim et al. (2018) described how the city was originally a fortressed zone bordered by its great mosque (*masjid raya*) and its market, which were seen as iconographic and communal structures which were stable over two centuries. The site of the royal enclosure, or *dalam*, was adjacent to Medan Khayyali with a river at its border. The *dalam*, shown as the dotted black line in Fig. 1.7, was the physical feature. The fort, in the rectangular

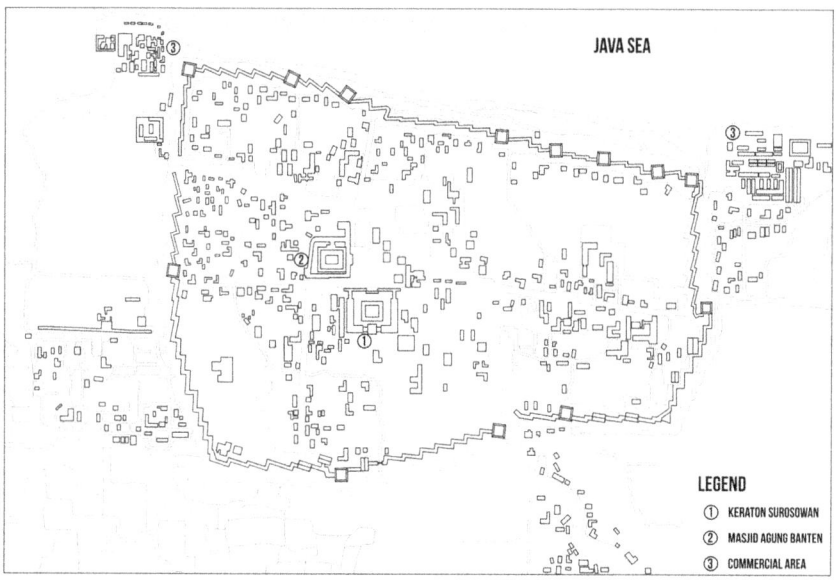

Fig. 1.7 A reconstructed Banten historic sixteenth-century city showing an organic clustering of *settlements around the sacred and symbolic centre of the city and aligned to maximise wind and views of the river*

area, acted as the most important administration site. Masjid Raya Baiturrahman (the Grand Mosque) is located to the north of *dalam* and was built during the reign of Iskandar Muda in 1612. The wide *padang* (open spaces) are located near the *dalam* of the king's palace, particularly for meeting and gathering with the *rakyat*. In the Florence map, those features that included the *dalam* were the two palaces, the customhouse, the two mosques, the laksamana's house, and the open spaces. *Dalam* is a complex used by the king and royal families.

Alor Setar, Kedah was basically founded in 1735 as the 8th Administrative Center of Kedah by the 19th Sultan of Kedah. Sultan Muham-mad Jiwa Zainal Adilin Mu'adzam Shah (1710–1778), Alor Setar is located inland by the right bank of the river, accessible around the sharp bend where the water terminal was located with direct access to the *padang*, alongside the terminal, the *masjid*, and across the *padang* to the east, with the Balai Besar oriented at such an angle and aligned with the *masjid* to capture the northeasterly and southwesterly prevailing winds of. The configuration is focal with the *padang* in the centre, the Balai Besar to the east, the *masjid* to the west, the metropolitan commercial centre to the south, bounded by the green and *alor* stream to the east, the river to the south and west, and the *kampung* neighbourhood beyond. The public realm includes pathways that lead to the *padang*, often shaded by large trees, which provide cool shade for walking bounded by shaded structures. The public realm also included the waterway as the journey travelled to experience the tapestry of the water's edge of the greenery, with *kampung* neighbourhoods that appeared from the green scenery that displayed the language of climatic origin, serene and blending with nature.

In every case, there is a topographical variant of an archetype that reflects a direct physical and visual link between the *istana* and the *masjid*, from the *padang* or *dataran* located at the *anjung* of the istana where public audience is received *and thus* formed the public front of the *istana* and to the *masjid* grounds. These cities had 'streets' that were engulfed in greenery since the public realm is heavily shaded by trees on each side of the street *and* bound by the facades of the *masjid* and the *istana and in between the façade elements of residential buildings on each side of the street filtered by big trees* with surrounding semi-enclosures of semi-open and shaded spaces.

A Comparative Characterisation

The cities discussed are compared with earlier core configurations of Trowulan, Majapahit and earlier trading cities in China, such as Chang'an (Table 1.1). Among the typo-configurations of public spaces, the first (represented by Melaka and Kuala Terengganu) followed closely the topographic form, in which public open spaces bordered a hill and estuary curve. In its original and indigenous eco-urbanist conditions, the hill was a high point which became not only a spiritual datum but also a visual node or focus onto the city population in the case of Melaka, and the hill-palace, field, mosque, and commercial promenade of the bridge were extremely compact with a direct visual axis between the palatial domain and the bridge-pavilion (as was historically verified). The close proximity of administration and commerce was ruptured by the colonial-led changes to Kota Melaka, from which the centre of pre-colonial public civic life was effectively destroyed and thus constituting the total disappearance of the original crest-located (rather than peak-located) center of the urban sacred space which included the main palace oriented towards the city centre. Similarities between the core morphological form of the city represented by the Aceh and Banten (Figs. 1.2 and 1.7) forms, where the river dissects the city distinctively and constitutes a promenade for people as it visually and virtually intersects the public domain, accompanying an almost uninterrupted public thoroughfare that allows shaded pedestrianised zones of constant walking along the river towards the public field or centre. This open field is characterised by its polygonal shape, and its shaded yet open space and large canopy trees had symbolic significance for the locality. It was almost as if an open-air public field was needed as a communal plaza but one which created historic imagery with borders surrounded by recognisable public architecture. In the case of Alor Setar and Melaka (Figs. 1.1 and 1.4) cities, the same public spaces,

Table 1.1 Comparing the morphologies of historic urban core forms: summating the temporal evolution of their basic morphologies and configurations of key structures, elements, and features

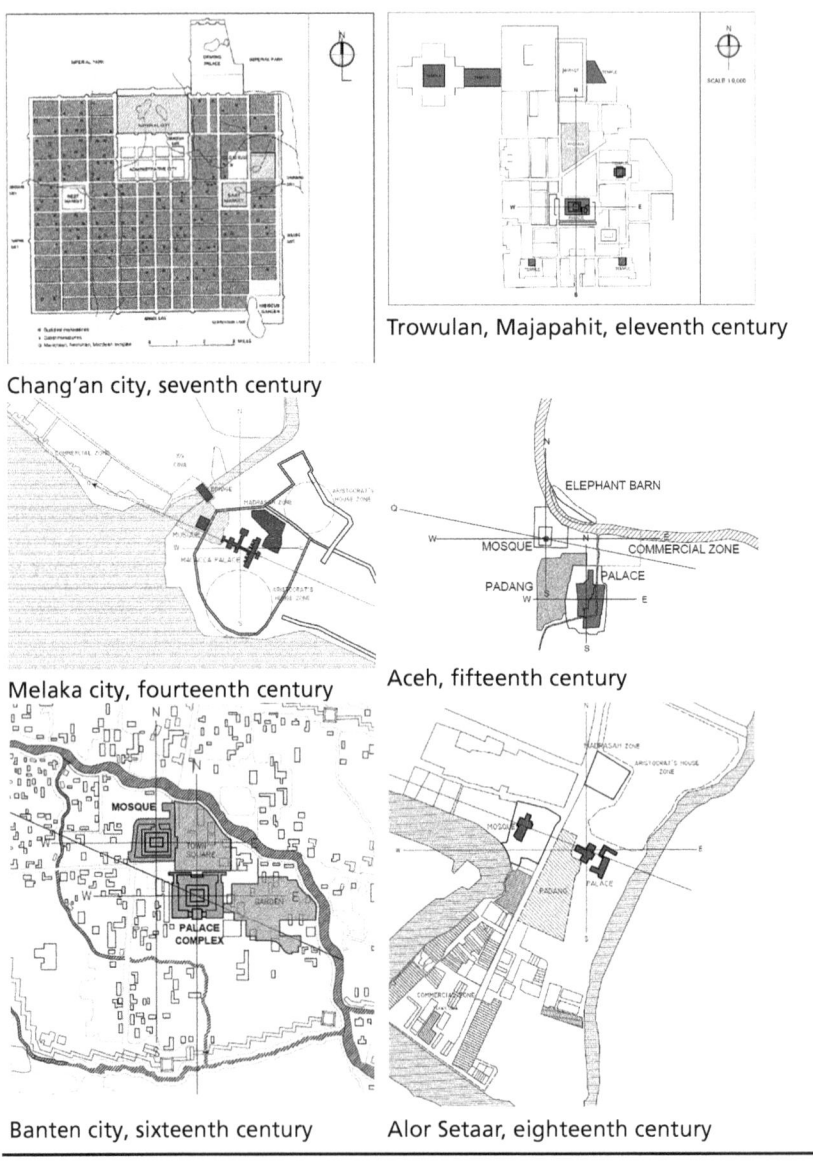

Chang'an city, seventh century

Trowulan, Majapahit, eleventh century

Melaka city, fourteenth century

Aceh, fifteenth century

Banten city, sixteenth century

Alor Setaar, eighteenth century

(continued)

Table 1.1 (continued)

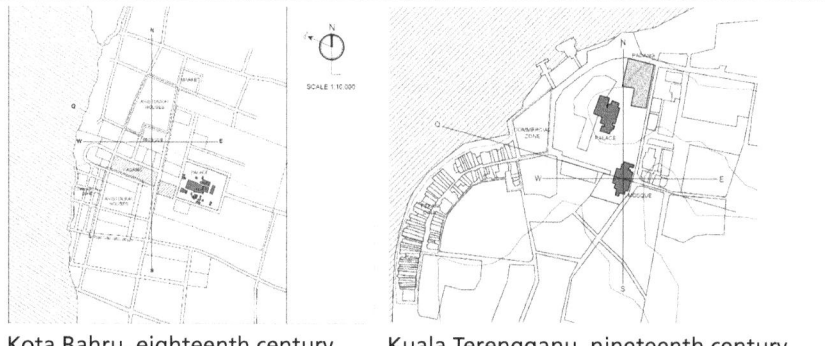

| Kota Bahru, eighteenth century | Kuala Terengganu, nineteenth century |

shaded zones beneath trees, and natural walkways form a compact core form, but the mosque and palace were set in an axial strong visual line with a distinct orientation due to the requirements of Qiblah (direction of Islamic prayer).

A comparison of the morphological evolutionary configurations of these past cities (Table 1.1) suggests how these configurations can be characterised by archetypes and eco-inflections of archetypes. The basic four-corner conception of urban elements consists of key structural elements which define the identity and historic landscape, varied according to site, climate, and topography. The *mandala* in the case of these littoral cities was never 'stamped' on the landscape but was always inflected to follow the curves and particularities of a given site. This recalls the observations of Alexander, Knapp, and Oliver about how vernacular settlements are not only culturally meaningful but point forwards to paths of sustainability due to the alignment between past urban forms, ecological patterns, and climate. They recall variations of Widodo's model of the South East Asian city, an urban form surrounded by waterscapes such as coasts and estuaries that include a diasporic community, which represents similar forms of evolutionary urbanism across several cities at around the same era. This is due to the simultaneous presence of an administrative centre with local settlement and includes diaspora communities living harmoniously in different zones and seen as "a layered reading of the city.

Lessons for the Future

The current rise of transit-friendly developments in new cities or new suburbs, reflects the rise of residential and mixed developments around a neighborhood transit station to major train stations, and these modern trends must again learn from the past in reinstating its sense of place or communal identity. Such focal points are needed for communities in response to the need for points of activity and revitalising adjacent neighbourhoods or residential areas. This is never more crucial than in parts of urban developments in recent years, where there is the development of a network of Mass Rapid Transit (MRT) stations, including in Malaysia and Indonesia, which was initially planned, and executed in order to encourage public transport while lowering carbon emissions in cities. Yet till present day, these transit stations have not yet evolved their potentials and have yet to be effective at constituting an axis or cohesive tool for the community and thus, improving the livability of surrounding communities. Such transit stations must again play their role—as in past transport route such as rivers and coastlines—as to become a focal point for the community and reinstate their criticality in their central locations—recalling the traditional centric nature of the *padang* in the traditional cities—which are again to be made easily accessible on foot, and light modes of transport, and to provide amenities, and which, amongst others, can encourage local businesses to supply the necessary services on location or take part in local public movements and activities. To become a prominent facet of urban life, a transit facility must again become a setting for community interaction and a place that accommodates a diversity of commercial activities and businesses, thus learning from historic urbanism, which suggests a recognisable public place, bordered by facilities which must be recognisable public spaces that act as focal points for a variety of activities and service establishments, such as open-air fresh produce markets, coffee shops, spiritual rest areas and facilities, branch bank offices, and health clinics, including services and uses which are permanent. Transit centres are essentially spaces of the public realm, and if made tropically benign including being effectively shaded, such spaces can congeal to become a visible focal point of the community in the historic urban cores, while creating a venue for community activities and events which reinforce their central roles. The common elements of traditional morphologies must again reinstall their original eco-urbanist elements, such as green open spaces, large trees, and proximity and presence of water to provide both a visual relief and a city's or transit centre's image, through the intersection of human acitivity, as well as strengthening the historically-based sense of place.

Taking the river routes as archetypes of modern public transportation routes, recent developments in urban design have highlighted the lessons such as 'pre-existing' past patterns of vernacular-based urbanism to both sustainable agendas and urban regeneration policies. Carmona reports that recent theories in urban design have been concerned with 'an emerging tradition of sustainable urbanism' and cited Brown et al.'s identification of 'four convergent lines of thinking in sustainable urbanism: (1) the need for vibrant walkable neighbourhoods that attract creative classes; (2) the emergence of downtowns with increasing demand for urban living; (3) an awareness of the growing obesity which has spread due to car-dependent urbanism; and (4) a growing interest in the potential of urban form to reduce the carbon footprint of mankind. The focus on the traditional city form and features is seen as an approach to sustainability, and its implementation can be re-invigorated by the re-emergence of the urban vernacular in order to fulfil the rising agenda of sustainability and sustainable development. Hillier has highlighted emerging ideas of sustainability and urban syntax which are linked to a more organic-form planning of the built environment. This echoes the earlier ideas in the writings of Alexander (1987) in his *A New Theory of Urban Design*, which summates that cities '… *must recapture the process by which cities develop organically* …' in order '*to create a new theoretical framework, to remedy the defects of cities today*'.

Conclusions

Past patterns should be compared with those of the present, and approaches and principles that represent patterns and past ethos can suggest sustainable patterns that can achieve the twin goals of sustainable development and urban heritage regeneration. In particular, much of the South East Asian conservation of cultural heritage and urban planning must include a site's topography, geomorphology, ecology and natural features, its built environment, both historic and contemporary, its infrastructures above and below ground, its open spaces and gardens, its land-use patterns and spatial organisation, perceptions and visual relationships, as well as all other elements of the overall urban structure and morphology. The overall aim is to highlight the essential historic layers within the multiple and evolving layers of morphology through typo-morphology methods according to the spatial reconstruction to recreate an identifiable and memorable branding of the tropical Asian context.

References

Alexander, C. (1987). *A new theory of urban design.* Oxford University Press.

Cakaric, J. (2010). Water phenomenon: Urban morphology transformation. *Facta universitatis—series Architecture and Civil Engineering, 8*(4). https://doi.org/10.2298/FUACE1004375C

Han, W., & Beisi, J. (2016). Urban morphology of commercial port cities and shophouses in Southeast Asia. *Procedia Engineering, 142*, 190–197.

Ibrahim, I., Abdul Latip, N. S., Jahn Kassim, P. S., Harun, N. Z., Mohd Noor, N., & Kamaruddin, K. (2018). *Historical "intimacy" in Malay urban core configurations: A Comparative analysis.* Proceedings of INHERIT conference Sarawak.

Jahn Kassim, P. S. (2002). The 'curves of nature'—The organic inflections of modern regionalism and ecological architecture. *An Urbanising Context, WIT Transactions on Ecology and the Environment, 57.* WIT Press. https://doi.org/10.2495/DN020231

Miksic, J. (2018). Khao Sam Kaeo: An early Port-City between the Indian Ocean and the South China Sea ed. by Berenice Bellina. *Journal of the Malaysian Branch of the Royal Asiatic Society, 91*(2), 155–159.

Miksic, J. N. (2009). Nail of the world: Mandalas and axes. *Arts Asiatiques, tome 64*, 134–145. https://doi.org/10.3406/arasi.2009.1694

Munoz, P. M. (2006). *Early kingdoms of the Indonesian archipelago and the Malay peninsula.* Didier Millet, Csi.

Schumacher, T. (1971). Contextualism: Urban ideals and deformations. *Casabella, 79–86*, 359–360.

Tambiah, S. J. (2013). The galactic polity in Southeast Asia. *HAU: Journal of Ethnographic Theory, 3*(3), 503–534. Harvard University.

Widodo, J. (2018). Historical morphology of coastal cities in Southeast Asia. In *Routledge handbook of urbanization in Southeast Asia* (pp. 391–399). Routledge.

Wiryomartono, B. (2012, 2013, December) Urbanism, place and culture in the Malay world: The politics of domain from pre-colonial to post-colonial era. *City, Culture and Society, 4*(4), 217–227.

2

River and City: Microclimatic Ameliorations and Accretions of the Ancient Urban Grain

Kamariah Kamaruddin, Illyani Ibrahim, and Nyimas Umi Kalsum

Introduction

The river lies at the heart of the dynamic historical evolution of cities of maritime Southeast Asia, and the early growth of cities was primarily driven by the river—the "giver" of its life. Southeast Asian trade routes gave rise to water-based urban communities, and traders, visitors, and administrators settled and shaped cities around the growth of ports and river–estuary settlements. Cities grew initially as a trading and administrative urban sites in edges and estuaries. Andaya (2008, p. 22) asserts in his observation of the link between historical geographies and the sociocultural nature of the archipelago:

K. Kamaruddin (✉) • I. Ibrahim
International Islamic University Malaysia, Jalan Gombak, Malaysia
e-mail: illyani_i@iium.edu.my

N. U. Kalsum
Universitas Islam Negeri Raden Fatah Palembang, Palembang, Indonesia

...the people were named after a particular river or stretch of river, stream or coast. In this maritime world, rivers and seas formed unities, while land formed the link between bodies of water...

Tarling (1999, p. 197) defines a conception of how the Southeast Asian maritime populations saw their environment:

... The critical link between these two forces of mountain and sea were the rivers, for they were the channels through which the rainwater that fell on the mountains flowed down, ultimately to merge with the sea. These river basins contained the earliest polities of island South East Asia...and shaped the political dynamic between them.

The maritime topography and past urban forms had a general microclimate due not only to their proximity to water and location and evolvements adjacent to rivers, estuaries, and coastal areas but also to the interspersing of urban and vegetal massing as a result of urban texture, fabric, and landscape. For example, the city of Brunei in Borneo is known for its villages in water. Land-river morphology in the Nusantara is still found in Banjarmasin, a city of canals that grew radially from a network of rivers and canals. Since the Banjar people are highly dependent on the Borito River and Martapura River as their main transportation network system, city settlements and human activities grew from connections to the river. Schophuys (1969) described the city built on a network of canals in the form of Anjir and based its name on the Banjarmasin River and its subsidiaries, including, among others, Sei Jingah, Sei bilu, Handil Bakti, and Antasan Kecil. A total of 102 rivers flow through Banjarmasin, thus forming a unique city character of incredibly intricate networks of rivers, streams, and canals.

A more linear form of settlement took shape in Kuala Kangsar, the royal seat of the Perak State, which had begun as a result of resettlement following the downfall of ancient Melaka. A settlement grew further inland along a main river route that had evolved as a public realm along the Perak River, primarily known as Kota Lama Kiri and Kota Lama Kanan. The morphology is described as follows by Airiess (2003):

...the settlement of the geography of the pre-modern world can be viewed as a quest by a riparian-oriented peoples footholds to maximize opportunities for the exploitation of both land and water resources to exploit the full range of resources that entered into trade and local consumption, land-based settlements functioned as nodes for water transport, penetrating upriver into a densely forested interior, along the coast, or seaward for external trade. The importance of river mouth and the confluence of two rivers as foci as settlements is apparent throughout the lowland tracts of the Malay culture world in the western half of insular Southeast Asia where the place name 'kuala' meaning river mouth and 'muara', a confluence of two rivers, have been adopted as common generic settlement... (sic).

Key public structures and spaces were planned along the waterway of Sungai Perak. Its evolvement recalls what Kathirithamby-Wells (1993) called the link of rivers with estuaries connecting the *hulu* (upstream) and *hilir* (*downstream*) of the river in the peninsular site:

...The nineteenth century Peninsular states, contributed to its characterisation as essentially coastal and estuarine, with the focus of political and economic control at the kuala or river-mouth...inherent in the character of the riverine Malay states was a dual orientation of another nature, based on hulu-hilir relations vital for their commercial identity...."; and urban settlement grew through a set of competing river systems based on hulu-hilir relations. (Miksic, 2018; Airiess, 2003)

The name Kuala Kangsar is believed to be derived from *Kuala Karong-Sa*, which means a hundred less one or the 99th tributary that flows into the Perak River. The settlement spread across the gentle undulating land along the banks to accommodate the growing community, but its core and historical part of town still sit quietly on the high grounds by the bend of the river. Later the Perak monarch constructed his palace at Bukit Chandan (Fig. 2.1), across the Perak River, which served as a public highway back then and where originally major economic activities took place on boats, which had evolved into an accretion of urban commercial zones—the floating market.

The river were the source of daily water for drinking, fisheries, trade, and transportation. The settlements were built along the wetlands on the

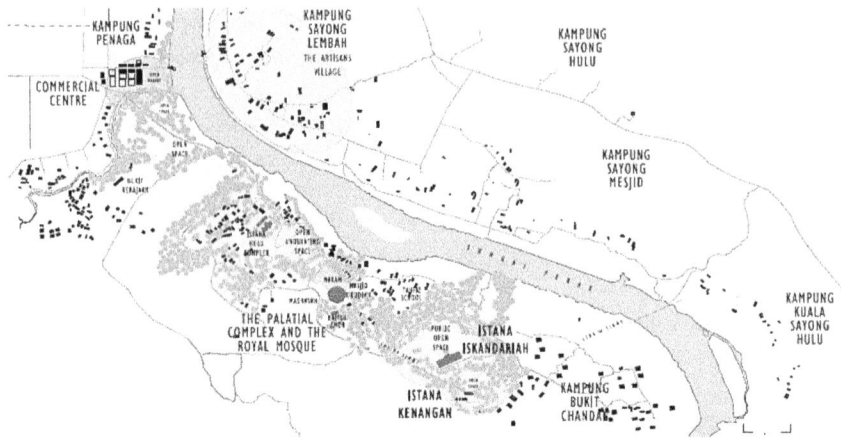

Fig. 2.1 Reconstruction of linear urban layout of royal zone in Bukit Chandan Kuala Kangsar in 1930s. (Copyright: Kamariah Kamaruddin)

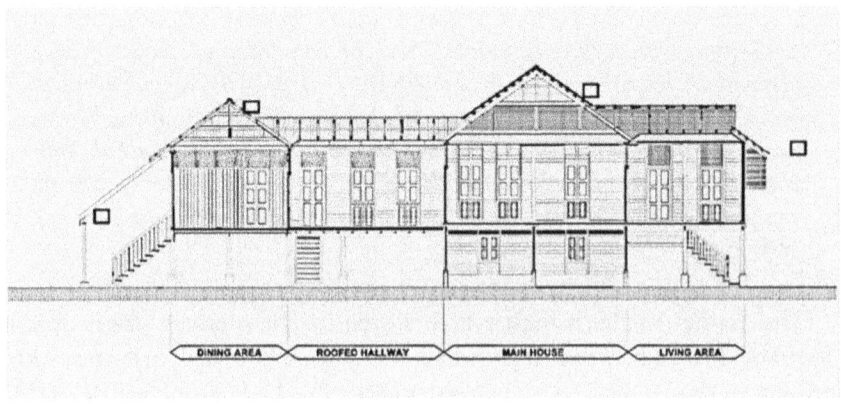

Fig. 2.2 Example of Malay house with double frontage, in Perak state. (Source: IIUM Heritage Center, 2016)

edge of the river that directly connected to the river transportation network. Riverfront houses had two faces with the main face directed to the river. Formerly, each riverfront house had a terrace with a boat dock (Fig. 2.2). Thus, originally, past settlements based on these river functions not only determined the size of the buffer area but also affected the layout, spatial zoning, and orientation of the buildings.

Urban grain reflects the granularity of a local settlement and economy and essentially provides a description of the pattern of plots in an urban configuration. It is described as fine urban grained when this pattern is dominated by small plots and coarse-grained by larger plots. Typically the urban grain of the historic core is finer as it gets nearer to the water's edge, offers a range of benefits, such as mixed use, ownership, residential and commercial uses, streetscapes, and street life in urban centers.

The reconstruction and morphology of the past traditional urban core of Kota Melaka as a trading city in the sixteenth century highlights how common patterns in the urban texture had evolved due to the denser zones by the water's edge. The urban fabric of Melaka historically grew from its origins in the fifteenth century. Bausani, citing Aroujo, described the nature of the habitation and settlement around Melaka port:

> "…at least 10,000 houses which were situated along the coast and the river of Melaka…" Quoting Giovanni, he adds that "…the town is situated near the sea-shore thickly strewn with houses and rooms stretches for three leagues which is most beautiful to see…"

These were interspersed with large common public zones, including boat landings, which constitute open spaces or public zones that directly face the river, and zones of highly dense clusters of commercial and residential areas in between.

Palembang City, Sumatera

The historical and triadic forces of river, land, and estuary are never more evident than in the city of Palembang. Its original morphology was intrinsically linked with the water and remains one of the deepest and most layered historical cities in the region. Its melding of Buddhist, Islamic, post-Islamic and colonial–postcolonial histories remains one of its unique characteristics. As an ancient city whose roots and genesis can be traced to the first century CE, a salient feature of the city has been described by historians and geographers as being submerged in, or surrounded by, water. Even its toponym comes from the combination of the word *pe*, meaning condition, and *lembang* or *lembeng*, meaning low-lying land whose tree roots are swelled due to submersion in water.

Its historic core became a walled city with three fortresses in 1682, following the fall of the Demak Sultanate. As the settlement flourished along the Musi River banks, the dynamics of the water city was still identified by a conglomeration of structures and houses built on rafts. Through legislation, the portion downstream of Seberang Ilir, where the palace was located, was intended for residents of Palembang, whereas foreigners who were not citizens of Palembang live on the opposite bank of the palace, called Seberang Ulu.

The extensive river and tributary systems of Palembang are the result of downstream and upstream settlements of the Musi River, resulting in multiple settlements on either side of its channel. Along these sites are dense river-based settlements, historically from the era of Srivijaya arising from the conglomerations of its so-called sea-people and sea-nomads, who controlled the maritime traffic through both the Melaka Straits and the river routes. The city's grip on trade and its dynamics meant it played a central role in Srivijaya, a maritime civilization and city by the eighth to twelfth centuries. As communities evolved and occupied "water" peripheral settlements or offshore spaces—originally "floating villages," i.e., seacraft-based activity—with their own public zones and residences, a layered and syncretic city grew in connections between the wide estuary and long breadth of the Musi River, from an evolving historical realm that encompassed the hulu area of Rawas, Lematang, and Pasemah and the *hilir* areas that open to the wide estuary and, eventually, the Straits of Malacca.

Oktarini (2018) observes on a macroscale that the Musi River itself can be divided into three zones: upstream, middle, and downstream. In the earlier maps of middle and downstream urban patterns, the roads and street network face the main river route. Fitri and Triyadi (2015) describe the essential life force of the Musi River as a determining parameter in the present urban morphology of Palembang. Romdhoni (2020) found that the original layer post-Srivijaya was a *"spatial configuration built during the Sultanate Palembang Darussalam; with urban fabric mainly clustered around the main transportation route, the river, and such accretive clustering also occur around the 'royal' centre containing the palace which marks the domain and centre of power, while certain forms grown from, and around such centers."*

Oktarini (2018) further described the architectural forms on the Palembang River: "The settlements in the upstream zone are not oriented to the river. In the middle zone, every riverfront house has two faces with the main direction to the land, whereas in the downstream zone, the riverfront house has two faces with the main orientation to the river. This indicates that the higher the level of river dependence, the more the settlement will be oriented to the river. People's dependence on rivers influences their adaptation, as manifested in the typology of buildings. In the upstream where river functions have little effect on people's lives, people avoid erosion by keeping away settlement from the river banks (Figs. 2.2 and 2.3).

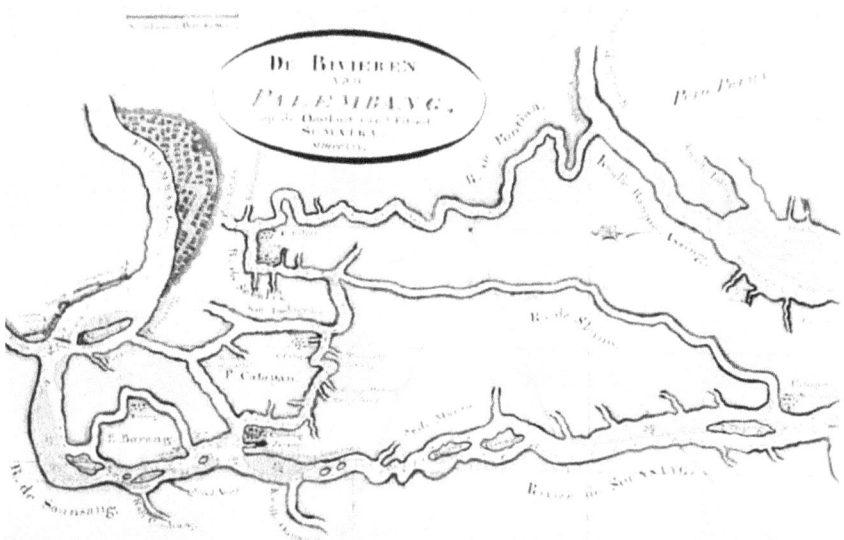

Fig. 2.3 Palembang: a map drawn by the Dutch in 1819 showing the accretive organic form of the river settlement. (Source: Anonymous. The Rivers of Palembang, on the East Coast of the Island of Sumatra. 1: 460,000. National Archief, 4. VELH 187, 1819)

The microclimatic conditions and wind pattern can influence the urban pattern and grain in the evolving city. The urban grain (Fig. 2.4) can be linked to the forces of accretion, which can be defined as *a growth or increase by the gradual accumulation of additional layers or matter*. Sanders and Baker (2016) make reference to accreted pattern that:

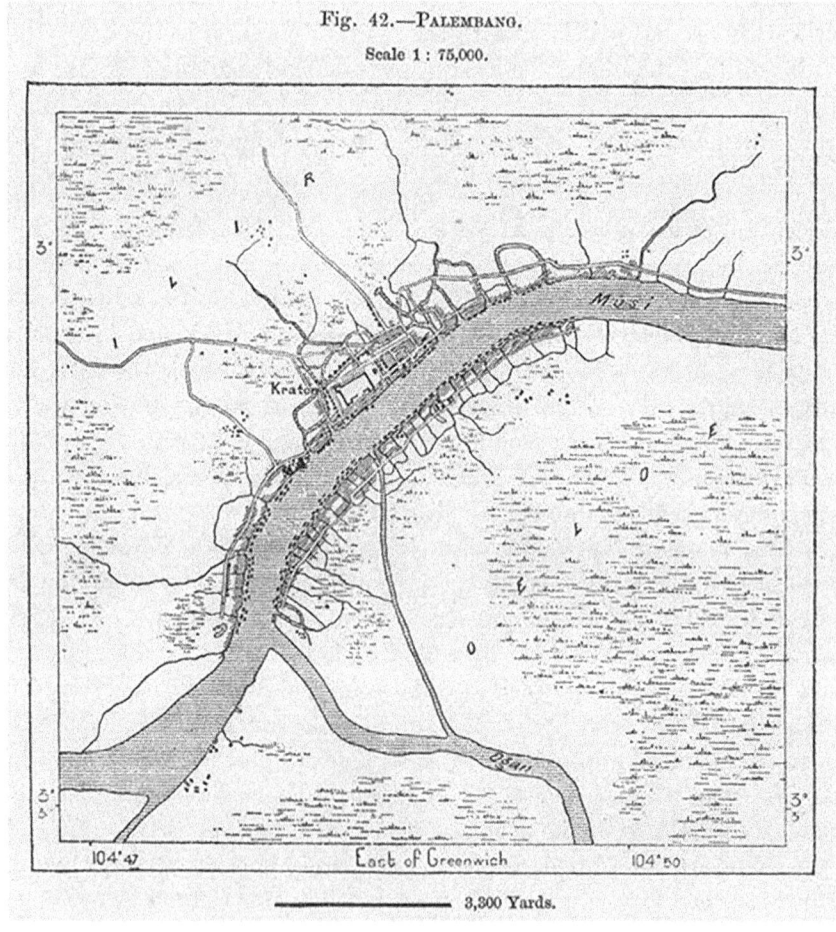

Fig. 42.—PALEMBANG.
Scale 1 : 75,000.

Fig. 2.4 Palembang urban fabric morphology pattern and form as it changes from early 1800s to 1885. (Map source; Major W.L. de Sturler. Plan of the Town of Palembang. 1:2,400. National Archief, 4. VELH 362, 1822)

Fig. 2.5 The river-accretive patterns of urban grain of Pontianak city, Borneo. (Adapted from Vahid Moosavi, 2022)

…has been a strong foci for urban morphological study that conceptualizes the urban landscape." Boeing (2019) defines and refers to accretion in the case where street networks may be planned according to clear organizing principles or may evolve organically through accretion, but their configurations and orientations help define a city's spatial logic and order.

These cities, where urban patterns grew through accretion, may lack a clearly defined orientation but can still be well structured in terms of complex human dynamics and land use (Hanson, 1989).

Accretion is thus the gradual accumulation of form which in most cases results in finer urban granularity around and near water sources or routes (Fig. 2.5).

i) **Pontianak, West Kalimantan**

Found along the Kapuas River, the capital city of West Kalimantan, the city of Pontianak evolved at the confluence of the Kapuas River, which is a total of 1,143 km (710 mi) long and up to 700 m (2,300 ft) wide at its delta; with a total area of 98,740 km² (38,120 sq mi), the river basin covers more than 67% of West Kalimantan. The river originates near the center of Borneo, south of the Indonesia–Malaysia border, in the area between the western slope of the Müller Mountain Range, which runs through the island center, and the southern slope of the Upper Kapuas Range (Indonesian: Kapuas Hulu), which is located more to the west (Fig. 2.5).

The historic core of Pontianak reveals that original urban grains are an evolvement of both local and Dutch patterns of settlement from the 1800s (Fig. 2.6). Essentially its morphology and fabric are a result of the interlacing of urban canals throughout the city and in riverside zones,

Fig. 2.6 The river-edge finer urban grain of the City of Pontianak by 1934

while its historic core is affected by its evolution from the Malay Sultanate system. Alqadrie (2010) found that the urban pattern phenomena of Pontianak City during "special functions" as the Waterfront City and Malay Sultanate evolvement and express a spatial planning system that affected the shape and arrangement characteristics of a Malay Sultanate city in Southeast Asia:

> *The dynamics of the city are affected by changes in global civilization and natural resources. The potential of lural and multicultural societies is a phenomenon for the process of formation (metamorphosis) and the functioning of the city. Morphology is not only related to the physical and geometric shapes, but concerning influence factors from ideas, spatial planning character and key events that change the basic idea.*

A mapping and tracing the morphological changes in Pontianak (Chandra Bayu, 2007) highlighted how the river that had instigated these urban evolvements and developments. Its resultant urban and typo morphological forms were linked closely to the traditional river-based cities network. Canals, morphology, fabric and urban grain can potentially able to be utilised for further microclimatic outcomes.

Urban Ventilation and the Urban Fabric

Ma and Chen (2021) found that under hotter climate conditions, the river exerts a significant microclimatic effect, due to the cooling and wetting capacity of what is termed the urban river corridors. With past development along rivers acting as trade routes, the function of the river is not merely transport, but climatic. It was eventually translated into the adjacent urban fabric and reflected a characteristic of the urban morphology of tropical cities of the past. Urban blocks with low building height and low site coverage will naturally allow wind that will help enhance ventilation efficiency. Urban development intensity will naturally gravitate on riparian zones that hold valuable natural landscape resources. In relation to modern development, increasing interspersing water around the urban canyons and pathways between blocks would allow wind flow to further

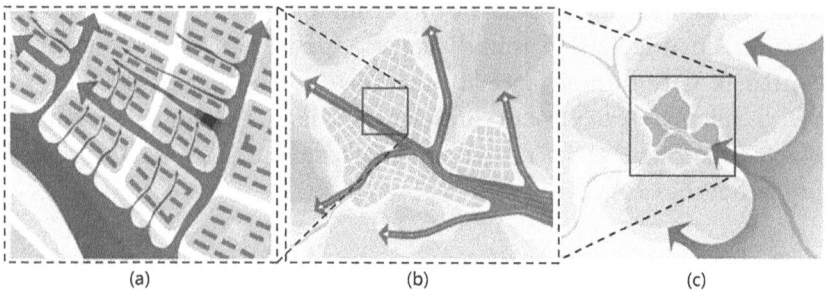

Fig. 2.7 Urban morphology, urban fabric, and ventilation corridors—from micro to macro scale (Tong & Tian, 2021)

penetrate into the body of the city. The longer axis of the corridor should be at a small angle with the dominant wind direction, and (Tong & Tian, 2021) observed that the angle between these corridors and urban spaces impact on how the effect of the ventilation corridor can exert its influence (Fig. 2.7) The direction of the ventilation corridor is within 30° of the prevailing wind (Oke, 1988).

The interspersing of wide-open spaces with high-density clustering in the past traditional city of the tropics can be found in cities such as Melaka, Palembang, and Pontianak, Borneo. The region has been described as communities in water (Bowring, 2019) and its microclimatic effect historically benefitted from the water. The microclimate of littoral cities in the Southeast Asian archipelago was originally described as cool by past travelers. Mills (1930) explained that Eredia documented a salubrious, cool tropical environment, in contrast to an urban heat island (UHI) typical of the region. Hence, historically, heterogenic cities grew from mercantile centres located in the coastal littoral zones and the cities were seeded from maritime activities that evolved throughout time in sea river estuaries or as river settlements. Their urban morphological characteristics evolved from these quasi-aquatic communities in the Southeast Asian archipelago that arose from a symbiosis between river communities, trade routes, and interior resources. Syafrina et al. (2020) found in their study of measuring and modeling the impact of river canals in Pontianak at least a 0.5° impact of the water canals on urban temperatures in peak daytime.

The cities has potential as the riverfront urban fabric and economic driver. It facilitate the distribution of ventilation as the wind path from the river can disperse and bring cooler air from the riverfront urban area into the urban fabric. This not only alleviates discomfort but reduces UHI impacts (Fig. 2.7).

In traditional cities, the conditions of finer and higher urban grain closer to rivers and water would not only allow visual interspersing experience of water but increasing urban canyons and pathways between blocks and physical bodies would then allow wind flow to further penetrate the body of the city. Ma and Chen (2021) found that under hotter climate conditions, the river exerts a significant microclimatic effect on riverside zones, and its cooling and wetting capacity is called the effect of the urban river corridors. Urban ventilation corridors are typically large open spaces, such as main roads, connected open spaces, landscaping, nonconstruction sites, building line setback zones, low-rise buildings, and urban structures that run through high-rise buildings. A public open space, the road intersection, a park, and connected roads have formed a continuous ventilation corridor.

Under hot and humid conditions, cool wind from the seaside or riverside can significantly decrease urban temperatures due to elevated cool air advection, increased atmospheric mixing, and sometimes the associated appearance of cloud cover (He, 2018; Papanastasiou & Kittas, 2012). There has been evidence that there is always a wind speed threshold, in proportion to the urban population scale, above which the UHI phenomenon of a specific city can be eliminated (He, 2018). The implication of wind ventilation for UHI mitigation is linked, among others, to localized urban morphology. Srifuengfung (2012) in his study of hot humid conditions in Bangkok and reiterated that under conditions of high density in cities, including those with historic cores, there is a need to plan and manage heights and density for urban microclimatic conditions:

>…the densest and most congested urban areas… as the importance of urban redevelopment design is that it could possibly make a linkage between public health and urban planning and explore collaborative strategies and tangible actions for healthier population. Thus, the systematic evaluation of urban ventilation performance is becoming an urgent problem and a challenge.

Urban Fabric and Heightened Densities

Urban morphological patterns can affect the ventilative effect of the urban fabric and potentially block the intended effect of river corridors. Yet a characteristic of the urban morphology of tropical cities of the past still preserved including the interspersing of naturally low-rise development. A high density with open spaces such as padang, boat landings and royal enclaves, can naturally facilitate wind corridors from the river or estuary. Choi et al. (2009) observed that urban expansion characterized by a high-density downtown morphological pattern can gradually affect urban wind speed per year.

Guo et al. (2017) had also indicated that urban enclosed city blocks, strip apartments in rows, and, especially, high-rise buildings with a large podium bulk can be unfavorable to natural ventilation and could reduce the mean wind speed by up to 78% relative to the approaching speed. Based on ventilation paths, hybrid buildings with different heights, building stilts, and increasing building height while decreasing their land coverage could improve the urban ventilation performance. In urban cores, the central conflict is due to economic factors; riverfront urban development intensity will naturally gravitate to river edges or riparian zones because these hold valuable natural landscape resources. Tong and Tian (2021) proposed that a balance between spatial form and ventilation in a riverfront area can be struck if a clustering pattern of urban riverfront development with dense urban grain–low-rise blocks is interspersed with open spaces or blocks with low development intensity located between these clusters.

Comparing the wind patterns of Melaka as in Fig. 2.6, and the approximation of the orientation of palace and mosque, it is clear that these key buildings of the public realm were optimally sized and sited to harness ambient conditions for bioclimatic design and comfort. Any axial readjustment was merely asserted for security and visual-based purposes reasons (as per Fig. 2.6).

Thus, in tropical cities, the conditions of finer and higher urban grain closer to rivers and water courses would not only allow a visual interspersing experience of water, but the increasing urban canyons and pathways between blocks and physical bodies would not only allow wind flow to further penetrate into the body of the city but evolve a particular profile of the city. As Čakarić (2010) insightfully observes:

> *Watercourses can be crucial information of city types following the consequences caused to the urban morphology and its transformation. But water as an ecological force asserts the generation of "urban forms and plan or design elements", as it affects the aesthetic quality of the visual representation of a city's silhouette.*

The vantage point of the water allows proximity to water, view point of water, and some degree of urban cooling. The dense mass and grain of the city is built from organic assemblage that existed over the centuries, also includes with the addition of 'void' structure from activity and trade along rivers and sea routes. Due to the fundamental role of waterways, the increased settlement increased the density on the water's edge producing an image of the city reflected by travelers' remarks and tales about structures that "arose from water" and whose skyline layered each other, arising from and approximating multiple craggy coastal topographies.

In Melaka, Kuala Terengganu or Palembang and Brunei (Fig. 2.6), and the historic form of Singapore, the profile of the city itself is supported so as to be resilient to the rise and fall of water levels. Structures and seascapes are part of the same unity and physical structures, and spaces grow to accommodate both public and private life. From the edges of the water, the city generally rises into a broken-up skyline that dominates the image of the cities of the region. Originally the profile of the city rose vertically in varied steep pitches and extended horizontally into land in deep hierarchical forms seen as fragments of the total settlement, ending in an orchestration of multiple skylines, resonating from the accretive nature of the urban grain of the littoral city. Its physical structures are seen as growing from the competitive necessity of access to water. Its broken-up skyline dominates the image of the city, coupled with the deep and steep fragments of its multiple roof lines. The river's edge in Pontianak, Borneo, reflects a water–land dynamic that creates a particular hybrid eco-urbanism waterscape that should be preserved and sustained in reflecting the original proximities and views of water bodies and rivers (Fig. 2.7). These structures are a combination of "light" and "mass" with

Fig. 2.8 Original fine-grained accretive nature of Southeast Asian city: sketch of old Singapore in 1800s (Source: Adila Shahrin (2014), credit to illustrator: Wafiy Harith)

steps and piers repeatedly found fronting the river, which reflects how the city and its people have a strong visual or physical connection to a river (Yassin et al., 2009, p. 3 cited.) (Fig. 2.8)

Such hybrid formations should be improved yet preserved to demonstrate the phenomenon of the residents that live above the water adapting and using the Kapuas River as their place to grow and cultivate their domestic life, transactions, and productions. Connected floating corridors, the water and riverside picturesque scene create an ameliorative effect to facilitate comfortable microclimatic conditions while reflecting the urban identity and sustaining the urban economy. Both climate and city can consolidate into a vernacular coastal assemblage characterized by a combination of eco-urbanism, water urbanism, and the tropical character of urban-architecture forms (Fig. 2.9).

Fig. 2.9 Water adjacency and steps are the unique feature of Pontianak's city traditional riverside zones

Conclusions

Ikaputra (2019) observed how there is a lack of (theoretical) reference (or narratives) regarding waterfront culture for urbanism, urban education, and practice in Indonesia and the wider region, thereby highlighting how the localized eco-urbanism narratives of place seem to be missing, and thus place identities and associated opportunities go undeveloped. Erham and Hamzah (2014) interestingly compared Melaka and Makassar and how the planning of a reclaimed hill zone of Melaka went against its coastal characteristic, as compared with Makassar, where the waterfront and coastal morphologies were still preserved. This reiterated Hall's (2010) description of the historical nature of maritime trade and how it must eventually develop into the city, including their urban grain, which were tied by their participation in international maritime trade. Their conceptual cosmopolis is based upon commercial networking among coastal ports that shared an international orientation, a dual functionality as ports and political entities, and a flexible capacity to rapidly adapt to new circumstances. Their centrifugal and centripetal roles gave rise to an urban grain and fabric that provide a cooling effect, whose microclimatic had paralleled uplands, jungles, and outlying regions far from the metropolis. The hierarchical nature of the cosmopolis urban network in Southeast Asia can produce an identity that show patterns that reflect varied clustering. The river and the city of the Nusantara must again evoke an alignment of main and tributary patterns that conforms to prevailing wind regime patterns. Reconstructions of the urban core of precolonial eras are examined in the light of climate parameters, and outcomes highlight key characteristics needed to facilitate outdoor urban comfort through urban ventilation. The conditions of finer and higher urban grain nearer river and water-edges not only allowed the visual experience of water, but the increasing urban canyons and pathways between blocks and physical bodies would facilitate and accelerate wind flow to penetrate into the body of the city.

The pattern or morphology of the traditional urbanism of these cities basically grew from the life of rivers including 'estuaries', thus evolved into having certain identifiable formal and geographical similarities between one another. From the aspect of planning, such patterns highlight how the original layers of the city are patterns that have functional relations and pay homage to rivers and estuaries, and they recall a green eco-urbanism approach that can give lessons to new forms of sustainable urbanism, which must focus on landscape and water bodies aligned with greenery to ameliorate the effects of climate change.

References

Airriess, C. A. (2003). The ecologies of "Kuala" and "Muara" settlements in the pre-modern Malay culture world. *Journal of the Malaysian Branch of the Royal Asiatic Society, 76*(1(284)), 81–98. http://www.jstor.org/stable/41493488

Alqadrie, R. D. W. (2010). *14876/1-1/1438/00* (Unpublished thesis). Morfologi Pontianak City, Gajah Mada University.

Andaya, L. Y. (2008). Malayu antecedents. In *Leaves of the same tree* (pp. 18–48). University of Hawaii Press.

Bakar, Y. A. (2010). Foreign Documents and the Descriptions of Melaka between AD 1505–1511.

Bausani, A. (1970). *Lettera di Giovanni da Empoli* (p. 132). Roma.

Bayu, C. (2007). *Perubahan Pola Ruang Perkotaan Dalam Transformasi Sosial Budaya Masyarakat Tepian Sungai di Pontianak, Kalimantan Barat.* Program Pascasarjana, Magister Teknik Arsitektur, Universitas Diponegoro Semarang.

Boeing, G. (2019). Urban spatial order: Street network orientation, configuration, and entropy. *Applied Network Science.* https://doi.org/10.1007/s41109-019-0189-1

Bowring, P. (2019). *Empire of the winds: The global role of Asia's Great Archipelago.* I. B. Tauris.

Čakarić, J. (2010). Water phenomenon: Urban morphology transformation. *Facta universitatis-series: Architecture and Civil Engineering, 8*(4), 375–388.

Choi, G., Collins, D., Ren, G., & Trewin, B. (2009). Changes in means and extreme events of temperature and precipitation in the Asia-Pacific Network region, 1955–2007. *International Journal of Climatology, 29,* 1906–1925.

Erham, A., & Hamzah, A. (2014). The morphology of urban waterfront tourism: The local identity portray in Melaka and Makassar. *Urban Economics & Regional Studies eJournal, 7*(155), 14.

Fitri, M., & Triyadi, S. (2015). Community cultures in creating the place-bound identity in Musi Riparian, Palembang. *Procedia-Social and Behavioral Sciences, 184,* 394–400.

Guo, P., Zhu, P., Wang, S., Duan, D., & Jin, Y. (2017). Improving natural ventilation performance in a high-density urban district: A building morphology method. *Procedia Engineering, 205,* 952–958.

Hall, D. G. E. (1970). *A history of Southeast Asia.* Macmillan.

Hall, K. R. (2009). Ports-of-trade, maritime diasporas, and networks of trade and cultural integration in the Bay of Bengal region of the Indian Ocean: c. 1300–1500. *Journal of the Economic and Social History of the Orient, 53*(1–2), 109–145.

Hall, K. R. (2010). *A history of early Southeast Asia: Maritime trade and societal development, 100–1500.* Rowman & Littlefield Publishers.

Hanson, J. (1989). Order and Structure in Urban Design: The Plans for the Rebuilding of London after the Great Fire of 1666. *Ekistics, 56*(334/335), 22–42.

He, B.-J. (2018). Potentials of meteorological characteristics and synoptic conditions to mitigate urban heat island effects. *Urban Climate, 24*, 26–33. https://doi.org/10.1002/joc.3370010304

Ikaputra, I. (2019). Linear settlement as the identity of Kotagede Heritage city. *DIMENSI (Journal of Architecture and Built Environment), 46*(1), 43–50.

Kathirithamby-Wells, J. (1993). Hulu-hilir unity and conflict: Malay statecraft in East Sumatra before the mid-nineteenth century. *Archipel, 45*, 77–96.

Kumar Das, G., & Datta, S. (2014). Man-made environmental degradation at Sunderbans. *Reason—A Technical Journal, 13*(89). https://doi.org/10.21843/reas/2014/89-106/108127

Kompas.com. (2009). *Matinya Anjir, Matinya Peradaban Sungai.* https://oto-motif.kompas.com/read/2009/02/14/05390877/~Oase~Mata%20Air

Ma, T., & Chen, T. (2021). River corridor ventilation analysis and riverfront planning strategy in Tianjin's urban core area. In E3S Web of Conferences (Vol. 237, p. 04022). EDP Sciences.

Miksic, J. N. (2018). *Sejarah Awal.* BAB Publishing Indonesia.

Mills, J. V. (1930). Eredia's description of Malaca, Meridional India, and Cathay. *Journal of the Malayan Branch of the Royal Asiatic Society, 8*(109), 1–288.

Moosavi, V. (2022). Urban morphology meets deep learning: Exploring urban forms in one million cities, town and villages across the planet. In *Machine learning and the city: Applications in architecture and urban design* (pp. 379–392). John Wiley & Sons.

Oke, T. (1988). Street design and urban canopy layer climate. *Energy and Buildings, 11*(1–3), 103–113.

Oktarini, M. F. (2018. December). The settlement morphology along the Musi River. *International Journal of Built Environmental and Scientific Research, 2*(2), 97–104.

Papanastasiou, D. K., & Kittas, C. (2012). Maximum urban heat island intensity in a medium-sized coastal Mediterranean city. *Theoretical and Applied Climatology, 107*, 407–416. https://doi.org/10.1007/s00704-011-0491-z

Romdhoni, M. F. (2020). Historical Evolution of Placemaking in Historic City of Palembang, Indonesia. *International Journal of Built Environment and Scientific Research, 4*(2), 85–100.

Sanders, P. S., & Baker, D. (2016). Applying urban morphology theory to design practice. *Journal of Urban Design, 21*(2), 1–21.

Schophuys, H. J. (1969). Perspectives of Lifting Water for Irrigation and Drainage in Indonesia in General in Sumatra and Kalimantan in Particular, with 1 Graph and 47 Maps, Bogor.

Shahrin, A. (2014). 22 incredible before and after pictures that reveal the transformation of Singapore. thesmartlocal.com, redrawn and adapted from photo by illustrator Wafiy Harith.

Srifuengfung, S. (2012). Relationship between urban morphological properties and ventilation in the intensely developed areas of inner Bangkok. *AU Journal of Technology, 16*(2), 63–73.

Syafrina, A., Koerniawan, M. D., Novianto, D., & Hiroatsu, F. (2020). Influence of urban water body on thermal environment in Pontianak city. *Journal of Asian Institute of Low Carbon Design, 8*, 163–166.

Tarling, N. (1999). *The Cambridge History of South East Asia, Volume one, Part one. From early times to c. 1500.* Cambridge University Press.

The book of Duarte Barbosa. (1918–1921). Translated by M. Longworth Dames, vol. 2. Hakluyt Society, 2d Series, Nrs. 44, 49. (Malacca in Nr. 49).

Tong, M., & Tian, T. (2021). River corridor ventilation analysis and riverfront planning strategy in Tianjin's urban core area. In R. Weerasinghe & C. Fang (Eds.), *3rd international symposium on Architecture Research Frontiers and Ecological Environment (ARFEE 2020)* (Vol. 237). Zhangjiajie, China. E3S Web of Conferences.

Yassin, A. B. M., Eves, C., & McDonagh, J. (2009). Waterfront development for residential property in Malaysia. In *Proceedings from the PRRES conference 2009—The 15th annual conference of the Pacific Rim Real Estate Society.* University of Technology Sydney.

3

The Mound and the Malay Nusantara Historic Landscape

Nurhaya Baniyamin, Mazarina Zain, and Mansor Ibrahim

Historic urbanscapes in Southeast Asia are characterised by geographical landforms such as hills, mounds, and mountains. The nature of its archipelago and its mountain ranges which act like a straddling backbone to its diverse landmass have evolved not only local belief systems and worldviews, but emphasise its crucial role in the region's historic ecosystem . Thus the planning and conservation of future sites and regions must address the critical role of these landforms and in light of climate change and environmental disasters, this is even more critical. Since time immemorial, its sacred role as horizontal and vertical axis was regarded as a way to reach the domains of the universe, yet in the present time, it must again find its universal role as a necessary part of the region's ecological, natural conservation and developmental policy due to topographic and ecologic significance in historic urban landscapes and urbanscapes.

N. Baniyamin (✉) • M. Zain • M. Ibrahim
International Islamic University Malaysia (IIUM), Kuala Lumpur, Malaysia
e-mail: Nurhaya@iium.edu.my; mazarina.zain@live.iium.edu.my;
Profmansor@iium.edu.my

© The Editor(s) (if applicable) and The Author(s), under exclusive license to Springer
Nature Singapore Pte Ltd. 2023
S. Jahn Kassim et al. (eds.), *Eco-Urbanism and the South East Asian City*,
https://doi.org/10.1007/978-981-19-1637-3_3

Introduction

The existence and formation of historic urbanscapes in Southeast Asia are characterised by geographical landforms such as hills, mounds, and mountains. Other than river sites, mounds and mountains are geo-topographical landmarks that attract people to set up settlements in the area. Initially, the existence of the early kingdoms in the Malay peninsula included marking strategic trade routes for traders heading to the region (Adnan Jusoh et al., 2017; Hassan & Ramli, 2018). Such geographical and topographical conditions of the sites—mountains, hills, and mounds—thus acted as a seed to the beginnings of cities, and they combine their axial forces to the embryonic seeding of rivers and seashores into fertile physical conditions which evolved into cities. The isolating mountain scopes of Sumatera and the peninsula, for instance, are framed, among others, by the Barisan Mountains, which run nearly without a break from Lampung in the south to Aceh in the north. Shaped through structural collapse brought about by subduction of the Indian Ocean plate under the Sunda Shelf, the two equal reaches and boundless volcanic action, which rose around 2000 meters, while the eastern heights range from 800 to 1500 meters high.

The mountain or mound in Southeast Asian communities thus forms not only physical but cultural landscapes and plays a crucial role in defining the identity of a place due to the nature of the topography of the archipelago. Over the centuries, there was evidence of how the locals had avoided altering the original landscape, instead simply adapting their urban layout to preexisting geographical features (Munoz, 2006).

The Mound and Cosmography

The word 'mound' is used instead of mountain to encompass all forms of distinctive higher ground. The primal and axial role of mounds and mountains in local history reflects not only their topographical and physical axes but resonates from a time when the hill mound claimed a primal role in the cosmology and cosmography of the region. From time immemorial through to the era of the Islamic periods, key hill mounds and hills represented, in Malay cultural geography, physical topographical features that are crucial markers and 'place-making' backdrops. As a result, the conception of 'place' or 'city' in the Malay worldview was a centre straddling hills, mountains, and the sea. Tarling (1999, p. 197) gives a conception of how Malays saw their environment in the past:

> ... In traditional Malay belief, both the source of river waters and the home of ancestral spirits were high on the hill mound slopes; the highest reaches of the hill mounds were thus thought of as holy places and the source of beneficent forces that bestowed well-being upon the people.

This was how some of the key cities in the Southeast Asian world had evolved against this powerful backdrop, which perpetuated the iconography and images of the city across time (Table 3.1). From the rise of Melaka to Palembang, Pengkalan Bujang, and Kuala Kangsar, these cities are centres of life, essentially striding hill mounds or hillocks. As Munoz (2006) summarises:

> ... In the archipelago, one can find the following associations of political centres and sacred mountains of hills.

What is defined in such heterogeneous cities was a connection between two points and the mark of a sacred centre, from which leaders asserted or extended their authority through spiritual means and from an emphasis on the sacred. The banks of the River Musi and the slopes of the hill have yielded various inscriptions, as well as large remnants of pottery and ceramics, rather than large, monumental, and ornate remains. These reflect a thriving city and its spiritual centre that began between the seventh and thirteenth centuries, with the main centre described as a

Table 3.1 Adapted from Munoz (2006)

Palembang	Bukit Siguntang
Kedah	Gunong Jerai
Holing	Dieng
Sailendra/Sanjaya	Gunong Merapi
Singosari, Majapahit	Gunong Penanggungan

mandala from which other 'mandalas' federated into an intricate web of kinship, political and familial ties, rather than military, creating an empire of mandalas tied by trade.

In ancient communities, this allows the realm of the divine to be personified or expressed. The verticality of the hill mound is seen as holding up sacred and powerful forces and essentially piercing the cosmic domain. They are seen as containers of a mystic essence. This worldview emerges from a cosmological outlook that sees the world and it is surrounded by hierarchically layered cosmic domains. The upper layer is considered 'other worlds' and often equated with different physical and existential meanings. This hill mound is thus a pure cosmic stratum that hovers over and administers a lower stratum of the earth, landscape objects and living beings, and schemas of plants, animals, and humans. An 'axis' is both a horizontal and vertical enabler. The vertical axis was regarded as a way to reach and travel through this hierarchically layered though coinciding domains of the universe. Thus, because of their power and status as 'enabler', a sort of portal to the immortal realm, they were seen as physical, metaphysical, and spiritual gateways.

Symbolically and cosmologically, such steepness reflects the hill mound form—which essentially 'pierce' through the mortal world into the abode of the outer world and receives the wisdom of the sacred domain. Thus, the hill mound is humanity's constant struggle to lift from its mortality, thereby manifesting as a structure steeply arising from its landscape as if piercing the atmosphere and reaching the celestial realm. Religious structures with multiple terraces are part of the 'Asian' hill mound concept, looking like a hill with terraced rice fields. One may discuss these structures as a range within a spectrum of fully religious to a full conflation of the spiritual and the political. The structures reflect a hill mound that defines the search for the sacred in the pure religious realms. Gennep (1960b) highlights a key conception that can be related to the Asian consciousness and outlook:

> … *the incompatibility between the profane and the sacred worlds that man cannot pass from one to the other without going through an intermediate stage. This liminal stage that bridges the two states must be transformative for the rite to be complete.*

The pervasive concept of *Meru* can be traced to its physical genesis: an active volcano hill mound or *Sumeru* in the region. The island hill mound exerts a forceful and powerful effect on the psyche of populations. It permeates and pervades the arts, artisanal skill and architecture of Indian and Southeast Asian architecture. Mabbett (1983b) contends that the representative substance of Meru as a cosmic organizing principle and the conceptual underpinnings or viewpoints rotating around the pivot of the Meru represent a point of connection with the heavens that would then convert into foci of power, not merely religious sanctuaries.

Mabbett (1983) suggests

What will emerge is that whatever its historical origins, Mount Meru became much more than a feature on the cosmographic map. Meru rose in a third dimension; in doing so, it pierced the heavens; in piercing the heavens, it transcended time as well as space; in transcending time it became a magical tool for the rupture of the plane.

Mounds and the Cities

Even in cities or dynastic centres, without a distinctive hill mound or hillock presence, an artificial one will be built as a reflection of the climatic and cultural meaning of these structures.

The seed and beginning of the urban core of ninth-century Srivijaya were located between the area of Bukit Siguntang and Sabokingking in Palembang. It was from this seed that a polity began which later federated the communities residing along the river, eventually forming a city and settlement between the hill mound—Bukit Siguntang, the sacred centre—and the river where archaeological remnants and inscriptions can be found. It was known that they named their centre *Kedatuan* and, by extension, their federation Srivijaya (meaning 'auspicious victory' in Sanskrit).

An 'artificial' example is the gunongan structure in the heritage core of Banda Aceh, which until today has been seen as a strange structure, a peculiarity not found in any other Southeast Asian city. Known to have been constructed by the then sultan in loving tribute to his queen, the *gunongan* was known as a part of a form of love or pleasure garden built as a tribute to his endearing love. This artificial mini-hill mound maze structure in the Aceh—a seventeenth-century structure built by an Aceh sultan for his Malay consort—represents a reminder of the sacredness of the hill mound in itself in the psyche of the community and how it represented the meaning of an elevated life. It is seen and believed to be a portal and an axis to a higher world. The establishment of the city itself was an evolution of such a place identification. Wessing (1988) describes the structure: As was mentioned previously, the *gunongan* is a three-storey, octagonal, flower-shaped structure from the centre of which protrudes a pillar. The walls enclosing the upper levels undulate, giving the impression both of waves and flower petals. The entrance to the hill mound is on the southern face. Upon entering one finds oneself in a narrow passageway (*gua* = cave) that extends a short way into the hill mound. In the end, this passageway abruptly turns to the left and becomes a stairway at the top of which one emerges through a hole onto the next level. The top of the stairway is constructed so that while emerging from the hole one is turned in such a way as to be facing east with the centre of the hill mound to one's left. One can now walk forward, take a couple of steps down and go along the gallery that leads around the hill mound on this level.

Hill Mound, Cosmography and the Sacred

An 'enabler' or 'conduit' of the sacred, a 'portal to the heavens', the hill mound, in ancient times, was seen as a vehicle or vertex that elevates the 'mundane' to the 'semi-spiritual' or 'immortal' level. It is this sacred tool that is the hill mound, and in ancient times it is a recurring and re-evoking phenomenon that reflects a city's connection between heaven and earth. Thus, beginning from the time during which those who live in realms close to the hill mound are seen as partaking in the sacred abode of the immortals, the image of the hill mound has reinvented itself across time and region. The hill mound or hillock plays this function and performs the need to 'enable' an elevated form of existence, a sanctuary or abode. Kings and the powerful were thus in continuous and constant search of such conduits.

According to Mabbett (1983b), the hill mound persona or icon is related to structures seen as a kind of spiritual 'enabler', an ecological structure or shape allowing the ancients to elevate from the abilities of 'mere mortals' to those of the 'immortals'.

The Hill Mound: Sea Duality in Planning and Siting

The various cities in Sumatera, the Malay peninsula, and Java have evolved morphologically based on the axis. Rukayah et al. (2013b) read the original layer of Jepara and Semarang and describe the underlying axis as the palimpsest of present cities in the archipelago:

> …if we look at a map of the ancient port city and sultanate on the northern coast of Java, we find a city layout that is naturally used Northern-Southern axis to face circulation path (sea/river). (Heuken, 1997)

Researchers can use the urban spatial of Jepara city centre to reinforce that assertion. The city pivot of Jepara was at the place of the sloping hill on the eastern side and the ocean on the western side. There are contentions that long ago Mount Muria was a volcanic island isolated from the central area island of Java. If the estimated location of the palace was overlooking the sea, the position would be on the eastern side. The eventual axis is not only cosmological but a functional form from a security and aesthetic perspective. The vista would allow easy visual sighting of the commercial 'downtown' area of the city.

Yogyakarta, shaped before the Dutch presence, was planned based upon a strong imaginary axis between Merapi Mountain in the north and the South Ocean in the south with Yogyakarta located in the centre (Karsono and Wahid 2008). Historically, the birth of the city of Yogyakarta was related to the dissension among family members in the kingdom of Mataram. Metaphysically, it was shaped by a cosmological axis, one that cannot be separated from other axes, such as the axial alignment of the Merapi Mountain, Keraton, and South Ocean. This order reflects a certain Majapahit influence in spatial ordering.

Mound and River

The basic connection between these two powers of slope hill and ocean were the streams, for they were the channels through which the water on the sloping hill streamed down, eventually converging with the ocean. These river basins—between the sea and hill mound—contain the earliest polities of the island in Southeast Asia and had eventually shaped the political dynamics between them. The observations of Tarling (1999, p. 197) of the local cultural worldview, which had evolved in life and cities straddling hill mounds and seas, gave rise to its cultural landscapes, urbanism, and the particularities of its cities:

> …In the traditional Malay view of the world, there was a powerful duality, a landscape dominated by high and steep hill mounds and seas whose horizons seem unreachable.…

Mound and City-Shore Dynamism: The Southeast Asian Cosmography

Communities evolved as conurbations and settlements that grew and consolidated at the foot of key hill mounds and hills. In Sumatera, Malaysia, Thailand, Java, and Vietnam, it is the topographically linear and cosmographically vertical physical present character of a hill mound or mountainous form or range that impacts the culture and economy of the littoral region. Its profiles and peaks are natural attractors to communities and traders, travellers and sailors, and at times pose challenging barriers and divide landmasses in two. The geographical and topographical conditions of the region were defined by the visual presence of these mountains, hills, and mounds, which generally overlooked a valley or estuary. These mounds acted like seeds spurring the emergence and growth of cities and, eventually, the embryonic seeding of communities along rivers and their arteries, since the physical conditions which could evolve into cities were always a combination of both trade and agriculture.

The dividing hill mound ranges of Sumatera and the Peninsula, for example, are characteristic beacons that evolved into representations of the spiritual and the sacred over time. The sacred peaks contained within the Barisan Mountains, which extend to those within the hill mound ranges in Java, run almost without interruption from their cities to those in Lampung in the south to Aceh in the north. Formed historically and geographically through tectonic folding caused by the subduction of the Indian Ocean plate under the Sunda Shelf, the parallel ranges were the basis of widespread volcanic activity, and their geographical character created a cultural and spiritual persona of the hill mound itself. Some of these rose to around 2000 to 3000 metres. The eastern elevations were lower, ranging from 800 to 1500 metres high.

It is at the foot of these hill mounds, for example, where the earliest littoral settlements emerged. Amongst the hill mound ranges are those known as the bone of the peninsula (Paul Wheatley, 1961), which divided and caused settlements to evolve on land and sites that are much lower, rich in minerals and fertile soil, attracting settlements at the foothills of these mound ranges. These are also found in particular in the geo-topography of Sumatera, and, much like the Malay Peninsula, it is the Titiwangsa Mountain range that divides the protruding landmass of the peninsula. It was the hill mounds that had 'beckoned' or attracted venturing traders and seafarers throughout the centuries. Kedah's Mount Jerai was a beacon, serving a role to seafarers from the West. Their landings eventually made the Merbok and Bujang valley a bustling port and commercial centre with a metallurgy industry. Like Campa and Aceh cities, it was a regular stop for travellers and traders. On a less important note, other sites, such as Patani and Bukit Jugra, were hailed as landmarks for Arab Mariners, as was Bukit Puteri in eastern Kuala Terengganu.

The critical triadic link between trade, commercial topography, and climatic and ecological conditions that had characterised these maritime cities was its formation between the two topographical and ecological forces of hill mound and water. Ocean waterways were the channels through which the water that fell on the slope hills streamed down, at last, to converge with the ocean. It was this eco-coupling of water sources, i.e. river basins—between sea and hill mound—that seeded the earliest polities of island Southeast Asia and had eventually shaped the political dynamic between them as observed by Tarling (1999, p. 197). The Malay cultural worldview was formed by the straddling of hill mound and sea, which gave rise to its urbanism and the particularities of its cities. Tarling further summarises for the evolution of Malay civilisation within Southeast Asia:

...In the traditional Malay view of the world, there was a powerful duality, a landscape dominated by high and steep hill mounds and seas whose horizons seem un-reachable....

Mound, Climate, and the City

It is critical to assert that in the local psyche, the conception of a city differs from that in the West. In the local conception, 'place' or 'city' is a combination of natural, ecological, and artificial features. Thus, the conception of mounds is connected not only to their striking profiles impinging upon the local psyche and daily cycles but to the fact that their climatic environment was associated with the sacred, a 'purer' and 'calmer' state of mind, a higher level of living, due to the cleaner and breathable 'zone' of life. These conceptions of the climate surrounding mountainous forms were eventually embedded in the sociocultural life of the locals and gradually became expressed and engraved in iconographic and symbolic forms in cities and building traditions.

Thus, the profile or symbol eventually came to identify the sacred realm of kinds, a dynastic and monastic way of life, which eventually evolved into symbolising the abode of kings. A condition of existence or life is a state above others, a purer 'life zone', and so creates a stronger, wiser, and higher mind and spirit. The mound—because of these climatic advantages—was eventually associated with a higher supra-being, related to an intelligent and 'meditative' climatic zone that ensured the wisdom of kings and nobilities. Thus, the *gunongan* not only became associated with an intangible axis that shapes cities as levers towards the heavens but resonated with a climatically benign space within the tropical zone. It became a symbol representing a high place, with cool, thin oxygen, steep slopes full of groves, and fertile lands. These were seen as both benevolent and powerful, endowing resources to those at the foot of the hill mounds, where there is usually a fertile plain.

From a hill mound there is always a wide view below. The higher the hill mound, the wider the visible horizon, impacting consciousness, creating a wider perspective, and no longer focused on details. It creates a different and elevated vantage point, and one gains a different perspective and a higher form of one's awareness. Ascetics who have reached the peak of consciousness have been known to approach, from the peak, a form of clarity or the truth, clearly seeing the injustices of communities below, thus raising awareness about the conditions of the surrounding community.

Transcending the Earth

In the Nusantara, the *gunongan* profile which adorns the architectural and urban boundaries creates a sense of layering. These often symbolise a transition from one stage to the next, virtually the marking of movement from the profane to the sacred. The discourse in planning and architecture within the Malay historical context is profuse with the mention of 'threshold and transition'. These shifts advance topographically and transiently, yet they portray the resultant urban space architecture as one that reacts to and progresses in a comprehension of space as a series of thresholds, as moving through the transitional and transformative, rather than just a collection of standalone structures. In several regions, it was the hill mound or *gunongan* motif or profile which adorned the notion of transitional space and created two different types of spatial experiences or functions, while a threshold is a momentary step into two fixed states. Similar to Sirivijaya, Champa had been a federated maritime civilisation that evolved on a strip of land extending for more than a thousand kilometres along the coast of Central Vietnam.

Mound as Gateways

As 'idealisations' and 'perfections', they were labelled in the names of cities, and the mound must be seen as this 'cosmic' enabler or tool. It is as a means and an embodiment towards immortality and within which the soul can reach a kind of salvation and attain a level of spiritual redemption. Thus, through time the mound is seen as a portal embodying a threshold into the sacred.

The mound later evolved as profiles in ornamental motifs often located as the symbolic threshold of the transitional space, whether the gateway, the entrance to a city, or a doorway. It normally denotes the stages in cultural rites of passage between two disparate spaces in design and urban communities. The transitional experience gives a relationship from which standards can be drawn for the plan of an extraordinary space or site. It is described by layering and equivocalness and can change the occupant of that space as they travel through it. The experience of the space poses a discontinuity and leads occupants to question their surroundings, leading to heightened awareness of the space as a transformative threshold between distinct spaces. The ritualistic acts and religious traditions of the Southeast Asian world use the hill mound as an avatar, a representation of the sacred. This necessitates the heightening of the perception of thresholds and movements—rather than buildings—through transitional spaces, which continually transforms these mundane to meaningful spaces in their everyday life. The hill mound elevates the space or the city, by gracing the gateway or entrance, creating a transformative space based on history and advancing the perception of the threshold.

Mound as Artisanal Element

The genesis of the mound in architectural traditions may have stemmed from its formations in the arts and artisanal traditions of the locale in the Southeast Asian world. Chiong and Ghulam Sarwar (2018) discuss how the symbols of both the hill mound and the tree had developed concurrently and constituted a particularly unique motif of the Malay Nusantara, in both its theatrical and building arts. Based on the significance of hill mounds and trees within the region given the situation, it is entirely conceivable that such a hill mound tree developed uniquely within the Nusantara. In this case, the tree is known as *pohon beringin*, is seen as a symbol of 'life', and is symbolic of the cosmos in miniature and a microcosm of the universe. The same sacred role of the hill mound is personified in this field of art, visually divided into three levels with a large tree motif standing at the centre. The tree motif is described as a symbol of totality, the cosmic whole, or the unity between upper and lower worlds.

The motif has recurringly been used to symbolise a space-to-space transition. In Indonesia, gateways at times take on the form of hill mounds or split hill mounds, while in Malaysia, timber gates are adorned with ornate hill-mound-like motifs and elements, the *gunongan*. In addition, the meaning of *gunongan* in a building is the same as the symbolism of the *pohon budi* in the play of *wayang kulit*, which means nature, world, or life. In the Kelantanese *gunongan* motif, the hill mound motif again appears as a motif, symbol, or icon accompanying such layering. In the traditions of Kelantan, which is steeped in the Langkasuka traditions of elaborate timber carvings, such reflections and imagery find their genesis in the histories of Patani and Thailand. In the palatial complexes of these regions, there is a fundamental public-to-private layering or zoning, with each zone preceded by gateways that are adorned at times, with the *gunongan* or hill mound motif.

The symbolism of the Meru is reflected in the split gates, which are characteristic and identifiable with Indonesia ancient sites. It is a unique and iconic structure that is a sight to behold. From sites to symbols, the *gunongan* is thus an element or artefact or building in the shape of a hill mound and its contents. Typically, and traditionally, the mound shape is found in the framing of a gate, including the palace gate, and when it is played (in the play of wayang kulit) the hill mounds are used as a palace.

Gunongan as Ornamentation

The types of *gunongan* are like mounds, cones, or forehead crowns that come either in a semi-circular or triangular shape, adorning or mounted on gateways or entrances. They are usually fully engraved or simple arrangements such as vertical or curved or sometimes made with a specific purpose depending on the owner's intent and status. This symbolism is prevalent for example in Northern Malaysia, i.e. Kelantan, along with other eastern coast states. The *gunongan* motif can usually be found at gates or gateways. The motif is placed at the part of the upper gateway and serves as the 'marker' to represent the entrance path and the separator or the point of the other two worlds, each with its purpose in the functioning of the building.

The hill mound is both a personification of forces and an axis planning tool in the Nusantara historical landscape. This chapter highlights the orientation of city configurations, which, historically in littoral Asia, have always used hill mounds as a datum or invisible lever. From the Jerai beacon of Kedah Valley to the cosmic centredness of Mount Meru, this chapter highlights the hill mound in meaning, imaginings, and planning role. It also delves into monuments and ornaments that have been found to mimic the hill mound, including the hill mound arising from the sea.

Hill mound symbolism dominates the local regalia significance, the position of the traditional sultanate's ornamented *cogan*, a ritual fan. It demonstrates that the fan's composition and critical symbolism reflect dynastic ecological propensities. It then relates local attributes to fundamental beliefs and cosmologies. As epitomised in the *cogan*, the profile reflects a hill mound's shape and thus embodies a form of sacredness, rooted in environmental intimacy and ecology, which diffuse into local thought and outlooks. These symbolisms reverberate in the architecture, at times syncretising with neighbouring royal influences to show a fusion of power in royal structures and sociocultural dominions. The *cogan*, a royal ceremonial fan, is the symbol of the Riau Sultanate and, within it, is a Malay inscription in Arabic script (known as Jawi), which is part of the hereditary sacred lines. Its leaf or hill mound shape evokes the symbolism of the *kayon* or *gunungan* found in the various *wayang* drama.

This fan's leaf-like shape alludes both to the pointed shape of the ubiquitous betel leaf/*sireh* and, in documents of earlier origins, to a legend suggesting Iskandar was named after a leaf which miraculously healed his mother. The hill mound or *gunongan* is metamorphosed into the tree motif found in various artistic traditions in Southeast Asia, including the region's shadow puppet artistry in which the form is known as *gunongan*, *kekayon*, or *waringan*, and is used as a backdrop and weaved from the local palm leaf.

Penanggungan Mountain in Majapahit Civilisation

The largest Hindu civilisation was the Majapahit kingdom from the thirteenth to sixteenth centuries, which last over two centuries. Penanggungan Mountain was a sacred hill mound on Eastern Java and played a crucial role in the legendary Hindu mountain in Java where the worship of the mountain is closely related to the syncretistic cult of Shiva-Buddha in the thirteenth century (Katkova, 2016). Penaggungan Mountain is a central peak and consists of four smaller hill mounds—Bekel Mountain, Gajah Mungku Mountain, Keluncup Mountain, and Sarakelapa Mountain. The main religion under the Majapahit civilisation was Ciwa-Buddhism, in which this cosmographic concept was the main influence in society and became the primary aspect in the creation of architectural forms. The other factors that shaped architectural form were climate, building materials, construction, local technology, and natural landforms. The cosmographic idea in the customary state is to regulate territory, space, and buildings.

Balinese civilisation under the Majapahit Kingdom was an advanced culture of Majapahit, on which was based their traditional architecture. Wind and water were believed to flow from the sacred hill mound to the sea and back again to the hill mound. In Balinese cosmology, the architectural concept was harmonisation between humans and the environment. This balancing concept was called *manik ring cecupu*, according to which architecture was a child of nature. Ciwa-Buddhist cosmological concepts strongly influenced the local cultural context until the Majapahit kingdom was able to come up with a sustainable approach to developing a sensible technology in building design. This sustainable and sensible technology can be seen and is still well preserved to the present day in Balinese traditional settlements from over a hundred years ago. The concept of embodying the universe reflects an effort by the Pakuwon community in Trowulan civilisation, who aimed to harmonise themselves with nature:

Humans do not subdue the forces of nature, but the human synergizes itself with the smaller natural environment. (Winarto et al., 2015)

Dissemination design with space and region was plainly in an enclosed yard. Huge and small residential units were isolated by the open space and a wide road. In the Majapahit settlement idea, *bale ageng* was put on or close to the sacred area in a settlement near the temple, and *bale ageng* was in the middle of the street or open space and functioned as a shared space and gathering area for the community (Winarto et al., 2015). In the Ciwa-Buddhist cosmological concept, the axis for building orientation was towards Penanggungan Mountain in the southeast, and the settlement was aligned with the environment and led to the emergence of Trowulan civilisation as a garden city with trees in open spaces. According to the Ciwa-Buddhist cosmological concept, the street axis followed the axis of the sacred hill mound on the southeast and the sea on the north side.

The Hill Mound as 'Breaker' and 'Beacon': Palembang and Melaka

The hill mound, in the history of the Southeast Asian city, is both a 'breaker' and 'beacon'. The establishment of the city itself was an evolution of such a place identification. Munoz (2006) describes the ancient practices of pre-Islamic societies in the Southeast Asian world

Once this was done, the political centre was erected on a hill mound or a hill close to the compound of the chieftain (kedatuan or kraton). When no hill mound or natural hill was available, an artificial hillock was created.

Melaka and Palembang were kingdoms with both a pre-Islamic and Islamic history; what is common is that their political centre, *kedatuan, kraton,* or capital, was located on a site close to a sacred hill or hill mound

(Munoz, 2006). The 'breaker' refers to the linear and vertical physical character of a hill mound or mountain range, which, in terms of topography, divides a landmass in two. The geographical and topographical conditions of the site, such as hills and mounds, have acted like a seed to the beginnings of cities, and then proceeds to the embryonic seeding of rivers and seashores as physical conditions which had evolved into cities. The dividing hill mound ranges of Sumatera and the peninsula, for example, are the characteristic highlands formed by the Barisan Mountains, which run almost without interruption from Lampung in the south to Aceh in the north.

In the western interior of Palembang, there is the Pasemah Lebar, which occupies the broad plain of Air Lematang, a tributary of the Palembang (this region was an important source of elephant tusk, rattan, 'dragon's blood', alum, pulas twine, cotton, and sulphur) (Airriess 2003). It was this region of the upper Musi River that royal tribute and monopolies played a role to ensure the flow of hulu resources towards the capital. Similarly, in the eastern boundary of the Malay world, cities grew particularly in southeastern Borneo, and the shallow gulf lying between two hill mound ranges was gradually filled in by the sediment from several rivers. The first Malay *kraton* or Tanjung Pura, established at the head of the gulf, gradually became an inland centre as accretion progressed. The hill mound ranges are known as the bone of the peninsula (Wolters, 1962) which divides and causes settlements to evolve upon land and sites that are much lower because they are rich in minerals and fertile soil, attracting settlements at the foot of the ranges. They are also found especially in the geo-topography of Sumatera, much as with the Malay Peninsula; it is the Titiwangsa Mountain range that divides the protruding landmass of the peninsula.

'Beacon' refers to how the hill mounds had 'beckoned' or attracted venturing traders and seafarers throughout the centuries. Kedah's Mount Jerai was a beacon, playing an alignment and navigational role, and had eventually made the Merbok and Bujang valley a constant stopping point for traders, and Bukit Jugra was praised as a landmark for Arab mariners, as was Bukit Puteri in Kuala Terengganu.

Jugra Hill and the History of Selangor

The royal town of Jugra evolved from a natural physical landform of hill mounds with a river and coastal area. Located in the northern part of Kuala Langat, along the Langat River to the Straits of Malacca in the southern part of Selangor state, Malaysia, it marks the starting point from Nuang Hill on the Titiwangsa Range towards the Straits of Malacca. Jugra Hill was a landmark that guided traders and sailors from the Straits of Malacca. There was a lighthouse in the Jugra Hill that functioned as an important security controller to guide sailors from the Straits of Malacca to stop over at Jugra during their trading voyage. According to Zainab Roslan et al. (2017), the domestic or foreign traders who stopped at Jugra were from China, the Arabian Peninsula, and Europe.

To the present day, Jugra Hill is a landmark of the Langat River (Fig. 3.1) and plays an important role as a feeding point to transport tins from the tin mine at Rekoh, Ulu Langat, to the nearby jetty based in the royal town of Jugra, which was also known as Bandar Temasya (Gullick,

Fig. 3.1 Orientation of Istana Bandar towards Langat River (Adapted from Zain et al. (2021))

1998). From Bandar Temasya, the tins were brought down to the port at Kuala Jugra using a bullock cart and exported by steamship from the port. Langat River was one of the local transportation sources since travel on roads took longer compared to waterways. Owing to its significant contribution as waterways, a shortcut canal between Sungai Langat and the Straits of Malacca at the Jugra inlet was built by Americans, which later turn into a channel that could be traversed by large cargo ships from Bandar Langat to Jugra Hill to transport goods.

Epilogue

Mounds were not only physical but metaphysical and spiritual centres of the universe in the Malay worldview. Their topographical meaning is linked to an eco-consonance that arises naturally from the landscape and topography. In the planning and development of cities and settlement in the present time, too often the sacredness, significance, and eco-importance of the hill mound or hill ranges are not given sufficient attention, and developers continue to carelessly cut or even level off these key features and elements. The levelling of hills on the periphery of modern cities and suburbs continues to the present day and has been the source of various disasters, such as landslides and structural failures.

References

Airriess, C. (2003). The ecologies of "kuala" and "muara" settlements in the pre-modern malay culture world. *Journal of the Malaysian Branch of the Royal Asiatic Society, 76*(1), 81–98. Retrieved November 10, 2020, from http://www.jstor.org/stable/41493488

Bakri, A. F., Yusuf, A. N., & Jaini, N. (2012). Managing heritage assets: Issues, challenges and the future of historic Bukit Jugra, Selangor. *Procedia - Social and Behavioral Sciences, 68*, 341–352. https://doi.org/10.1016/j.sbspro.2012.12.232

Bargeos, W. (2012). Urbanism, place and culture in the Malay world: The politics of domain from pre-colonial to the post-colonial era. *City, Culture and Society, 4*(4), 217–227.

Boeing, G. (2019). Urban spatial order: Street network orientation, configuration, and entropy. *Applied Network Science.* https://doi.org/10.1007/s41109-019-0189-1

Chiong, F. W. E., & Ghulam Sarwar, G. Y. (2018). The visual elements in the Pohon Beringin figure of the Kelantan Shadow Play. *Malaysian Journal of Performing and Visual Arts, 4,* 63–78.

Cotterell, A. (2014). *A history of South-East Asia.* Marshall Cavendish International Asia Pte Ltd.

De Freitas, I. V., Sousa, C., & Ramazanova, M. (2020). Historical landscape monitoring through residents' perceptions for tourism: The world heritage Porto City. *Tourism Planning & Development, 18,* 1–20. https://doi.org/10.1080/21568316.2020.1769717

Denpaiboon, C. (2001). *Transformation by modernization of the traditional waterfront settlements in the context of their coexistence with aquatic environment: A case study of Raft House and Pillar House in Thailand.* Kyoto University.

Geoff Wade, L. T. (2012). *Anthony Reid and the study of the Southeast Asian past.* Institute of Southeast Asian Studies, NUS Singapore.

Gravagnuolo, A., & Girard, L. F. (2017). Multicriteria tools for the implementation of historic urban landscape. *Quality Innovation Prosperity, 21,* 186–201. https://doi.org/10.12776/QIP.V21I1.792

Gullick, J. M. (1998). *The History of Selangor* (2nd ed.). The Malaysian Branch of the Royal Asiatic Society.

Hans-Dieter Evers, R. K. (2000). *Southeast Asian urbanism: The meaning and power of social space.* LIT VerlagMünster.

Harun, N. Z., Jaffar, N., & Jahn Kassim, P. S. (2020). *Physical attributes significant in preserving the social sustainability of the traditional Malay settlement "reframing the vernacular: Politics, semiotics and representation".* Springer.

Hassan, Z., & Ramli, Z. (2018). Archaeological research in Kedah: Prehistoric and Proto-historic sites. *Selected Topics on Archaeology, History and Culture in the Malay World,* 87–98. https://doi.org/10.1007/978-981-10-5669-7_7

Heuken, A. (1997). Tempat-tempat bersejarah di Jakarta. Yayasan Cipta Loka Caraka. ISBN 6027039574, 9786027039575 Length 458 pages.

Hussain, M. A., Yazid, M., Yunos, M., & Ismail, N. A. (2020). A review of the elements of nature and the Malay cultural landscape through Malay literature. *Sustainability, 12,* 1–13.

Jahn Kassim, P. S., Ibrahim, I., Harun, N. Z., & Kamaruddin, K. (2018). Ecological urbanism in the tropics studies on the sustainable dimensions of

Malay traditional urban centers. *International Journal of Engineering & Technology*.

Jessup, H. (1985). *Dutch architectural visions of the Indonesian tradition*. Source: Muqarnas, vol. 3, pp. 138–161. Brill.

Jusoh, A., Sauman, Y., Nayan, N., & Ramli, Z. (2017). Archaeotourism and its attractiveness in the context of heritage tourism in Malaysia. *International Journal of Academic Research in Business and Social Sciences, 7*(4). https://doi.org/10.6007/ijarbss/v7-i4/2923

Karsono, B., & Wahid, J. (2008). *Imaginary axis as a basic morphology in the city of Yogyakarta-Indonesia*. 2nd International Conference on Built Environment in Developing Countries, Penang, Malaysia.

Kathirithamby-Wells, J. (1993). Hulu-hilir unity and conflict: Malay statecraft in East Sumatra before the mid-nineteenth century. *Archipel, 45*(1993), 77–96.

Katkova, I. R. (2016). *Mountains in Javanese Sacral Topography*.

Mabbett, I. W. (1983a). The symbolism of mount Meru. *History of Religions, 23*(1), 64–83.

Mabbett, W. (1983b). *The symbolism of Mount Meru, history of religions*. (Vol. 23, pp. 64–83). The University of Chicago Press.

Milner, A. C. (2011). *The Malays*. Wiley-Blackwell.

Munoz, P. M. (2006). *Early kingdoms of the Indonesian Archipelago and the Malay Peninsula*. Didier Millet, CSI.

Nasir, A. H. (1990). Kota-kota Melayu. Percetakan Dewan Bahasa dan Pustaka.

Prabowo, B. N., et al. (2020). *Historic urban landscape (HUL) approach in Kota Lama Semarang: Mapping The layer of physical development through the chronological history*. IOP Conf. Ser.: Earth Environ. Sci. 402 012020.

Proceedings of the AcE-Bs 2013 Hanoi *ASEAN* Conference on Environment-Behaviour Studies Hanoi Architectural University, Hanoi, Vietnam, 19–22 March 2013 "Cultural Sustainability in the Built and Natural Environment." Available Online at www.e-iph.co.uk AicE-Bs2016Edinburgh7thAsia-Pacific International Conference on Environment-Behaviour Studies, St Leonard Hall, Edinburgh University, United Kingdom, 27–30 July 20162398-4287 © 2016.

Roslan, Z., Shin, C., Ramli, Z., & Er, A. C. (2017). Local community perception on the importance of cultural-natural heritage protection and conservation: A case study in Jugra, Kuala Langat, Selangor, Malaysia. *Journal of Food, Agriculture and Environment, 15*(2), 107–110.

Rukayah, R., Puguh, D. R., & Setiyorini, E. S. S. (2013a). Morphology of traditional city Center in Semarang: Towards adaptive re-use in urban heritage.

Rukayah, R., Roesmanto, T., & Sukawi, S. (2013b). The sustainability concept of Alun-alun as a model of urban design in the future. *Procedia – Social and Behavioral Sciences, 85*. https://doi.org/10.1016/j.sbspro.2013.08.390

Sabtu, S., Mahat, R., Amin, Y., Price, D., Bradley, D., & Maah, M. (2015). Thermoluminescence dating analysis at the site of an ancient brick structure at Pengkalan Bujang, Malaysia. *Applied Radiation and Isotopes: Including Data, Instrumentation and Methods for Use in Agriculture, Industry and Medicine, 105*, 182–187. https://doi.org/10.1016/j.apradiso.2015.08.024

Srinurak, N., & Mishima, N. (2017). Urban Axis and City shape evaluation through spatial configuration in 'Lan Na' Northern Thailand historic city. *City Territ Archit, 4*, 10. https://doi.org/10.1186/s40410-017-0067-z

Stark, M. (2015). Southeast Asian urbanism: From early city to Classical state. In N. Yoffee (Ed.), *The Cambridge world history* (pp. 74–93). Cambridge University Press.

Tarling, N. (1999). *The Cambridge history of South East Asia, volume one, part one. From early times to c. 1500.* Cambridge University Press.

UNESCO. (2011). *Recommendation on the historic urban landscape*. November.

van Gennep, A. (1960a). *The rites of passage*. University of Chicago Press.

van Gennep, A. (1960b). *The rites of passage*. The Chicago University Press. (original French, 1908). from Salet, W. (2018). Sifting through transition: Revisiting 'rites of passage'. *Transactions of the Association of European School of Planning 2*(2018), 1–8.

Wessing, R. (1988). The Gunongan in Banda Aceh, Indonesia: Agni's fire in Allah's paradise? *Archipel, 35*(1), 157–194.

Winarto, Y., Santosa, H. R., & Ekasiwi, S. N. N. (2015). The climate conscious concept of Majapahit settlement in Trowulan, East Java. *Procedia - Social and Behavioral Sciences, 179*, 318–329. https://doi.org/10.1016/j.sbspro.2015.02.435

Wolters, O. (1962). Paul Wheatley: The Golden Khersonese: Studies in the historical geography of the Malay Peninsula before A.D. 1500. (Malayan Historical Studies.) xxxiii, 388 pp., front. Kuala Lumpur: University of Malaya Press, 1961. (Distributed by Oxford University Press. 45s.). *Bulletin of the School of Oriental and African Studies, 25*(3), 638–639. https://doi.org/10.1017/S0041977X00069822

Zain, M., Baniyamin, N., Ibrahim, M., & Jahn Kassim, P. S. (2021). *Linking historical urban landscape, national identity and edutainment in a tourist heritage site: The Case of Jugra, Malaysia.* Proceedings of the Putrajaya International Built Environment, Technology and Engineering Conference (PIBEC09) 2021, 9.

4

The Malay 'Garden City': An Ethos of Malay Historic Urbanism

Nor Zalina Harun

Introduction

Reid (2005) points out that a characteristic of these cities was the weaving of the 'rural' and the 'urban'. '*How do we explain the liking of Southeast Asians, still evident today, for continuation in a "rural" pattern of life in the city, with coconut and fruit trees surrounding an open, wooden elevated house, in contrast to the compact urban models of the Mediterranean and China? Climate was obviously one factor. The treeless, congested quarters which the Chinese built of stone or brick beside the Southeast Asian market centres, and which Europeans began to emulate in Manila after the 1583 fire and in Batavia in the mid-seventeenth century, were stuffy, exposed to the sun, and unhealthy. By building on the ground, they suffered from problems of flooding and of drainage and waste disposal from which the typical elevated pole house of maritime Southeast Asia was immune. Eventually, these alien urban models became pestilential and were abandoned to the poorest urban inhabitants.*'

N. Z. Harun (✉)
Universiti Kebangsaan Malaysia (UKM), Bangi, Malaysia
e-mail: nzalina@ukm.edu.my

© The Editor(s) (if applicable) and The Author(s), under exclusive license to Springer Nature Singapore Pte Ltd. 2023
S. Jahn Kassim et al. (eds.), *Eco-Urbanism and the South East Asian City*,
https://doi.org/10.1007/978-981-19-1637-3_4

Tracing Historical Roots

The major sociocultural transition that resulted from the invasion of the West was the challenge of tracing gardens' true typology and identity. In order to recognise the propagation of information in Malay culture, including the notion of the Malay garden, the records and documents of such a garden rely heavily on the study of Malay literature such as old texts, folk tales, and poetry. One of the earliest depiction, 'Taman' (garden), is the mention of *taman* (Malay: garden) in *Hikayat Inderaputera*. The word *taman* appeared twenty-six times in the countenance of *mahligai* (princess's residence); *balai* (pavilion); water is referred to as *kolam* or *mandi* and *pagar jala-jala*; the word *taman larangan* or fortified garden appears twenty-six times representing a trellised fence.

The city of Aceh, for example, which was often the first Southeast Asian city-like experience for travelers from the West, was described at its height. To capture the ethos of the Malay city, which essentially privileges the garden and the green, over the artificial, one can survey the precolonial cities that once graced the littoral throughout Southeast Asia and its archipelago. One again recalls the description by traveler John Davis upon arriving, for the first time, at the mediaeval city of Aceh. Perhaps the reason was the particularly well-treed nature of Aceh, which covered its buildings and streets in a green veil. Hakluyt wrote in his book that the town of Achien is extremely spacious and constructed of solid wood. It is surrounded by houses elevated approximately six to seven feet above the ground.

> ...*Neither could we go into any place, but we found houses and great concourse of people: so that I think the town spreadeth over the whole land.*

Reid (2005) reports on how a French Jesuit left a more lyrical description of the same city even in its decline almost a century later:

> *Imagine a forest of coconut trees, bamboos, pineapples and bananas, through the midst of which passes quite a beautiful river all covered with boats; put in this forest an incredible number of houses made of canes, reeds and bark, and arrange them in such a manner that they sometimes form streets, sometimes*

separate quarters: divide these various quarters by meadows and woods: spread throughout this forest as many people as you see in your towns, when they are well populated; you will form a pretty accurate idea of Achen [Aceh] and you will agree that a city of this new style can give pleasure to passing strangers.... Everything is neglected and natural, rustic and even a little wild. When one is at anchor one sees not a single vestige or appearance of a city, because the great trees along the shore hide all its houses.

The presence of a traditional Malay garden in the Malay Archipelago was recorded as early as the second century, in the form of a palace garden intended for royal pleasure. Gardens are gradually created through harmonious interactions between nature and cultural values and are seen as part of the Malay cultural landscape translated into compound garden architecture.

Malay manuscripts represented the Malay manuscripts as the work of written Jawi (based on Arabic alphabet) in scripted signature using the Malay version produced between the sixteenth and the nineteenth centuries. Malay manuscripts were written on materials such as paper, leather, palmyra leaves, bamboo, ivory, wood, and cloth with long-lasting and permanent materials. It has also been found that Arabic scripts had a major influence on the Malay language. In the manner of Persian letters, Malay-Jawi was based on the Arabic alphabet along with some extra letters. Jawi was created according to the rules of Persian letters. As a result, Arab-Malay or Malay-Jawi letters were able to adapt, incorporate, arrange, and be structured, and this greatly enhanced the language of Malay and thus added to the culture of Malay.

Nevertheless, histories of various royal Malay gardens are recounted in classical Malay manuscripts, such as the city garden of the Langkasuka Empire, the palace garden of the Majapahit Kingdom, the palace garden of the Malacca Sultanate, and the pleasure garden of the Acehnese Sultanate. This chapter presents a critical assessment of the life of the traditional Malay garden recorded from the second to the eighteenth centuries by examining its garden identity with a detailed investigation of nine selected well-known classical Malay manuscripts written between the thirteenth and seventeenth centuries during the flowering of the literary age.

A History of the *Taman*

Malay reference to the traditional garden and to *taman* in a local sense (such as Hikayat Inderaputera) could therefore be explained in the form of walls, public pavilions, and water elements with private women's spaces. They were often landscaped with diverse plants and trees with special roles and mythical animals. The garden often physically epitomised calm and relaxation.

More detailed descriptions of the classical Malay garden can also be found in earlier histories of Malay manuscripts, for example, *Hikayat Raja-raja Pasai*, *Hikayat Merong Mahawangsa*, *Hikayat Hang Tuah*, and many other pieces of classical Malay literature. In this study, nine famous traditional Malay manuscripts, including *Sulalatus al-Salatin* (*Malay Annals*), *Bustan al-Salatin*, *Hikayat Merong Mahawangsa*, *Hikayat Hang Tuah*, *Hikayat Hang Tuah*, *Hikayat Inderaputera*, *Hikayat Acheh*, *Hikayat Raja-raja Pasai*, and *Hikayat Patani Pasai*, were taken from the literature on the traditional Malay garden. The inclusion criteria include ancient Malay manuscripts written between the thirteenth and eighteenth centuries. The examined manuscripts were evaluated and graded on the basis of the significant garden's elements. The approach sets the parameters for creating an assessment of the existing landscape practise in Malaysia; specifically, the Malay garden design principle for representing the landscape's identity.

One of the earliest textual confirmations of the management of gardens in the Malay urban centre and in its earliest history is the existence of sago palm plantations around Palembang. This textual evidence is found in the Old Malay inscription from Talang Tuwo (684 CE), known to be written by King Jayanāga shortly after the founding of his new polity in Srivijaya. On the occasion of his creation of a garden (*parlak*), other gardens are alluded to in the historical text:

> Here is His Majesty's wish: That everything that is planted (tanam) here, coconut palms (ñiyur, Malay niur), areca palms (pinang, M. id.), sugar palms (hanāu, M. enau), sago palms (rumviyah, M. rumbia), and the various trees whose fruits can be eaten, as well as the hāur, vuluh and pattung bamboos, etc.; and also that the other gardens with dams, ponds and all the good works done by me, may be for the good of all beings, mobile or immobile, and may be for

them the best means of obtaining joy. If they are hungry at a halt or on the road,
let them find food, and water to drink. May all the swidden fields (huma) and
gardens (parlak) made by them be full [of crops]. May the livestock of all kinds
reared by them, and also the slaves owned by them prosper.

This text is described by historians as an encouragement for populating the new harbour city. Sago and other palm trees producing food (and useful otherwise) are encouraged to be planted (*tanam*), which implies domesticated rather than wild forms: coconut (*Cocos nucifera*), sugar palm (*Arenga saccharifera*, producing palm drink, sugar, a lower-grade starch, and ijok rope), and areca nut (*Areca catechu*, used in betel chewing). The inscription continues with the royal wish that the people's swidden fields (*huma*) and gardens (*parlak*) will be very productive. In a later era, the planting of sago trees in royal gardens finds an echo in a late-nineteenth-century map of Jambi (where the Srivijaya capital was transferred after the eleventh century): along the old meander of Danau Sipin, at the foot of the sultan's palace, not far from the Solok Sipin site dating to Srivijaya times, one finds a 'Sago garden belonging to [Sultan] Pangeran Wiro Kusumo'.

The multiple layering and spirit of the garden in the Malay city is characterized by the sixteenth-century gardens of Kota Melaka, which has been described in detail as very dense yet whose urban life and man-made city is close to the hinterland. A description is usefully given by Manual Eredia in the sixteenth century: *The flora of the district may be divided into three different classes, aromatic trees, fruit-bearing, and medicinal trees, and wild forest trees: the same applies to the plants and herbs.*

Among the aromatic and scented trees there is the 'Aguila' a tall stout tree with
leaves like an Olive: the pith inside is bitter and oily. The 'Aguila' is differenti-
ated by an extra thin skin on the outside of the bark; if it loses this skin, the tree
decays after 3 months through exposure to the weather, and then, owing to this
decay, it exhales the scent which comes from the pith. 'Calamba' is derived from
the oiliest pith of the same tree. 'Bejuim' called 'Caminham' is another tall stout
tree: the gum or liquor which oozes and exudes from clefts and holes in the bark
we call 'Bejuim'. It is the same with the camphor tree: it is a tall stout tree, and
the camphor-liquor flows from the holes in the bark: the scented wood is much
used in the carpenter's craft, for beds and tables of superior grade. One finds

different species both of camphor and of 'bejuim'. There occur in the country many other scented woods, of which we will not make particular mention here.

Among the fruit-trees, the 'Doryão' is a big, very tall tree: the fruit resembles a round head, and is covered with green pyramidal pricks: when ripe, it turns yellow, the skin is all thorny, and it splits open at the point into divisions and compartments like an orange-blossom: within these divisions are the lumps of fruit substance, sweet and very delicious, having the consistency of blanc-mange, with a stone concealed inside each lump. One finds many species of this fruit: the best and most creamy is the 'Doryaó Tambaga', which to my mind is the finest fruit in the world.

Eredia refers to Melaka as a city built in orchards, referring to the prevalence of fruit such as the mangosteen:

…Mangostan, as a 'tree of no great height, bears a fruit which is round like the orange, with a thick rind: while unripe it is yellow, and after ripening it turns red: in the hollow interior lie its sweet juicy portions flavored like the cloves of a head of garlic and containing a stone: this fruit is useful in illness as it is juicy and refreshing'.

Other fruits found within the city itself include the following:

The 'Tampôe' is another tree of the same height: it bears a fruit with a thick rind, the color of cinnamon: in the hollow interior lie sweet portions flavored like the cloves of a head of garlic and containing a stone: as it is sweet and rather hot, they distill from it a wine which resembles Moscatel.

There are other native fruits such as 'bachoés', 'rambotans', 'rambes', 'chintês', 'champadas', 'buasducos', 'romany', and others so numerous that we cannot now mention them, nor can we mention the other foreign fruits, that is to say, the fruits of India Intra-Ganges: for the country of Indostan and the Peninsula of the Promontory of Chory or Cape Comoryn have different natural characteristics from this other country of Ujontana in India Extra-Ganges. For the trees of the one place do not produce fruit in the other place: I mean to say, the trees of Ujontana do not produce fruit in Indostan: more likely are the trees of Indostan to produce fruit in Ujontana.

The Melakan hinterland is often described as an extension of the inner-city garden, in which there is an extension of the essential character of the Malay garden as both a symbolic and productive element. Eredia described the Melaka hinterland as having valuable spices and where *the 'trees of cinnamon', 'cana fist oía', and 'tamarindi'* are found. Throughout history, forests are described as jungles or woods containing many kinds of big and tall trees for constructing boats and which yield gum and oil of which considerable shipments are made. Yet descriptions of the Melaka or Malay hinterland are replete with productive elements.

The forests in Malaya were known to contain particular types of Brasil-wood trees, many species of gum-bearing trees, and numerous cotton trees. There are many species of plants, both cultivated and wild, particularly aromatic plants: round pepper, long pepper, 'renriure lancas' (another and hotter species) 'choncor', country saffron, 'casumba' (resembling European saffron), and aromatic 'betre', besides numerous other plants which cannot be discussed in a short space. As Eredia described: '*The wild palms called "Nypeiras" resemble the palms of India in shape and leaf—(they are somewhat bigger than those date-palms); they have a big, stumpy base and grow in the swampy land.*

Key Features of the *Taman*: Hardscapes and Elements

Detailed descriptions of the classical Malay garden can be found in earlier histories of Malay manuscripts, for example, *Hikayat Raja-raja Pasai*, *Hikayat Merong Mahawangsa*, and *Hikayat Hang Tuah*; many other pieces of classical Malay literature mention certain recurring elements of the *taman*. In a study of nine famous traditional Malay manuscripts, including *Sulalatus al-Salatin* (*Malay Annals*), *Bustan al-Salatin*, *Hikayat Merong Mahawangsa*, *Hikayat Hang Tuah*, *Hikayat Hang Tuah*, *Hikayat Inderaputera*, *Hikayat Acheh*, *Hikayat Raja-raja Pasai*, and *Hikayat Patani Pasai*, seven principles or elements repeatedly describe the gardens of the old Malay Kingdom and what defines its spatial structure, softscape elements, hardscape elements, culture, and beliefs. These can be summarized as follows.

Encircled by Walls or Clouds

These walls are known as forts or fortifications and are a major component of the royal institution's physical architecture. In terms of construction function, the distinction between the two categories was that fortifications were employed for defensive purposes and may also have been used for urban administrative functions. As a means of displaying their dominance and providing security from invaders, fortifications were fundamental components of early Malay culture. This is owing to the frequent battles and tensions that happened between the second century CE and the early fifteenth century CE Western arrival in the Malay Archipelago's kingdoms. In addition, the hierarchy and splendor of Malay's ancestry signified the sturdy building of the fort, independent of its functions. It is evidenced by the construction of a sequence of forts adjacent to one another, which has become a custom among the Malay Kingdom's rulers with each change of leadership and the establishment of new areas or empires.

1. Accessed by the Main Door

The typical Malay garden was enclosed by walls in a royal complex and accessed from different directions by the main door, as an entry door and other doors. The palace's primary entrance was richly ornamented with a meticulously arranged collection of plants and served as the venue for formal greetings.

2. The Presence of the Pavilion or Balai

The presence of *balai* was formally or informally accommodated for two reasons, primarily as a royal meeting venue as well as royal seat. The *balai* overlooked the countryside with unhindered views and was typically located near water elements, such as canals and *kolam* (pool and pond). It refers to the tradition of sitting and assembling or *duduk and kumpul*. The *balai* was for either the royal seat or the king's hall. Courts and their components were created in traditional Malay gardens to direct the area and facilitate ritual ceremonies. For example, in the courtyard of the Garden of the Majapahit Empire, a sacred edifice was housed by Shiva and the priest. The king, however, converted the courtyard into a mosque following the conversion of the empire to Islam.

In the traditional Malay garden, there is a courtyard and its components built to direct the space and accommodate religious practices.

3. A Range of Planting Species by Function

Plants have a unique symbolism, significance, and purposefu sequence of traditional and modern times in the Malay culture that may be connected with the Malaysian garden identity.

4. Water Components

Canals, reservoirs, basin and lakes symbolised cleanliness in the Malay landscape. A baths is considered a highly civilised and hygienic act owing to the rainy and hot tropical weather. During the coronation of the Malay sultanates, known as *Raja Bersiram* in Malay ceremonial custom, the bath was part of the essential ceremony.

5. Arts and Cultural Elements in Malay Landscape

Arts and cultural elements in the Malay landscape were a testament to this declaration as a highly evolved and sophisticated society. Complicated and beautiful carved wood decorations in royal Malay garden walls, doors, or fences were among the artistic and cultural influences in the Malay countryside.

The Garden (*Taman*) as City

At the peak or apotheosis of Malay civilisation, the garden itself can be described as a microcosm of the Malay city, or the city in miniature. Epitomising the Malay garden, the archetypical city itself is the royal garden within the city, such as the *Taman Ghairah* in Aceh with its symbolic *gunongan*, as described in the Malay manuscript *the Bustan*. The royal garden, or *Taman Ghairah*, is described as a large square covered with many coloured stones and planted with all sorts of flowers and fruit trees. *Cutting through this garden was a river Darul-'Ishki, which was described as 'a stream of cool pure water that sprang from the mountains and had been diverted from its original course to run through the garden and the palace grounds'.*

Wessing describes how "*… the Bustan details at great length all the features of the Taman Ghairah and the perfection to which they have been executed. About the Gunongan it says*:

> *… And right in the middle of that square [of the garden] there is a mountain on which stands a tower, a place for sitting in state, named Gegunungan Menara Permata (the Mountain of the Jeweled Tower); its posts are made of copper and its roof covering is made of silver, resembling the scales of the sago palm, and its peak is made of pinchbeck. When hit by the rays of the sun its reflection is radiant. Inside of it are several jewels of varied colors and Solomite and … And there are planted on that mountain several flowers such as frangipanni and red and white roses and seri-gading [Nyctanthes arbor tristis] and at the side of the mountain, toward the bank of the river [there is] a carved stone platform named Kembang Lela Mas-hadi and in it its upstream direction a sapphire coloured stone platform called laced lotus [Kembang Seroja].*

This particular structure and garden previously built by Sultan Iskandar Muda of Aceh can be said to be, essentially, the epitome or peak evolvement of the traditional elements as described by Harun and Amni (2019) in their elementary characterisation of the Malay Garden.

Budi as 'Ethos' of the Garden

Budi in the garden is, amongst other things, attained by the layering of any built landscape with life-giving elemental zones, i.e. that of orchards, fruit trees, and herbs planted for olfactory, medicinal, and subsistence purposes, endowing the built and vegetative environment with beneficial elements. The reconstruction and historical and theoretical construct of the Malay garden pose a challenge because little physical evidence has survived. Yet the remnants and presence of a traditional archetypal Malay garden in the Malay Archipelago can be traced to evidences and inscriptions recorded as early as the second century, in the form of a city garden, a productive garden, and a palace garden intended for royal pleasure. Histories of various royal Malay gardens were recounted in classical Malay manuscripts, such as the city garden of the Langkasuka Empire, the palace garden of the Majapahit Kingdom, the palace garden of the Malacca sultanate, and the pleasure garden of the Acehnese sultanate. The Malay reference to the traditional garden and to *taman* in a local sense (such as *Hikayat Inderaputera*) could therefore be explained in the form of walls, public pavilions, and water elements with private women's spaces. They were often landscaped with diverse types of plants and trees with special roles and mythical animals. The garden often physically epitomised calm and relaxation. Gardens were, for the Malays, gradually created through harmonious interactions between nature and cultural values and are an integral part of the Malay historic cultural landscape.

References

Hakluyt, R., & David, R. (1981). Hakluyt's Voyages: A Selection. In Richard David (Ed.), Chatto & Windus, The University of Michigan, 258–260.

Harun, N., & Amni, S. (2019). The existence and identity of the traditional Malay garden. In M. Zen & N. Harun (Eds.), *Islamic relevance in landscape architecture*. IIUM Press.

Reid, A. (2005). *An Indonesian frontier: Acehnese and other histories of Sumatra. Asia Research Institute*. National University of Singapore. Singapore University Press.

5

Bioclimatic Alignments of the *Alun Alun*: A Genealogy of the Nusantara Open Space

Shireen Jahn Kassim and Nor Zallina Harun

Framework

This chapter attempts to the genesis and the evolution of the 'alun alun' or the 'padang'; a local urban space type which has undergone successive changes and morphological inflections and layerings over time. Present discourses on the *padang* have highlighted its hybrid journey, from that of a simple open space in front of an administrator's residence to the ceremonial forms and squares that evolved during the colonial era of the Nusantara region and nations. Through a reconstructed narrative, it attempts to reroot the meaning and narrative of the 'alun alun' or the *padang*, as a key element of urbanism in the region, and identify its formal and evolving changes into its palimpsest and hybrid forms; from its

S. Jahn Kassim (✉)
International Islamic University Malaysia, Jalan Gombak, Malaysia

N. Z. Harun
Institute of Malay World and Civilisation, Universiti Kebangsaan Malaysia, Bangi, Malaysia

© The Editor(s) (if applicable) and The Author(s), under exclusive license to Springer Nature Singapore Pte Ltd. 2023
S. Jahn Kassim et al. (eds.), *Eco-Urbanism and the South East Asian City*,
https://doi.org/10.1007/978-981-19-1637-3_5

root form. As the chapter muses over its earlier pre-colonial origins, it suggest that this urban space-type arise not from external imports—such as similar Western-linked and Middle-Eastern linked space type—or merely the outcome of unplanned spaces—but from its roots in the notion of the 'sacred' space and the regional history of the sacrosanct contract between the ruler and the common people. This space has a closer link with the notion of 'urban spectacle' and the very 'emptiness' of this space, have subjected its interpretation to the rhizomic character of the region. For example, Kien Lai (2010) intertwines its original root and evolvement as a local archetype with the same space-type arising from post-colonial discourses, highlighting it as a

> *Legacy of British colonial urbanism, its continued maintenance has created tenuous and contrasting relationships with their evolving metropolitan cityscapes, the padang originated with 15th century Isfahan.*

Hidayat and Widrakara (2018) assert a similar intertwining or layering of the 'external' appropriations upon the local form and goes further in acknowledging and expressing the difficulties in historically separating the external (colonial) from the internal (local) readings of the space in their discussion of the hybrid forms and the Nusantara-based origins of the *alun alun*:

> *This crossing is a condition of meeting between two things (or more). In the condition of this crossing, authenticity becomes irrelevant because all things are a 'cross' between one thing and another, between the original and the non-original, between the one here and the one there,*

More importantly, Hidayat and Widrakara (2018) recognise an 'original' layer beneath the colonial-based evolution of such urban space-form. Basundoro (2015) observes that the colonial-linked layering of the *alun alun* of Malang, Indonesia. Fyre (2018), in his discourse on walls, interestingly suggests that in cities and civilisations within which no significant physical fortresses or walls are found as their archaeological remnants, their lack of protective enclosure is partly due to their cities' security mechanisms being complemented by other urban space-types measures such as 'empty' space which the local army but which later evolve into more complex spaces due to the essentials of sociopolitical or civilised life. Frye (2018) observes that exceptions in the formations of historic cities—such as the city of the Spartans which rejected fortified settlements and—others which rejected massive fortification whose dwellers settle in an open space for the outside world to see—as the city would be:

....*defended by their 'walls of men.*

The significance of the *alun alun* historically is thus related to the social-political character of the local population, which perceived a sacred and intense bond between the ruler who held a sacred position but bound by a historic social contract with the people. Later, it would play a socio-communal role in the city or center of settlement, and some observed its fundamental social role as a 'glue' (NorZalina Harun, 2017) of local societies and populations, allowing a daily cycle of activities that marked the key events of local communities and which embody the needed fusion of its urban social hierarchies.

Tracing Origins

The *padang* or alin alun—a key component of the public realm of Malay–Nusantara urbanism—has essentially a compact but free-form character; which recalls the common central space of local neighbourhoods which a common central area is surrounded by houses which face its center and each other, and this centric, yet organic form, grew from the vernacular low-density settlements of the region—the *kampung*. The *padang (or alun alun)* can be seen as an evolvement of an even smaller unit of space—the *Halaman rumah*—the open space of the garden characteristic of the Malay vernacular house compound which is then surrounded by trees and after that, a series of randomly arranged houses. Zalina and Farhana (2020) in their mapping of the residuals of vernacular 'kampung' settlements in Melaka, found many of these compounds were based on an overriding 'communal' configuration and layout, reflect the community-centric character of the Malay village or lifestyle, in which the open spaces were never fully enclosed or bounded on all sides, but more of an over-riding 'C' shape. On the higher level and at the macro-scale of set-tlement, the palace, mosque and market place would enclosed these open spaces. Yet even with the *masjid/surau* structures the grounds were not enclosed but were functioning as green spaces bounded by other interfac-ing elements and smaller spaces such as the city wall, fencing and screen-ing device, and gateways, which suggest restrictions on public access to the centre and a formal entryway that could restrict the open flow of people.

As for the origins of the public *padang* to the *alun alun* of twelfth-century civilisations in the Nusantara, in the case of cities and communi-ties in Java, the open space was commonly located in front of the local ruler's residence palace and was in fact the hub of the local society. The royal court of the time was commonly housed in a public-private structure and fronted by a wide and turfed open space which was sur-rounded by huge shady trees . There was an overriding quality of this spa-tial type, where there was a visual continuity between the pavillion-like royal court which acts as an outdoor room and the width and breath of the par-tially enclosed square. The semi-enclosure character of this space was only later made more gridded and 'square-like', during the colonial years, as the original space became fortified with administrative buildings oand rows of large, matured trees planted in straight lines that act as continu-ous features linking one end to another. Thus by the 1800s, the *alun alun* or *padang* evolved into a central urban element which recalled the 'town square' and which then became like a conscious and deliberate urban tool in reminding the presence of the colonial administration, and thus a sym-bol of the new 'rulers' and the rules. The urban space thus became a rep-resentation of the direct administrative apparatus and support structures during the colonial times. As civilisation moved into organised polities, and the evolvement of maritime, the same spaces in the same centres, became not only a site for ceremonies and parades but continually used also as a public place to execute criminals. In certain locations and com-munities, in the event of the certain crimes, at times, the *padang* became a tool for the public implementation of law and punishment.

To trace the genealogy of the 'alun alun' and the padang, one must return to the genesis. As discussed earlier, in historical terms, this genesis begins from the unit of the village; however, in a larger-scale of urban sites in pre-colonial times, the genesis has evolved into 'a large green open space, or *alun alun,* common found in front of courtyards and the princely residences of Nusantara. An example is the early depiction of the morphology or shape of the square is in the illustration of the old Banten city, of the sixteenth century (see 'Banten' in Chapter 1); where the open space is part and parcel of the compact an centric nature of the city. To differentiate the genesis and genealogical roots of a form of the archetype, and to the original idea and function of the *alun alun*, one must refer back to the morphological studies of the Malay-Nusantara traditional cities and urban sites (examples are Jahn Kassim, et.al., 2019; Pasaribu, 2019; Ibrahim, 2020). In such mapping and reconstructions, the layer that one encounters in the centre of these cities a fragmentation of the rigid square, which can be argued almost like a deformation or inflection. with paths that flows into it from various directions, thus having multi-directional 'corridors' allowing the necessary tropical breathability of the urban space.

The Evolution

Another example is the *alun alun* became the centre of the royal cities and symbols of power in Java and the rest of the Malay- Nusantara world. Tracing earlier forms particularly found in cities from the time of amongst others, the center of the kingdom of Majapahit whose mapped reconstruction has not been clearly found till now (Miksin, 2009) but whose remnants recall a more fragmented form of the mandala, rather than the rigid mandala-based nature of key agragrian cities such as Angkor. The open space is planned for its vistas and viewpoints, and deliberately formed by the surrounding structures or buildings to form a planned configuration but with particularities and inflections—where, of course, the process of formation was not the same from one city to another. Based on historical investigations and archaeological excavations of Trowulan (Miksic, 2009) and the royal cities of Mataram Islam such as Kotagede, Karta, and Karatsuba, a recurring pattern was the inflection variations of the triadic nature of the configuration of *padang*, palace, and mosque. The cities which had the *alun alun* in front of the palace, was planned such that the combination of the *alun alun* and palace had created a harmony of function and interdependence between the two. There was evidence *of a unified design since the beginning of its planning* and construction. The *alun alun* was believed to be organised, inserted and sustained because it was needed by the typology of the palace itself; it was a negative space, yet a green space that became visually and environmentally unified with the palace. The *alun alun* and palace of Yogyakarta and Surakarta for example, can be argued as the last remnants of the Javanese heritage, has a more preserve palimpsest of the original open space, which still function in terms of communcal roles, while the *alun alun* or padang of the original 15th century city of Melaka, for example, is all but erased. Both form and ecological elements such as the large shady tree which was still part of the urban character was still preserved in the Dutch era, and it resonated its original Malay royal-based urban role as the green core of the city and state; as Melaka was historically both a city and a state at the same time. As it grew from a maritime Southeast Asian city-state that strategically was located midway between 'the turn of two monsoonal winds' and at the mouth of a large navigational river and deltaic plain, allowing ships to easily navigate and berth, the open space still remained as a separator or protective yet ceremonial urban element, however by the 1920s, with the advent of the motorcar, the green core as an eco-urbanist element has all but disappeared. The hill—which historically became a natural defensive tool and the 'royal' site which was bordered by orchards and a large field grew into a dense community still resonate its green continuity which was once represented by royal enclaves, and which other public structures including mosques, and artisanal and commercial neighbourhoods were located. The same open greenery, coupled with pavillions (part of which was the bridge, which will be discussed in Chapter 15) which housed mercantile and maritime activities, and the presence of large shady trees were the urban tropical continuum which carried on on the opposite side of the river into the busy multicultural commercial zone.

Reconstructing the Roots of the *Padang*

At the heart of historic Nusantara, is a green nexus and open garden in the centre of the city and is known as where the grass grows, and in certain parts of the Nusantara, where the large banyan trees stand at the four corners. This particular Javanese-linked form of the *alun alun*, consists of either a central or peripheral large tree, originated in the time of the sultanate and so was not a democratic or administrative space in the modern sense of the word. Nevertheless, it was a civic space which was part of the public realm and fully accessible by the masses. It was a space where certain demands could be made directly to the monarch. In certain cities, it was placed north to the *bupati's pendopo* (regent's administration office with a front yard), with a city mosque on the west side following the late Islamic adjustment of the cosmos.

As the *alun alun* typology locally evolved, and transformed into the *padang*, the shape-morphology and formal-spatial character due to the influence of other space typologies, including the cultural influence became a norm in Southeast Asia. Thus, there occured a cross-cultural evolution, and later, a reading of its evolution had often the resulted in a tracing of the roots of this space from origins outside the region, rather than linking such spaces to the very social-cultural nature of this region. This is not surprising as the region is one beset by multiple rhizomatic influences crossing its archipelagic geo-political zones. Thus, confusion as to the origins and genesis of architecture and urban types and forms is not new.

Thus the *padang* has been asserted as an element originating from the squares of Europe and the four-square gardens of Isfahan and Mughal cities. Yet the local type is quintessentially different from its imported counterpart, though the original space-type may have been influenced by the eventual pressures of colonial and by particular notionsof the public square as g imported from the West. The character of the original Malay–Nusantara urban core is defined and characterised by a certain compactness in configuration, the centricness of the green open space—representing the centredness of the city—and by a fragmented, polygonal form, rather than a gridded, formal and axial form. Though such grids and axial bearings may have influenced the space throughout time, a reconstruction of precolonial urban coreswill highlight that such indigenous urban patterns and configurations were not merely a product of superfluous or 'left-over' urban space, but, like its open-air architecture, a historical product of both ecology, topography, climate and history. The fabric of the urban core in the region was primarily affected by these four factors, and the local populace had intuitively configured and located its key structures, vegetation and spaces between key structures, in such as way as to preserve the necessity of microclimate and to ensure the extension of the essentially 'climatic' sanctuary of the public realm which began from the royal structure or space, which constitutes the palace, and later whose continuum include the mosque, and key structures around them. Traditionally these were located comparatively close to each other, bordering rivers and estuaries, thus the coolin and microclimatic effects of these water and monsoonal adjancies would have been harnessed to enhance the city as part of its role as a network of tropical trading nodes, ports and routes. The increasing density of the city which surrounded green urban cores due to other accretions such trading stalls, structures, and associated aristocratic structures nearby would have been intuitively planned so as not to impede such microclimatic cooling and be seen as a continuum of the royal sanctuary and gardens.

Large trees are natural elements that create shaded zones and natural boundaries extending from the properties, and the historical buildings in tropical Asia should be depicted as extending urban spaces and shaded zones with the presence of such large trees. Trees, under the tropical environment, must be considered as urban elements assembled around urban spaces and causing urban experiences in the tropical city. By grouping these natural elements and their properties, the city takes on a unified form which can be classified as a truly culturally resonant sustainable city with a distraction of its own. The emergence of native trees, shade, and wildlife as a support to the notion of the city is an area that is recognised as having a significant local character which is identifiable from the inside and used for exterior reference.

Definition: From Primordial Space to *Padang*

The very meaning of the word *alun alun* reflects its original meaning. The word itself suggests its actual origin whose function and form differs substantially from the Western notion of the field. The term *alun* can be literally translated as a centre around wave-like formations or shapes. Thus, *alun alun* means multiple waves. It suggests the notion of masses seen as waves, where a central and primal function of this space is a kind of negative space (without walls) that invites the gathering of people. This definition harks and traces back to the primordial notion of the *padang* or *alun alun*. The ancient Malay world and polities arose from the central contract between king and subjects. For the people in Malay thought and cosmology it is an abiding and active contract. The sacredness of the contract reverberates even in the urban form as it is that which creates a deep link, and space becomes a reflection of this link. The *alun alun* thus connotes a space that is meant to contain a sea of people which is typically in wave-like formations. The Islamic religious influence could also be a factor in its continuity in the urban histories, and this includes the religious belief on the *padang mashyar* or the primordial field of souls—consolidating the idea of a wide-open space as a spectacle facilitation between subject and king, with the belief in the eventual judgement between souls and a Divine sovereign.

Trees, Gardens, and Fields

The central roots of form of the *alun alun* is as a space or an 'urban container' of 'souls and human subjects or in short, of the masses. Under this notion, though the space is essentially an open space, the regional form of such spaces must render is shaded, embraced, and protected by trees—and often, a single large protective tree. This has a similar mirror form of religious connotation and spiritual meaning, held . in the belief of the 'tree' in heaven or the sacred 'Sidratul Muntaha' of Islamic teachings. Although the archetype form of tree, open space and fluid boundaries are ancient, Wiryomartono (2014) traces the first formal *alun alun* to the complex and settlement of Singasari in Java. However, he mentions an even earlier genesis related to sacred open spaces surrounding the temples of Java which were needed for ritual movements such as circulation. Tracing these to even earlier forms, these sacred spaces are generally populated by a tree in the middle surrounded by a boundary or wall. In Javanese tradition, as described in Negarakartagama (1222), the *alun alun* is generally described with several banyan (shady) trees. At times, each tree is enclosed by a city wall. Thus, the notion of the open space in the region and culture is now even earlier than the twelfth or thirteenth century. The role of the *alun alun* or *padang* in the Malay city or public realm is related to its origins. Its nexus is more than just a royal field, but throughout the centuries, it evolved into multiple variants. In its original form, it was never a rigid square. Its green area was originally bordered by trees and greenery instead of buildings. There are often identifying and local species and the large trees form a 'soft edge' to the centre. Later these characterised the Malay city but were unfortunately gradually decimated by colonialists and later development, who at times, made it a definitive square or blank grid . erasing its central and primordial nature and role as green sacred center.

Climate Alignments

The polygonal character and form of the Malay *padang*, which is its original form at times overwhelmed by the square stamp, becomes not only a recollection of the socio-polities of the local region, but a bioclimatic tool that engaged with the multidirectional nature of wind directions. Wind forces in the region are known for its multi-directional behaviour, rather than having a main direction throughout the year. Its 'fragmented' spatial form and orientation reflect the climatic and ecological characterisation of the Nusantara region. A look at cartographic evidence highlights how the *padang* was essentially of a multi-directional and fragmented character, with trees in the middle of it (Fig. 5.1). for example, Hidayat and Widrakara (2018) observed a similar climatic alignment in their city in Indonesia:

> *Like the alun alun in other cities, the alun alun of Probolinggo has four (4) unequal sides, according to four wind directions (south, west, north, and east), where the four sides have different characteristics.*

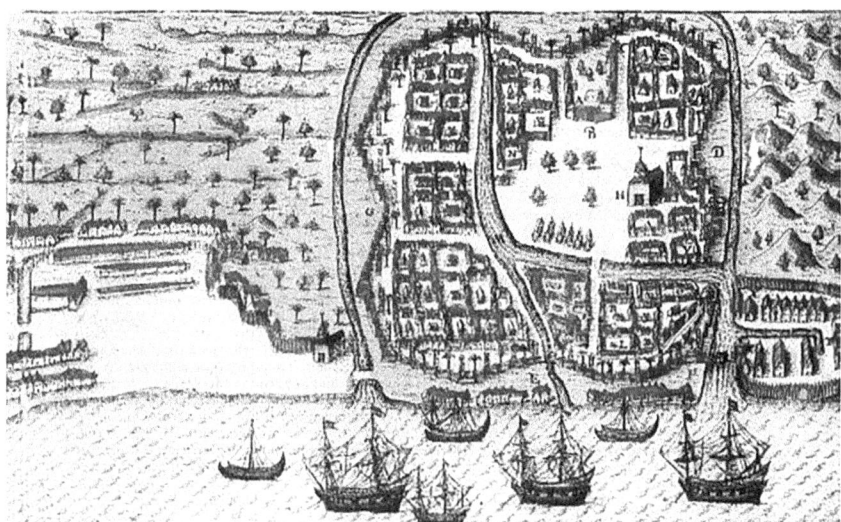

Fig. 5.1 An old visualisaton of the ancient Malay city of Banten and its fragmented yet polygonal centre and green space. (Source: Orientalische Indien ("Little Voyages"), Johann Theodor de Bry (1560–1623) and Johann Israel de Bry (1565–1609), 1599)

Markus and Morris (1980), suggested and identified that in the tropical climate, an urban configuration of a staggered layout of buildings and structures, is in general, more facilitative, under hot humid regions. Similarly inverting the principle, an open space which has a staggered and multidiretional form will be more effective in terms of wind-driven ventilation for cooling throughout the year. The multi-directional nature of wind—for example in the annual wind regimes of cities Nusantara, such as from Semarang, to North Jakarta (Banten), to Palembang, to Melaka and sites on the West coast of Malaysia—demonstrate varied behavior yet a common locational wind character summarised in their wind metereological reports, where the wind rose, depict patterns which are more multidirectional where the longer 'fingers' of the rose represented higher frequencies of wind from that direction are mixed with the 'shorter' fingers or duration of wind.

Table 5.1 compares the historic form or shape of the local Alun Alun or 'padang' in several sites in the Nusantara against the sites "wind Rose"

Table 5.1 The Multifaceted forms of Historical Padang and Alun-Alun of the Nusantara—Selected cities and locational site wind conditions

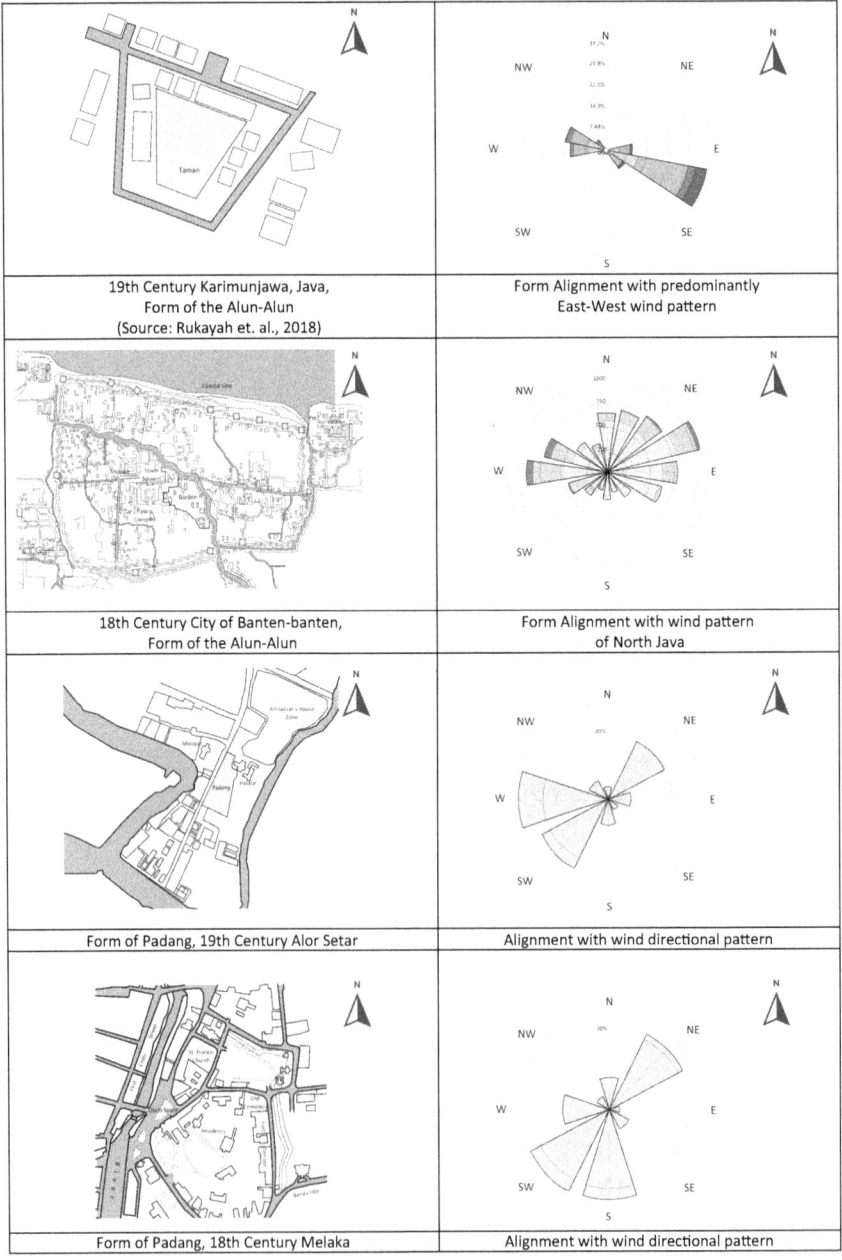

19th Century Karimunjawa, Java, Form of the Alun-Alun (Source: Rukayah et. al., 2018)	Form Alignment with predominantly East-West wind pattern
18th Century City of Banten-banten, Form of the Alun-Alun	Form Alignment with wind pattern of North Java
Form of Padang, 19th Century Alor Setar	Alignment with wind directional pattern
Form of Padang, 18th Century Melaka	Alignment with wind directional pattern

which summates the magnitude and directional behaviour of local wind patterns. This comparison suggests a degree of bioclimatic alignment between the site's annual wind behaviour which varies according to location and the polygonal and multifaceted shape of the local alun-alub or Padang. Wind is crucial to the climatic conditions for urban tropical comfort, and it mirrors the morphology of the Alun Alun or Padang which had evolved from the historic social-cultural history of place. Their eventual forms had evolved according to the inherent local knowledge of place and climatic forces. Overall, the longer perimeter length of these open spaces seem to face the higher frequencies of prevailing wind directions and higher speeds of wind, thus annually, the spaces are able to capture the multidirectional wind movement so crucial to tropical comfort in public spaces. However in certain sites, these intended conditions would have changed due to additions of buildings and obstructions.

Overall, Nusantara sites are characterised by multi-directional wind regimes, rather than a dominant direction of wind. Only in extreme coastal areas, such as Melaka, Banten, and Terengganu, does a slightly dominant pattern emerge. In such coastal sites, the winds are influenced by the monsoon seasons, for example, on Malaysia's east coast, namely the northeast monsoon with two short inter-monsoons. The northeast monsoon occurs from November till March and brings higher-speed winds to the peninsula. The first affected areas of the strong northeast monsoon are in the east coast areas. Thus Nugrahanti et al. (2018) highlighted the interlinking of other urban elements in the cooling of public spaces, with the necessity of air movement under tropical humid conditions:

Other research conducted by Hong found that tree arrangement, building layout patterns and their orientations with respect to wind have significant effects on the outdoor wind environment. Furthermore, long facades of the building, which are parallel to the prevailing wind direction, can accelerate horizontal vortex airflow at the edges and obtain pleasant thermal comfort and wind environment at the pedestrian level. In line with Hong, Olgyay (1961) stated that houses are separated to utilize air movements which generate a scattered and loose layout.

The Dutch, for example, included the *alun alun* in the movement of the capital, with the same compound planning of the surroundings in Indonesian urban centres. It became enclosed by streets that led to the market, bus station, and a commercial and cultural centre in the surrounding area. The evolution of the *padang* had originated from a polygonal-form continuous field (between palace and mosque) in Malaysia and only later did it become 'adapted' to the characteristic 'squares' of the colonial city. The padang of Alor Setar was initially a trapezoidal form (see Chap. 1), and it was only by the early 1930s that it was morphed into a formal square, with less greenery and a decrease in large trees due to Colonial efforts of introducing a central highway across the city, and consciously dividing the sacred center with a highway/road between palace and mosque. Historically these large trees were integral elements of the *padang in the city*.

Similarly, in Javanese cities, the *alun alun* were ecologically characterised by a large central tree or several trees in an informal order and as it evolved, these had lined their borders in a mor gridded manner. In all cases, these had created shaded zones, natural boundaries, and a sense of enclosure in the center. It is observed that in many cities, in their original layer of typo-morphological patterns, the urban streets seemed to overlap with and diffuse organically into these open *padang or medan*. They did not end at the edge with the open space but legibly continued into it (Nor Zalina Harun, 2000). In certain cases, such open pavilions would symbolically enhance the open spaces, and at the same time, they would blend between the streets and often served as a gateway to a local event or local parade or religious ceremonial event.

The padang and its trees, in a tropical environment, are inseparable and crucial in terms of microclimate and must be considered as urban elements assembled around urban spaces and causing a shaded urban enclosure experience in the tropical city. By grouping these natural elements and their properties, the city takes on a unified form and the emergence of native trees, shade, and wildlife as a support to the notion of the city as an area which is recognised as having a significant local character which is identifiable from the inside and also used for exterior reference. It is in the preservation of its form or layout and the natural and built properties that its heritage value can be increased, which would also enhance the authenticity of the urban fabric, its climatic environment and its tropical identity (Fig. 5.2).

Figure 5.2. A reconstruction of the historic center and green padang of Alor Setar, Malaysia before the 1920s. the area near the Masjid Zahir and Balai Besar are surrounded by green fields with an array of Jacaranda trees during the 1800s. The observation of an Alor Setar wind rose diagram illustrates the incoming prevailing wind from the direction. The magnitude (strength) of prevailing wind averaged between 0.3 and 3.5 m/s (Figs. 5.3 and 5.4).

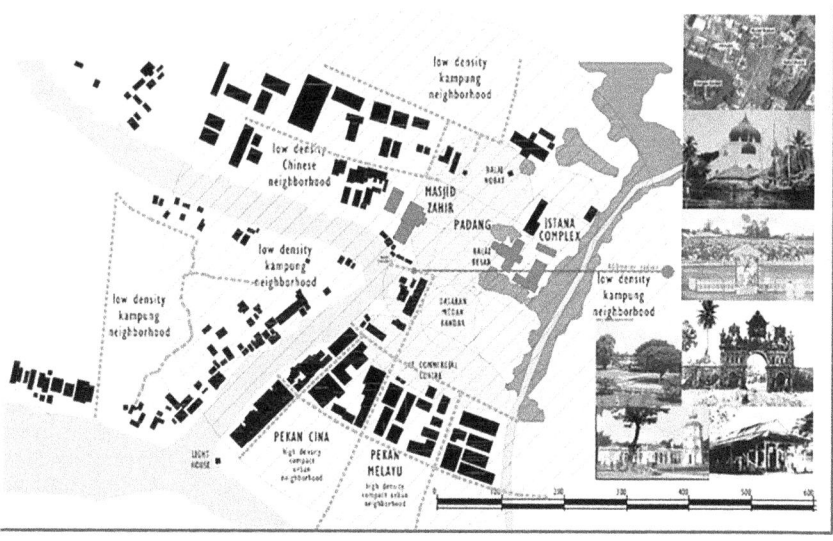

Fig. 5.2 Estimation of origi*dang* within urban morphology of historic core of Alor Setar before 1900s (Kamaruddin & Ismail, 2011)

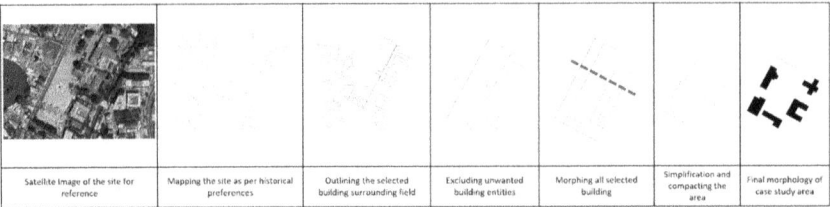

| Satellite Image of the site for reference | Mapping the site as per historical preferences | Outlining the selected building surrounding field | Excluding unwanted building entities | Morphing all selected building | Simplification and compacting the area | Final morphology of case study area |

Fig. 5.3 Summary of the urban center and green space site of Alor Setar, the reconstruction of the morphology and the mapping of site area and its eventual modelling process in the wind and comfort simulation using local wind average data and directional conditions

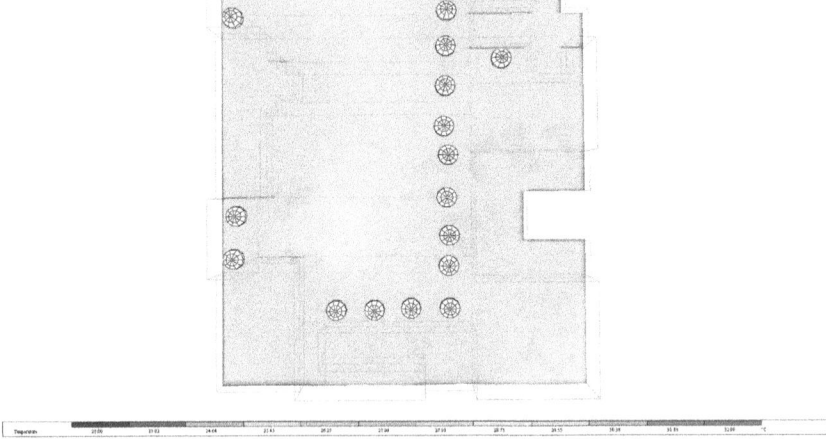

Fig. 5.4 Simulation Results suggest the combined cool environment results from the directional and morphological form of the "pasang" space, the original presence of grass and greenery and the presence of large jacaranda trees historically at site

Climate, open space and Morphology: A simulation of urban comfort conditions

To illustrate the climatic impact of the combination of fragmented open space with their original lined shaded trees, a computational dynamic simulation using the software Micro Flo (by Integrated Environmental

Solutions) is undertaken. The open space is modelled in its original dimension, and surrounded by key structures as in Figure 5.2 and whose simplification in terms of modelling in summarised in Fig. 5.3. The results are presented in Figure 5.4 and beyond.

Preliminary results of the external airflow simulation of the cooling impact of the green space and its original tree-lined and fragmented central *padang* as undertaken and found for the padang of Alor Setar; within which the environment surrounding Masjid Zahir, Balai Besar, and other prominent historical buildings were modelled with greenery along with wind directional character, its average value including turbulence occurrences and an analysis of the temperature profile in the presence of large shady trees and the original green grassed turf of the center as found in Figure 5.2.

Conclusions

Along with its loss of social role, the padang and *alun alun* are increasingly losing its critical position as a climatic and ecological 'green' counterbalancing strategy in the need for enhancing urban microclimate in tropical urbanism. Cooling sensations reported by travellers to these cities and foreigners who evoke descriptions of a bioclimatic past in their diaries and documents are increasingly absent in present urban cores which are hard-paved and lack shading elements. Recalling a time when the cooling tropics were associated with a city, there was a continuous cool and shade with no sudden ruptures or drastic temperature differences between indoor and outdoor environments. To resonate with Relph (2014), one must begin with the urban core. The *padang* is not only a sociohistorical element, but a bioclimatic element arising from the roots of the *padang* as a 'field of men' and the present conservation direction of the historic urban landscape must include this challenging, often misconstrued, locally derived form. Its original bioclimatic form must be differentiated from its external counterparts, and those spaces which were hybrid evolvements from external influences.

The Alun alun or *padang*—rather than its original role as a communal site and a climatic urban device—has increasingly became a gridded stamp merely to evoke the adminstration of man over man, or of humans over nature, rather than its original role as a social and eco-urbanist public space. At times, this typology of public space still retains its communal function, and where greenery is maintained and preserved there are still at present a multitude of people which are using it, but throughout the loss of its original archetypal form and climatic function has been transformed into a gridded symbol, which together with concrete structures glass-walled space and a lack of permeability, has contributed even more to the rising urban heat island of tropical cities. With the emergence of green urbanism, it is hoped that the original forms of padang or *alun alun* is recognised in its key role as part of the region's historic urban landscape and, the beautification of the *padang* and its green identity is crucial to the identity, vibrancy, and vitality of the region's tropical cities' everyday life.

References

Abdul Rashid, M. S., & Amat, S. C. (2009, July 20–21). *The traditional Malay architecture: Between aesthetics and symbolism.* Proceedings of the Intellectual Property and Heritage Issues in the Built Environment seminar, Malaysia Intellectual Properties and Pusat Warisan Seni Melayu, University Teknologi MARA (UiTM), Renaissance Hotel.

Basundoro, P. (2015). The two alun alun of Malang (1930–1960). In F. Colombijn & J. Cote (Eds.), *Cars, Conduits and Kampongs* (pp. 272–299).

Durrans, B. (2005). *'Malay design: Towards an anthropological perspective', seminar on Spirit and form in Malay design.* Department of Museums and Antiquities.

Farhana, M. F., Illyani, I., Zalina, H. N., et al. (2018). Analysis of the composition of malay traditional house compound: A case study of kg Seri Tanjung, Melaka. *Planning Malaysia.*

Frye, D. (2018). *Walls: A history of civilization in blood and brick.* Simon and Schuster.

Gell, A. (1998). *Art and agency: An anthropological theory.* Clarendon Press.

Gunawan, S. R., Nindyo, S. O. E. W. A. R. N. O., Ikaputra, I., & Bakti, S. E. T. I. A. W. A. N. (2013). Colonial and traditional urban space in Java: A morphological study of ten cities. *DIMENSI: Journal of Architecture and Built Environment, 40*(2), 77–88.

Hidayat, A., & Widrakara, Y. A. (2018). *Postcolonial study on alun alun area in Probolinggo City*. Duta Wacana Christian University.

Ikaputra. (1999). *Personal Space, dalam Paper Seminar pada acara Arsitek(tur) Kontemporer Indonesia, Tarumanagara Tapes, Jurusan Arsitektur, FT* (pp. 17–18). Universitas Tarumanagara.

Ikaputra. (2004). Towards open and accessible PublicPlaces, conflict and compromise dalam proceedings managing conflicts in public spaces trough Urban Design, 1st international seminar National Symposium, Exhibition,and workshop in Urban Design. In B. Prayitno, Poerwadi, A. T. Setiawan, & D. P. Aji (Eds.), *Master Program in Urban Design, Postgraduate Program*. Gadjah Mada University.

Kamaruddin, Z., & Ismail, S. (2011). Configuration of carved components and its layout patterns in Malay timber houses. *International Journal of Architectural Research, 5*(1), 7–21.

Kamarudin, Z., & Said, I. (2009). Principal orders in the composition of woodcarvings and its layouts in Kelantan and Terengganu traditional houses. *UTM Journal, 3*, 12–23.

Khudori, D. (2002). *Menuju kampung pemerdekaan: membangun masyarakat sipil dari akar-akarnya: belajar dari Romo Mangun di pinggir Kali Code*. Yayasan Pondok Rakyat.

Kompas. (2008a, Agustus 13). *Jemelah PTS di Yogya Terlalu Banyak*. Jakarta.

Kompas. (2008b, Juli 19). *Seturan Menuju Kawasan Hiburan*. Jakarta.

Kompas. (2008c, Agustus 16). *Si Petruk Tujuh Belasan di Mal*. Jakarta.

Krier, R. (1979). *Urban space*. Academy.

Lai, C. K. (2010). Maidan to Padang: Reinventions of urban fields in Malaysia and Singapore. *Traditional Dwellings and Settlements Review*, 55–70.

Lang, J. (2006). *Urban design*. Routledge.

Lim, M., & Padawangi, R. (2008). Contesting alun alun: Power relations, identities and the production of urban space in Bandung. *Indonesia. International Development Planning Review, 30*(3), 307.

Nāgarakṛtāgama. n.d. Javanese epic poem written in 1365 by Prapañcā.

Othman, R. (2005a). '*Malay art of woodcarving: Derivation and transformation of form and content*', seminar on Spirit and form in Malay design. Department of Museums and Antiquities.

Othman, R. (2005b). The language of the Langkasukan motif. *Indonesia and the Malay World, 33*(96), 97–111.

Rajab, T., & Safwat, N. F. (1997). *The harmony of letters: Islamic calligraphy from the Tareq Rajab museum*. Asian Civilisations Museum.

Rukayah, R. S., Susilo, E. S., Pringgenies, D., & Agus Tri Setyo, W. (2018). The Alun-Alun Karimunjawa as Economic Space in the Coastal City as Alun-Alun in the City Center in Java. *Proceedings of the 2nd Southeast Asian Academic Forum on Sustainable Development* (SEA-AFSID 2018), 168(2009), 342–347. https://doi.org/10.2991/aebmr.k.210305.061

Said, I., & Abdullah, A. S. (2010). *Spesies-spesies Kayu dalam Seni Ukiran Melayu.* Penerbit UTM Press.

Spiro, K. (1992). *The City Assembled: The elements of urban form through history.*

Sunaryo, R. G., Soewarno, N., & Setiawan, B. (2010). *Posisi Ruang Publik dalam Transformasi Konsepsi Urbanitas Kota Indonesia.* Doctoral dissertation, Petra Christian University.

Sunaryo, R. G., Soewarno, N., & Setiawan, B. (2013). *The transformation of urban public space in Yogyakarta a search for specific identity & character.* Doctoral dissertation, IVA-ICRA, Institute for Comparative Research in Architecture and Department of Architecture and Pla.

Tohid, M. S. (2006). *Ethical values in Malay Woodcarving—A case study of Wan Mustaffa Wan Su's Work.* M.A. thesis, Fine Arts, Universiti Teknologi Mara (UiTM).

Wiryomartono, B. (2014). *Perspectives on traditional settlements and communities: Home, form and culture in Indonesia.* Springer Science & Business Media.

Xu, Q., & Xu, Z. (2020). What can urban design learn from changing winds? *The Journal of Public Space, 5*(2), 7–22.

6

Traditional Compactness of the Urban Core: 'Walkability' and the Malay Public Realm

Illyani Ibrahim

Introduction

Cities in tropical Asia have long served as centres of commerce. Their historic urban cores first functioned as commercial centres, containing all the features that constitute a city. However, these forms have disappeared without a trace because the materials used can be easily destroyed by external factors, such as rainfall and heat, over the years.

Urban space is conceptualised as 'all kinds of space between buildings in cities and other localities as urban space' (Krier, 1979). The intimacy between the urban forms is based on what the community thinks of each time. Intimacy is one of the key parameters of the urban design principle, which explains the proximity between physical features. Intimacy was first described by philosopher Martin Heidegger as 'man's relation to things' and by Dekkers (2011) as 'proximity'. The notion of intimacy and community

I. Ibrahim (✉)
International Islamic University Malaysia, Jalan Gombak, Selangor, Malaysia
e-mail: illyani_i@iium.edu.my

stems from an understanding of the cultural influences that diffuse at the heart of particular settlements. Proximity has also been used to explain the relationship between people and things. Urban forms can be expressed through the concept of proximity by showing the influence of the community's culture on the surroundings. Proximity can also be used to describe the social and cultural relationships of a community with a particular place, thereby providing insight into the characteristics of the community. Density and intimacy in the public space of an urban core can also be used to (i) identify the space's traditional character that has disappeared following modern urbanisation and (ii) gain insights into the intimacy of the traditional urban core and settlement areas. This chapter suggests that the character of intimacy between the royal elements has persisted over time.

Maritime cities such as Srivijaya, Melaka, Aceh, Banten, and the north Javanese ports are situated at river mouths, which flush out swampy coastal fringes. The cities were typically administrative and economically based since the rivers facilitated communication to collect export staples, such as jungle produce, gold, and pepper (Kathirithamby-Wells, 2008). These cities are characterised by a combination of polity, culture, and population, which are closely related to the urban form.

A public realm is defined as spaces in an urban environment that are open and physically accessible to residents (Fleming et al., 1985, in Talen, 2000). Walking is the simplest mode of movement from ancient times until now and represents the best mode of human interaction with the urban environment. However, after the Industrial Revolution and the widespread advent of the automobile, the structure of cities faced major changes as vehicular movement became dominant (Jou, 2011). However, in the past, walkability provided accessibility, increased land-use efficiency, and improved liveability. A public space can be understood through its physical attributes. The promotion of a 'living community' is strengthened by establishing shared open spaces, walkways, and other public gathering places (Christoforidis, 1994).

Traditional Cities

The traditional city in maritime South East Asia is explained by Kathirithamby-Wells (2008) as a 'central urban complex' and 'an inherent structure in terms of its parts and their different functions'. The distinction between the city as an urban centre and its rural surroundings is reflected in the traditional Javanese view of *negara* (Kathirithamby-Wells, 2008). The same paper defines *negara* in the fourteenth century as 'all where one can go out (of his compound) without passing through paddy fields'.

The traditional city is enormously compact and walkable from one place to another. Traditional cities are divided into two general types: traditional coastal cities and traditional inland cities. A traditional coastal city is a city located near the coastal area and usually has a fort for safety measures. The factors that drove the building of a coastal city were economic contributions and accessibility to transportation. The traditional inland city is usually located near the mountains. In Peninsular Malaysia, the traditional urban core is located in the coastal area. It is very organically driven factors and parameters. Such characteristics can be discerned by comparing the difference between the urban configurations of Asian and European locations or, even more significantly, before and after the colonial era in South East Asia. Asian urban centres lack the roots and identity grounding found in European heritage cities, until the present times.

Traditional urban form is a combination of space bounded by monuments and buildings. The urban core area comprises palaces, a *padang*, a market, and a mosque. Compared to other inland areas, the urban core is the most compact area because it is usually administered by a sultanate. The coastal city was designed as a fortified city for defensive purposes.

Urban design in the traditional Malay world is also filled with embellishing interfacing features, such as the *serambi* (verandah), *anjung* (porticoes), *kolong* (under floor space), and *wakaf/bangsal* (pavilion or shed); they provide shaded spaces for comfort and a walkable distance for the public within urban limits.

South East Asian Traditional Cities

Southeast Asian archaeologists have described nucleated settlements as urban areas on the coasts and river networks, where the inhabitants engage in trade and agriculture. Most of the mainland areas in South East Asia have ceremonial centres that also serve political, economic, and social functions (Stark, 2015). Stark (2015) discussed urban cores as being in several places, such as Ayutthaya (1350–1767 CE) in Central Thailand, Pagan in the Irrawaddy Basin (849–1298 CE), and Mahapahit in East Central Java. Another study on the urban core of Angkor identified the concentration of stone temples, linear canal segments, and embankment features (Evans et al., 2007). During the eighteenth century, the core of a traditional town in Singapore at Kampong Gelam included a padang, districts of traders, craftsmen, and pilgrim brokers (Tajudeen, 2005).

According to Stark (2015), the rulers lived in these urban centres, and change in rulers generally entailed a change in location of the polity centre. A walled urban centre refers to arteries that stretched from the capital to secondary centres throughout a polity's realm. Another historical area, Kathmandu, has an urban core comprising palaces, temples, and houses, built from the fifteenth to the eighteenth centuries (Rai, 2008).

Scholars refer to the urban core using various terms, such as 'urban centre' or 'core area'. Urban core refers to the main area, particularly of a royal residence, administration, and commerce. Cities in Asia have served as centres of trade for a long time. The historical urban cores initially functioned as city centres for trade. Urban cores typically include all features that form a city. In tropical Asian remnants, the urban form was decimated without a trace because the materials used were quickly destroyed by external factors, such as rainfall and heat, over the years. The concept of urban space refers to 'all kinds of space between buildings in towns and other localities as urban space' (Krier, 1979).

The latest study of urbanists used a five-minute walk to indicate the primary access standard relating to time, which is based on the typical size of a neighbourhood—about a quarter-mile from the centre to the edge (Steuteville, 2021).

South East Asia's Traditional Urban Core

The five main core components of South East Asia's traditional urban core are the palace, *padang*, masjid, market, and settlement. These components represent an Islamic identity with the placement of the masjid in the centre of the urban core. Each of these components has its form and function.

During historical time, a palace was a place for administration and the residence of the royal family. The palace was fortified mainly for security purposes. A palace can have one building or several structures, each being used for different functions. Ordinary people can enter the palace until *Balai Penghadapan*, but the rest of the area is restricted for the nobles.

The *masjid* is one of South East Asia's traditional elements located near the palace. *Masjid* is where Muslims perform prayer and is also a place of madrasah for disseminating knowledge and education about the values of Islam.

An open field or *padang* is a public space where royals and the people gather or for the coronation of the royalty. A *padang* is a green area with some parts of trees located at the edge of the area. The *padang* can also be used for the public realm. It possesses a kind of cultural-religious aura or charge, not merely for administrative purposes. Because the *padang* is an open area, it is permeable, allowing people to walk through it from any area. Certain features differentiate between colonial and Middle East squares of *padang*. The South East Asian *padang* is not precisely square because it follows the natural urban form. It is characterised by not being rigid with a path for the public to enter the *padang*.

In those days, the market was near the river to make it easy to sell goods to the community. The position of the market, therefore, is not at the centre of the urban core. The function of the market is primarily for social and economic purposes. The market is also located outside the fortified areas.

The last component of the public realm is settlements, which refer to places where people live. In those days, people preferred to live near rivers, which acted as a means of transportation. Settlements were established in various villages and surrounded the royal palace.

The Compactness of Traditional Urban Core

Compactness, defined by nearness or short distances, is characterised by the link between public places, such as between a palace and a mosque, or between a palace and a *padang*. In those days, the traditional urban core was compact; all public places were accessible and within walking distance. Such a feature made it easier for people to carry out their daily activities and socialise because they were close to each other. However, many of these attributes have disappeared in connection with modernisation. Some of the attributes were left unattended without proper maintenance, and some were replaced with asphalt and concrete.

On the other hand, the materials used in European buildings, such as bricks and stone, are more durable. The compactness of the urban form was related to how the community thought of that particular time. Compactness is one of the key parameters of the urban design principle; it explains the closeness between physical features. Compactness was first discussed by the philosopher Martin Heidegger as a man's 'rapport with things' and as 'nearness' by Dekkers (2011). The notion of compactness and community arose from the understanding of the influence of culture on the centre of these settlements. Nearness also explains the relation between *man* and *thing*. Urban forms can be expressed through the locational concept by showing the impact of a community's culture on its surroundings. South East Asia's urban forms have constituted several elements of an urban form, such as a fort, fortification, or a stockade, and the forms were also the administrative centre for South East Asia's rulers during the splendour of South East Asia's kingdom (Harun & Jalil, 2014). Nearness can also be used to describe the society and culture of people in particular places. The relationship of the people to place can shed light on features of the community.

Spatial Configuration of Urban Core

Spatial configuration is a two-dimensional (2D) map of an urban core that shows the relationship between built and unbuilt spaces. Some spaces are gridded, some are organic, and some have an irregular geometry. Sociocultural aspects can be understood based on the 2D dimensional system. Traditional Western settlements typically have a gridded geometry, whereas South East Asia's traditional settlements are more irregular and organic. Maps can be used to analyse interactions between buildings and surrounding areas, such as neighbourhoods, among others. The anaysis can also provide an understanding of the patterns of the study area in terms of the linkage and sense of place. Estimation of walkability is done based on the location of the public realm, which has fundamental effects on movement choices, primarily by walking. There are three rankings; high walkability (red), medium walkability (blue), and low walkability (yellow).

1. Urban core of Kota Bharu: tracing original patterns

Kota Bharu is the administrative centre of Kelantan and is located in the north-east of the Malaysian Peninsula. The spatial configuration (Fig. 6.1) of Kota Bharu shows that the palaces (Istana Balai Besar and Istana Jahar) are close to Masjid Muhammadi and a *padang*. The *padang*, which is orientated towards Sungai Kelantan, indicates that Sungai Kelantan was frequently used as the main form of transportation by

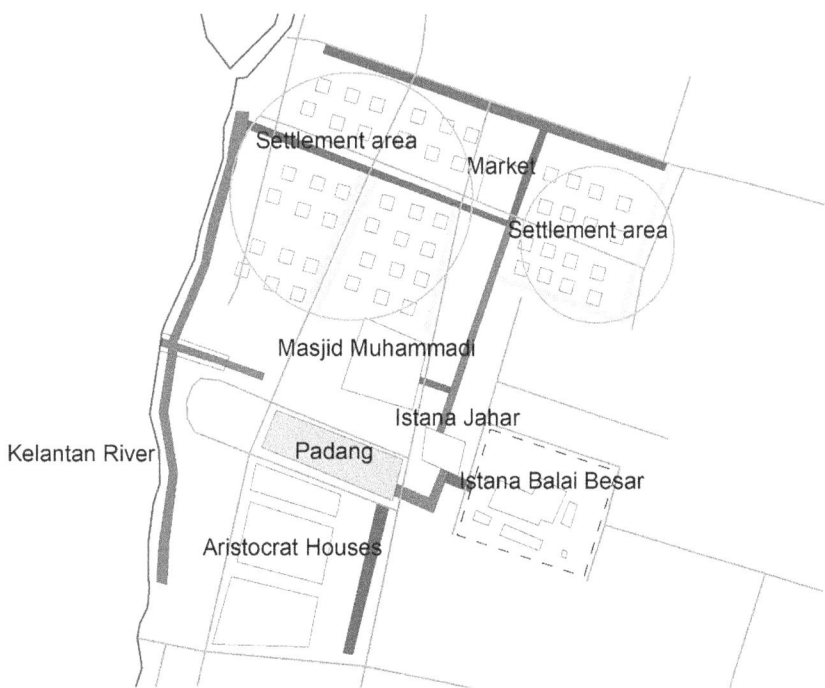

Fig. 6.1 Urban core at Kota Bharu (adapted from Muzium of Kelantan)

royalty. The map (Fig. 6.1) also shows that the market is close to the settlement. The *padang* is a rectangular green field and is associated with a natural urban form.

2. Kuala Terengganu

The capital city of Terengganu, Kuala Terengganu, is located on the east coast of Peninsular South East Asia. The urban core is located at the estuary of the Terengganu River. The map (Fig. 6.2) shows that the palace (Istana Hijau) is the centre of the urban core. Pasar Payang is located near the river and the settlement. The palace is situated in the centre, between the *padang* and Masjid Abidin. The urban core of Kuala Terengganu shows that the palace is surrounded by a *padang*, a market, a *masjid*, and settlements, indicating the importance of royalty during that time. The shape of the *padang* is not exactly square because it was designed to follow the natural urban form.

Fig. 6.2 Urban core at Kuala Terengganu [adapted from Syala et al. (2018) and Noor Fazamimah (2007)]

Fig. 6.3 Urban core at Alor Setar [Adapted from JahnKassim et al., 2018)]

3. Alor Setar

Alor Setar is the capital city of Kedah. Figure 6.3 shows that the central core of the city consists of a palace and a *padang*. The *padang* is surrounded by important buildings in the urban core, such as the *masjid*, the palace, and the market. An atmosphere of openness can be seen in the absence of a fortress or wall around the city. It is worth noting the existence of elements such as trees in the *padang*. The *padang* in Alor Setar is also not exactly square. A market is located near Sungai Kedah and the settlement and is bounded by the river. Another settlement is close to the *masjid*.

The findings confirm clear Islamic images and identities in the case studies of the South East Asian landscape, evidently from the closeness of the *masjid*, palace, and *padang*. The compact urban core results in a compactness in the case studies. The mosque's strategic location makes it a place for communities, learning, social gatherings, and celebrations.

Walkability around Public Realm

This section discusses walkability in the public realm based on a distance analysis. Table 6.1 summarises the distances between the historical palaces and other physical elements, such as the *masjid*, *padang*, settlement, and market.

Three urban cores were used to examine walkability. To compare the distance of the historical royal urban core, the distances between the palace and the public spaces (such as the *masjid*, *padang*, market, and the settlement) were analysed. On average, the distance between the palaces and the *masjid* is 170 metres, between the palace and *padang* is 130 metres, between the palace and settlement is 300 metres, and between the palace and market is 280 metres. Among all the public realms, the distance between the palace and *padang* is the shortest (130 metres). This explains the importance of *padang* as a meeting place between ruler and people.

It can be seen that the distances are less than 400 metres, which is within the walkability distance, indicating that intimacy existed in the study area. All distances are less than a ten-minute walk, consistent with the primary access standard (Steuteville, 2021). The walkability has led to a liveable environment in the urban core.

The coloured lines indicate the estimation of walkability around the urban core. The high walkability is estimated along the river since that is where the main hubs of transportation are located, like the walkway along Istana to the market. The walkability around the market to the settlement is considered medium. Low walkability is found around the settlement area. From historical concerns, the impact of urban policy

Table 6.1 Distance and time taken (minutes) of historical palaces with physical elements (metres)

Historical Royal Town	Palace	Masjid	Padang	Settlement	Market
Alor Setar	Istana Kota Setar	200	100	300	200
		3 min	2 min	5 min	3 min
Kota Bharu	Istana Balai Besar	100	200	200	230
		2 min	3 min	3 min	3 min
Kuala Terengganu	Istana Hijau	200	100	350	400
		3 min	2 min	5 min	6 min
Average (±10 m)	–	170	130	300	280

suggests that these areas need to be preserved, such as by improving these walkway areas and enhancing the pedestrian urban design, because these are historical walkways.

Discussion

Comparison of the quantified measures for the three urban core case studies showed similarities between the urban cores in measurement. All the public realms were close to each other, at a distance of less than a ten-minute walk. Such findings suggest a clear, legible distinction of all public realm. Similarities were noted in all case studies as follows: (i) all urban cores are located near a river; (ii) there is high compactness between the settlements and the market and *masjid*; and (iii) there is high compactness between the *padang* and the palace and *masjid*. Ibrahim et al. (2020) found that the Malay royal urban core does obey the urban design principles of intimacy and walkability.

Lai (2019) and Uma (2002) claimed that *padang* is a legacy of British colonial urbanism, but this is no true. It is worth noting that most researchers are biased towards British counterparts. The British open square is called an open square with a geometric grid layout. However, the traditional South East Asian *padang* is not necessarily square; it can occur in any form based on the local topography. The *padang* is highly permeable because it is accessible, and it creates a network for walking through it. It is an open space that is visually and physically accessible to all, without exception. The case study urban cores also existed before the arrival of the British, and major physical royal elements have not changed to this day, particularly the elements of palace, *masjid*, and *padang*. Noor Fazamimah (2007) explained that one of the physical components of South East Asia's traditional urban core is the *padang*, which is usually located across from the grand palace.

To make cities more walkable and eliminate a dependence on cars, urban patterns must reflect eco-urbanism. Thus, there is a need to re-engage with the historical precedents and return to a more traditional planning strategy.

Conclusion

This chapter attempted to show that the compactness of South East Asia's traditional urban core still exists because a clear distinction between the public realms remains evident. The similarities indicate that urban cores are near rivers, and there is high compactness (i) between the settlement, market, and *masjid* and (ii) between *padang*, palace, and *masjid*. From an urban planning perspective, the essence of this traditional urbanism is the incorporation of open spaces and other public spaces in pedestrian areas, which promote walking.

References

Christoforidis, A. (1994). New alternatives to the suburb: Neo-traditional developments. *Journal of Planning Literature, 8*(4), 429–440.

Dekkers, W. (2011). Dwelling, house and home: Towards a home-led perspective on dementia care. *Medicine, Health Care, and Philosophy, 14*(3), 291–300. https://doi.org/10.1007/s11019-011-9307-2

Evans, D., Pottier, C., Fletcher, R., Hensley, S., Tapley, I., Milne, A., & M. B. (2007). A comprehensive archaeological map of the world's largest preindustrial settlement complex at Angkor, Cambodia. *Proceedings of the National Academy of Science, 104*, 14277–14282.

Harun, S. N., & Jalil, R. A. (2014). The history and characteristics of Malay early towns in Peninsular Malaysia. *Asian Journal of Humanities and Social Studies, 2*(3), 403–409. www.ajouronline.com

Ibrahim, I., Jahn Kassim, P. S., & Abdullah, A. (2020). Historical Intimacy in Malay Urban Core Configurations: A Comparative Analysis. *Culture & History Digital Journal, 9*(2).

JahnKassim, P. S., Ibrahim, I., Harun, N. Z., & Kamaruddin, K. (2018). Ecological urbanism in the tropics studies on the sustainable dimensions of Malay Traditional Urban Centers. *International Journal of. Engineering & Technology, 7*(3.9), 93–99.

Jou, K. K. (2011). Pedestrian areas and sustainable development. *World Academy of Science, Engineering and Technology, 77*(5), 483–490. https://doi.org/10.5281/zenodo.1082615

Kathirithamby-Wells, J. (2008). The Islamic city: Melaka to Jogjakarta, c. 1500–1800. *Modern Asian Studies, 20*(2), 333–351. https://doi.org/10.1017/S0026749X0000086X

Krier, R. (1979). *Urban space (Stadtxaum)*. Rizzoli.

Lai, C.-K. (2019). Maidan to Padang: Reinventions of urban fields in Malaysia and Singapore. *International Association for the Study of Traditional Environments (IASTE), 21*(2), 55–70.

Noor Fazamimah, M. A. (2007). *Role of cultural landscape in improving the identity of the Kuala Terengganu Town centre as a Malay Historic Town*. Universiti Teknologi Malaysia.

Rai, R. (2008). Threats to the spirit of the place. In *16th General Assembly of ICOMOS—Québec 2008*.

Stark, M. T. (2015). *Early Mainland Southeast Asian landscapes in the first millennium a.d. January 2008.* https://doi.org/10.1146/annurev.anthro.35.081705.123157

Steuteville, R. (2021). The 15-minute neighborhood gets its 15 minutes of fame. *Public Square A CTU Journal*. https://www.cnu.org/publicsquare/2021/01/25/15-minute-neighborhood-gets-its-15-minutes-fame

Syala, N., Kassim, S. J., & Abdullah, A. (2018). Islamic influence in traditional Malay settlement—The Case of Kuala Terengganu. In *SLAH 2017 1st International conference of Islamic Architectural HeritageAt: Kuala Lumpur, Malaysia, July*.

Tajudeen, I. (2005). Reading the traditional city of maritime Southeast Asia. *Journal of Southeast Asian Architecture, 8*, 1–25.

Talen, E. (2000). Measuring the public realm: A case study. *Journal of Architectural and Planning Research, 17*(4), 257–278.

Uma, G. D. (2002). *Singapore's 100 historic places*. National Heritage Board.

7

Animals and the City: A Southeast Asian Historical Perspective

Noor Hanita Abdul Majid

More recent discourses in urban ecology, urban geography, and urban planning have led to the realisation, as an outcome of the Covid-19 pandemic, of the need to emphasize the benefits to human health and well-being of green space and green infrastructure (e.g. parks, living walls) that would allow animals and their ecosystems to thrive in urban environments. To recentre the foci in public policy discussions of creating a greener, more sustainable, and more resilient cities, considerations for the habitat of fauna and wildlife animals must be re-instated in discussions about future cities in all aspects, including architecture, infrastructure, and urban design. These must include the social dynamics of people and animals, including wildlife, particularly in considerations of and in relation to landscaping, parks, open space, air, and water. Owens and Wolch (2017) discussed concerns about the consideration of animals in connection with a robust urban theory in the age of ecology. Animals

N. H. Abdul Majid (✉)
Kulliyyah of Architecture and Environmental Design, International Islamic University Malaysia, Selangor, Malaysia

© The Editor(s) (if applicable) and The Author(s), under exclusive license to Springer Nature Singapore Pte Ltd. 2023
S. Jahn Kassim et al. (eds.), *Eco-Urbanism and the South East Asian City*,
https://doi.org/10.1007/978-981-19-1637-3_7

become part of the planning decision for cities and the allocation of places suitable for animals, such as parks and zoos. Nevertheless, in the early days of city planning, animals were part of city development rather than separate aspects requiring their own town planning decisions. Fauna plays a vital role in animal-related transportation in planning the buildings and the streets. The planning of streets and buildings in early towns and villages made way for animals used for transport, like elephants, horses, and even bull or oxen. Wilson (2016) discussed the elephants in the city of Chiang Mai that were part of daily human activities but now have been reduced to artistic and cultural depictions and, through the incorporation of elephant images, imbued within the built environment in the city.

Throughout history, traditional cities offered special places for animals, either to rear them or use them for transportation, food, or creating a sanctuary for replenishment as war machines. In the 1700s, cities in Southeast Asia such as Aceh in Indonesia and Nakhon Si Thammarat and Patani in Thailand provides zones for animals. Human daily activities intertwined and interconnected with animals at many different levels, with some used as transportation for people and goods, for agriculture and food sources, and even as war machines. Domesticated elephants were important assets for the royals and valuable resources to the rulers. Animals, whatever their significance or function to humans, were part of a city's ecological growth.

Pioneering the research on the role of animals in the past will increase the understanding of the making and unmaking of places and landscapes (Wilbert, 2009) in the city. Forman (2019) described how cities were unique due to their evolvement in a cultural context. Historical traditions and legends are filled with mentions and incidents featuring local fauna and species of animals. John Hadidian (1998) remarks that it is a human predisposition to love living things, including animals. Malay cities of the past are excellent examples that carried almost sacred resonance in terms of being sites or 'sanctuaries' that celebrated animals. Apfelback et al. (2020) proposed the concept of 'wildlife-inclusive urban design' that integrates animal needs into urban planning and design process. The concept is proposed to be inserted at different stages of the urban planning cycle. The existence of animals has not only made urban life better for people but also solving urban conflicts and humanely dealing with animals.

The ecology of cities is intertwined with the people's culture and beliefs featuring animals' involvement in its development and is best defined as patterns, processes, and changes involving people, their beliefs, socioculture, and physical dimensions within the city area. Fauna was considered and integrated with the planning of streets and orientation of layouts of buildings. Planning decisions must accommodate the routes and width of spaces and streets to make way for animals used for transport, like horses, elephants, or even oxen.

Etymology of Place

The etymology of naming places in Southeast Asia is commonly associated with heritage, language, culture, animals, plants, and incidents, among others (Mills, 2011). The co-existence of animals and humans in cities is seen through how places were named. The animals became part of place names due to either a significant incident at a specific spot or origin of the city or part of a visual sighting or a memorable experience of a specific act of animals. History has tales of how places and sites were named after animals or incidents involving animals, such as the name of Singapore as Singapura (*singa*/lion and *Pura*/city), Langkawi Island (*lang*/eagle and *kawi*/red), and Kuching, Sarawak (*kucing*/cat). Language emerges from direct human interactions and relationships with the physical, social, and spiritual environments. Thus, place names represent a narrative and identity of sites, capturing the notion that 'an entire way of understanding is indigenous and intertwined with that place'. Animals are significantly linked to key legends and embedded in myths, thoughts, traditions, and historical narratives and have always been included in symbols and representations as part of local sociobelief systems and history.

Establishment of Cities Due to Incidents Involving Fauna

Historic cities are previously eco sites, with animals having a significant presence in certain places. The etymology of place could have been through sighting, a specific act, or places where animals roam.[1] Repeated stories were told in the naming of places in Southeast Asian cities related to elephants. The key importance of elephants in history of the region is that they can be found in large numbers, which led to many places being named after elephants or *gajah*: Kubu Gajah (Elephant Fort), Batu Gajah (Elephant Stone), Alor Gajah (Elephant Stream), Gajah Mati (Dead Elephant), and others.

Cities may also acquire their names in connection with flocks of animals found in certain places. Bullocks (*kerbau*) bathed in a creek that flows through the city of Singapore in the early 1900s. There is a place near the Bukit Timah area in Singapore named Kandang Kerbau that is due to the existence of buffalo stables in that area (Fig. 7.1).

In Thailand, elephants are associated with the cosmological aspects of Buddhism and were portrayed in many forms and artwork such as murals, stone carvings, ceramic, fashion, jewellery, and others. The animals roamed freely in cities and were part of the civilisation. Until about 800 years ago, the city of Chiang Mai co-existed with elephants as part of human daily transactions and activities. Nevertheless, now the animal prevails and is represented in the built environment as 'guardians' at temples, incorporated and displayed as sculptures in the built environment and a variety of elephant-themed jewellery, clothing, handbags, prints, carvings, cards, statues, and various goods.

---

[1] The city of Phoenix, Arkansas, United States of America was named after a mythical bird, the phoenix. The city adopted the name as it was built and developed from the ruin of an old civilisation just as a phoenix would rise from the ashes. The city of Buffalo, United States received its name from a nearby creek called Buffalo Creek. British military engineer Captain John Montresor has referred to the name in his journal of 1764, which may be the earliest recorded appearance of the name.

WASHING BULLOCKS, SINGAPORE.

Fig. 7.1 Coolies Washing Bullocks, Singapore in 1910. Source: Courtesy of National Archives of Singapore

Fauna in Functional and Symbolic Roles

Urban planning, in traditional Southeast Asia, configured street dimensions to allow provisions for the animals used for transportation, including considerations for traditional royal parades with floats in animal figurines such as the *Burung Petalawati* and *Gagak Sura*. The significant planning of cities up to the buildings' detailed designs has incorporated animal figures, both real and mythical.

Elephants, associated with the pride and strength of past kingdoms, are instrumental to the power and military might of cities in the history of Thailand, Cambodia, India, and the Malay Kingdoms of Melaka, Pahang, Langkasuka, and many others, including Aceh. Langkasuka, for example, had its army of elephants, thanks to their size and strength, deter strikes from enemies. Elephants are mainly seen as the core of a royal's strength and thus are associated with civilisations' military might (Nurul Izzati et al., 2004). Their critical role resonated in the planning of routes for travel and communication for trade and strengthening

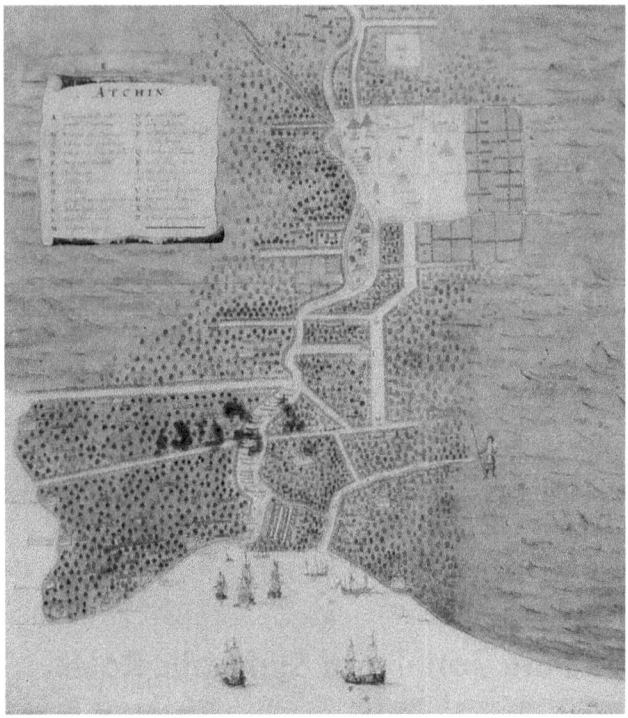

Fig. 7.2 Dutch Map of Aceh in 17th Century Showing Elephant Island and Elephant on Palace Grounds. (Source: Reid Anthony, Ito Takeshi. A Precious Dutch Map of Aceh, c. 1645. In: Archipel, volume 57, 1999)

sociopolitical ties. The animal was found in high numbers in the Sunda Plateau and surrounding areas, such as Indo-China and Thailand.

Aceh's map in the seventeenth century, as formed by the Dutch (Reid & Ito, 1999), showed evidence of elephants inside the royal enclosure *(dalem)* and surrounding areas of the palace grounds. The elephants are placed near the open square *(medan khayyali)* and an island outside the palace grounds. The island marked a special ground where the elephants were kept for royal usage (Fig. 7.2). The Aceh map is evidence of how elephants are part of planning for a Malay city, and Fig. 7.2 shows a bird house on palace grounds. During the reign of Sultan Iskandar Muda (1607–1636), his army cavalry consisted of 1000 elephants, used for war, and welcomed foreign delegates (Dinas Kebudayaan dan Pariwisata,

Aceh). The Sultan chose elephants over horses to ride in wars; when he rode on elephants, his army would ride on horses. Similar planning that incorporated animals into the ancient city planning can be seen in Patani and Nakhon Sittamarat, Thailand. The animals are included in planning and were given a place within the cities.

Animals are also inscribed in the plan of the walled city of Ligor (now known as Nakhon Sithamarat) circa 1825, representing the walled city and its surroundings. The plan is full of details, with architecture, nature, bridges, animals, and people. Elephants and horses are depicted in enclosures within the inner city wall. Inside the city, walls are houses, presumably houses of aristocrats, wat or temples, and fruit groves. De la Mare noted that the open space in the city of Ligor 'is extremely rural and full of fruit trees' (Munro-Hay, 2000). The open or tree-filled spaces within the wall suggest an ecologically friendly environment between humans and the environment in the city setting.

Architectural Reverberations

As key symbols of military strength for kingdoms of the past, ancient Chinese records recorded how elephants were used to send tributes from the kingdom of Langkasuka to China's emperor in the years 502–507, 511, 515, 518, 520, 531, and 568 AD. Schafer (1957) wrote about Malay court pages entrusted by the Chinese Emperor Fei to muster two elephants. Sulalat as Salatin (Samad, 1996) is a piece of evidence that elephants had a particular position in Malay society and are often dubbed 'elite animals' because they played a significant role, especially for kings, rulers, and officials (Nurul Izzati et al., 2004). It was recorded that Admiral Hang Tuah, an very famous Malay admiral, bought six elephants from Siam to be presented to China's emperor. Figure 7.3 showed the Forbidden City's open space in early 1400 with elephants and horses as part of a delegation visiting Emperor Ming.

The only animal given special entry to the palace grounds are elephants. Many historical records noted that elephants were used to carry foreign delegates, envoys, and messages right to the audience hall. Sultan Alauddin-din Ri'ayat Shah of Aceh received a letter from Queen Elizabeth

Fig. 7.3 Illustration in Garden Arbor (1853) showing elephants brought by guests to Emperor Ming. (Source: Illustration published in German magazine Die Gartenlaube (1853), p. 445)

to witness the letter being carried by the elephants from the palace gates to the throne. Hence, the palace gates, the reception, and the throne area were designed to accommodate the size and proportion of elephants and entourage. The gates of Istana Balai Besar, Kelantan, were built without a roof to allow the entry of elephants to the palace grounds.

The relationship between animals and architecture is also evident in the design of traditional Malay houses, specifically the houses of royals and nobles who owned and used the elephant for transport. Their abode was explicitly designed for them to ride on elephants. They mounted elephants through an opening resembling a door with no stairs leading to it, known as *pintu malim*, without going to the ground. The inhabitants directly boarded the elephants without climbing up the back of the animal. Some long roof houses in Terengganu and Pahang, for example Rumah Serambi Pahang owned by the late Headman of Mukim Kelola, Jerantut, Ismail Khatib Bakar. Figure 7.4 have high stilts that allow elephants to move underneath the houses. The bracings for the

Fig. 7.4 The height and the one way bracings for the columns allow for elephants to move underneath the house. The opening also allow direct mounting on the elephant directly from the house

stilts are also designed parallel to the elephant route to allow movement without barriers (Fig. 7.4).

Past Planning of Cities: Animals as Transportation

The establishment of cities is also due to goods and transportation. Trans-peninsular routes or *Jalan Penarikan* or *Rentasan Purba* have been established in Malayan Peninsula since the third century, where writers have documented approximately seven routes through rivers and land (Mohd Zamberi, 2011; Mohd Kasri, 2010). Mohd Zamberi attributed the success of the Kingdom of Langkasuka to the trans-peninsular routes, where elephants were used for the transport of goods and rides for people across land and rivers.

The natural routes taken through the jungles are natural animal trails that did not significantly tamper with the ecological state of the rainforest

Fig. 7.5 This 1897 photograph showed elephants by the Perak River further downstream at Kuala Kangsar. (Source: National Archives)

environment. Though elephants, bulls, and horses were the 'machines' used for clearing land and built villages that would develop into towns and, later, cities, the routes that were taken by the animals eventually evolved into roads or streets when the villages developed into towns and cities. Figure 7.5 shows a dirt road used by the elephants along the Perak River that is part of the federal road system in Perak. The use of elephants as a means of transportation and army for war is recorded in many socio-political literature writings. As the biggest animal on land, elephants were used as vehicles or land transportation up to the early 1900s. Elephants were a popular means to transport goods over land routes in the 1800s. Both elephants and water buffalo were made to work at the founding of cities and settlements.

Among the established routes are those from Kedah to Siam and the Langkasuka Route in Kedah Tua (Ancient Kingdom of Kedah). Titi Gajah (meaning Elephant Bridge) in Kedah is a key route elephants took to bring tribute to the King of Siam. The elephants were part of the crucial means of transportation during that time that took goods and people to ports, to be further transported by water. After the downfall of Pelabuhan Merbok in the Ancient Kingdom of Kedah, Bagan or Butterworth in Penang/Pulau Pinang assumed the transport hub's role for that time. The etymology of Kampung Gajah (Elephant Village) and Kubang Gajah (Elephant Puddle) in Perak shows the elephants' existence and the trail that links important sites. In fact, the elephants or *gajah* were then used to name places owing to their crucial role at the beginning of urban sites, which has a historical link to the animal.

Seedings of Towns

Transportation routes used by fauna, specifically elephants, were important instigators to the birth of towns and cities. Pendang, Kedah, was established due to the elephant's importance to support the political structure between Kedah and Siam in the seventeenth century (Andaya & Andaya, 1984). Kedah sends delegates to Siam with gold and silver flowers, or *Bunga Emas*, as a tribute using elephants as the main transport. The places along the route assumed the names related to elephants; the well or bathing spot for elephants on their way back from sending the tribute was called Kubang Anak Gajah (wallow of elephants), and the place to bury dead elephants was called Kampung Gajah Mati (the village of the dead elephant). Other places named after elephants are *Titi Gajah* (Elephants' Bridge), Kampung Gajah Putih (Village of the White Elephant), and Kampung Gajah (Village of Elephants); many other places in Malaysia have tales related to elephants.

Elephants' size and proportion are vital considerations in planning streets or roads in Malay towns. Cultural rituals and celebrations had to accommodate the large numbers of men and animals. Royals always travelled or hosted festivals for the people, using animals on streets and roads. The royals and the rich mainly used elephants as a means of transport and in rituals and festivals. Hence, there were many records on elephants and their names in Malay historical texts and stories. The old Malay cities have the road clearance and the gateway were designed for the parade of elephants to go through it. Also, the canopied seats' height was considered in the design for the gateway headroom clearance. Elephants were royal regalia, the symbol of strength and wealth for rulers, and the planning of cities considered their existence by providing infrastructures for them as a means of transport. Horses were also a popular means of transport even before the colonial period. It was the primary transportation means and a symbol of status for royals and nobilities (Nurul Izzati et al., 2015).

Historical Urban Infrastructure in Colonial Southeast Asia

During the colonial period, British officials used horse carriages or gharries as opposed to the more common bullock carts. However, public works departments recorded that bullock carts were the primary transportation mode in Malaya in 1890 (JKR, 2011; Abdul Talib, 2017). The Malaysian Tatler reported about 18,000 bullock carts in the Straits Settlements (Penang, Melaka, and Singapore). The bullock carts were used to transport goods near the waterfront and warehouses. Figure 7.7 shows that the roads were wide enough for two-way traffic. Even though without applying the public works departments' standards, the road allowance is sufficient to accommodate the bullock carts. Traffic lined up properly on dirt roads even without proper markings.

The natural circulation routes evolved to more planned streets as part of town planning. Figure 7.5 shows how the houses were arranged along dirt roads in a village in Penang, Malaysia. The roads allowed for animal-driven transport to utilize them as a communication route. As time went by, the 'natural path' developed into more structured roads to aid the transport of people and goods. Time has shown that the dirt roads in old villages and towns evolved into modern streets. The once dirt roads, graced by bullock carts and gharries, were transformed into modern streets. Interestingly, even the early dirt roads had an ingrained traffic system, a 'two-way road system' used by carts, rickshaws, and pedestrians.

The animals were indirectly a part of towns' planning during the colonial years and were considered in the building design and street systems in Southeast Asia. For instance, the early towns in Malaya show evidence of buildings in rows, sometimes functioning as shops and a combination of shops and houses, or shophouses. The buildings indicated the streets' sides, which created a linear pattern intersected by perpendicular roads. Even without proper markings of lanes or parking spaces, there were invisible territorial suggestions that allowed for gharries, carts, or even animals to be parked alongside rows of buildings. The bullock carts were confined near godowns or in villages and small towns. They were also part of the city centre of Kuala Lumpur.

The streets in the early eco-cities were large and built wide enough to accommodate traffic, elephants, horses and oxen, trishaws, and even cars. The large width was not only for traffic but also for parking and loading and unloading activities. Figure 7.6 shows the different built environments in Taiping, Perak, Malaysia, marking different years, types of animal transport, street width, and building types. Figure 7.6 shows that there was enough space for parking animal-driven carts in front of shophouses and allowed for loading and unloading goods.

The dominant building typology in early planning were single-storey shophouses with attap roofs lined up on both sides of a street. The street

Fig. 7.6 Elephant at Kelian Pauh, the old name for Taiping/Taiping Old Town. (Source: *Malayan Information Agency, London, from the collection of Arkib Negara Malaysia*)

Fig. 7.7 *Itik pulang petang* as a repetitive motif that is commonly used in carvings in Malay buildings. (Source: author)

is wide and used by animals (as transport for people and goods) and pedestrians. A double-storey shophouse typology of a later development with clay tiles still exists today. Both shophouse types created a datum for roads with an understood hierarchy of circulation routes for vehicles, parking spaces, and walkways. Figure 7.6 showed the Taiping market with two animals mainly used for transport: horses and oxen used to transport goods to and from the market.

In the early days, Kuala Lumpur streets have ample space between the buildings without proper demarcation of traffic flow or parking spaces. The generous width provisions for the roads suited the later development of Kuala Lumpur. Through the years of development, the roads that were then considered spacious with 'freeways' but understood traffic circulations changed to narrow streets with strict provisions of one- or two-way traffic circulation. Nevertheless, the allowance for road width in the early inception period allowed for a complex road system in towns or cities.

In the early period of city development, traditional streets were freeways for versatile use of transportation modes. Streets were developed with strict line forming a border decided by buildings on both sides. The street accommodates traditional fauna-based transport and modern transportation to serve private and public usages. At least four transportation means were used in Singapore circa the 1930s: bullock carts, rickshaws, electric trolleys/buses, and cars.

Mythical Animals and Iconography

In addition to the animals used for transport in daily activities, some animals are important in cultural rituals. Humans' close relationships to animals from the earliest times may be traced to animals' spiritual/mystical nature. Animals were seen as a personification of strength, bravery, or skill and represented and used in many forms. For example, on the east coast of Peninsular Malaysia, celebrations included ornamentation using mythical animals for parades to celebrate occasions such as the circumcision of young princes. In this instance, the dimensions of streets should also consider royal parades with floats in the form of mystical animal figurines such as Burung Petala Indera, Burung Petalawati, Jentayu, and Gagak Sura.

Old town planning in Southeast Asia often shared common building typologies and open spaces: the palace, masjid, market, houses, and open space. Such planning is prevalent in Asia and is evident in royal towns in Malaysia too. An example is Kota Bharu, Kelantan (a state on the east coast of Peninsular Malaysia), which has all the mentioned built environment elements. The city also encompasses an open space used for royal and public functions near palace grounds. The open space is also a site for a celestial bird procession for the circumcision rites for the Kelantanese nobility.

The procession commences from the palatial gate and continues throughout the main avenues to an area known as Batu Peringatan/ Memorial Plaque in Padang Bank, Kota Bharu, Kelantan. The open space is surrounded by the royal palace, the mosque, commercial buildings, and residences. The constructed mythical bird, Burung Petala Indera, was approximately 6 metres high, carrying a wooden pavilion of 9 square metres with two-tiered singgora-tiled roofs that could seat six passengers. Reid, a photographer for *The Straits Times Annual* in Kelantan, noted that several large trees in Kota Bharu were removed to manoeuvre the colossal monument during the celebration that may have affected the ecological stability of the place. The procession was attended by the male relatives of the prince (dozens of sons from noble families and older relatives), more than 300 military personnel, palace officials, maidens, and 100 persons to carry the bird's portable base.

Traditional artistic performances also accompanied the large-scale parade on the moving stage. The entourage ends with a platform of Rebana Besar or royal percussions (PPSK, 2015). According to Sheppard (1965), the float base sides were so crowded that people almost suffocated. Hence, the streets and open space dimensions needed to accommodate the throngs of people in the parade.

Fauna-Based Ornamentations

Architectural elements and ornamentation in the cities are an outcome of the sociocultural dynamics and evolution of the place. The ornamentations impart messages of social status when applied to buildings (Norhaiza, 2009). The palaces, houses belonging to the royals or aristocrats, for example, were adorned with carvings that originated from motifs developed through time. In Southeast Asian cities, fauna-based ornamentations are associated with the Hindu-Buddhist era and may have been associated with the presence of animals close to human settlements. The fauna motifs of the Kala, Garuda/mythical bird, and Naga/dragon (Farish & Khoo, 2003) symbolised protectors of a building, space, or city. The fauna-based ornamentations were subject to modifications to abstract shapes or were depicted as flora motifs after Islam's coming (Zumahiran & Ismail, 2008).

Traditional houses have motifs resembling animals and carry different meanings. The animal associated with palaces or houses is found around the house. The traditional houses of Cambodia depict the carving of a rooster on the roof finials known as 'chicken tail'. Malaysia and Indonesia share motifs and semantics related to animals, such as *itik pulang petang* (the act of ducks walking in a row) (Fig. 7.7), *lebah bergantung* (the hanging bees), which are depicted in a repetitive motif that adorned fascia boards or *papan cantik*. Linear motifs are commonly seen on elongated decorative panels. *Kepala cicak* (lizard head) describes the corner design for fascia board decoration used at roof ends. The same transformation of the *kepala cicak* (lizard head) motifs to flora-based motifs is seen at fascia board corners. After Islam arrived, the fauna figures used as ornamentation were stylised to resemble flora motifs or abstract forms. The *sulur bayur* motifs based on vegetal motifs are used in masjids to replace protective figures such as naga/dragon, and Garuda can be seen at Masjid Kapitan Keling and Masjid Kg Hulu in Melaka.

Smaller decorative carvings were incorporated into walls, fascia boards, roof barges, and other architectural elements from the Malay world. The decorative elements are believed to be the protective spirits for a building. The decoration element at the end of a roof ridge was adorned with dragonheads as a protective figure. After Islam's arrival, the ridge end was also designed with what is known as *ekor itik* or ducktail, which is more abstract.

Urban Assimilation of Fauna

The urban presence of animals and wildlife is affected by urbanisation or the development of cities as they struggle to live in ever-changing natural habitats. In turn, wild animals search for food in cities and are seen as pests. As monkeys, stray dogs and cats, bears, wild boars, and others try to survive and scavenge, confrontations between nature and humans are replayed. William Lynn (a research scientist in the George Perkins Marsh Institute at Clark University), in an article for the Animal and Society Institute, observed how animals continued to live at the periphery of cities. In Southeast Asian cities, the types of animals may vary from elephants, boars, pigs, monkeys, pigeons, crows, or other small insects. The changing spatial characteristics of cities have transformed human relationships with urban animals, wild and domestic. The city's biodiversity needs to be preserved alongside the development that took place to maintain a well-balanced eco-city environment.

Conclusions

Fauna and flora, as part of a city's ecology, are gradually diminishing. The presence of fauna or animals through the folds of history has marked their importance and influence on contemporary cities today. The animals are part of decision factors in the start of 'modern' cities and development of urban ecology. Atkins (2012) asserted that animal-centredness has emerged and is discussed in areas of the arts and humanities, social sciences, and studies of urban ecosystems, which showed their importance in ecology. Animals' existence has always been part of the natural system that evolves in balance with the development of traditional cities. Despite the importance of animals in evolution, origins, and eventually designing or planning of the cities, their role had not been widely mentioned, written about or discussed. The phenomenon or historical events involving fauna, should be brought to the fore of future cities in for a sustainable approach. The influence of fauna in these past cities is undeniable. The involvement of animals in eco-cities can be seen at many levels of cities' establishment. The cultural context of the Southeast Asian cities, the core of this discussion, cannot be viewed without animals, which were part of the ecosystem and planning. Fauna affected the development of cities, including the evolution and establishment of circulation, transport systems, and architecture. The rich sociocultural context within a region is radically affected by external influences and urbanism that had given way to historical changes that involved imported ideas, systems, and foreign technologies. A new vision and concept of wildlife-inclusive urban design must integrate animal life, in terms of zones and ecosystems, into future cities' urban planning and design processes. Taking the experience of Southeast Asian cities where animals were a fundamental principle in planning and development, it is critical that a new eco-urbanism of cities be realised.

References

Abdul Talib, A. (2017). Public transport system; from bullock cart to MRT. July 30, 2017 https://www.nst.com.my/opinion/columnists/2017/07/262104/public-transport-system-bullock-cart-mrt

Andaya, L. Y., & Andaya, B. W. (1984). *A history of Malaysia.*, ISBN 0312381212 (pp. 65–68).

Apfelbeck, B., Snep, R., Hauck, T., Ferguson, J., Holy, M., Jakoby, C., MacIvor, J. S., Schär, L., Taylor, M., & Weisser, W. (2020). Designing wildlife-inclusive cities that support human-animal co-existence. *Landscape and Urban Planning, 200.* https://doi.org/10.1016/j.landurbplan.2020.103817

Atkins, P. (2012). Introduction, Animal Cities. Animal Cities (pp. 1–17) Edition: 1Chapter: Introduction Ashgate Publisher.

Farish, A. N., & Khoo, E. (2003). *Spirit of wood: The art of Malay woodcarving.* Periplus Editions (HK) LTD.

Forman, R. T. T. (2019). *Towns, ecology, and the land.* Cambridge University Press.

Hadidian, J. (1998). Urban wildlife. In M. Bekoff & C. A. Meaney (Eds.), *Encyclopedia of animal rights and animal welfare* (pp. 341–342). Greenwood Press. In Lynn (2004). http://pp-sk.blogspot.com/2015/05/sebalik-nama-padang-merdeka-kota-bharu.html; https://www.jstor.org/stable/1579643

Kementerian Kerja Raya (JKR). (2011). Roads in Malaysia. Jabatan Kerja Raya/ Public Works Department, Malaysia.

Mills, A. D. (2011). *A dictionary of British place names.* Oxford University Press.

Mohd Kasri, S. (2010). Tinjauan ke laluan Lama Kedah -Siamzaman kesultanan Silam, dlm. Ishak Saat and Mohd Akbal Abdullah, Isu-isu terpilih dalam sejarah politik dan perjuangan, Penerbit YTHM, 2010, hlm 3.

Mohd Zamberi, A. M. (2011). *Langkasuka Negara Malayu Pertama.* Kuala Lumpur: Anjung Media.

Munro-Hay, S. C. (2000). A Plan of Nakhon Sri Thammarat (Southern Thailand) of c. 1825 in the Collection of the Royal Asiatic Society. *Journal of the Royal Asiatic Society*, April 2000, Third Series, Vol. 10, No. 1 (April, 2000), Cambridge University Press on behalf of the Royal Asiatic Society of Great Britain and Ireland pp. 61–70 Stable URL: https://www.jstor.org/ stable/25187931

Norhaiza, M. (2009). Ukiran Kayu Warisan Melayu. Kayu Perbadanan Kemajuan Kraftangan Malaysia. Mantera Communication Sdn. Bhd.

Nurul Izzati, Md M., Adnan Jusoh, Khairi Ariffin, Nabir Abdullah dan Kamal Kamaruddin (2004). Fungsi Gajah Dalam Kesultanan Melaka dan Aceh: Satu Persamaan Budaya. In Taufiqul Hulam; Eddy Asnawi; Adriansah; Jeni Wardi; Yalid; Nining Sudiar; Sudaryanto; Elvira Asril; Fiqru Mafar (Eds). Prosiding: Konferensi Internasional, Hubungan Indonesia Malaysia Ke-8 (The 8th international conference on Indonesia-Malaysia relations, Universitas Lancang Kuning, Pekanbaru, 23–25 September 2004.

Nurul Izzati, M. M., Jusoh, A., Arrifin, K., Abdullah, N., & Kamaruddin, M. K. (2015). Penggunaan Tenaga Haiwan sebagai Medium Pengangkutan dalam Masyarakat Melayu Tradisional [The use of domesticated animals as a medium of transportation in traditional Malay society]. *International Journal of the Malay World and Civilisation, 3*(2), 53–61.

Owens, M., & Wolch, J. (2017). In L. Kalof (Ed.), *Lively cities: People, animals, and urban ecosystems*. The Oxford Handbook of Animal Studies. Oxford Handbook Online.

Persatuan Pecinta Sejarah Kelantan. (2015). Sebalik Nama Padang Merdeka, Kota Bharu: Siri Orang Kito. Monday, May 4, 2015. Source: Retrieved October 4, 2020, from https://www.researchgate.net/publication/327646565_NASKHAH_MANTRA_GAJAH_DALAM_SEJARAH_SOSIOBUDAYA_MASYARAKAT_MELAYU_MANTRA_GAJAH_IN_SOCIOCULTURAL_HISTORY_OF_MALAY_SOCIETY

Reid, A., & Ito, T. (1999). A precious dutch map of Aceh, c. 1645. In Archipel, volume 57, 1999. L'horizon nousantarien.

Samad, A. (Ed.). (1996). *Sulalatus Salatin – Sejarah Melayu*. Dewan Bahasa dan Pustaka.

Schafer, E. H. (1957). War elephants in ancient and medieval China. *Oriens, 10*(2), 289–291. https://doi.org/10.2307/1579643

Sheppard, M. (1965). Glimpses of Kelantan. Kota Bharu: Perbadanan Muzium Negeri Kelantan 1995: 414–417 "The giant bird," Malay civilization. Retrieved September 27, 2020, from http://malaycivilization.com.my/omeka/items/show/154436

Dinas Kebudayaan dan Pariwisata Aceh. Sultan Iskandar Muda merupakan Raja Aceh yang terkenal kerana dizamannya dari 1607 sampai 1636 Kerajaan Aceh Darussalam mencapai puncak kejayaannya. Source: sindonews.com. http://disbudpar.acehprov.go.id/kisah-raja-aceh-dan-seribu-pasukan-gajah/

Wilbert, C. (2009). Animal geographies. In R. Kitchin & N. Thrift (Eds.), *International encyclopedia of human geography, Volume 1* (pp. 122–126). Elsevier.

Wilson, L. (2016). Elephants in the city. The nature of cities. Posted 7 August 2016. https://www.thenatureofcities.com/2016/08/07/elephants-in-the-city/

Zumahiran, K., & Ismail, S. (2008). Placement of woodcarving in Malay timber houses of Kelantan and Terengganu. In Z. Baba (Ed.), *Warisan Seni Ukir Kayu Melayu* (pp. 129–141). ATMA, Universiti Kebangsaan Malaysia.

Part II

8

From Archipelago to Architecture: The Sacred Center and the Pillared Space

Shireen Jahn Kassim and Mansor Ibrahim

Introduction

Andaya (2008) describes maritime Southeast Asia as a region evolving from a network of centers or *mandalas*. Such mandalas are often described as having "centers" with a gravitation of peripheral settlements and a confluence of the sacred and the "mundane" zones of the city. This centric pattern stems from the conurbations of the micro with the macro, from the regional network to architecctural and urban spaces. Their core administrative and peripheral nodes are organized in a centric pattern, gravitating toward, and orbiting around, a central node. There were no

S. Jahn Kassim (✉)
International Islamic University Malaysia, Jalan Gombak, Malaysia

M. Ibrahim
Department of Urban and Regional Planning, Kulliyyah of Architecture and Environmental Design, International Islamic University Malaysia, Jalan Gombak, Malaysia
e-mail: profmansor@iium.edu.my

distinctive physical boundaries. In all scales, between the center and the periphery; the "center" can be part of a network, which is then a part of a larger network with their own centers. These centers of these networks and subnetworks are subsequently made distinctive and identifiable structures by building or enhancing upon natural formations of elements found within the local ecology and topography. This particular character of enhancing the centrality of the center is a particular essence of the archipelago, and which are at times, marked by a dense and profiled combination of structures including natural and man-made whether in tersm of, architecture, and urban space. Yet many of these centers have disappeared due to the perishable nature of construction and the overlayering of development as a result of colonization.

Centricness within the archipelago

Centricness in both architectural and regional terms begins with the notion, and an identification, of boundaries within the archipelago, which must include extensions of both land and water. With reference to how Andaya (2008) uses the word *kedatuan*, it can be argued that this denotes a fluid boundary and center, which in turn, represent the core or center of settlement in a local region, thus denoting a *center* that grew from the seed of an original city. In maritime Asia, the historic seed generally had connotations of sacredness and kingship. And alongside this, the elements of a sanctuary. For example, in centers which represent the earliest origins of the city in the Malay world, i.e., from Srivijayan centers, to the time of Islam. Such centers represent the position of power and administration conjoined with a spiritual heightening of urban space, as one approaches the center within a collection of galactic configurations and regions that include both land and water. In terms of the Nusantara , the 'beginning' of the center has been described by Kulkule in relation, to the era and region of Srivijaya as

> initially presented by a typical mandala structure: a very strong center surrounded by concentric rings of decreasing authority.

What defined the urban center or 'centricness' of Srivijaya was thus its fluidity and federative character—instead of the usual coercive loyalty that had characterised the earlier nagara eras—and such centricness had pervaded both land *and* water. Srivijaya was united by an intricate web of political and familial ties of kinship. Initially helmed by Palembang, then the Muara Jambi, it became the stopping point for Chinese Buddhist pilgrims on their way to India. As Srivijaya continued to grow; its extensions by the year 1000 saw how it controlled most of the region, but it soon lost to Chola, an Indian maritime and commercial kingdom that had found Srivijaya to be an obstacle on the sea route between South and East Asia. Its origins were traced to a site located between the area of Bukit Siguntang and Sabokingking in Palembang, Indonesia—a site that can be defined as between the *mountain* and the *river*. This had once grown into a federated realm of the communities residing along the river and became a city and settlement formed between the mountain—*Bukit Siguntang*—and the river. Jambi and Palembang were exactly midway between the extreme boundary of its federative states, which are linked by common interest and trade, i.e., Langkasuka to the north and Central Java to the south (Fig. 8.1).

Srivijaya continued to grow and was seen as a power on both sea and land routes. By the end of the twelfth century Srivijaya had been reduced to a small kingdom, and its dominant role in Sumatra had been taken by *Malayu* (based in Jambi), at the time a vassal of Java.

Munoz (2006) describes how

the hill of Bukit Siguntang was probably the sacred center of the kingdom, while its administrative center was the Kedatuan of the maharajas.

Srivijaya as Center

It was during this era that the city center, known as *Kedatuan*, and, by extension, the Federation Srivijaya were seen as the center. Archeological and epigraphic remnants reflect a thriving city and a spiritual center that flourished between the 7th and 13th centuries in Sumatera. Although these physical remnants are scarce, documents and inscriptions reveal a main center and its mandala, which can be described as an intricate web of kinship, political, and familial ties rather than military, created an

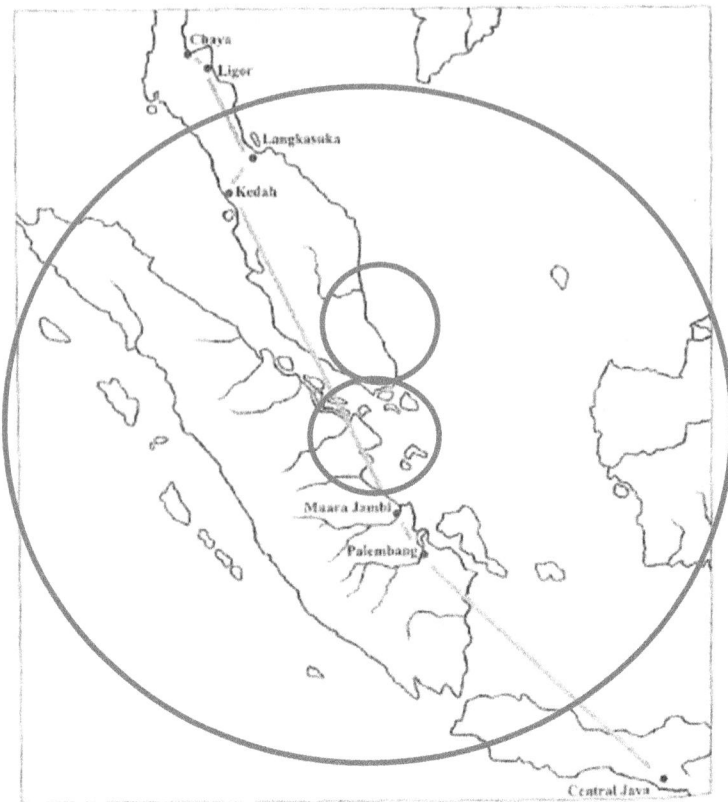

Fig. 8.1 The central position of Muara Jambi, known as a pre-Islamic Buddhist learning center with its peripheral northern node of Langkasuka, its transit center Lembah Bujang (Kedah) within the entire realm of Srivijaya ending at the southern peripheral center of Central Java. (*Red circle* by authors)

empire of mandalas connected by trade above all. The Srivijayan Domain was, as Manguin (1968) defined it, rooted in its sacred beginning—its basic archetype is as described by Kulke (1993): Srivijaya

> *initially presented a typical mandala structure: a very strong centre surrounded by concentric rings of decreasing authority.*

Historically, Srivijaya's center was one in which religious activities were fused with commerce and the stability and peace afforded by its centrality, a confluence of spiritual learning and thriving of commerce. The duality of the sacred and the ceremonial had permeated the center of civilizations and characterised its ambience, thus the following discussion is intended to reconcile the remnants of this center as found in the region once known as Srivijaya. Excavations in Srivijaya showed the dominance of the Buddhist belief system in the pre-Islamic era of Sumatera, which later led to the beginnings of the Malayu. Traders were drawn to the Malay region primarily in search of gold, aromatic woods, and spices such as cloves, brought from the eastern part of the archipelago (Andaya & Andaya, 2016, pp. 19–20). Remains of these interactions are found in mainland Southeast Asia and the Malay Archipelago, along the isthmus of the Malay Peninsula, around the coast of the Gulf of Siam and of the southern part of Vietnam, and later in the archipelago from the western part to the east; these remains include inscriptions in Indian languages and scripts (Mabbett, 1977), yet a summary by Stewart Gordon (2007, pp. 183–184) essentializes the core of the sacred history of the region, which lies in the dominance of Buddhism and, later, Islam on the polities. He observes as follows:

> The great Asian world benefited from two major universalizing religions: Islam and Buddhism. Both addressed universal human needs and recruited on the basis of relatively simple personal commitment rather than ethnicity, region, language, or gender. Both required long-distance travel in pursuit of knowledge and training and built institutions that promoted and supported such travel. At the height of Buddhism, there was a chain of monasteries, rest houses, and sites of worship stretching across Central Asia, Afghanistan, India, Southeast Asia, China, Japan, and Korea. Islamic patronage eventually developed madrasas and rest houses that stretched from Spain across North Africa, through the Middle East, into both Central Asia and India, and certain cities of Southeast Asia and China. These institutions made it possible for believers to find shelter and worship with other thousands of miles from home. In both religions, building rest houses, establishing markets for traders, and planting trees for shade along roads were acts of religious merit.

Perhaps a representation of the coupling of the sacred and the ceremonial can be found in the ancient cities of Burma, for example, the Amarapura palace in Burma (Fig. 8.1) has a dual profile, of a palace (made from public and private zones) and of a temple. Similarly, Wheatley (1961) describes the northern peripheral tip or node of Patani as the northern horizon of this Srivijayan pre-Islamic sacred realm:

> *The final emergence of Langkasuka as a kingdom in the sixth century was concurrent with, and doubtless contingent upon, the decline of Funan around the ninth. It came to form a unit in the Sri Vijaya thalassocracy.*

Wheatley (1961) and Munoz (2006) identify the southern boundary of this sacred Srivijayan realm and, thus, the southern horizon of the Srivijaya realm as the Sailendra dynasty and its center:

> *In central Java, (there was) a rivalry of two interrelated lines of aspiring paramount rulers, one supporting Shivaism Hinduism (the Sanjaya) and the other supporting Mahayana Buddhism (the Shailendra, who had commercial and family connections with Srivijaya). The best known and most impressive of these are the Borobudur, the largest Buddhist edifice in the ancient world (constructed between about 770 and 820 and located northwest of present-day Yogyakarta) and the magnificent complex of Hindu structures at Parmanand, located east of Yogyakarta and completed a quarter-century later.*

The pre-Islamic core religious layer was that of Buddhism, as attested by several historians such as Prasad (2014):

> *… any religious center would have a "core" character, and it would add additional features to its "core" in the course of time, basically to negotiate changing socio-economic and religious situations. The intended relationship between the "core" and add-ons, at least from the perspective of the Buddhist Sangha, was not that of equality. The add-ons were expected to be subordinate to the core personality of these Buddhist religious centers.*

The Era of Islam

The notion of the sacred and the overlayering of such sacred charges with the ceremonial and the ruling polity continue to characterize the urban centers in the era of Islam. The interplay between religion and political centers, physically and symbolically, translated into a compositional and

Figs. 8.2 and 8.3 Physical coupling of mosque and palace as a symbol of original Malay city represented by Gunong Sahilan and Kalimantan center complex

skyline coupling of its structures, when seen from a distance. Some of the earliest profiled cities consist of the profile and presence of the Istana— the residence, administrative center, and symbol of the monarch—which is located as an alignment with the physical and spatial form of the mosque. The urban core city was then consistently planned by the axis of *qiblah*, and the proximity of the mosque and palace was determined by function and formation, the location of mountains, seas, and rivers (Figs. 8.2 and 8.3).

A more axial *coupling* of mosque and palace, as the old city center, is found in Pontianak, another Malay city built in the 1700s where the center of the ruler is represented by a traditional tiered structure, which is the axial alignment of the Kadriah complex, combined with the urban recharging of a public *field* or *padang* and its boundaries. It later exerted social and economic influence on the urban layout and architectural form, and these became "agents" or instigators of change or development, and developments and settlements grew around the palace within which the mosque and palace were sited within visual proximity. As Jahn Kassim et al. (2018) stated:

> *The symbolic coupling of the mosque-palace complex is again seen in a historic urban core on the eastern region of the Malay world, the Kadriah palace-mosque binary in Pontianak, a Malay city in West Kalimantan and on the confluence of the Kapuas River. Primarily due to its geographical isolation it has throughout centuries, it has been less affected by Colonial rupturing and layering of development across time.*

The mosque was built by the pioneer Sultan Alkadrie, who had disembarked to the downstream of the Kapuas River together with his envoys on fourteen boats. It was known that Alkadrie's entourage, which reached the confluence of the Kapuas River and Landak River on 23 October 1771, had cleared the area near the estuary to start a new settlement. From this spot, the new Pontianak sultanate was founded, and a royal palace and royal mosque were built to mark the sacred center or core.

Alkadrie died in 1808 AD, and his son Usman oversaw the completion of the new mosque by 1827. Yet the overall archetype of the mosque remains unchanged to the present day, i.e., its multitiered pyramidal roofs. There are three tiers of roofs, topped with a fourth tier in the form of a bell-shaped cupola. Mosques and palaces were typically sited and configured within an open green field or arena, which then had further symbolically charged the center as the palaces were configured to heighten the position of the monarch. Their configuration reflected the original Melaka city compact configuration, as always influenced by a river, which often acted as a lifeline and the main artery for transportation for seafarers and fishermen (Ooi, 1990). Public spaces often consisted of a huge area located in front of the palace, marketplace, and religious buildings (Fig. 8.4).

The city of Melaka can be seen as the center of a growing mandala, as it took over the central role of overlapping mandalas or sultanates. Thus, the historical documents highlighted in Fig. 8.1 reveal the centrist nature of the city of Melaka, arising from a medieval riverine and sea estuary, with dense clustering around a riverine settlement and patterns that reflect a feudal socioeconomic system. The pattern is organic but mainly clustered around the main transportation route, the river, and clustering also occurs around the royal palace, which marks the domain and center of power (Fig. 8.5).

Wheatley (1961) further describes the centering of Melaka transregionally and the judicious overlaying of the religious realm and center, which created an atmosphere of urbanity and peace—and the dynamism of commerce:

The pivotal position of Malacca (was represented by its location) at the junction of the Indian, China and Java seas. Malacca is (essentially both a city and a

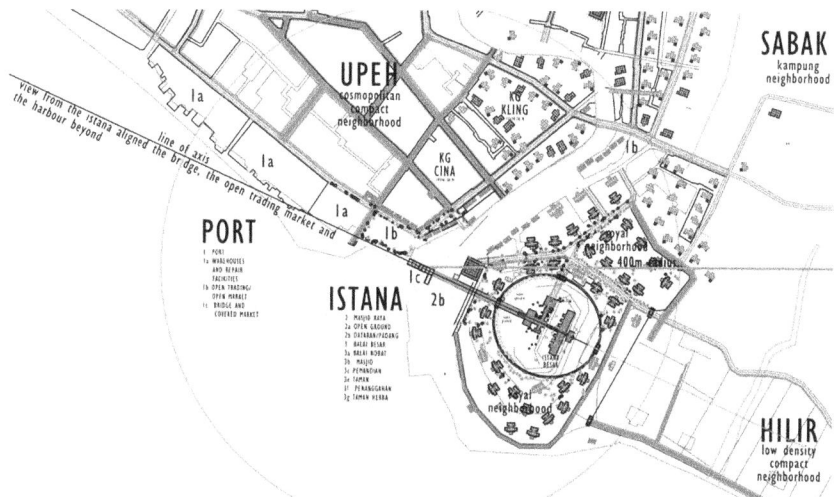

Fig. 8.4 Duality of mosque and palace in sixteenth-century Kota Melaka: a morphological reconstruction of the precolonial indigenous Melaka city, showing an archetypical pattern reflecting littoral configurations that gravitate along the river and coastal line with a lower density but with higher vegetation around the palatial core and higher densities in the commercial districts. (Copyright: Kamariah Kamaruddin)

region) surrounded by seas and lands, whose (center) lies in the middle, and (from which) the trade and commerce between different nations for a thousand leagues on every hand must (eventually) come to Malacca.

Its sixteenth-century morphological layout reflected a similar close coupling of the sociopolitical structure of the time, where political power was characterized by a closeness with its religious hierarchy. These eventually evolved into an intimacy of the city center, where the configuration of the streets and closeness of key structures were brought together by the proximity of commercial and spiritual activities. In the case of the Melaka, the duality is made distinct due to the elevation and heightened backdrop afforded by the hill. Thus, the Melaka palace as described by Sherwin (1981) is "*Surrounded by a wide field then followed by a mosque.*"

The site and location of the original Melaka mosque was found to historically refer to the site where the present Portuguese Fortaleza was built

Fig. 8.5 The sacred "central" position of Melaka amidst the Melaka realm at its peak during the fifteenth and sixteenth centuries. (Source: Wheatley, 1961, circle by authors.)

(Jahn Kassim et al., 2018). Similar configurations are found in the city of Banten in West Java, where the coupling of palace and mosque is seen with the localized tiered Javanese-style mosque and palace, which were built during the reign of Sultan Maulana Yusuf, the third sultan of the Banten Sultanate, in Dzulhijjah 966 (1566 CE). A semiopen pavilion *pawestren* (side hall, used as a female praying hall) was added during the reign of Maulana Muhammad (1580–1586). Later, the southern *serambi* (porch) of the mosque was converted into a structure containing about fifteen graves. In 1632, a 24-meter minaret was added to this palace–mosque complex. Designed by a Chinese man named Cek-ban-cut, it reflected the same tapered full masonry minaret characteristic of Melaka and Palembang, all around the fifteenth to sixteenth centuries.

The coupling of mosque and palace, linked by a *padang* and the "pillared" space continuum of the Balai Besar (Audience Hall), can be seen in the urban royal center of Kedah's capital, Alor Setar, which was once known not only for its palace and market complex but as a center of Islamic learning. Its center had multiple *madrasah*s, which had originally surrounded the royal center or enclave.

It was also known that Sultan Sulaiman Shah (1602–1619 M), with a royal seat in *Kota Siputih*, had appointed an *ulama* from Hijaz, Syarif Aznan (Uthmaniah). In the sixteenth and seventeenth centuries, the role of the city as a center of religious teaching found support from the sultans and was an integral factor in the development of the informal Islamic *pondok* system. These *pondok*s were established by many religious teachers who had traveled and come from Patani due to the instabilities in the region. Sultan Ahmad Tajuddin al-Mukaram Syah (1854–1879) and Sultan Abdul Hamid Halim Syah (1882–1943 HM), for example, were known to be supporters of the establishment of Islamic *pondok* institutions. During the period 1850–1935, more than 60 *ulama* in Kedah taught in many *pondok*s located in many districts in Kedah, Pulau Pisang, Kubang Pasu, Yan, Sik, Langgar, and Tunjang, for example. Two prominent *ulama* had their *pondok* in Kota Setar, Haji Salleh, and Hj Wan Sulaiman bin Wan Sidik. Tuan Hj Salleh lived in the era of the twenty-fourth sultan of Kedah, Sultan Ahmad Tajuddin Mukarram Shah, who came from Penaga to Kota Setar and established his *pondok* in the area of Limbong Kapal in the southern region of Alor Setar. The *pondok* then developed into a *madrasah* (formal Islamic school). After the demise of Haji Salleh, the madrasah was replaced by the Old Sessions Court Building in 1931. (Haji Salleh was buried in the compound of the building. The grave is marked by a tombstone of Acehnese design.) It was during the reign of Sultan Abdul Hamid Halim Syah (1882–1943 HM) that the Religious Affairs Office of Kedah (Pejabat Agama Islam Negeri Kedah) established the learning centers at Limbong Kapal and authorized Hj Wan Sulaiman bin Wan Sidik (one of the people responsible for the establishment of the *pondok* system) to administer, and later move, the *madrasah* at Limbong Kapal to Madrasah al Hamidiyyah. Similarly, Kota Bahru, Kelantan, was originally a center populated with *madrasahs*, mixed in with public structures in the city. The original *madrasah* reflects the original style of the Malay world with its slender, proportional columns and open and recessed façades. The activity of Islamic learning is likewise seen in the town of Kota Bahru, which now exists only in partial reconstructions, documents, lithographs, and urban heritage.

The Pillared Space—Architectural Nature of the Center

The center, in terms of architectural language and space, is characteristically formed and associated with a pillared space. This refers to a structure that is essentially open air and supported by a column-based structure (Fig. 8.1), which represents a kind of recurring spatial character from pre- and post-Islam. It is a recurring three-dimensional form that can be classified as both sacred and communal, as well as climatic, at the same time. These open pavilion type structures are found in all historic complexes of South East Asia, and they represent the communal nature of worship and the close relationship between ruler and ruled. They are representative of the sociocultural nature of the population (Wolters, 2008): *The relationship between the ruler and divinity in early South East Asia is the aspect most visibly signified by inscriptions and monuments. But the complementary aspect was the ruler's relationship with his people; it, too, was a religious one and attracted venerating followers.*

Essentially such a space is a simple pavilion with a roof supported by exposed columns. Yet in South East Asia, these can be said to have three subtypes: the experiential "liminal" pillared space, the "peripheral" pillared space, and the centric pillar. The pillared space can be grouped into three generic subcategories:

1. A space with a dominant central pillar;
2. A space populated by columns, posts, or poles with no walls or without the visual experience of walls; and
3. A space constructed mainly of columns with walls inserted within the overall form without disturbing the integrity of the form.

The notion of the center can be translated architecturally, i.e., from the macro *regional* space to the micro *building* space, through the notion of the pillared space, which can be traced to variations on four centralized pillars or single central pillared spaces that recur throughout Southeast Asia, while the notion of the pillared space in architectural terms seems inseparable from the social and religious significance of its sites and locations. The pillared space is a seed of the so-called tectonic approach in architecture, where space is conceptualized as movement both horizontally and vertically and encapsulates Asian outlooks where space is seen as a liminal[1] experience rather than quantifiable volume, signifying the transitional period or phase of a rite of passage, which reflects the inherent nature of human development and evolvement. It arises from the cosmovision of ancient times that views the structure of the universe as having pillars with deep cosmological meanings. Thus, translated to the earthly scale, the construction of vernacular space becomes not just an outcome of building but enfolds a sacred infusion of cosmology and, therefore, a city's identity.

Architecturally, Janson and Tigges (2014) put it best in describing not only the architectural form but its spatial quality. In their book *Fundamental Concepts of Architecture: The Vocabulary of Spatial Situations*, the pillared space embodies a specific experience through space and

---

[1] The idea of liminality was introduced into the field of anthropology in 1909 by Arnold Van Gennep in his work Les Rites de Passage.

imposes a certain psychological dimension on the human psyche and experience:

> *The hall for public (functions), (had) urban functions which has large openings, and in some, no walls at all. The decisive aspect is the roof, which, given its considerable size, must either span a large space or rest on supports. In the first instance, the space offers great freedom of movement and flexibility of use. In the second, the supports guide movement through space, thereby endowing it with a special rhythm. In elongated covered promenades, the mode of movement is oriented to striding up and down, hence ... the movement is conducive to conversation or contemplation. There is a liberating sense of breadth. The rhythmisation is affected by vaulting panels, and perhaps also by audible reverberations.*

They describe its architectonic qualities as follows:

> *... the number of columns or pillars give the space structure, while movement is guided by resultant zones, tracks or naves. Visitors may have the impressions of wandering amongst the trunks of the forest as though in a shadowy grove ...*

As Tigges (2014) says: *it must be population by columns and the columns must be close enough for the experience of pillars.* Meister (1985) usefully suggests that the evolution of any pillared hall begins with its timber constructional roots. The evolution of a pillared hall occur at different rates throughout Asia, and its origins point to its beginnings as a form of timber construction and its building traditions, arising from its roots in the construction process which elevated the central pillar or a series of centric pillars. Meister (1985) proposes, in the case of temples and within the context of India, an evolution of forms of religious structures and highlights how one evolved into the other in India:

> *The contrast of these two temples between a pillared, primarily wooden, tradition and a masonic tradition, with stone enclosing an inner cell—between the forest of the ascetic and the mountainof Siva-plays a significant role in the development of temple architecture nnorth India ... One represents a palatial or domestik form of architecture, with open pillared spaces, as also reflected on temple walls through out south India and on some brick temples in south*

Kosala; the other the cave-stone representing the mountain within which the divine presence is made manifest …

Across Asia are scaled variants of this form of liminal space, in which a progression space populated by columns is still in a liminal phase or progressing into the central space, fused with the experience of liminality as space is seen as an experience in progression, rather than a static physical form. The word liminality is derived from the Latin word *limen*, meaning threshold. According to dictionary.com liminality is

> *the transitional period or phase of a rite of passage, during which the participant lacks social status or rank, remains anonymous, shows obedience and humility, and follows prescribed forms of conduct, dress, etc.*

Indian temples are known for their liminal mandapas, which in anthropological studies represent the notion of liminality. In Indian architecture and traditions, the mandapa (also spelled mantapa or mandapam) in Indian architecture is a pillared outdoor hall or pavilion for public rituals. It embodies a space-type and is thus seen as a progression, a dynamic concept rather than a static idea of space. Malawaraarachchi (1999), in her master's thesis, attributes to architecture in Indian traditions the central characteristic of being progressively experienced, not just seen. Progression, in the context of the religious architecture of India, refers to a certain transitory state from the profane and the sacred:

> *What at times has been seen as the quality of ambiguity or disorientation that occurs in the middle stage of a rite of passage, when participants no longer hold their pre-ritual status but have not yet begun the transition to the status they will hold when the rite is complete, pillared space is a strategy in manifesting such liminality.*—Malawaraarachchi (1999)

By the pillared peripheral space, one refers to a subtype or pattern in which walls are inserted into the integrity of the pillared structure. Walls are elements inserted between pillars, becoming a dynamic part of the formation of the structure, and do not appear as dominant or as separate in the overall form or space. This pattern is seen throughout the region,

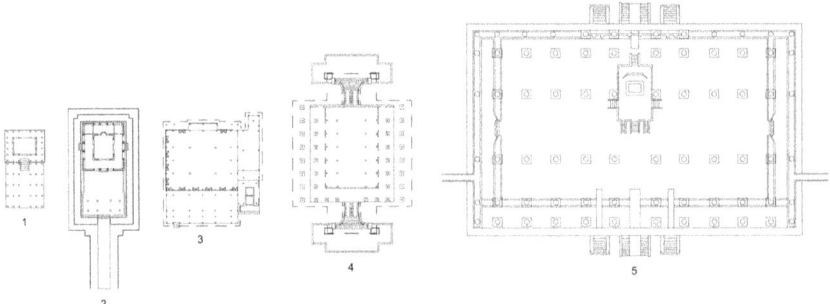

Fig. 8.6 From left: **(1)** Candi Lemah Bujang, **(2)** Masjid Kerisik, **(3)** Masjid Kampung Laut, **(4)** Istana Indragiri and **(5)** Hall of Supreme Harmony, Forbidden City

from the halls of Indianized temples of Southeast Asia to ancient mosques and to sixteenth-century architectural marvels, where walls become part of a single form of pillared structure. In certain traditional typologies, the pillared space represents a kind of antispace, the antithesis of the centering of the building. In approaching the sacred space in the temples of Cambodia, for example, the mandapa precedes the front room of a temple. The Kratons of Java show the same pattern, just like how the hall of Supreme Harmony in historic China reflected one structure in which walls were inserted and which could only be discerned as one gets closer to the dominance single roof type form (Fig. 8.6).

The same pattern of emergence, expansion, and proliferation expressed in a single temple is reflected in the development of architectural forms during the course of various traditions. This unfolding takes place both in the details and at the level of the whole composition. The effect observed in a single, developed temple, of one form putting forth another, which in turn emits another, and so on, is brought about by a cumulative extrapolation and successive incorporation of temple designs: a new design springing from an old one, while preserving the old one within the new.

The Central Pillar—Symbolism and Significance

The single pillar or the central pillar pattern in space has been repeated many times across Asia. Across space and time, the single pillar stood as a symbol of protection and, later, as a symbol of victory and dominance of a leader over his population. This single pillar, whether fashioned in timber, stone, or metal, translates into a kind of protector, spanning from a simple invisible protection to the protection and centeredness and significance of kings and warlords. From a simple house to an entire city or nation, the sole pillar seems to give meaning to space that goes beyond the physical and quantifiable. In earlier communities, the process of erecting a main pillar was undertaken as one of the most important and ceremonial phases of house construction. The building of a traditional or indigenous house in the Malay Southeast Asian ritualistic tradition typically began with the erection of the central column or post, i.e., the tiang seri, the axis mundi of the traditional Malay space-universe. The construction of any building begins by digging a hole for this central post, accompanied by the recitation of a charm. The tiang seri, the axis mundi of the traditional Malay space, over time became a representation of what Rappenglück (2012) usefully described as a recurring universal phenomenon and pattern that echoes throughout all vernacular communities:

> Human self-awareness defines a topocentric system of observation and order at any spatiotemporal point. Even an out-of-body state is bounded to a certain reference point of perception, which sets an origin. Hence the human motive to centre the world is an anthropological a priori. By holding the body upright, the human sense of balance (equilibrioception) determines the first world axis, which is a vertical one and fixed by a line between the zenith, the observer's location, and the nadir.

One of the few surviving ancient timber-based mosques in Indonesia is found within the complex of Cirebon Palace. Known as Langgar Alit, it was built by Cakrabuana at the end of the fifteenth century and is the oldest soko tunggal structure known on Java Island. Built with one central pillar and twelve perimeter columns supporting a two-tiered pyramidal roof structure, Langgar Alit was used by the sultan on religious occasions, such as the commemoration of Nuzul Qur'ān (revelation of the Qur'ān), Isra', and Mi'raj, as well as the annual distribution of alms before the 'Id prayers (Fig. 8.7).

Fig. 8.7 Sole pillar or soko tunggal of Masjid Keraton Soko Tunggal, Jogjakarta, Indonesia 1972. (Source: illustration by Wafiy Harith and authors)

The Islamic Era: Constructional Roots of Pillared Space

Derived from ancient Javanese architectural elements, the pendopo evolved into common ritual spaces primarily intended for ceremonies and for semipublic purposes such as receiving guests in the compounds. Sometimes they were constructed as standalone structures or attached to a walled inner structure (dalem). The pendopo or pandhapa then evolved and morphed into a fundamental element of Javanese architecture, a large pavilion-like structure built on columns. The first variant is the archetypical Javanese construction incorporating four central timbers, which later became the four central columns in mosques. The guru or "teacher" refers to the eventual evolution of a centric form of architecture, which evolved into the recognizable form of the *soko guru* or four wooden beams, with the word *soko* referring to the four main posts. These *soko guru* systems thus act as main structural columns/posts that not only support the dominant roof but define the space. Hence, what was a construction system that basically supports the roof directly became a culturally defined form, with the word *pendopo* characterizing this space and essentially referring to a structure with columns but no walls.

In her mapping of these Nusantara timber variants, Sharif (2014) describes the pillared columnar spaces of the vernacular mosque as beginning with the basic model of the pyramidal timber mosques. Masjid At-Taqwa Nusa Tenggara (seventeenth century) and Masjid Kampung Laut in Malay Peninsula (eighteenth century) (Fig. 8.8) are early timber mosques with *soko guru* (principal pillars) and supporting pillars arranged in an established pattern that characterizes the space within the mosque. The *soko guru*, made of massive solid pieces of wood, supports a multi-tiered roof configuration. In the later Masjid Agung Demak and Masjid Agung Cirebon Kasepuhan, smaller pieces of wood were held together with metal bands, forming the central pillars. These types of pillars are known as *soko tatal* (Ashadi, 2006, p. 35).

The central *soko guru* and arrangement of columns at equal distances are followed by layers of perimeter columns defining the boundary of the space, which thereby creates the experiential uniqueness of the pillared space of the universal Nusantara mosque. The main structural columns/posts of a Javanese space (the *soko guru*) support directly the roof and not the wall. Each of these four main posts sits on top of an umpak, a three-dimensional trapezoidal stone that acts as a transition between the post and the foundation. The peripheral pillared spaces are typologies or patterns that are essentially single volume but walled to denote, separate, and define spaces.

The tectonic four-column form evolved into more complex variants across time and space. In each case, the column is a dominant element and rests on what was termed the umpak, which is a masonry base, generally of square or trapezoidal form. Over time, the simple *umpak* form was expressed in multiple stylizations. The same stylizations repeat across buildings and traditional indigenous houses in Southeast Asia. Roesmanto (2002) discusses how the joglo column elements were brought into the structural stylization of the Nusantara house following the Islamic era in Indonesia. The pillared space then became a space that was stylized and aestheticized, from the essential mosque to house, and in each case

Fig. 8.8 Soko Guru of Masjid Keramat, Kerinci, Indonesia (1800s). (Source: authors)

dominated by pillars and resting on bases, which over time evolved into pedestals and composite elements.

Conclusions

This chapter highlights how the conceptions of the center in Southeast Asia and the Malay world and the character of pillared spaces as being intrinsic in the traditional urban experience have evolved from the macro (region) into the micro (architectural and spatial terms) scale in terms of forms. The center is celebrated as a location within and between a body of water and a land continuum and later developed as the confluence of the sacred and the mundane, which resonated in traditional urban design and architecture. These allowed microclimatic identity and elements to permeate the city, architecture, space, and structures. Evers and Korf (2000) compare the stark differences between past and present urban forms in the region:

The lack of linkage between the city and the place is visible …. The centre of political power in these states was the palace (istana), this was surrounded by royal villages, inhabited by retailers and craftsmen. The central square opens to the Sultan palace. The main mosque is found next to the Padang …

A reconstruction of past urban cores, key symbols, public spaces, and landscapes highlights the bioclimatic nature of urban planning and these semiopen forms, which integrate to form different variations of enclosed and open architectural and urban layouts. The city was arguably a different center, seen in its dual significance of sanctity and ceremony, rather than merely the center of a settlement or a riverine settlement. There were clear demarcations between public and private zones within these cities, which demonstrated elements of urbanism, such as public spaces, walkways, and connected buildings, collectively forming a kind of bioclimatic urban design pattern. The tropical urbanism of the precolonial world had orbited and gravitated around the centers, which exhibited elements of an urban life before the massive revolution of modern times.

References

Andaya, B. W., & Andaya, L. Y. (2016). *A history of Malaysia*. Macmillan International Higher Education.

Andaya, L. Y. (2008). *Malayu antecedents. In leaves of the same tree* (pp. 18–48). University of Hawaii Press.

Ashadi. (2006). *Warisan Walisongo*. Lorong Semesta.

Evers, H.-D., & Korff, R. (2000). Southeast Asian Urbanism: The Meaning and Power of Social Space (L. V. Münster (ed.)).

Gordon, S. (2007). *When Asia Was the World: Traveling Merchants, Scholars, Warriors, and Monks Who Created the "Riches of the East"*. Da Capo Press.

Jahn Kassim, P. S. J., Kamaruddin, K., Ibrahim, I., & Harun, N. (2018). A tropicalized urban design framework from morphological patterns of precolonial maritime centers of the Malay world. *Geopolotica Informatica, 1*.

Janson, A., & Tigges, F. (2014). Fundamental Concepts of Architecture. In *Fundamental Concepts of Architecture*. Birkhäuser.

Kulke, H. (1993). "Kadātuan Śrīvijaya"-Empire or Kraton of Śrīvijaya? A Reassessment of the Epigraphical Evidence. *Bulletin de l'Ecole française d'Extrême-Orient*, 159–180.

Mabbett, I. W. (1977). The 'Indianization' of Southeast Asia: Reflections on the historical sources. *Journal of Southeast Asian Studies., 8*(2), 143–161.

Malawaraarachchi, R. H. (1999). *Spatial progression in architecture: an examination of the concept of mainstream architecture.* Master of Science dissertation, University of Moratuwa.

Meister, M. W. (1985). Symbol and surface: Masonic and Pillared Wall-structures in North India. *Artibus Asiae, 46*(1/2), 129–148. Published by: Artibus Asiae Publishers.

Munoz, P. M. (2006). *Early kingdoms of the Indonesian archipelago and the Malay peninsula.* Didier Millet, Csi.

Ooi, G. L. (1990). *Town councils in Singapore: Self-determination for public housing estates* (Occasional Paper No. 4). Singapore: Institute of Policy Studies.

Paul Wheatley. (1961). The golden Khersonese: Studies in the historical geography of the Malay Peninsula before A.D. 1500. (Malayan Historical Studies), p. 388, front. University of Malaya Press. (Distributed by Oxford University Press. 45s.).

Prasad, B. N. (2014). Cultic relationships between Buddhism and Brahmanism in the 'last Stronghold'of Indian Buddhism. *Buddhist Studies Review, 30*(2), 181–199.

Rappenglück, M. A. (2012, June 11–14). *The housing of the world: The significance of cosmographic concepts for habitation.* Presented at Nexus 2012: Relationships between architecture and mathematics.

Roesmanto, T. (2002). A study of traditional house of northern Central Java-a case study of Demak and Jepara. *Journal of Asian architecture and building engineering, 1*(2), 219–226.

Sharif, H. M. (2014). Mosques in island Southeast Asia (15th-20th century). *Journal of Architecture, Planning and Construction Management, 4*(2).

Sherwin, M. D. (1981). The palace of Sultan Mansur Shah at Malacca. *Journal of the Society of Architectural Historians, 40*(2), 101–107.

Wolters, O. W. (2008). *Early Southeast Asia: Selected Essays* (No. 43). SEAP Publications.

9

The 'Punctured' Pavilions

Noor Hanita Abdul Majid and Shireen Jahn Kassim

The Basic Archetype

While the term *pillared space* highlights how such open columnar structures had permeated and characterised the notion of the sacred urban 'centre' of South East Asian cities, the term *punctured* pavilions refers to how such columnar characters evolved and pervaded as intrinsic elements of architecture and urban design. In the most basic unit, the punctured pavilion recalls the traditional *pendapa* or *pendopo* (Indonesian spelling: *pendapa*, nonstandard spelling: *pendopo*). The *pendapa* can be thought of as the most fundamental element of the tropical vernacular architecture, defined as a pavilion-like structure built on columns. Either square or

N. H. Abdul Majid (✉)
Kulliyyah of Architecture and Environmental Design, International Islamic University Malaysia (IIUM), Jalan Gombak, Malaysia

S. Jahn Kassim
Faculty of Architecture and Environmental Design (KAED), International Islamic University Malaysia, Jalan Gombak, Malaysia

rectangular in plan, it is open on all sides and provides shelter from the sun and rain while, crucially, allowing the admission of breeze and daylight.

Historical Origins

The word *pendapa* is cognate to the Sanskrit word *mandapa* (hall). The Dutch writer Multatuli in his colonial reformist novel Max Havelaar described the *pendapa* thus:

> *After a broad-brimmed hat, an umbrella, or a hollow tree, a 'pendopo' is certainly the simplest representation of the idea roof.*

If derived from ancient Javanese architectural elements, the *pendapa* may have begun as a humble open structure. In the context of South East Asia, the *pendopo* is better known as the traditional structure of the *wakaf.*

The most basic form of a punctured pavilion that resembles the *wakaf* or *pendopo* is the four columns with a square-based plinth. However, in Java, the four columns, known as *saka guru* or *soko guru* in Javanese, are the main posts that support the roof of a structure without walls, which is the basic form of the *pendopo.* The pavilion-type structure is basic to Javanese mosques and houses. The *soko guru* is one of the most fundamental elements in Javanese architecture because it supports the entire roof of the building.

The same structural concept is found in Malaysia in the form of a *wakaf.* A four-column *wakaf* in Malaysia also forms the basic structure that is sometimes developed into elongated form with additional columns that resulted in a basic long roof form. The basic form of a square base with four columns is a popular structure in the east coast states of Malaysia: Kelantan, Terengganu, and Pahang. Figures 9.1 and 9.2 show the plan and form of a basic *wakaf.* The *wakaf* are punctured pavilions that are commonly used as a place for gathering, socialising, and resting. Traditionally, one would build a *wakaf* for public use as an act of good deeds, which is also how the structure derived its name, the concept of waqaf in Islam. It is built by the people for the people. The *wakaf* structures are placed at junctions of roads to give shelter for the locals as well

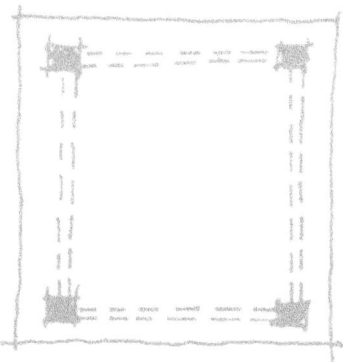

Fig. 9.1   Plan of a basic form of punctured pavilion, known as *wakaf* or *pendopo*

Fig. 9.2   Basic form of punctured pavilion with four columns. (Source: Author)

as travellers. The *wakaf* is also a multifunctional structure for the people, for resting on a journey or after working in the fields, praying, eating, teaching of the Quran to children, reciting the Quran, *wirid*, and praying for the deceased. A *wakaf* also functions as an additional shelter when accompanied by larger buildings. In short, a *wakaf* functions in relation to where it is sited.

In Java, the *pendopo* assumes the function of a common ritual space primarily intended for ceremonies and for a variety of purposes such as receiving guests. In the compounds of the Javanese house, the *pendopo* at times is constructed as a stand-alone structure (Fig. 9.3) or, at times, attached to a walled inner space (*dalem*). The traditional Javanese houses, between two gates in Kota Gede, Jogjakarta, is a rudimentary example of free-standing *pendopo* and *joglo* houses. The *joglo* houses have an attached *pringgitan* or *serambi* or colonnade space to the *dalem/omah* or house (Ikaputra, 2019; Heritage Studies Report IIUM, 2006). The *pendopo* is an open layout structure constructed from four basic columns called *soko guru*. The Javanese *pendopo* usually has a distinctive *tumpang sari*, which is a set of horizontal beams that are stacked in a tapering layout upwards and creating a decorative ceiling to the centre of the *soko guru*. The

Fig. 9.3 Layout plan of between two gates houses showing basic form of punc-tured pavilion with four basic columns. (Source: Ikaputra, 2019)

pendopo is used, for example, to entertain guests, practice, and perform traditional music. In addition, the *pringgitan* is located between the *pendopo* and the house/*omah*/*dalem* is in the form of a semi-open space, a colonnaded space, veranda, or *serambi*. It is a semi-open space in contrast to the *pendopo* that is a public domain.

Mohd Shariff (2014) argues that the notion of the Nusantara mosque arises from variations in the essential *pendopo* and the evolvement of this Nusantara type based on varied functions and requirements of the community. These became forms which were variations that arose from the basic type. However, the *pendopo* can also be built as an extension area from the main prayer halls. The evolution of the *pendopo* in mosques is

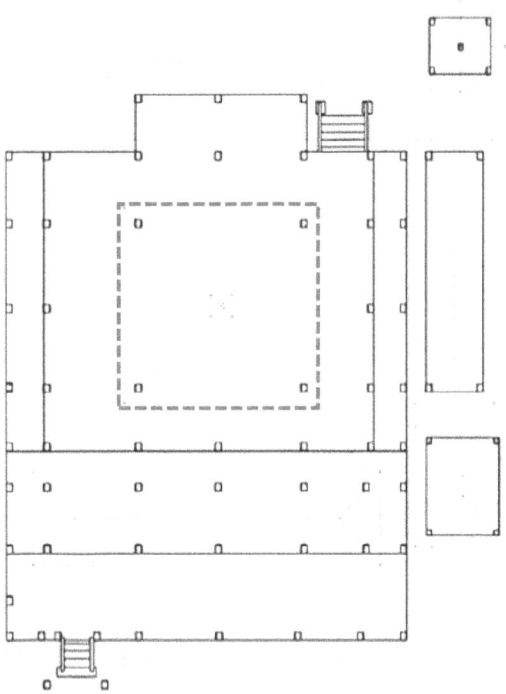

Fig. 9.4 Plan of masjid Kg Laut at Nilam Puri with added *balai lintang* (perpendicular pavilion) to east side of praying hall (Source: Authors)

traceable in the form of *pendopo* (in Javanese mosques) and *balai lintang* in Malay mosques. The *balai lintang* is also supported by a veranda, *serambi*, or colonnades on the north and east sides of the prayer halls to provide overflow praying space.

The basic structure of Malaysia's oldest mosque Masjid Kampung Laut can be seen as a derivation of the pavilion (Fig. 9.5). A later development saw the addition of a *pendopo* or a *balai lintang* on the east side of the prayer hall. *Balai lintang* is a common punctured structure added as an annex to traditional masjids in Malaysia. Both mosques of the long roof and pyramidal roof typologies can have annexes in the form of *balai lintang*, an open pavilion attached to the main prayer hall on the eastern or main entrance.

The *pendopo* at the old mosques of Jawa, Indonesia, can be seen as a prevalent punctured structure; Masjid Demak, Masjid Surakarta (Great Mosque of Kraton Surakarta), and Masjid Agung Sumenep, Madura, are among them. The figures show the open pavilion on the east side of the

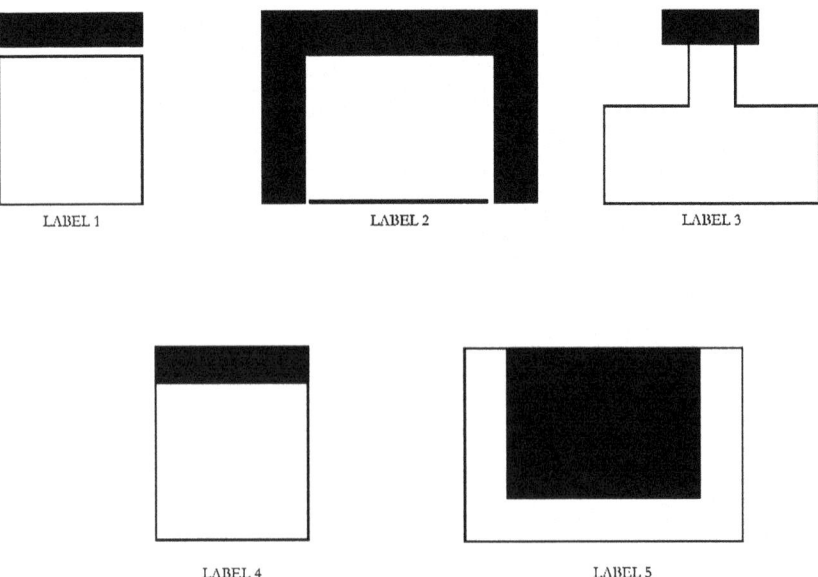

Fig. 9.5 Abstractions of evolvement of punctured pavilions as extensions of architecture

prayer hall or the main entrance to the mosque. It functions similarly to the *balai lintang* in Malay mosques. Budi (2004) in his review of the origins of Javanese mosques asserted that Javanese mosques have a veranda, either on the front or on the side, known as *surambi* or *siambi* (by Javanese) and *tepas masdjid* (by Sundanese).

From Mosque to Aristocratic Residences

The aristocratic residences of Kuala Kangsar, Perak, Malaysia, beautifully manifested the unmistakable relationship between residences and the outdoors. Both Baitul Rahmah and Bytul Anwar, built by Raja Harun al-Rashid (the crown prince of Perak) during the reign of Sultan Idris Shah, have porches, balconies, and perimeter zones in the form of colonnaded corridors. Baitul Rahmah is surrounded by large outdoor greenery that flows to the surrounding open space and the compounds of the nearby mosque and royal palace. Decorative columns and balustrades suggest the sensation of a punctured structure to the residence. The identical double-storey attached pavilion protruded to the front of the resident and created a Malay classical façade (Puteri Shireen et al., 2019). On the sides, colonnaded balconies are also adorned with carved timber columns, fascia boards, and balustrades. The adjacent walls are punctured with carvings in the form of ventilation grilles to allow air and daylight penetration into the internal spaces.

The same mimicry is evident at Bytul Anwar, further enhanced by tiered balconies on either side of the residence. Although not surrounded by colonnaded corridors, the tiered balconies or *sotoh* accentuates the open-air pavilion image suiting the public realm in eco-cities. Interviews with the descendants of the royal family reiterated that Raja Harun al-Rashid used the *sotoh* in the evenings to view the surrounding areas. Located on a small hill, the *sotoh*, which is a semi-open structure, flows to the green area that was then connected to the palace grounds of Iskandariah palace. Bytul Anwar can be seen as a modern derivation of this typological, modernized, refined, almost cosmopolitan form of a punctured pavilion. Besides the twin *sotohs*, the extended space, in the form of *anjung* on the first floor now created a semi-enclosed space on the ground floor with half brick wall with grilles. This space is a public area used to entertain guests and have performances.

The compactness of the house plan is balanced by the general climatic permeability of the ground floor (as seen in Bytul Anwar) and wide open-air perimeter zones (as seen in Baitul Rahmah, Kuala Kangsar), thus connecting artificial structures with water bodies and the urban perimeter grain along any river. This ground-level permeability between structures enhances and cools the city, the sense of cooling enhanced by the visual and sensorial capture and continuity of landscape elements, thereby bringing the shading and shadowy impact of orchards and the dynamism of light and shadow into the interiors. These aristocratic residences are permutations and evolvements of the notion of 'punctured' pavilions, whether stand-alone or extended pavilions extend from the sacred centre or the royal courts into green open spaces. It becomes part of a common space that is wide, turfed, and surrounded by huge shady trees that infuse the core of any centre of settlement with an overriding quality of shade. Thus, the urbanism in South East Asian roots of architecture and urban life depicts a shaded form of urbanism that is on a continuum from structure to nature. This spatial type is not similar to any outdoor room or enclosed square. The eco-urbanism context consists of permeable forms and interstitial spaces that increase the permeability between water perimeter and land, and such permeability between structures includes the elevated character of tropical architecture. The open structure that exists among orchards is recognizable as locally derived typologies of architecture and urbanism. The punctured royal courts are evident in many South East Asian cities: Alor Setar, Kedah and Kota Bharu, Kelantan and cities such as Pontianak, Kalimantan Barat, Inderagiri, Sumatera, Indonesia, and others. The Balai Besar Alor Setar, Kedah, Malaysia, was originally built in the 1700s by Sultan Muhammad Jiwa Zainal Adilin Mu'adzam Shah II for formal royal functions and coronations. The original structure was burnt and rebuilt again during the reign of Sultan Abdul Hamid Halim Shah in 1896 for the weddings of his five children. The structure took the form of a timber double-storey structure with colonnades with recesses and projections that are typical in this hot humid tropical climate. The Balai Besar is the biggest structure among many other *balai* or pavilion structures built in open areas representing the districts in Kedah state (Syed Mohammed Syed Hassan Shahaeudin dan MG Knowles, 1958). The open area was bounded by the Balai Besar, the Zahir Mosque, and the courthouse, which is the centre of Alor Setar. Both authors interviewed a government officer (Che Mohamed Deli), who was an eyewitness of the grand event. The pavilions were used to entertain guests. The scene described perfectly an eco-city with palaces, pavilions, mosques, open spaces, and rivers, with a continuum from structure to nature. The Balai Besar and the other pavilions erected are punctured pavilions as part of the eco-urbanism that has a very fine line to separating outdoors and indoors.

Istana Kadriah, Pontianak, Kalimantan Barat was originally built in 1771 and renovated to its current form in 1923. Originally, the palace has an elongated veranda or pavilion that is 50 metres long. The veranda was used to entertain guests and used mainly for the community during events and traditional ceremonies. The pavilion is a punctured structure or an outdoor room attached to the palace. The tectonic language of the South East Asian form is reiterated, and the basic form is expanded further into an extended space for rulers to view the open space on the palace grounds.

Recurring features of eco-urbanism include a palace, palace grounds or open space, mosque, market, and river, together with the houses of the commoners. It is interesting to note that the components and characteristics resemble the layout in Alor Setar (Chap. 1).

These tropical 'public' aspects of South East Asian architecture, including its aristocratic mansions, are characteristically 'punctured' by colonnades or enclosing columns as key elements of the language. These structures are not enclosed on the ground floor but allow airflow to permeate freely in their pavilion-like elevational characters, details, and identities.

Pavilions as Transitional Spaces

From basic spaces of the basic pavilion—*wakaf* or *pendopo*; veranda, *serambi*—evolved a series of transitional spaces which formed integrated social and climatic parts of the city or of a residence. The Istana Lima Laras, Sumatera, Indonesia, showcased a complex semi-outdoor veranda or pavilions linked at different levels to the central pavilion attached to the main entrance of the palace (Fig. 9.6). The semi-enclosed spaces habitually flow into the outdoor space of eco-cities that are customary mainly in a garden-like tropical setting like Istana Langkat, Sumatera.

The shaded and semi-enclosed nature of the punctured pavilion was strengthened by rows of large, mature trees that act as continuous features linking one end to another. Both pavilions and trees in the tropical context must be considered urban elements assembled around urban spaces and causing urban experiences in the tropical city.

Evolution of Punctured Pavilions

The development of pavilions can be traced from its basic four-column structure to annexes, as *serambi*, colonnade spaces in the form of veranda and peristyles. These spaces vary in terms of their size, morphology, and

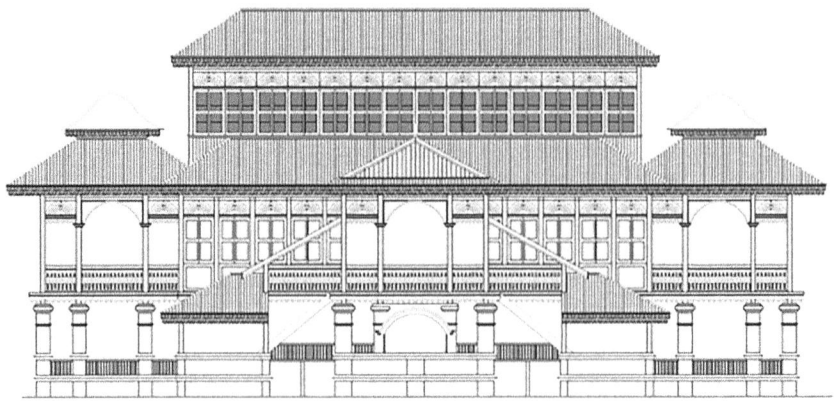

Fig. 9.6   Istana Lima Laras with complex outdoor pavilions. (Source: Author)

scale. The development is an emulated extension of tropical open-air pavilions to extensions of buildings with generous colonnaded walkways which face onto open green spaces or ground floor open air-permeable spaces.

These 'punctured pavilions' are essential to the original character of public realms. In South East Asian cities, their generally compact and organic planning, due to their maritime location, create urban spaces that are generally characterised by a palpable continuum between the royal zones and green landscape. These are provided by a typological principle broadly referred to as 'punctured pavilions', in which there is a constant puncturing of walls and the perimeter zones and the ground floor onto the outdoors. These may range from deep colonnaded porticoes to enclosing columnar-type structures to open-air structures and may be differentiated in terms of size, morphology, or scale, yet all emulate the pavilion and are varied extensions of the tropical open-air pavilion, from the basic four-pole type to the extensively colonnaded type. This varies from extensions of buildings generously spaced colonnaded walkways which face onto open greens or ground floor open air-permeable spaces.

Punctured Pavilion as Elevated Plane in Urban Context

The architectural vocabulary arising from the local vernacular of the tropical region reverberates as a localised form of the pilotis, interspersed with perforated and ornamented walls, large roof overhangs with gable boards to create sustainable (low energy without high solar gains) and comfort (minimally acceptable in terms of comfort and low visual glare) in the urban context. Thus, pavilions can be elevated on a pilotis, clad with perforated walls, shaded by extended roofs, and incorporated into eco-urban sites. Punctured pavilions captured the cool-layered and extended forms, pilastered or even balustraded elements, in line with the traditional ethos, to allow sun shading and naturally ventilated space. Roofs that are broad overhanging devices create pockets of cool shaded air as an intermediate outdoor area. Elevated planes or pavilions also act as cantilevers extending far beyond the wall line to provide shade for the space on the ground level. Having evolved from an ideal archetypal form, elevated planes or pavilions can become a template that will undergo any form of expressive deformation in the process of being adjusted to the context of type, function, and urban site and space.

Climatic Character

Some research has been conducted to assess the comfort performance of semi-outdoor spaces in Asia (e.g., Pitts, 2013; Nakano and Tanabe, 2020; Chun and Tamura, 2005; Jahn Kassim, 2018; Hui and Jiang, 2014). The findings shed light on the design and assessment of urban semi-outdoor environments. Due to the dynamic climatic conditions of South East Asian cities, the climatic conditions of semi-outdoor spaces cannot be controlled, although guidelines were proposed to achieve greater comfort. It was also discovered that people can accept a broader thermal environment in transitional spaces (Hui & Jiang, 2014). Transitional spaces that are carefully designed with appropriate passive design strategies can help achieve more energy-efficient usable outdoor and indoor spaces in buildings of the future.

The annual occurrence of flood and occasional occurrence of flash flood are similar climatic forces that have led to the evolution of the notion of pillared architecture as a kind of climatic resilience of the built form (Jahn Kassim et al., 2018). Cities on coastlines especially have architecture which evolved on higher poles and pillars due to annual flooding events. As present densities, capitals are increasingly faced with sudden monsoonal impact; a return to this alternative urban form that is flood-resistant, such as elevated planes in the form of punctured pavilions, must again evolve in the city, which can be referred to as a multi-level urbanism approach, with added enhancement such as the integration of water plazas, stepped areas, and lower public areas, for example. The containment of rising waters within these public areas—highlighted by elevated spaces and water bodies—will allow the public to move freely and safer at the upper levels in the event of sudden disasters.

An elevated city can function fully during so-called normal times and yet can be transformed into levels of refuge and protection during flash flood or monsoon emergency periods. Punctured pavilions could be explored further to take a larger form in the urban context. The idea of elevated-plane, semi-outdoor areas can be extended to create a large breathing structure with all the attributes of punctured pavilions.

Modern Interpretations

Inspired by the idea of the Malay pavilion and house, an interpretation of urban design principles involved combining the punctured and elevated forms, permeability, and landscape in two key projects, the Masjid Negara and the Singapore National Library. In the Masjid Negara, architect Hj Baharuddin transformed a Miesian cube into a tropical pavilion, whose comfort conditions are evident to the present day. The notion of permeability in the city and in urban life must be derived from an extension of the pavilion. Such attempts are fundamentally expressed in certain developments, for example by Ken Yeang's National Library ground floor plaza which not only provides shade in the city but an open ground zone or realm which combines eateries and the notion of permeability. This idea was coupled with the need to reduce the urban heat island effect and linking comfort conditions with ground-based heat sinks and multi-volume spaces populated by trees. Ken Yeang asserted that an elevated public realm as a form of a bioclimatic device can harvest and divert cleaner and faster air at higher levels down to the humid ground space which may be blocked by continuous low-rise building blocks. Traditional principles, founded upon the abstraction of history and local tradition as a source of reference for teminologies and values, becomes a tool contingent and dependent upon the achievement of comfort for pedestrian and city users at the body level and human scale. To achieve a city form with infused walkability, the notion of not only comfort but the pedestrian experience of security and safety as points of interest are fused with high-rise structures which can be strategically placed to ventilate the tropical city outdoors, and its form and urban microclimatic impact must couple both diversion of upper winds for comfort on the pedestrian level and the shadowing of pedestrian walkways and thoroughfares at critical times of the day. The key criterion must be the comfort of the pedestrian, and this includes large structures optimized for shaded outdoors and the optimum wind flow for comfort. Hence, though significant attempts have been made to evoke the tropicality of the past in shaded urban spaces, many of the colonnaded or shaded areas of past expressions were obliterated. In their place were put spaces that were defined by modernist driven styles, although some had distinctive elements of topicality, such as the extended spaces of Masjid Negara, which is richly populated with tall columns or 'in-between' spacescovered by linked walkways and infused with greenery. There are notable award-winning spaces which include the ground floor of National Library Singapore, which were an evolution of Yeang's bioclimatic principles of freeing the ground floor, but instead of a single-storey space, the multi-storey volume was enhanced by an open atrium inserted right through the library block into the ground floor, enabling it to breathe and admit external elements. To this day, the space is thermally comfortable, as the multi-volume space creates and enhances vortex actions of external wind patterns over the buildings, even though in midst of a dense city centre.

Conclusion: Punctured Pavilion in Eco-Urban Context

The urban permeable variations—punctured pavilions and open-air spaces, combined with natural elements and their properties—are essentially permutations and combinations of pavilions which are typologies that represent a return of the eco-urbanist ethos of the past. 'Punctured pavilions' refers to the nature of the edges of the city centre, or the nature of its main massing and its peripheral mass. As a whole, the defining principle of many South East Asian cities is one of elevation and permeability. Due to its evolvement in a tropical context, the city centre is surrounded by open, rather than closed, edges. Thus, the peripheral urban mass is essentially made up of variations of the essential archetype of tropical pavilions. Even a palace or large house with open ground is essentially a 'pavilion'. It is, in a nutshell, an open or 'punctured' form in which airflow can occur, as both people and air can move, rather than a compact and sealed form.

It is argued that, essentially, eco-urbanism is filled with punctured and pavilion-like boundaries and linkages. From their origins to the present, the public realm in the city's approximate variations of these 'punctured' spaces can be traced to the essential archetypical tropical pavilion. From extensions of a mosque to the colonnades of public structures and public zones of palaces to semi-outdoor spaces in traditional centres, these are essentially a series of alternating or differentiating extensions of the 'punctured' form. Even the open-air *serambi*, *wakaf*, or *pendapa* (*pendopo* in Javanese) can be seen as stand-alone or attached 'punctured pavilions'. They differ in terms of size, morphology, or scale, yet all emulate extensions of tropical open-air pavilions, from the basic four-pole type, and vary from extensions of buildings to generous colonnaded walkways which face out onto open green spaces or ground floor open air-permeable spaces. These should be spaces that allow an integration of native trees and shades and with the presence of wildlife which is identifiable from the inside and used for exterior reference. These semi-outdoor spaces are crucial to reinfuse identity into city form that must be the antithesis of sealed building blocks stamped onto plots of land. The underlying principle is to have open continuous spaces connecting both horizontal and vertical movement of people with insertions of punctured pavilions integrated naturally into the fabric of the city. The eco-city must again recall the cultural and climatic ethos as critical pathways and the variants, and innovations of these semi-open structures must again punctuate the city form, with public spaces and buildings.

References

Budi, B. (2004). A study on the history and development of the Javanese Mosque Part 1: A review of theories on the origin of the Javanese Mosque. *Journal of Asian Architecture and Building Engineering, 3*, 189–195. https://doi.org/10.3130/jaabe.3.189

Chun, C., & Tamura, A. (2005, May). Thermal comfort in urban transitional spaces. *Building and Environment, 40*(5), 633–639.

Heritage Studies Report IIUM (2006). *Between Two Gates*. Heritage Lab, Department of Architecture, Kulliyyah of Architecture and Environmental Design, International Islamic University, Kuala Lumpur. Unpublished report.

Hui, S. C. M., & Jiang, J. (2014). Assessment of thermal comfort in transitional spaces. In Proceedings of the Joint Symposium 2014: Change in Building Services for Future, 25 Nov 2014 (Tue), Kowloon Shangri-la Hotel, Tsim Sha Tsui East, Kowloon, Hong Kong, 13 pp.

Ikaputra. (2019, July). Linear settlement as the identity of Kotagede Heritage City. *Dimensi-Journal of Architecture and Built Environment, 46*(1), 43–50.

Jahn Kassim, S. (2018). Assessment of linkage between natural ventilation, thermal comfort and urban morphology of a semi-open plaza in the hot-humid climate. Readings in Construction Technology and Management (pp. Chapter 12). : IIUM Press.

Jahn Kassim, S., Abdul Majid, N. H., Mohd Nawawi, N., & Abdul Latip, N. S. (2018). The historicist city in the tropical climate: Conflations of identity, sustainability, permeability and walkability. Conference: 4th International Conference on Universal Design in the Built Environment 2015 (4th ICUDBE 2015) MUSAWAH: Sharing The World "Universal Design & Accessibility in Disaster Preparedness, Local Planning Development & Improvements and Four Generations Housing". Putrajaya Corporation, Putrajaya, Malaysia 23rd & 24th November 2015.

Nakano, J., & Tanabe, S.-I. (2020). Thermal adaptation and comfort zones in urban semi-outdoor environments. *Frontiers in Built Environment, 6*. https:// doi.org/10.3389/fbuil.2020.00034

Pitts, A. (2013, January). Thermal comfort in transition spaces. *Buildings, 3*, 122–142. https://doi.org/10.3390/buildings3010122

Puteri Shireen, J. K., Abdul Majid, N. H., Raja Abdul Qadir, T. A. Q., & Abdul Latip, N. S. (2019). Themes of classicality in the Malay architectural form: Principles from Aristocratic Realm. *Melayu: Jurnal Antarabangsa Dunia Melayu, 12*(1), 27–59.

Syed Mohammed Syed Hassan Shahaeudin, & M. G. Knowles. (1958). The three million dollar wedding. *The Malaya in History*. In Faisal Tehrani (2019). Perkahwinan berharga 3 juta pada 1906. malaysiakini.com (published 24 July 2019, 9:08 am. https://www.malaysiakini.com/columns/485155

10

Climate and Archetype: Vernacular House-Forms as Tropical Urban Ideations

Norwina Mohd Nawawi
and Shaiful Nadzri Shamsudin

The rise of the sustainable agenda must face the reality of tropical regions which must grow their own archetypes and models of sustainable urbanism. Urban principles derived from the local vernacular roots can contribute to the agenda of lowering carbon emissions in a congested city based on local conceptualisations derived from the region. To explore ideations within the local Malay form, one must develop structural and spatial vocabularies that can feed into urban design concepts that can evoke later, historical, and cultural forms, which coincides with the goals of green urbanism and the low carbon agenda.

N. M. Nawawi (✉)
International Islamic University Malaysia (IIUM),
Gombak, Selangor, Malaysia
e-mail: norwina@iium.edu.my

S. N. Shamsudin
University Sains Malaysia, Gelugor, Penang, Malaysia

Introduction

The image of the kampung or a typical village is often linked to traditional Malay settlements which have inspired the urban designers, architects and urban planners. The Malay traditions in the past were based on a strong belief and connections between their daily life and activities. According to Vuksanovic, (2000), vernacular built environment includes the spirit of belonging and true neighbourhood, is particularly reflected in the physical forms and the morphology of the kampong which reflect the evolution of time as it developed (Fig. 10.1).

The word kampung is often simplified today as 'village'. In fact, the term has a range of meanings, including its connotation of clustering that might refer to the character of urban conglomerations of town units. In Malay, the verb *berkampung* (to form a kampung) means to congregate or come together. At times, in Malay jargon, it is used to denote the gathering of a group of friends or neighbours for major festivities or even imply the notion of forming a residential group or settlement unit. There is also the Malay term *kampung halaman*, which literally translates as 'compound yard', to denote one's home village, town, or neighbourhood. Historically, these various meanings have been adopted in English through three

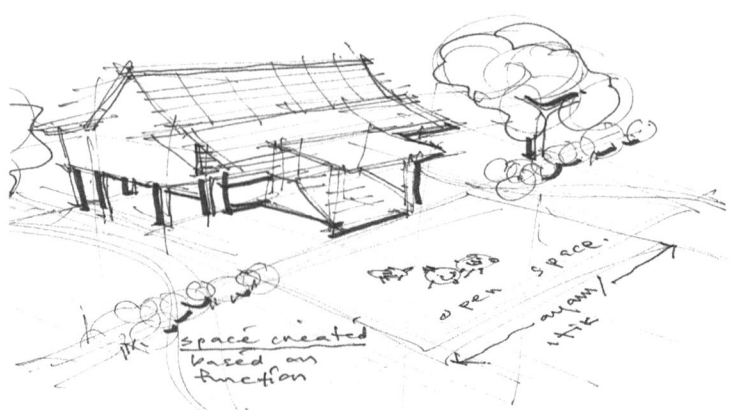

Fig. 10.1 Sketch of the open space or courtyard in front of a typical Malay house in a 'kampung' setting

versions of the same word: 'campong', 'compound', and 'kampong'. Excerpts from various dictionaries give the word origin or etymology of the English word 'compound' from the Malay word *kampung*, via Portuguese and Dutch adoptions, and also show the absorption of the words 'kampong' and 'campong' into English. The word 'kampung' may denote a spatial context where community relations are nurtured, but it is difficult to interpret the idea of a 'kampung' community in terms of spatial forms. In Malay culture and values, the word 'kampung' recalls the presence of a community spirit that goes beyond any physical form or preconceived idea. Although it conjures idyllic visions of the countryside, wide paddy fields, and sporadic settlements, the kampung has a connotation depicting the nature of human relationships, the dominance of communal interest over individuality, and, essentially, the presence of a generosity of spirit. Hence, to translate such values in terms of physical forms implies a kind of oxymoronic attempt to represent high ideals in specific architectural terms and forms. Yet, what we can glimpse and perhaps relate to the built environment the principles that involve the wafering of various approaches to high-rise residential spaces and architectural forms to evoke or resonate with the idea of the kampung. This is evident through the inclusion of physical spaces with the aim of nurturing the spirit of community and increasing the possibilities for interaction.

Urban form is not for its own sake but form from the needs of the community that grew together. The organisation of space is a reflection of its inherent value to the population and the fulfilment of a communal and not individual mission. Urbanism serves and reflects a sociospatial human need. The concept of a 'vertical' kampung in countries of the South East Asian region is thus a form that can resonate and capture such a community spirit. Urban forms, including architecture and spatial layout, must, thus, represent a resistance to the 'individualistic tendencies' of the modern or western world. The idealised creative insertions are critical 'crucibles' to induce a regeneration essence of community. In Jakarta, the problem of mass housing is at an acute juncture where slums and squatter settlements predominate over various areas around the central district. The growing sections of the population live amidst dire conditions such as extreme overcrowding and lack of basic infrastructure and services. The theme of the vertical kampung arises due to the need to preserve a sense of community and close-knit relations amidst urbanisation. This sense of community is vital for the population to grow and develop their social wellbeing.

Within this scenario, climate-based theoretical precepts, design strategies and key principles from the local vernacular can become a rare model for the tropical city. Ideas that link to forms that conflate with walkable pedestrian pathways are seldom heard. In modern urban setting buildings are spaced far apart from each other and thus they do not shade each other. The urban setting which are surrounded by heat island sources, the carbon lock-in effect of such models becomes acute and uncontrolled (Asaeda and Ca (1993). The more traditional idea of a city or urban form must therefore develop from local forms integrated with bioclimatic principles and a low energy position.

In Asian cities, the experience of walking through historical corridor streets and traditional squares is sporadic. Precincts in China, Sumatera, Malaysia, Thailand, and even Singapore still retain such urban forms. Yet old buildings and precincts are constantly being demolished to make way for the new and perceivably progressive models. The 'new' cities' urban form is generally gravitating towards the notion of compact sustainable cities and traditional morphologies derived from closer and more organic urban fabric and grain. The 'taller and bigger individual building volumes' inserted into modern developments contradict the need for the 'continuous enclosure' of buildings. Schumaker (1971) suggests how a traditional city is the complete reverse of the 'city in the park', that it is generally composed of isolated buildings and will present a city experience to the pedestrian as one that emphasises 'building volumes' rather than the spaces between buildings.

Under a tropical climate, realising the goals of low carbon cities cannot ignore the contribution of private vehicle use to the carbon equation. To achieve carbon targets, policies in urban design that involves individual buildings, and transportation issues must be addressed. The conflation of a low carbon city with aspects of nurturing place-identity must be seen as a strategy to ensure targets are met, and this includes reducing energy consumed by individual buildings by lowering carbon emissions of buildings and increasing the walkability of cities and reducing private vehicle usage. Culturally, this also coincides with the need to enhance locational identities of cities which can support economic growth in diverse areas such as tourism. To support a 'walkable' city in the tropics, climatic principles remain the main issue. While a compact city may have a denser urban fabric and narrower canyons, the reduced airflow within areas between buildings will be acute. Traditional ideas related to 'urban shade' must be explored in studies, and standards related to the level of adaptive outdoor comfort conditions can be implemented. The traditional principles of increased eave projection and projections of verandah-like spaces with shading must be reworked into the higher densities, finer urban grain, and narrower streets of sustainable tropical cities and implemented within morphological characteristics of traditional patterns and urban forms of the past. The organic character of old townships must be explored to understand and ascertain the overall layouts could result in the self-shading of buildings and occasional areas in between. Closer buildings not only create a self-shading mechanism but psychologically exude a feeling and perception of safety at the human scale pedestrian level when structures and buildings designed to be closer and, hence, are perceived to be close to one another. On the human scale and human level of visual perception, the incentive to walk is triggered when there is a psychological factor present as one perceives the likelihood of encoutering speeding vehicles is lesser as pathways or urban canyons are narrower.

Origins of the Modernist City

Modern theories of urban forms and city planning have principally been in conflict with the notion of the historicist city. The modern city seems to be an offshoot or a derivative of the ideas of the Ville Contemporaine, Le Corbusier's projected utopian vision where the poetics of spaces are translated into compact stand-alone high-rises in a city that would free the city's population from congestion (Le Corbusier, 2013). The 'modern' suggestions would return the urbanite to a pollution-free traditional environments for the population. To facilitate the transition of traditional communities to modern industrial societies, Le Corbusier had the optimistic belief that technology would pave a radical path in terms of urban form. His ideas, such as skyscrapers in parks, *pilotis* lifting structures from the ground, allowing traffic flow, gardens on roof terraces, and prioritising 'light and air' in high-density living, resulted in physical forms in a grid-like proposal that ultimately veer towards individual volumes that are set apart from each other. These ideas have been criticised by many. Yet the very conflation of Le Corbusier's ideas with economic efficiency meant that the international style would dominate any city. The roots of Le Corbusier's urbanistic principles can be traced to his ideas on the poetics of space, which in turn recalls his preoccupation with a modest house and modest life, set within a vast landscape. If one were to trace this phenomenon to the present, the idea of the individual block is inevitable because as one gravitates to the centre of a city—or what is known as the 'golden triangle'—it is the criterion of economic determinism and necessity that overrides all other rationales. Hence, one is faced with the recurring modern Asian city, which is basically the physical outcome of rising land values and economic necessities that require the grouping of people and services in high concentrations but perhaps should be based on the local vernacular tradition (Khosla, 1985) (Fig. 10.2).

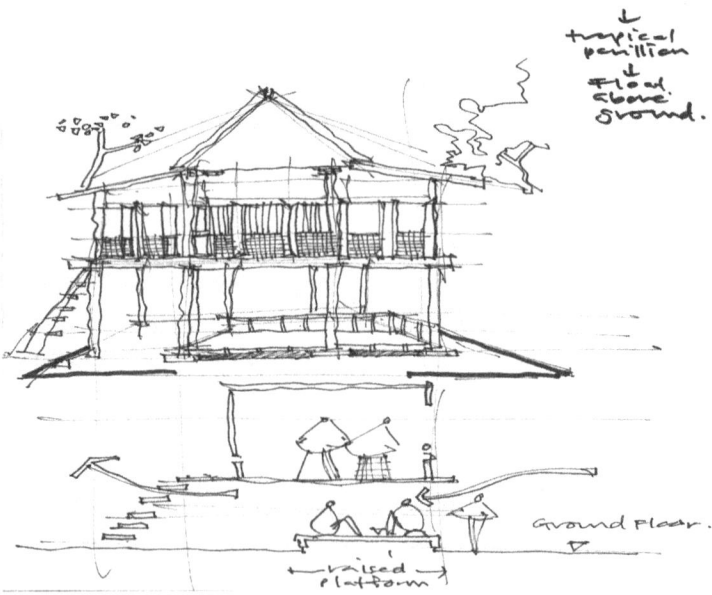

Fig. 10.2 Raised floor enhances the natural ventilation system throughout the house while serving as a multi-function area

Thermal comfort requirements and expectations in outdoor areas differ from indoor working environments due to the adaptive opportunities present in more external environments. There are various opportunities by urbanites and workers to adapt and achieve acceptable comfort throughout the day. In comparison, office or working environments are less 'flexible' in terms of adaptation—where the occupant occupies a specific location for work for a lengthy period of time (Busch, 1995; De Bear, 1995). When they are working, occupants are more aware of the limitations placed on their adaptation to their immediate thermal environments. They become more sensitive to any temperature departure from expectations.

Space and form in Malay traditions, for example, arise from functional needs, which have evolved through generations and their general organization and arrangements exude a strong utilitarian basis. Spatial layout reflects a hierarchy and layering that is the most crucial characteristic of the Malay form as it is born out of hierarchy of a series of connecting functions and cycles of home and family life. Space is divided between the public, the private, and the transitional or semi-public. The notion of privacy of the family is reflected in form and arrangement. Hence, while roof forms vary from region to region or state, house layout essentially obeys a certain hierarchy and progression in differentiating and facilitating public and private domains. Interiors are composed of spaces, namely, the verandah (*serambi*), the front house (anjung), the main house (*rumah ibu*), intermediate areas (*selang*), the kitchen (*dapur*), and the washing area (*pelantar*). Similar to other traditional houses in this region, the spaces underneath these houses are used for multiple purposes (Table 10.1).

In the Malay world, as with other parts of the tropical Nusantara (of the Malay Archipelago) region, the local vernacular house is a structure for shelter and family life. Fundamentally, this is the most basic type of residential form derived from the conventional post-and-beam structural system surmounted with a pitched roof with elevation above the ground (Tahir et al., 2009). The simplest kind of houses are covered with thatched or tiled roofs, enclosed with wooden or bamboo walls, perforated with windows and lattices, and, lastly, a platform floor raised on stilts, wooden posts, or masonry piers. Houses raised on stilts or posts

Table 10.1 Elements from the local vernacular Malay houses in their modern conceptions

Urban concept/ strategy/ parameter	Malay concept	Definition of Malay in tradition and potential urban extension of concept
Permeability	'kolong'/'telus'	Open and columnar space below vernacular house, traditionally formed to protect structures from flood and wildlife
Open space	'padang', 'alun alun'	Open plain or central field, which is a neutral patch of greenery linking key symbolic structures such as mosque and palace
Enclosure	'anjung', 'lanai'	Semi-outdoor areas, which are elevated and demarcated with collonades and balustrades
Mesh/boundary	'pagar musang'	Open-air grilles which allow ventilation yet reduce to intensity of solar gain by design and hence reduce tropical glare
Transitional zone	'balai'/'serambi'	Hierarchy of spatial experience of houses and palaces having a transitional space between public and private
Compound cul-de-sac	'kampung'	The English word 'compound' is derived from the Malay word 'kampung' which represents a common area which commands the frontage of surrounding buildings and which is enclosed between buildings
'pilotis'	'pelantar'	While pilotis refers to columns in Corbusian vocabulary, 'pelantar' refers to elevated timber floor or platform which recall the notion of tropical pavilion which seems to slightly float above the ground
Tectonic	'tanggam'	Timber traditions of Malay world recall emphasis on tectonic, which means to express construction and thus to express joints and connections, creating a language of columns, beams, wedges, and planes such as the solidity is punctured

have undercroft spaces (*kolong*) that are well-ventilated and cool yet are high enough to be used as a storage and activity space. The space underneath the house is often used for rest, work, storage, and keeping livestock. As a fully shaded area, it is frequently used in the afternoon for

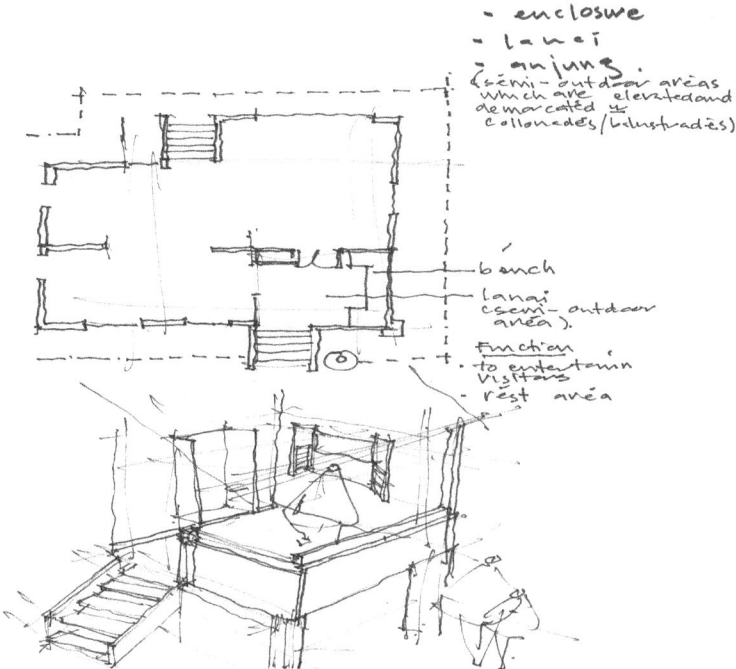

Fig. 10.3   Lanai or Anjung (Porch) in Malay vernacular architecture

food preparation, cooking, sewing, net mending, carpentry workshop space, resting, napping, or just hanging out with friends. The undercroft can also serve as a storage space for boats, farming implements, and utensils. Houses which are slightly raised have crawlspaces which can only be used for storage, as an animal pen or children's play area (Fig. 10.3).

The notion of permeability can arise from an extension of the idea of the *kolong*, which is basically the coupling of heat sinks and columnar populated open spaces on the ground and below occupied floors in order to extend the urban concept of public space. Rather than assuming urban setting as building blocks masses punctuated by pathways and roads around the ground level of cities that can be perceived as an open continuous space connecting both horizontal and vertical movement of people, there should be insertions of walkways with covered pathways through buildings and blocks. This insertion of covered walkways or path can also be punctuated by a vertical nodes of pocket parks and urban courtyards integrated naturally into the fabric of the city. Under equatorial conditions, such 'pockets' or punctuation of air can be utilised in terms of diverting the downward flow of air from increasing speeds from the higher levels of a multi-storey building and ventilate the stagnant air conditions at enclosed areas on the ground level. Past studies showed from trends in urban airflow and bioclimatic data that air stagnates within lower levels of urban pathways, including enclosed plazas or courtyards.

Hence, spaces and key high-rise structures can be strategically placed to ventilate the tropical city outdoors. The key criterion is, therefore, to allow for the optimum windflow for the pedestrians' comfort (Arnfield, 2003). Thus the creation of the sustainable city can extend the urban form arising from traditional elements yet be interspersed with high-rise blocks which are not merely located based on iconic purposes but more importantly as bioclimatic devices harvesting cleaner and faster air at higher levels down into the humid ground space, which may be blocked by continuous low-rise building blocks. Traditional principles, founded upon the abstraction of history and local tradition as a source of reference for terminologies and values, become a tool contingent and dependent upon the achievement of comfort for pedestrians and city users at the body level and human scale (Givoni, 1998). To achieve a city form with infused walkability, not only the notion of comfort but the pedestrian experience of security and safety as points of interest are important.

Hence, conflations of the traditional and sustainable tropical city can be founded upon local traditions, with its strategic massing of solid and void as well as permeability in the city spatial planning to increase comfort on the ground yet inserted with heightened points of interest to elevate the walking experience within a hot and humid climate. While pedestrians walk through, their experience is heightened by textures, traditional areas of interest such as heritage spots, information kiosks, niches and corners, spaces in between, low-lying eateries, and refined details of architecture to lessen the experience of thermal stress in a hot, humid environment. Recalling the Malay house forms and abstracting from such vernacular sources, shaded breezy areas can innovatively be created from the idea of *anjung* (external porch) and *serambi* (verandah) that recall spaces for resting and connections at the human scale to realistically and consistently encourage an environment conducive to walking with secure pedestrian movement.

A tradition in Malay architecture is rooted in the wide range of expression emerging from the simple elevated timber frame house tectonically and physically raised from the ground in respect to nature to socially inclusive dimensions. The Malay archetype is reminiscent of such roots, the rescaling of this elemental form in an urban setting with multiple modern functions must begin with multi-storey treatments that maintain a sense of proportion, order, and demonstrable balance while not losing a sense of human scale. To derive rules of form and harmony that can be replicated and recalled in urban buildings, the elements of a human scale vocabulary must be identified and then reinterpreted and expressed in spatial and facade systems. Buildings in a city need facade treatments' sense of belonging and identity more than anything else to remain culturally relevant as typical development takes place in zero lot sites and when urban boundaries pose constraints.

Any opportunity for sense of identity falls on the architectural expression contained within the articulation of space and the facade treatment. Hence, an understanding of the Malay archetypes is crucial in identifying patterns and abstractions that can characterise a language and grammar of Malay urban language based on traditions. With more complex building typologies, the variations and idiosyncrasies of site and typology must be related to essences found in variations of traditional cultural templates as contained within the Malay states or region. The localised vernacular design template as results of the tectonic and environmental facade pattern studies can develop into a highly stylised and rescaled grammar of architecture that can be implemented and applied at the urban scale. Steadfast on the essence of tradition, the exercise thus has not deviated from or losing the essential human-scale elements and proportions that mirror the nature of the Malay culture.

A range of expression and variations of facade treatments and proportions can be adapted to systems of walls, windows, openings, sunshades, screens, and verandahs. The grammar must reflect the rich traditions of the Malay world, as well as its historical confluence of many cultures and traditions, across time and states. The existence of various Malay palaces with a range of stylistic variations inadvertently represents the variations of archetype by time and region.

Urban elements can recall values, climatic sense, and cultural resonance. A synthesis of the systems that recall age-old climatic strategies should be inseparable from urban and architectural elements of design (Anderson, 2009). There is a need to re-think and re-cast the notion of universal modernism, and tradition should be part of the same coin implicitly. The present condition of being couched in a dichotomous relationship between tradition and modernity must find its way back to the sensibilities of the past. The challenge is to create a re-instigation and re-enactment of tradition in the modern world while allowing such a framework to be infused with sustainable principles and the rigor of the environmental sciences. Acclimatization adjustments are necessary for the mainly columnar type of language, where it transmutes into urban forms, and this must achieve a balance and sense of negotiation between cultural roots, climatic sensibilities, technology, functionality and resource availability or re-inculturation.

Conflating the Climatic and the Cultural

Any re-enactment of a historicist city with sustainable credentials must achieve minimal shaded comfort in open areas. If it does not achieve this, the city will return to its unsustainable state of individual modern highly air-conditioned blocks and structures with heated walkways and open plazas (Anderson, 2009). The principles from the Malay vernacular architectural design must conflate bioclimatic urban strategies in terms of optimised and well-oriented massing of low, medium, and high-rise building blocks into a range of layered and stratified urban forms adjusted to the hot, humid context. This will then fuse sustainable objectives into the struggle and effort to recreate the notion of the traditional city—without the literal 'copying' of history or reverting to traditional forms.

Hence forms applied to the city can have underlying principles:

i. Climatic aspects:
   - A respect for and consistency with proportions;

- The primary role of verandahs, projections, and shading devices—maintained at a similar ratio to traditional forms to maintain the aesthetic feel and sense of scale inserted with limited proportions of the old carvings from *past* houses and palaces;
- Openings of long shuttered windows, perforated ventilative and privacy screens, window and door louvres for both natural ventilated areas and areas requiring intermittent needs as well as in emergencies;
- Continuous open spaces underneath (the 'kolong' area) and around buildings, i.e. shaded and sheltered open spaces for people to utilise in an urban context such as the underneath spaces which may also have an accelerated wind effect;
- Of structural and fabrication material that will sustain and weathers well in the local context;
- Ratio of width and building height as well as open space or courtyard to regulate temperature;
- Appropriate vegetation for oxygen and shade at appropriate space; and
- Of form and make that accommodates the different climatic situation of the local context.

ii. Cultural Aspects:
  - Consideration for privacy as individual, family unit, organisation, community—in public, semi-public and private spaces with unwritten understanding of hierarchy, sacredness, and modesty;
  - Community consideration for socialisation, meetings and activities for different communities (age group, gender, ethnicity, faith) with open, extended, and accessible spaces at different levels, with a sense of place, space, and identity;
  - Consideration for security and sense of security and safety in surveillance through interlocking spaces, visual and audio connectivity;
  - Provision of spaces for learning and recreational activities across society;
  - Provision for trade and retail activities through spatial nooks and corners along the pathways within the neighbourhood units of cities at accessible distance;
  - With ambience that provides a sense of timelessness, memory with aesthetics; and
  - Allowance for growth and enrichment in time.

The vocabulary from the local vernacular can be developed not only into expressive urban design elements such as multi-layered walls and rhythmic columns, cool surfaces detailed into wall panels, gable boards, ornamented panels, shutters, and grilles, but these naturally converge into elements that are sustainable (low energy without high solar gains) and comfort (minimally acceptable in terms of comfort and low visual glare). Walls and windows are no longer merely blank surfaces. They should capture the cool layered and extended forms, pilastered, or even balustraded elements, in line with the traditional ethos, where shutters can be fully openned to allow in climatic elements. Roofs are broad over-hanging devices creating pockets of cool shaded air. Cantilevers extend far beyond the wall line to provide shade. It becomes again an architecture that is grounded in a new system of logic—a climatic and environmental one (Steemers, 1989). Grown from an ideal archetypical form, these elements can become a template that can undergo any form of expressive formation in the process of being adjusted to the context of type, function, urban site, and space. The vernacular archetype exhibits a rectilinear form, yet it has a pliable capability to evolve into forms which can combine ground rules of either a rational or a free-form organization.

The 'Permeable' Fabric

Pockets of semi-open spaces within city and buildings in the city can be adjusted with the adjacency of high-rises at critical orientations in order to create microclimate conditions amenable to social and commercial activities within the city structure. The challenge within the hot, humid context is not to commit these social networks and urban spaces to a lifetime of air-conditioning consumption. The airflow direction, magnitude, and distribution can be changed with the presence of high-rise building blocks within low-rise three- to four-storey developments in order to create conditions particularly significant for thermal comfort. The relationship and effect of urban morphology, the configuration of buildings, urban plazas and courtyards, and their impact in terms of natural ventilation and thermal comfort under dense city conditions should be further explored (Olgyay, 1963; Ali-Toudert and Bensalem, 2001). A pattern of high-rises interspersed with a medium-density scale of buildings to low-rise retail establishments—characteristic of a historicist city—can be organised to divert high winds and hence generate windy and comfortable conditions at lower levels in order to 'ventilate' in-between commercial and social centres within dense city environments similar to enclosed public plazas and atriums (Jahnkassim and Kenneth, 2000b). Negative and positive pressure zones can be created to induce wind flows to create a thermal sensation to cool pedestrians across ground-level pathways and public plazas. However, there must be a deeper understanding of the thermal sensation in city streets and across public semi-open spaces—where the parameters of thermal comfort in outdoor urban areas are interlinked with expectations of the city user (Jahnkassim and Kenneth, 2000a); Arnfield, 2003). These are affected by urban design parameters, the morphology of buildings, characteristics of surrounding surfaces and spaces, and commercial activities (Potvin, 2000). An understanding of the convective and radiative exchanges through actions of wind and differences in temperature and pressure will contribute towards the characteristics of microclimate (Lomas, 1991). Inner-city thermal conditions are affected and can be influenced by the following:

(i) The role of the vertical urban geometry and solar orientation in creating a different microclimate within a canyon or semi-open space or covered walkway or plaza;
(ii) The effects of these microclimatic changes on human outdoor thermal sensation; and
(iii) The effects of urban morphology on outdoor thermal comfort.

Plazas and public spaces can be created as pockets within the enclosure of low-rise structures or as an extended forecourt of large buildings (office/retail/residential) with Malay-based extended serambi-type spaces or semi-public or private space serving as a thoroughfare and seating areas for occupants or visitors. While modern architecture tends to focus on the aesthetic experiences of buildings, it is the quality of open and semi-open urban walkways and spaces that can improve the quality of urban life and enhance the isolation and social exclusion of city dwellers. The spatial elements has become more important due to current efforts in revitalising and rejuvenating old cities. Covered plazas and spatial extensions provide opportunities for eateries with low energy but enhanced semi-outdoor spaces by admitting airflow, inducing ventilation, and yet protecting from heavy rain. On the other hand, the solar gain is minimised, and overhead covers and canopies must not 'shut out' climate but filter outdoor environmental factors, for example rain and wind (Fikry, 1990 and Potvin, 2000). The aim is to reduce energy yet make the urban fabric and outdoor areas be a form of communicating with nature and reconnecting oneself to the rhythm and life of the climate where people can experience rain, wind, and daylight and yet be sheltered and not seal themselves in blank boxes, which would further commit the city to a lifetime of high energy consumption and perpetual health hazards (Jitkhajournwanich, 1994).

Pocket parks and wind-induced courtyards create a potential buffer zone that decreases energy transfer from building surfaces to the outdoor environment. This benefit must be fused with the goal to maximise natural ventilation through wind-induced ventilation and a stack effect in these plazas and adjacent occupied zones without air conditioning.

The Elevated Pedestrian Plane

Tropical cities have another factor which needs to be considered in increasing resilience—the occasional occurrence of flash floods. Cities on coastlines have annual events of flooding while dense capitals are increasingly faced with the sudden monsoonal impact. An alternative urban form that is flood-resistant will allow urbanites and city users to create pathways of safety and enable drastic reductions in losses of property and infrastructure (Han et al., 2002; Henrique, 2013). An open urban form with elevated public areas can then allow flooding with waters to rise over the height of the first storey, and where many of the critical services and functions will be on the second or third floor. The public sections of the city must be redeveloped and re-assigned into a new 'multi-level' urbanism approach, with critical functions relocated, and with added enhancement such as the integration of water plaza stepped areas and lower public areas (Jha et al., 2012). The containment of rising waters within these public areas will result in a lower loss of damaged property and will allow the public to move their belongings into safer upper levels in the event of sudden disasters. The cultural urban model must reflect the idea of an 'elevated' city they can also provide a working, reproducible model to replace the devastated areas of the cities. An elevated city can function fully during so-called normal times yet can be transformed into levels of refuge and protection during flashflood or monsoon emergency periods. The alternative urban forms become culturally aligned 'elevated' forms integrated with multi-purpose retarding basins which store flood waters for outflow control when necessary. Rainwater harvesting can also be integrated within such spaces and form part of a sustainable drainage system. The spatial planning and design can include a combination of strategies-combining water retention methods, water plazas, rainwater harvesting, and green infrastructure, with the lower ground floor areas freed to ensure open areas and functional areas moved to the levels above, which would be a new form of urbanism for the affected areas (Lennon et al., 2014). In Malaysia, the recent flood disasters include the unprecedented floods in Kelantan have caused an estimated RM 200 million in losses, with estimated losses of up to RM 932 million. There is a realization that structural damage is caused when the flow of floodwaters is checked and contained within a structure. The forces can cause structural damage to both sub-structure and superstructure elements. Hence what is now being focused on is that urban structures allowing floodwaters to have unhindered passage through a property could ensure significant reductions in repair costs. The concept of 'Sponge City' and 'Living with Flood' is currently being explored for innovative management of the prevailing issues.

Conclusion

Cities must return to the model of conflating climatic and cultural principles of the locality in order to both reclaim their space of identity and reverse the carbon lock-in effects of modern development (Bitan, 1992; Feireiss and Pitt, 2009). Urban forms and its architecture must be rethought, optimised, and manipulated to generate and induce wind flow for increased pleasantness and comfort under humid conditions (Fanger, 1972). By these approaches, as Asia modernises at a rapid pace, the notion of the historicist city—or a city built on historical elements grew from social and culture of the locality that are sustainable—must also be discussed. As old structures are demolished to make way for new gleaming glass boxes, the idea of the historicist-walkable city is gradually dying in modern Asian cities. Yet it is this reflected idea of the past ingenuity based on solid traditions that may perhaps throws a lifeline or hope to the persistently increasing global impact of carbon emissions to recovery. The concentration of carbon emissions is in modern cities, where buildings account for around 30 per cent and transportation, including private vehicles, account for 70 per cent of emissions. Transportation is one of the main sectors contributing the highest carbon emissions. Therefore to achieve low carbon targets, the specifications and strategies for reductions in energy demand and carbon emissions for a range of building types, land-use factors, transportation sectors and city or urban planning must be given due attention. Sustainability must be seen as a movement in which the city should re-instates its 'humanity' concerns over just economics. The construction wisdom and spatial dynamics of the long tradition must combine with innovative approaches to enhance the role of climate in the built environment in order to once again re-sensitise urban forms as resilient and humane habitat for the years ahead.

References

Ali-Toudert, F., & Bensalem, R. (2001, November). A methodology for a climatic urban design. In *Proceedings of the 18th conference on PLEA, Florianopolis, Brasil, 7*(9), 469–473.

Anderson, W. (2009) Homes for a changing climate: adapting our homes and communities to cope with the climate of the 21st century. Green Books.

Arnfield, J. (2003). Two decades of urban climate research: A review of turbulence, exchange energy and water, and the urban heat island. *International Journal of Climatology, 23*, 1–26.

Asaeda, T., & Ca, V. T. (1993). The subsurface transport of heat and moisture and its effects on the environment: A numerical model. *Boundry-Layer Meteorol, 65*, 159–179.

Bitan, A. (1992). The high climatic quality city of the future. *Atmos. Encir, 26B*, 313–329.

Busch, J. (1995). Thermal comfort in Thai air- conditioned and naturally ventilated offices. In F. Nicol, M. Humphreys, O. Sykes, & S. Roaf (Eds.), *Standards for thermal comfort—Indoor air temperatures for the 21st century* (p. 133). E & F. N. Spon.

De Bear, R. J. (1995). Thermal comfort in air-conditioned office buildings in the tropics. In F. Nicol, M. Humphreys, O. Sykes, & S. Roaf (Eds.), *Standards for thermal comfort—Indoor air temperatures for the 21st century* (pp. 122–129). E & FN Spon.

Fanger, P. O. (1972). *Thermal comfort—Analysis and applications in environmental engineering.* Mcgraw Hill Book Company.

Feireiss, K., & Pitt, B. (2009). Architecture in Times of Need: Make It Right: Rebuilding New Orleans Lower Ninth Ward. New York. Prestel.

Fikry, Ahmed. (1990). An Investigation into window shading devices to optimize the control of the internal environment: with special reference to subtropical climate, PhD thesis, University of Sheffield.

Givoni, B. (1998). *Climatic considerations in building and urban design.* Van Nostrand Reinhold.

Han, D., Davis, J., Hu, Z., Lan, G., Maren, E., & Twyman, C. (2002). *Design studies on flood-proof house.* University of Bristol Academic Report Sponsored by ICE R&D Enabling Fund.

Henrique, K. P. (2013). Housing Responses to Climate Change: Analyzing Architectures of Transition. In Flood-Prone Zones, Nature of Spatial Practices, 131–139. Retrieved from https://www.academia.edu/5363991/Housing_Responses_to_Climate_Change_Analyzing_architectures_of_transition_in_flood-prone_zones

Jahnkassim, P. S., & Kenneth, I. P. (2000a). Optimising for sun and light—the environmental performance of two bioclimatic highrises"; published in the Proceedings of the World Renewable Energy Congress 2000, Brighton, UK, July 2000.

Jahnkassim, P. S., & Kenneth, I. P. (200b). "Environmental and architectural impacts of bioclimatic highrises in a tropical climate" published/presented at the Sustainable Building 2000 International conference. 22–25 October 2000b, Maastricht, Netherlands.

Jha, A. K., Bloch, R., & Lamond, J. (2012). Cities and flooding: a guide to integrated urban flood risk management for the 21st century. World Bank Publications. Allocation and Utilization of the Local DRR and Management Fund.pdf. (n.d.).

Jitkhajournwanich, Kitchai. (1994). Expectation and experience of thermal comfort in transitional spaces: a field study of thermal environments in the hot-humid climate of Bangkok, PhD thesis, School of Architecture, University of Sheffield.

Khosla, Romi. (1985). Crashing through Western modernism into Asian reality. *Proceedings of the Seminar on Regionalism in Architecture*, Bangladesh, Dec 17–22, 1985, Singapore : Aga Khan Award for Architecture and Concept Media.

Le Corbusier. (2013). The City of Tomorrow and Its Planning. Dover Publication.

Lennon, M., Scott, M., & O'Neill, E. (2014). Urban design and adapting to flood risk: The role of green infrastructure. *Journal of Urban Design, 19*(5), 745–758.

Lomas, K. J. (1991). Dynamic thermal simulation models of buildings: New method for empirical validation. *Building Services Engineering Research and Technology, 12*(1), 25–37.

Olgyay, V. (1963). *Design with Climate: Bioclimatic approach to architectural regionalism*. Princeton Architectural Press.

Potvin, Andre. (2000). Assessing the microclimate of urban transitional spaces, Proceedings of Architecture, City and Environment, Proceedings of PLEA 2000, Cambridge, UK July 2000, pp. 581–586.

Schumacher, T. (1971). Contextualism: Urban ideals and deformations. *Casabella, 359-360*, 79–86.

Steemers, Koen. (1989). The performance of external shading devices—Proceedings of the 2nd European conference on architecture 4–8 December 1989, Paris, France.

Tahir, M. M., Usman, I., Ani, A. C., Surat, M., Abdullah, N., & Nor, M. M. (2009). Reinventing the Traditional Malay Architecture: Creating a Socially Sustainable and Responsive Community in Malaysia through the Introduction of the Raised Floor Innovation (Part1). Energy, Environment, Ecosystems, Development and Landscape Architecture Journal.

Vuksanovic, D. (2000). Vernacular Architecture—A Paradigm for Sustainable Building. *Proceedings of the 3rd International Conference for Teachers in Architecture* (TIA 2000), 10–12 July 2000, Sommerville College, Oxford University.

11

The Matriarch, the Matrilineal System, and the Minangkabau *Rumah Gadang*

Azizi Bahauddin

Introduction

A number of studies have discussed the Minangkabau community of Western Sumatera with its *perpatih* custom. The Minangkabau community of western Sumatera is probably one of the largest matrilineal societies in the world. Aside from the relative rarity of the matrilineal system itself, the Minangkabau matrilineal system has been of special interest to scholars because of its combination with patrilineally oriented Islam, 'how such a (matrilineal) system could work in conjunction with the patrilineal Islamic legal framework has excited a good deal of speculation' (Geertz, 1963). Seems like a contradiction between traditional customs and Islam, but they merged with each other to make this culture more apparent and unique and strengthening belief with customs.

A. Bahauddin (✉)
School of Housing, Building & Planning, Universiti Sains Malaysia, Penang, Malaysia

S. Jahn Kassim et al. (eds.), *Eco-Urbanism and the South East Asian City*, https://doi.org/10.1007/978-981-19-1637-3_11

Culture plays a major role in shaping the uniqueness and aesthetics in architectural elements of traditional homes (Fox, 1993). The traditional architecture can be explained by the study of related culture as both are interrelated (Hashim & Nasir, 2014; Yuan, 1987; Idrus, 1996). Its architectural components are seen to be able to produce sustainable design in harmony with the environment (Bahauddin, 2012). Hence, traditional architecture should be preserved due to the high aesthetic values that can be inherited by the present generation and generations to come (Ahmad, 2010). Minangkabau society is well known for its traditional and cultural home. The Minangkabau culture has existed since around 500 AD. The community and culture began in some areas of Western Sumatera (Fig. 11.1) known as *Wilayah Nan Tiga*, which consists of *Luhak Tanah Datar* as the first region, *Luhak Agam* as the second region, and *Luhak Lima Puluh Kota* as the newest province (Asri, 2004; Is, 2000; Jayatri, 2001; Widya, 2001; Soeroto, 2005). Pagarruyung in *Tanah Datar* was designated as the Minangkabau Government Centre (Idrus, 1996) and led by a king known as *Rajo Alam* (Kamaruzzaman, 2012). The

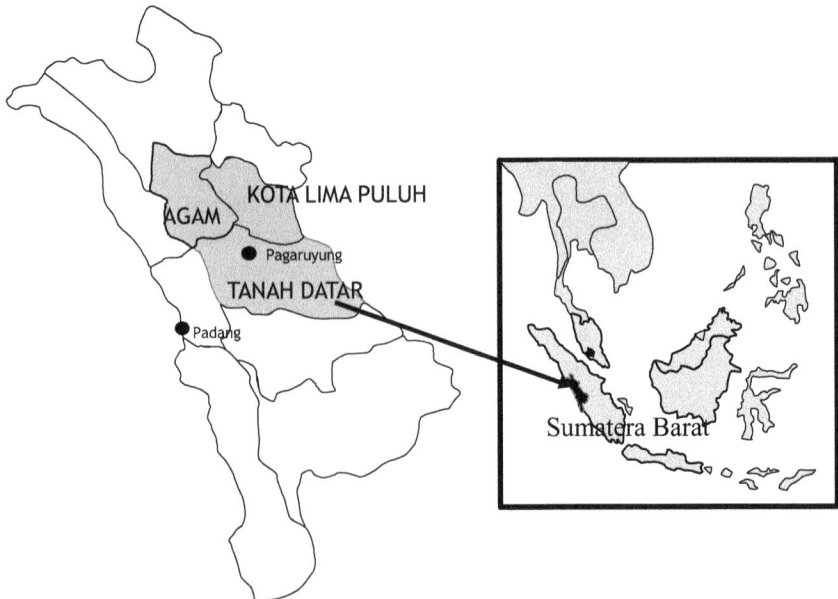

Fig. 11.1   Western Sumatera Minangkabau Region

Minangkabau Kingdom's glory and success have made it one of the few famous kingdoms throughout the Malay Archipelago (Abidin, 2012).

The Minangkabau house is also known as the *rumah gadang* as well as a place of residence. It was used as a symbol of a people and to hold a variety of rituals, customs, and family activities (Yovita, 2012; Idrus, 1996; Asri, 2004; Is, 2000; Widya, 2001). The physical shape is easily recognised for its multi-tiered concave roof (Figs. 11.2 and 11.3), and this is not seen in other traditional houses (Idrus, 1996). The concept of *alam takambang jadi guru* or nature as a guide is the foundation of the Minangkabau culture. It can sustain the culture embedded in the architecture that is compatible with the environment. The environment has become a source of natural science to the community. Minangkabau society adheres very strongly to the idea of using nature as a guide (Abidin, 2012). The interior layout reflects customs and occupants' behaviour (Is, 2000). The architectural uniqueness and greatness exist through the concept and philosophy of the community that is based strongly on matrilineal society (Soeroto, 2005). This matrilineal society is hundreds of years old (Nasroen, 1957; Ng, 2006; Ibrahim, 1993; Edison, 2010). Such a unique custom is thus reflected in

Fig. 11.2 Datuk Paduko Alam house in Lintau Buo, Tanah Datar (Bahauddin et al., 2012)

Fig. 11.3 Datuk Rajo Mangkuto Nan Putih in Payakumbuh, Lima Puluh Kota (Bahauddin et al., 2012)

the appearance of the interior layout of the house, and it is able to create harmonious relationships and integration with house occupants (Is, 2000).

Minangkabau Culture

According to Sanday (2002), there is an archetypal maternal symbol, a dominant symbol in anthropological terms, which condenses in the matriarch being primordial principles of conduct. Based on these principles, the mother/child bond is sacred, part of natural law. Being grounded in natural law, customs associated with matrilineal descent are treated as an inalienable part of the foundation of Minangkabau identity. The overarching defining principles of conduct in family, clan, and village life pivot around men and women connected through females to a common ancestress in a long-practised custom. Customs and Islam are two important components in Minangkabau culture seen as complementing each other. The phrase 'the custom is governed by Islamic rules and the Islamic rules are governed by the Koranic teachings' gives a very clear indication that Minangkabau customs are steeped in Islamic teachings, as these teachings were written in the Koran and *Hadith* (the words of the Prophet Muhammad), and they must be adhered to. Minangkabau society in the Malay Archipelago is known for its spiritual loyalty to Islam and holding fast to the faith. In the fourteenth century, the Minangkabau people received the advent of Islam and believed that Islam complements the culture (Soeroto, 2005; Nasroen, 1957). Components of this culture have been the core of life of the Minangkabau for years, a departure from animistic beliefs (Nasroen, 1957). Hence, the custom of the culture encompasses a very broad range of meaning as it includes regulations that guide the community to achieve happiness and success in both religious and non-religious affairs (Amir, 1997).

Customary rules and principles were established in the community through cultural philosophy. The concept of *alam takambang jadi guru* has become the dominant philosophy in Minangkabau culture (Soeroto, 2005; Manggis & Panghoeloe, 1982). In this concept, nature and human beings are interdependent and part of the environment created by the Almighty. Hence, the universe is used as a guide to educate people through mutual respect, love, and existing in harmony with the environment (Nasroen, 1957). Customary laws and regulations in Minangkabau culture are divided into four stages. Each level has a different law. The first stage is called 'the definite custom', the second is 'the created custom', the third is 'a customary tradition', and the fourth is 'the rites' (Hamka, 2006; Nasroen, 1957; Ibrahim, 1993). Each level has a basic role and functions involving customs that either can or cannot be changed. An unchangeable custom is a custom based on the Islamic faith, and the law of nature is mentioned as 'the definite custom' and 'the created custom', whereas changeable customs are 'the customary tradition' and 'the rites'. These changeable customs can be modified to suit the local community agreed upon through discussions guided by a set of rules and laws. This culture is divided into two systems of governance. The Koto Piliang was led by Datuk Ketemenggungan, an autocratic custom, whereas the Bodi Caniago was led by Datuk Perpatih, a democratic custom (Is, 2000; Widya, 2001; Hamka, 2006). However, they are both still being practiced in the same matrilineal kinship in which women would be given the privileges to accede to the lineage, inheritance, and the rights to voice opinions.

According to Kato (1978), there are four readily identifiable characteristics of the traditional Minangkabau system:

1. Descent and descent-group formation are organized according to the female line. Each village (*nagari*) consists of several ideally exogamous matriclans, or suku, which have distinct names, such as Melayu, Piliang, and Caniago.
2. A matrilineage is a corporate descent group with a ceremonially instituted male head called the *penghulu*. He is distinguished by a special title, e.g., Datuk Radjo Adie, which belongs to and stands for his lineage. To address a *penghulu* by other than his *datuk* title is a great offense to his lineage members. A lineage possesses communally owned properties, including agricultural land, houses, fishponds, heirlooms, and miscellaneous *adat* titles. In principle, ancestral property (*harta pusaka*) is inalienable and there is no individually owned property, particularly property of an immovable nature. A lineage is further divided into several sublineages (*paruik*). These also have their properly recognised male heads (*tungganai rumah*). Ancestral properties, or, more accurately, rights to their use (*ganggam bauntuak*) are assigned to sublineages for the benefit of their respective members.
3. The residential pattern is duolocal. After marriage, a husband moves to or near the house of his wife and stays there at night. But he continues to belong to his mother's house and frequently goes back there during the day.
4. Authority within a lineage or a sublineage is in the hands of the *mamaky*, not of the father. *Mamak* literally means maternal uncle, but the term can also refer to classificatory maternal uncles such as *penghulu* and *tungganai rumah*. The kin term which complements *mamak* is *kemanakan* to indicate a male.

The Matrilineal Kinship

The Minangkabau community in Western Sumatera is the largest community in the world that adheres to matrilineal kinship (Gilbert, 2002). The clan is classified as the fourth largest tribe in Indonesia and the only people who practice the matrilineal custom in this country. Through this tradition, women are given the privilege to inherit the lineage and heritage. The women were also given special positions with the title *bundo kanduang* (the matriarch) (Asri, 2004). The title is very apropos in describing the characteristics of a good leadership and a planner (Hermayulis, 2008), although the maternal brother, known as *mamak*, leads only in customary ceremonies (Asri, 2004). In contrast, men are only fathers to their children or husbands to wives and are considered outsiders or given titles such as *urang sumando* (Ibrahim, 1993; Selat, 1975). They are not given the right to inherit (Azwar, 2001). In general, *bundo kanduang* (matriarch) can control the economy by keeping an inherited estate and being a wife and mother who can maintain a family custom and religion (Hermayulis, 2008; Astuti, 2004). Women serve a very important function in the society, as expressed through their family lineage (Asri, 2004). In addition, they are also the strength of the community and supporters to men. The wisdom possessed by women would be able to make them better leaders of the community, thereby making the view of *bundo kanduang* (matriarch) important in a community's decision-making processes (Hermayulis, 2008). Three characteristics of the matrilineal kinship system constitute the strength of the community in keeping the culture alive (Fig. 11.4).

The title of a powerful mother or *bundo kanduang* is matriarchal, whereas the term for the descendants or followers of the custom is matrilineal and is still going strong to this day (Amir, 1997). The well-managed administrative, social, and economic systems cover all aspects of life, including the area of designing and constructing the *rumah gadang*. These practices involve women (usually in their roles as mothers) in activities that authenticate and regenerate or as a decision-maker, a term which is closer to the ethnographic details that nurture the social order. By this definition, the ethnographic context of matriarchy does not reflect female power over subjects or female power to subjugate, but female power (in their roles as mothers and senior women) to give different opinions and to bring the family together and regenerate social ties in the here-and-now and in the hereafter. Because this approach stresses the connection between the archetypal (or cosmological) and the social, rather than between power and politics, it cannot be interpreted as the female equivalent of patriarchy (Sanday,

Waris
keturunan
- mengikut
susur galur ibu
(matrilineal/matriarchal)

Perkahwinan
secara eksogami
secara berlainan
suku
(exogamy marriage)

Ciri-ciri matrilineal
(MATRILINEAL CHARACTERISTICS)

Kuasa ekonomi
dan harta pusaka
diwarisi oleh
kaum ibu
(inheritance rights)

Fig. 11.4 Characteristics of matrilineal kinship. (Adapted from Amir [20])

1998). The circulation in the house is designed according to the comfort of the women (Ng, 2006). This can be explained when all daughters are given the rights to their own rooms and when newly married daughters will be given a special treatment.

The *Rumah Gadang*

The traditional house in Minangkabau society is known as the *rumah gadang* because, apart from being a place of residence, it is also used as a venue for cultural ceremonies for the family or community (Is, 2000; Ahmad, 2010). The house has become a symbol of glory and the existence of a community (Asri, 2004; Soeroto, 2005; Erman et al., 1981). The construction is not simply to be owned by an individual but for the community. Therefore, all individuals in the same community have the right to use the *rumah gadang* to conduct ceremonies such as, for example, marriage, appointing leaders, coming of age, and funerals (Is, 2000). This house is inhabited by a large family (extended family), which can consist of several generations. Families residing in this house would be of three to four generations of mother to grandmother, grandmother, mother's family, and daughter. In general, the *rumah gadang* is occupied only by the maternal descendents and led by a brother of the mother. The leader is called *mamak tungganai* and carries the title *Datuk* or Your Excellency (Idrus, 1996; Erman et al., 1981). In addition to *mamak tungganai* (leader) each *rumah gadang* has a *bundo kanduang* (matriarch) with the title of *limpapeh nan gadang* or the beautifier and a protector. Her function is that of leader to the community and to other women (who have married daughters with children), and she manages all matters related to the family in the house. Until now, the house has remained in use and has been passed on to mothers and daughters for generations. It is considered one of the unique characteristics in the matrilineal system when mothers and daughters possess the right to inherit property, including the *rumah gadang*. It has become the pride of the community because the architecture is rich with cultural values based on the matrilineal kinship. Therefore, based on customary law, the house cannot be traded because it is the property of valuable inheritance bequeathed by the ancestors over time (Is, 2000; Soeroto, 2005). In addition, the beneficiaries must also have the characteristics of individuals who adhere to the customs and qualify to inherit the house according to the law (Is, 2000).

In general, there are two types of *rumah gadang* (Asri, 2004; Is, 2000; Jayatri, 2001; Widya, 2001; Soeroto, 2005). The *rumah gadang* design with verandas was established by the community under the Koto Piliang influence, whereas the *rumah gadang* without verandas was by the community of Bodi Caniago (Is, 2000). A large number of *rumah gadang* with verandas are located in the area of Luhak Tanah Datar, whereas *rumah gadang* without verandas are mostly found in the Luhak Agam and Luhak Lima Puluh Kota (Asri, 2004; Is, 2000; Jayatri, 2001; Widya, 2001; Soeroto, 2005). The significant differences in these two types of houses can be seen in the amount of internal floor spaces. The Koto Piliang rumah gadang has verandas and a high floor, and the Bodi

a   c

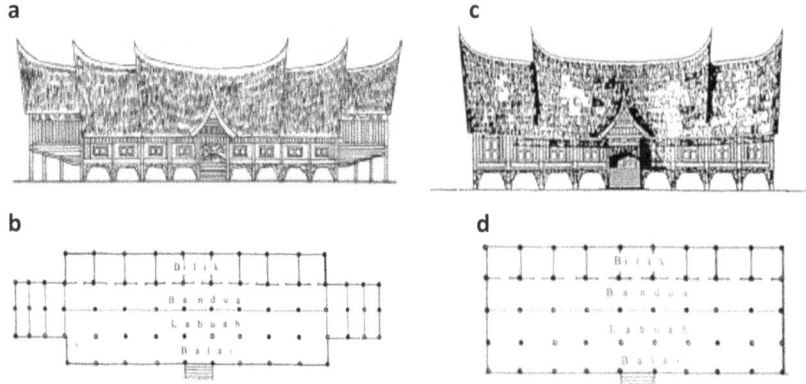

b   d

Fig. 11.5 Differences between *rumah gadang* with and without *anjung* (verandas) (Bahauddin et al., 2012). (**a**) Front Elevation. (**b**) Floor Plan—Koto Piliang Minangkabau House. (**c**) Front Elevation. (**d**) Floor Plan Bodi Caniago Minangkabau House

Caniago house is the opposite (Fig. 11.5). These differences exist through the result of the system of governance practiced by both leaders. The Koto Piliang practices principles that distinguish levels of autocracy of leaders reflected in the multiple levels of floors. The Bodi Caniago *rumah gadang* is without verandas and influenced by democratic principles. However, the layout of the interior space and the physical form of these *rumah gadang* has more similarities than differences. The house design is rectangular and elongated, and the interior layout is divided into three areas, the space at the front, the middle part as the main space, and the space at the back.

The kitchen area was prepared in accordance with requirements and is outside the house. The interior layout is divided into *lanja* or bays and spaces (Fig. 11.6). Specifically, the distance from the front to the back room is known as a *lanja* or a bay and the distance from the right side to the left side is known as a *ruang* or space (Asri, 2004). The space on the right side is known as the beginning, whereas the space on the left side is known as the ending. The *lanja* is divided into four bays known as the *lanja/bilik* (room), *bandua* (ante room), *labuah* (open space), and *balai* (foyer). The floor height of the *lanja/bilik* (room) is

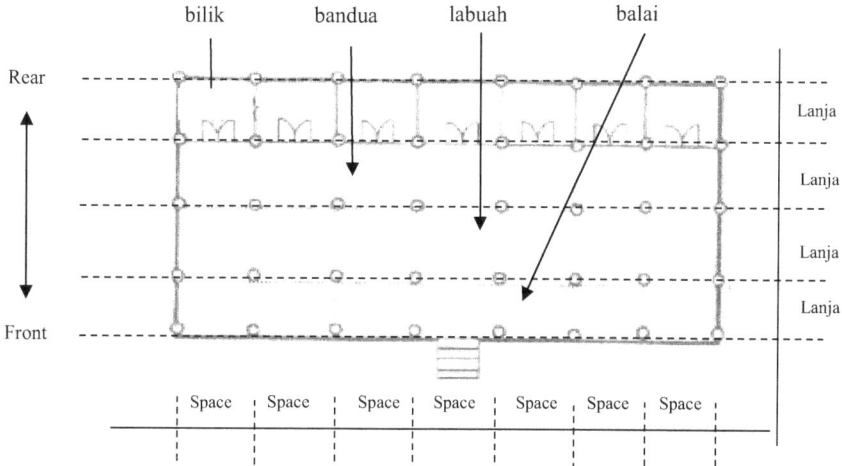

Fig. 11.6 Floor plan of Datuk Rajo Mantro Alam House, Nagari Koto Nan Ampek, Payakumbuh, Lima Puluh Kota (Bahauddin et al., 2012)

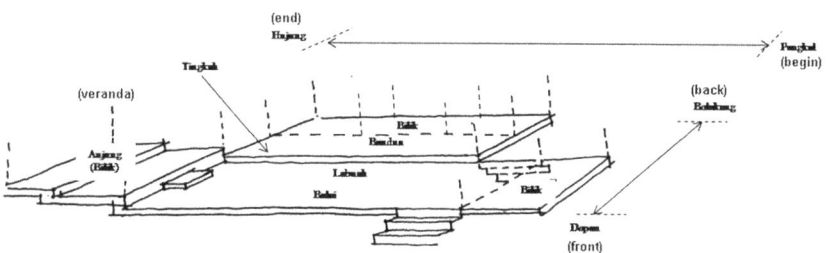

Fig. 11.7 Different heights of floors (Bahauddin et al., 2013)

the same as the *lanja bandua* (ante room) but higher than the *lanja labuah* (open space) and *balai* (foyer) (Fig. 11.7). This floor is raised 20 cm and is known as the *tingkah* or level. In Koto Piliang style, the verandas will be at the tip either of the left or right side of the base, or on both sides. The *anjung* (veranda) is raised higher than the *lanja bandua* (ante room) (Fig. 11.8).

The layout of the house includes indoor and outdoor spaces (Fig. 11.9). It has separate spaces for men and women. This separation of spaces remains a priority in the matrilineal custom requiring women to be

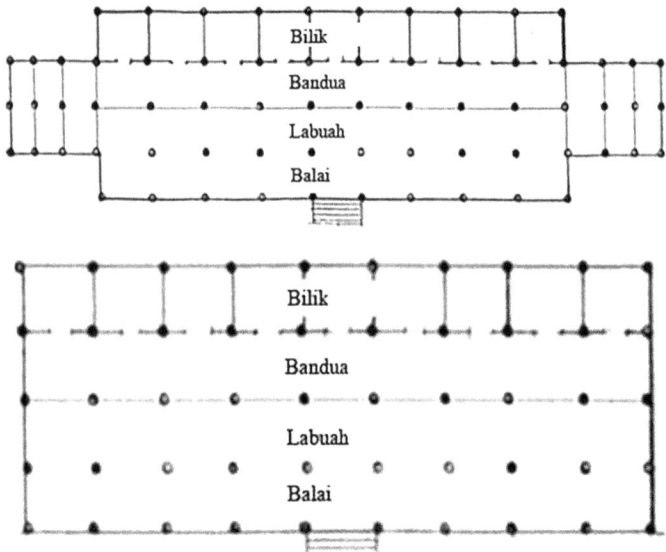

Fig. 11.8 Differences between ceremonial house with and without *anjung* (verandas) (Bahauddin et al., 2012)

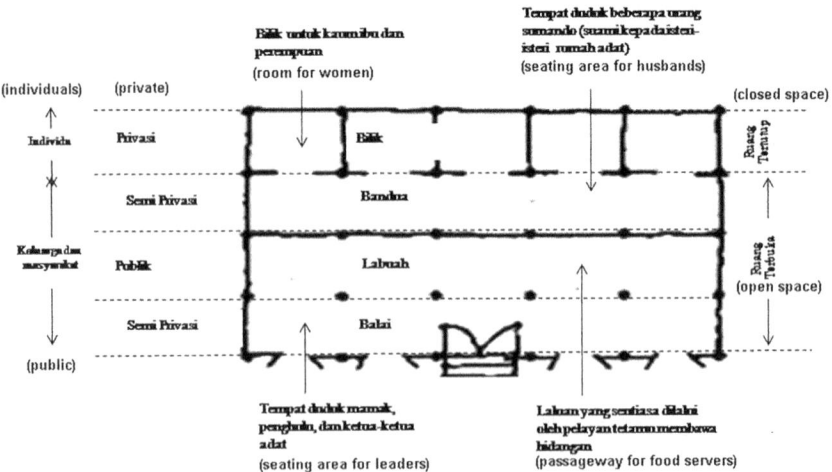

Fig. 11.9 Distribution function concept and interior space layout (Bahauddin et al., 2013)

protected and respected, especially for the dignity of the *bundo kanduang* (matriarch) (Is, 2000).

Spaces in the house are divided into front or middle space and back. The front room or centre space is an open area consisting of the *lanja balai* (foyer), *labuah* (open space), *bandua* (ante room) and is used as a main space for carrying out community meetings (Asri, 2004). The back space is an enclosed area consisting of the *lanja bilik* (room) reserved for married daughters. In general, the rooms at the back or at the side of the space are private and not everyone is allowed to enter them.

The interior layout of the house is divided into three spaces, private, semi-private, and public (Asri, 2004; Is, 2000). Such spatial distributions indirectly divide these spaces for individual, family, and community activities either for daily chores or during a celebration. The *lanja bilik* (room) at the back is used to provide shelter to the women and their husbands, the *urang sumando*, as well as their children.

This space is categorised as private and used only for individual activities, whereas the *lanja balai* (foyer), *labuah* (open space), and *bandua* (ante room) are used as family and communal activity spaces. The *lanja bandua* (ante room) and *lanja bala* (foyer) are semi-private spaces because they are used as the family seating area for several *urang sumando*—husbands and women, the *mamak* (brother of the mother's side), the leader of the community, and the leaders for performing rituals (Is, 2000). The *lanja bandua* (ante room) also serves as a waiting area for house occupants. The *lanja balai* (foyer) serves as a seating area for male guests during rituals and is known as the honourable chamber. The *lanja labuah* (open space) is also a public space that is a circulation area for food servers during ceremonies. This layout in the space planning gives comfort in concordance with the family and the community's social hierarchies. Thus, during a ceremony, everyone in attendance is aware of his/her position in the house. In this house, a married daughter is given the privilege of having a room (Asri, 2004; Ng, 2006). Newly married couples are given privacy and have special rooms at the house end (Fig. 11.10). If there are new married couples, the couples who had gotten married earlier will move to the middle room. The process continues until there is no room left for the old couples, triggering the need to build a new home. The internal circulation is designed and laid out to provide comfort and

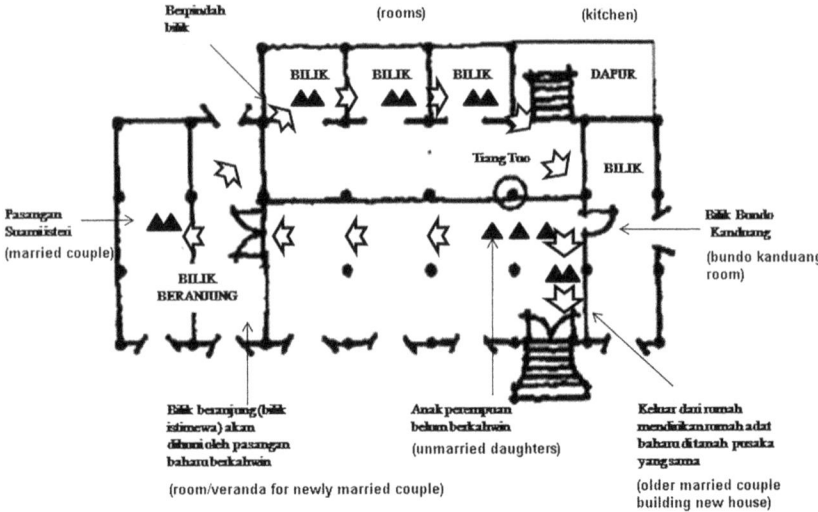

Fig. 11.10 Space circulation for married daughters (Bahauddin et al., 2013)

security to occupants (Ng, 2006; Azwar, 2001). The verandas are used as seating areas for honoured guests such as the community and ritual leaders. The veranda space at times is also used as a bedroom for the newly married daughter with a more private location. The floor is raised both on the right and left ends.

Cultural and Architectural Sustainability

The architectural features of the *rumah gadang* stem from the values of society adhering to customs and culture (Is, 2000). The culture is reflected in the fact that the architecture is centred on rituals, philosophy, and old beliefs as practised in the matrilineal system (Soeroto, 2005; Erman et al., 1981).

The ukang tuo or a skilled constructor and *bundo kanduang* (matriarch) would take a few days to determine the appropriate site. The determination of this site based on the elements of rituals and customs and cultural beliefs has been passed on through generations. Problematic sites will be abandoned due to the beliefs that the residents and family may encounter domestic problems if they still live at the site, for the Minangkabau people still strongly believe in the existence of supernatural elements (Asri, 2004). In practice, the determination of a location to build a house requires investigation before the construction work can take place. This belief takes into consideration the safety of occupants as practised in sustainable architecture and the environment. It demonstrates that the sustainability of the architecture and culture go hand in hand to guide the harmony and well-being of the community. Minangkabau culture cannot be separated from the *rumah gadang*. The body size measurements of *bundo kanduang* (matriarch) will be used to build the house. This is in view of the importance of the main occupant of the house, the owner and heir, who spends her life in the house. Positions of her standing, sitting, and lying down will determine the house comfort scales such as for windows, doors, and floor heights in the house. The window height is based on a woman of adult height sitting in a cross-legged position, in a position that allows her to look out into the surroundings (Asri, 2004). Based on the requirements of the ventilation system and lighting, the house used nature as an element of energy. Air and light vents were designed on the walls of the building. Shapes were carved with motifs from nature such as plants (Fig. 11.11) and geometry (Fig. 11.12).

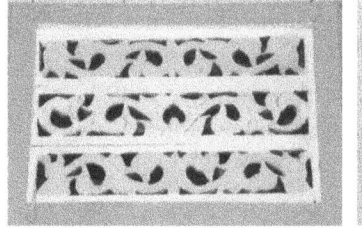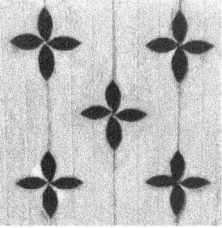

Fig. 11.11 Air and light vents carved with plant motifs (Bahauddin et al., 2013)

Fig. 11.12 Carved geometrical motifs (Bahauddin et al., 2013)

Architectural Sustainability

The architectural components were introduced according to functions, culture, and architecture, which provide for harmony and comfort to individuals, families, and communities. Thus, the cultural sustainability of the architecture has remained and is still passed down to today's generation. It cannot be denied that when constructing this type of house, it is perceived as one of unique cultural heritage of architectural importance derived from cultural elements such as from the matrilineal system. It is made stronger with the influence of a tribal society, lineage, ethnicity, and maternal authority, as well as the inheritance of the estate. The elements of this culture have been embedded from the early stages of the construction of the house until it is in use (Bahauddin et al., 2014). This clearly shows that the philosophical and cultural traditions in using the universe as a guide direct the community towards the right way of life or celebrate ritualistic ceremonies in a comfortable and harmonious state, housed by a traditional architectural environment and culture in view of their sustainable conditions. The cultural philosophy of nature was manifested in the house through the vagaries of decorative carvings on the walls, ventilation systems, and natural lighting systems. Its walls are decorated with carvings and quirks of nature such as plants that symbolise the nature of the Minangkabau cultural philosophy.

Climatic Considerations

The people believe that nature can give peace to humans. Moreover, natural elements, such as sunlight and ventilation, can have a big impact on energy saving in a traditional house (Bahauddin, 2012). The people build a house based on the configuration of a human body, where the roof is assumed to be the head, the walls are the body, and pillars serve as legs (Idrus, 1996). Therefore, all these elements have important functions in the house. Overall, these elements have a cultural philosophy in turning a house into a sustainable building. A high curved sloping roof structure (Fig. 11.13) is not only designed to provide cool ventilation in the house, but the roof, being taper-shaped, is capable of draining rainwater at appropriate speed throughout the year. Initially, the material used to make the roof is of *ijuk* or palm fronds, which allow cool natural air into the house, but now the roof material is made of zinc. The roof over the staircase can provide shade from the sun in the hot season and cover during the rainy season.

House columns are assumed to be part of the foot and the first architectural component to be erected in a house construction. These columns

Fig. 11.13 Curved roof (Bahauddin et al., 2012)

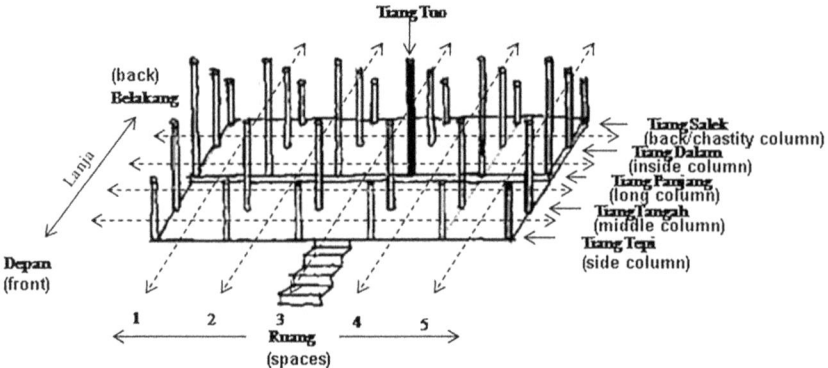

Fig. 11.14 Column positions for five-space *rumah gadang* (Bahauddin et al., 2012)

(Fig. 11.14) have names and functions, including the *tiang tepi*—side columns, *tiang tangah*—middle columns, *tiang panjang*—long columns, *tiang dalam*—inside columns, and *tiang salek*—back columns. There are also two additional types of columns: *tiang temban*—intermediate columns, and *tiang anjung*—columns for verandas in the Koto Piliang house. There is also a column called *tiang tuo*—the main column. According to custom and ritual beliefs, the *tiang tuo* must be mounted first before the other row of columns is installed. In practical terms, the *tiang tuo* indicates the limit of the front and back and beginning and end of the house (Is, 2000).

Additionally, during construction, the *bundo kanduang* (matriarch) will be given the honour to pull a rope tied to the column along with the community as a symbolic gesture to introduce the homeowners to the community. The influence demonstrates a strong matrilineal kinship in the *rumah gadang*. After the *tiang tuo* is erected, other columns are laid with the distance between columns at approximately five *eto* (50 cm) or 250 cm or 8 feet (Is, 2000; Idrus, 1996). Side columns called *tiang penegur/tiang tepi* are columns that are supposed to greet guests before they enter the house. This is followed by the *tiang tangah*—the middle columns, known as the eight columns symbolising servers during ceremonies held in the house. The *tiang panjang*, the long column, is also known as the unity column, the tallest among the columns; and the *tiang tuo* is among these long columns. The *tiang dalam* is located between the *lanja bandua* and a room known as the *putri berkurung*—the hidden princess, as the rooms can only be owned by women. The *tiang salek* is also known as the chastity column that protects the dignity of women in rooms away from prying eyes. These columns are installed with a five-degree slope. The structure is flexible and strong, able to withstand earthquakes, which occur frequently. The stronger the tremors, the stronger the columns become. The floor is mounted high, supported by tall columns. The idea is to provide security to inhabitants and protect residents from the threat of wild and poisonous animals and avoid the threat of floods that can occur at any time. In addition, this structure is also capable of channelling cool air under the house and into the house. The sun is also able to shine directly underneath the house and can reduce the moisture trapped in the space, which can be used for other functions. The *rumah gadang* are apparent in applying the construction system of mortise and tenon joint.

Analysis

The creative community uses the universe as a guide. They use resources that are available to make a perfect house without the use of modern materials. Such a system would result in the construction of the building structure that is flexible in the event of an earthquake. The wall structure is one of the key elements in the house. The analogy is that the human body is viewed as a wall that is beautifully decorated with accessories and carvings of various means according to function. An important requirement inherent in the house's wall is the numbers of openings in the front and reduced at the back. The purpose of these windows is to create natural ventilation to provide fresh and cool air in the house. Bedrooms have no windows to avoid intrusions into the room through the windows. However, the walls are made of bamboo that can provide natural ventilation to compensate for the lack of windows.

The Strength of *Adat* in the Matriarchal Structure and Its Slow Shift

The Minangkabau, known as the largest matriarchal society in the world, has an underlying matrilineal organisation that governs by inheritance, property, and the *adat* (custom). It remains strong to this day despite numerous external factors. The untouchable elements in long-lived customs and traditions are permitted and even a conflict based on these elements can become irrefutable. An oppositional mode appears every time a new element arises in which the *adat* remains secure and untouched. Some new elements will be completely rejected whilst others will be integrated. Such a dualistic concept helps the 'traditional' lifestyle to survive, and the new elements can become part of it. This structure can be seen throughout the history of the heartland of West Sumatera. The *adat* distinguishes between different levels of importance (Stark, 2013):

- *Adat nan sabana adat* (the *adat* which is truly *(sebenar) adat*): This *adat* is the core of the Minangkabau way of life related to the religion, namely Islam. This means it governs what is allowed or forbidden according to the religion (Anwar, 1997). But it also contains the matrilineal way of life (Amir, 2007).
- *Adat nan diadatkan* (the *adat* which was made to *adat*): This *adat* takes the words and sayings conveyed by the ancestors as points of reference. Parts of this *adat* never change (Anwar, 1997). It could be a core element with a flexible element allowing the acceptance of decisions passed through consensus.
- The other two forms of *adat*, *adat istiadat* and the *adat nan teradat*. The *adat nan teradat* (the *adat* that accidentally became *adat*) covers lifestyle (Amir, 2007), and *adat istiadat* regulates daily ceremonies like marriage and birth; however, these differ from village to village.

The many categories of the *adat* indicate how the customs are deeply embedded in the cultural attributes of the community brought on through generations. The Minangkabau *matriarchaat* has managed to resist and accommodate the patrilineal influences of immigrant kings, traders, and religious proselytizers. To this day, the Minangkabau people are aware of the threat to their 'matriarchal' customs posed by modernity (Sanday, 2002). In Minangkabau, the conflict is not only recognised but institutionalised within the system itself. Conflict is seen dialectically as essential to achieving the integration of society (Abdullah, 1966). Experts argue that if peripheral elements are allowed to change, core elements will remain fundamentally the same (Errington, 1984). In 1999, the central government promoted an autonomous regional government in the various districts. This policy aimed to support the numerous cultures and societies of the country. Many local governments in West Sumatera promoted the unique Minangkabau way of life. The term *desa* was replaced by the term *nagari* in 2001 (Sanday, 2002). Many government buildings use the 'traditional' architecture. These are signs that the local government wants to promote the established lifestyle.

Conclusions

The influences of the matrilineal system and the leadership of the matriarch are apparent in the *rumah gadang*. In Western Sumatera, the differences in the Minangkabau house design with and without verandas of different levels are caused by the differences in the governance of the customary systems of Bodi Caniago and Koto Piliang. However, the matrilineal influence on the architecture is very apparent. The womenfolk are the main beneficiaries, along with residents inhabiting the house and authorities that have the right to design a home formed in a unique way. Even the men are given small roles during a celebratory ceremony. Architectural elements in the ceremonial house reflect the culture and customs of the matrilineal society that need to be acknowledged by the unique culture of Minangkabau society. The strength of the matrilineal influence can be seen in the layout of the interior, as space design is dominated and controlled by the women. Spaces for the young, older, unmarried, newly married, and 'have been married' women are adequately provided. The architectural features and design of the Minangkabau house can have an impact on sustainable design that fit the culture and natural environment. Sustainability can be seen in the beliefs, philosophies, and rituals alone, but less so in the reduction of energy and resources used in modern technology. Ultimately, the layout of the space is consistently creating spaces to provide harmonious social relations, involving the lives of individuals, families, and communities in connection with the environment. Such approaches to design can provide comfort and harmony to occupants living with nature.

References

Abdullah, T. (1966, Oct.). *Adat and Islam: An examination of conflict in Minangkabau* (pp. 2–24). Indonesia No. 2. Southeast Asia Program Publications: Cornell University Press.

Abidin, M. J. (2012). *Tinjauan Tentang Nilai-nilai Dasar Adat Minangkabau.*

Ahmad, A. G. (2010). *Pemuliharaan bangunan warisan di Malaysia: Pengalaman dan cabaran masa hadapan.* Penerbit Universiti Sains Malaysia.

Amir, M. S. (1997). *Adat Minangkabau: Pola dan tujuan hidup orang Minang* (Vol. 38). Mutiara Sumber Widya.

Amir, M. S. (2007). *Adat Minangkabau. Pola dan Tujuan Hidup Orang Minang.* PT Mutiara-Sumber Widya.

Anwar, C. (1997). *Hukum Adat Indonesia. Meninjau Hukum Adat Minangkabau.* PT Rineka Cipta.

Asri, S. (2004). *Prinsip-prinsip pembinaan rumah adat minangkabau.* Doctoral dissertation, Universiti Teknologi Malaysia.

Astuti, F. (2004). *Perempuan dalam seni pertunjukan minangkabau: Suatu tinjauan gender* (pp. 1–211). Kalika.

Azwar, W. (2001). *Matrilokal dan status perempuan dalam tradisi bajapuik: studi kasus tentang perempuan dalam tradisi bajapuik.* Galang Press.

Bahauddin, A. (2012). The traditional malay Melaka house of Malaysia: The architectural and cultural heritage in Kazimee. *BA Heritage and Sustainability in the Islamic Bulit Environment,* 93–110.

Bahauddin, A., Hardono, S., Abdullah, A., & Maliki, N. Z. (2012). The Minangkabau house: Architectural and cultural elements. *WIT Transactions on Ecology and the Environmental, 165,* 20.

Bahauddin, A., Hardono, S., Abdullah, A., & Maliki, N. Z. (2013). The Minangkabau house–a vision of sustainable culture and architecture. *International Journal of Design & Nature and Ecodynamics, 8*(4), 311–324.

Bahauddin, A., Aldrin, A. B., & Zarifah, M. N. (2014). The matrilineal architectural values of the construction of the Minangkabau house. *Journal of Architecture and Built Environment, 41*, 55–56.

Edison & Nasrun. (2010). *Tambo Minangkabau: Budaya Dan Hukum Adat Di Minangkabau* (p. 2). Kristal Multimedia.

Erman, M., Boestami, Moechtar, M. S., Zaiful, A., & Nusjirwan, A. (1981). *Rumah Gadang Minangkabau*. Proyek Pengembangan Permuseuman Sumatera Barat.

Errington, F. K. (1984). *Manners and meaning in West Sumatra. The social context of consciousness*. Yale University Press.

Fox, J. J. (1993). Comparative perspectives on Austronesian houses: An introductory essay. *Inside Austronesian houses: Perspectives on domestic designs for living, 1*–28.

Geertz, H. (1963). *Indonesian cultures and communities* (p. 84). HRAF Press: New Haven.

Gilbert, K. (2002). Living contradictions. *The Women's Review of Books, 20*(1), 25–26.

Hamka. (2006). *Islam dan Adat Minangkabau* (p. 7–17, 161–171). Pustaka Dini.

Hashim, W., & Nasir, A. H. (2014). *The traditional southeast Asian house*. ITBM.

Hermayulis. (2008). Peranan dan Kedudukan Perempuan Melayu dalam Masyarakat Matrilineal Hildred Geertz. In T. Ruth & McVey (Ed.), *Indonesian Cultures and Communities*. Rev. ed. (New Haven: HRAF, 1967), p. 80.

Ibrahim, N. (1993). *Adat Perpatih: perbezaan dan bersamaannya dengan adat Temenggung*. Fajar Bakti.

Idrus, Y. (1996). *Rumah tradisional Negeri Sembilan : Satu analisis Seni BIna Melayu* (p. 1-3, 5-9, 116-129). Fajar Bakti.

Is, S. (2000). *Kajian Nilai-Nilai Budaya Pada Ekspresi Tata Ruang Dalam Rumah Adat Minangkabau: Kes Kajian Luhak Tanah Datar Sumatera Barat* (pp. 1, 4–5, 42–44, 66, 84–87, 105, 131–132, 136–147,180, 182, 185–186). Tesis PhD, Universiti Teknologi Malaysia, Johor.

Jayatri, A. (2001). *Rencana Induk Lanskap Kawasan Wisata Budaya Komplek Istana Pagaruyung, Sumatera Barat*. Doctoral dissertation, Bogor Agricultural University (IPB).

Kamaruzzaman. (2012). *Budaya Alam Minangkabau: Falsafah & Arsitektur Istano Basa Pagaruyung Serta Objek Wisata Lainnya* (pp. 1–4). Tanah Datar.

Kato, T. (1978, April). *Change and continuity in the Minangkabau matrilineal system* (pp. 1–16). JSTOR. No.25. Cornell University Press; Southeast Asia Program Publications at Cornell University.

Manggis, M. R., & Panghoeloe, D. R. (1982). *Minangkabau: sejarah ringkas dan adatnya*. Penerbit Mutiara.

Nasroen, M. (1957). *Dasar Falsafah Adat Minangkabau* (p. 23, 25–26, 33, 44–45). Bulan Bintang.

Ng, C. (2006). Raising the house post and feeding the husband-givers: The spatial categories of social reproduction among the Minangkabau. *Inside Austronesian houses, 121*.

Sanday, P. R. (1998). *Matriarchy as a sociocultural form: An old debate in a new light*. Paper presented at the 16th congress of the Indo-pacific prehistory.

Sanday, P. R. (2002). *Women at the Center. Life in a modern matriarchy*. Cornell University Press.

Selat, N. (1975). *Sistem Sosial Adat Perpatih* (p. 29–52, 120–124). Utusan Melayu (M) Berhad.

Soeroto, M. (2005). *Pustaka Budaya & Arsitektur* (p. 1–4, 21, 34). Myrtle Publishing.

Stark, A. (2013). The matrilineal system of the Minangkabau and its persistence throughout history: A structural perspective Southeast Asia: A multidisciplinary journal. *Vol, 13*, 1–13.

Widya, D. (2001). *Kajian Arsitektur Rumah Tinggal Tradisional Minangkabau Nagari Panyalaian Kabupaten Tanah Datar* (p. 2, 30–31, 42 50). Tesis Sarjana, Universitas Diponegoro.

Yovita, W. (2012). *Budaya Matrilineal Masyarakat Minangkabau Pada Arsitektur Rumah Gadang*. The Minangkabau Matrilineal Culture of the Minangkabau Big House Architecture. Retrieved February 14, 2012, from http://www.scribd.com/doc/46656529/Budaya-Matrilineal-Masyarakat-Minangkabau-pada-Arsitektur-Minangkabau

Yuan, L. J. (1987). *The southeast Asian house: Rediscovering southeast Asiansia's indigenous shelter system*. Institut Masyarakat.

12

The Layered Space: Permutations of the Portico

Tengku Anis Qarihah Raja Abdul Kadir,
Nurhaya Baniyamin, and Shireen Jahn Kassim

The portico is the essence of tropical form and represents the quintessential architectural character of the South East Asian tropics. The variations of the verandah, 'anjung' and 'serambi', can be seen as the 'permutations' of the tropical portico. The portico can be broken down and mapped to unearth a corpus of frontage 'layered' layouts and configurations. In the discourse of tropical architecture, the portico is a part of public space and differs from the 'balcony', which remains an elemental attachment to form, rather than an inherent part of the main structure and space, evolving through centuries as a container of community life. This chapter represents a series of 'open air' deep spaces which occupy a range of frontages of palatial

T. A. Qarihah Raja Abdul Kadir
Centre of Studies Architecture, College of Built Environment, Universiti Teknologi MARA (UiTM), Shah Alam, Malaysia
e-mail: tengku.anis@uitm.edu.my

N. Baniyamin • S. J. Kassim
International Islamic University Malaysia, Kuala Lumpur, Malaysia
e-mail: Nurhaya@iium.edu.my

© The Editor(s) (if applicable) and The Author(s), under exclusive license to Springer Nature Singapore Pte Ltd. 2023
S. Jahn Kassim et al. (eds.), *Eco-Urbanism and the South East Asian City*,
https://doi.org/10.1007/978-981-19-1637-3_12

architecture in South East Asia. The focus on the palatial or aristocratic form stems from the fact that the 'portico', in the case of this complex building type, constitutes the traditional public realm, within which public events and transactions are played out in tropical Asian public life.

On closer inspection, the morphology and typology of these spaces vary according to region or state, particularly in the Malay Nusantara. Seen as the varied expressions of the regions and cultural public realm, they are richly diverse yet seen as having a common root, and it is asserted that they evolved genealogically from the essential archetype of Malay vernacular form. This root form—from the Malay vernacular—has been emphasised in many studies (Mohamad Rasdi et al., 2005; Jahn Kassim et al., 2017) as a common universal origin of local architecture. The chapter begins with a typological case study, which reveals the three essential types of public-private divisions of space, from which a series of varied spaces of the 'portico', showcasing a grammar of Malay architecture, genealogically and climatically rooted and not detached from their social, climatic, and environmental contexts, is discussed.

Introduction

Cultural aspects of place concern meanings related to the environment (Wan Ismail, 2012). A person's perceptions of what entails human quality of life or well-being are shaped by community customs and traditions (Masri et al., 2015). Social and cultural values are mainly contextual, intertwined with the community's way of life, which represents customs, traditions, beliefs, and essential determinants of norms and moral etiquette. Architecture is a manifestation of these intermingling cultural practices (Rashid, 2014). Typological mappings of architectural form are crucial in the absence of a universal framework of theory of space and architecture and thus are necessary for the development of a theoretical framework.

In a region marked by extreme cultural (and architectural) diversity, South East Asian architecture can be said to be combinations, evolutions, and permutations of the tropical portico (constituting the container of public life) with private space. The mappings of these layouts, forms, and facades change across time and space, depicting a rich variation of both space and embellishment, yet they demonstrate and unfold from a common root. The root can be described as the essence of the semi-outdoor space, known as the *anjung* or *serambi* in the Malay region, which have contributed not only to a universal resource in efforts to create, evoke, and apply a modern vernacular but which have also been used in classifying the region's vernacular architecture in regional terms, rather than parochial or nationalistic. The connections of root and variation of form can be unearthed both spatially and stylistically.

The following discussion begins with an attempt to describe the roots of this space and then proceeds to describe how they are located and framed within the public-private divisions of spaces in Malay palaces. Although historically these palaces are linked to idiosyncrasies of the monarch or aristocracy and may have evolved by different events, personalities, and conditions, they still reflect a unifying intrinsic value of a historical continuum in the culture of South East Asia in general and the Malay world in particular—the inherent integration of public spaces as tropical semi-open-air spaces within the seemingly private and compact nature of palaces. Tropical space, in architecture and anthropology, thus reflects a life world and social hierarchies of the local culture, which essentially arise from the nature and cycles of climate. These spaces, examined in greater depth, are inevitably linked and conflated with specific daily and annual cycles and variations, and thus adaptations, in the climatic context of place. Thus, there may be countless variations, yet a recurring spatial transposition and transmutation will evolve from generation to generation and will transfer from one typology to another, i.e. from the house to the palatial scale.

Portico Space

The Malay sociocultural view on the attributes of life, therefore, is the inclusion of cultural values essentially which traces to spaces within the 'house'. In this context, therefore, it signifies a co-existence of people and the environment in line with their cultural values. There exists a combination of the custom-based designation of space within interior spatial organisation. Cosmologically, Idrus (1996) and Masri (2012) emphasised the house form as particularly characterised by the integration or fusion between outdoor and indoor. Thus the *serambi* is an extremely essential part of local architecture, which reflects a particularity of architectural form as a result of the tropical climate and the strong communal values of the population. This is, generally, the 'face' of the house, and its status and position in daily life are symbolised by assertive decorative wood-carvings and ornamental traditions in curved, expressive, and convoluted patterns, emerging from the traditions of woodcarvers and artisans observing ecological forms.

For example, from sociocultural perspectives, the perceivable in spaces, i.e. outdoor and indoor rooms, reflects a culturally linked arrangement and design concept, and Malay families would occupy these spaces in the evenings, and over time, it became a place to receive guests with observed cultural diplomacy and subtlety in the manner of showing respect in receiving guests, acknowledgement of guest status or rank within their social organisation structure and communicating sociocultural boundaries based on the concept of *mahram* (unmarriageable kin) (Wahab et al., 2014) guidance in Islam. The design of these spaces over time inculcated and ensured any persons is to be of *adab* (appropriate manners similar with cultural norms and/or moral etiquette). As Islam influenced the region, Islamic viewpoints of sociocultural interaction (*menjaga batas-batas syarak*) and privacy affected the divisions through defining domains for male and female (Jani & Hussain, 2014). Traditionally the activities occurring in the *serambi* significantly show the cultural manner in which they are managed and executed in their norms and moral etiquette. For instance, the two most significant sociocultural values inculcated within the design of *serambi* are the positioning of the main entrance and the sequencing of future extension for *serambi* space. Essentially, the porch (*rumah tangga*) acts as an open space prior to the main entrance at the *serambi* designated for male guests (Idrus, 1996; Masri, 2012). The main entrance by design is purposively positioned asymmetrically to the overall *serambi* facade.

From *Anjung* to *Balai Penghadapan*

A veranda is a transitional space which is located between the external environment and the interior environment of a building. In tropical life, it inhabits and celebrates the connection between the external and the interior environment. The transitional space acts as a function of linking building residents to the outside surroundings. The transitional space was considered a supplemental space to optimise the comfort of the indoor environment. The gradual spatial transition allows a person entering it to adapt his/her thermal comfort expectations, from the hot outdoors to the cool indoors and vice versa. South East Asian urbanism and its traditions had in their evolutionary existence their own distinctive forms, features, and identities. These had dynamically evolved throughout the centuries and different eras.

What binds local forms is that they are characterised by a layered quality, a variation of semi-outdoor 'porticoes' which evolved from a basic counterpart—the *anjung* or *serambi*. In houses, mansions, and palaces of different sizes and functions, these exhibit different scales, layers, and extent of being elevated and ornamented. The *serambi or anjung* can be defined as a characteristic 'outdoor room' or large protruding veranda which extends from the main body of the house or living room spaces. The Malay word 'se·ram·bi' literally means 'a space that is extended'. The root of this tropical portico in the house can be traced to two main types, either a normal veranda or extension of the living area or the hanging veranda or *serambi gantung* or a split-level veranda. It is the first space in which locals greet guests, entertain, and serve visitors. Sometimes, the portico was built semi-enclosed with lattice detailing or fully enclosed by walls and windows to allow the free flow of air.

Anjung, on the other hand, is more enclosed—like an extended and enclosed porch. These spaces or rooms are extended from the main spaces, whether to the right or left. The rooms are also usually raised up one or two steps to delineate them and are even used as temporary bedrooms and protruding parts at the front of the main building. The *anjung* is a marker or a fulcrum to a home. At times these serve as a final transition space between the public and the private forms.

In the traditional Malay house, the original vernacular elements of the traditional *anjung* and *serambi* are one of the key definitive features of the vernacular. Interiors were composed of specific functions yet within spaces that differed in cool comfort and diffusion of light, namely, the veranda (*serambi*), the front house (*anjung*), the main house (*rumah ibu*), intermediate areas (*selang*), the kitchen (*dapur*), and the washing area (*pelantar*).

While its variants differ, essentially the *serambi* is a covered portico in which the host or owner of the house sits with guests and relaxes and enjoys the evening and night air. At times, it stands at the left and right parts of the house and seen extending from the main building. The veranda often extends to the rear and adjacent to the main room. It is lower in the main room, distinguished by finishing with the surrounding wall or pole position for each corner. It is a symbol of the habit of culture, evolved through centuries with the prevailing climate culture and lifestyle of the traditional population.

While the Malay Nusantara is essentially patriarchal and rooted in the *Temenggung* traditions, *serambi* precedes a longitudinal space. It is a semi-open 'room' attached to the *rumah ibu* (main house). Spatially, the *Temenggung* tradition causes a deep hierarchy of the private realm and a distinctive separation between male and female. The spatial arrangement infused the safeguarding of Islamic views of sociocultural interaction (*menjaga adab dan syarak*) and privacy through defining domains for male and female (Jani & Hussain, 2014). In the Minangkabau, on the other hand, the *serambi* is generally wide ranging from left to right of the house walls, rooted in their matrilineal social organisation and the practice of *merantau* culture. Thus, as presented in Chap. 10, their spatial organisation is wide, rather than 'deep'. Space arises from the principles of communal adjacency, efficiency in family activities, and a spatial hierarchy that uses floor levels differentiated longitudinally. Significantly, the name given to the type of *serambi* is indicative of this inter-relativity. In Negeri Sembilan, *Rumah ibu* is called *Rumah Tengah* (Middle House) (Idrus, 1996). It shows incremental differences from site to site; two of the most significant sociocultural values inculcated within the design of *serambi* are the positioning of the main entrance and the sequencing of future extensions for *serambi* space. On the whole, the space reflects how

Malays observed cultural diplomacy and subtlety in the manner of showing respect to guests, acknowledgement of guest status or rank within their social organisation structure, and communicating sociocultural boundaries.

The analysis of typology of Malay palaces, a critical element of Malay urbanism, reveals frontage spaces which are layered into projections and promenades that continue into landscaped shaded areas and interact seamlessly with the surrounding landscape, other buildings, and outdoor spaces. Then these continue into extensions of other public buildings, such as mosques and madrasahs, which are at times used as a public gathering space and extend into pavilions and bazaars centred around the coolness afforded by the river. Malay civilisations were maritime in nature that grew up near or astride rivers which had particularly thrived from the fifteenth to late nineteenth centuries. Their urban centres, which occupy symbolically charged fields between the palace and the mosque, grew into cities and urban zones. The sites of palaces and gardens are in fact their public urban spaces with the palatial complexes having a 'public extension' which represents the 'urban space of its time'.

Such a shaded continuum of public spaces held functions related to government and were centres of quasi-urban life exhibiting traditional archetypical forms of open-air squares and shaded portico courtyards. Legends in the Malay world refer to the seafaring life in 'the sea of *Malayu*' (Andaya, 2010) within which trade and maritime activities once dominated everyday life and which had eventually become part of the semiotic and spatial expressions of the region and its origins. The geography of the *Malayu Nusantara* is such that its diversified lands lay dispersed in an archipelago and are historically perceived as '*a vast network of seas, hindered by passages of land*' rather than land hindered by swathes of seas (Andaya, 2010). As the tropical climate is an intrinsic factor in the shaping and characterisation of such forms, the forms and its terminologies arise from the presence of radiant cooling at night and from the sociocultural needs of families and communities, of such wide, elevated, and projected portico spaces in houses and palaces.

From Pre-Islam to Post-Islam

To understand the variation of the portico in the region, one must review the entire evolution of palatial configurations, seen as different permutations and combinations of the public and the private, the 'wide' and the 'deep' from the fifteenth century onwards. These frontages are, in essence, a continuum of public spaces and public arena. They are essentially tropical shaded structures and halls, spatially and functionally enlarged and tectonically ornamented. Between the basic unit of the house and the complex place, there are varying sizes and scales, each with different combinations between portico, walkways, frontages of aristocratic homes, and pavilion-type spaces. From afar, these frontages appear as a unified front and appear as collonaded recesses or shaded projections and, in their most enhanced versions, as projections, ornamented by delicate artisanal embellishment, crafted as a status symbol of the elite or the aristocracy, elevating space with associated brackets, finials, filigrees, and balustrades.

The typology of the portico can be said to originate from the humble *serambi* or *anjung* space of the residential domestic type. It is an inherent space-type in vernacular architecture from which emerge variants of the *pendopo* or *joglo*, whose forms and articulations predate the Islamic era in the Nusantara region. The most basic *joglo* house was essentially two main spaces, one internal and one external and both constituting an artificial habitat in which cultural values are manifested via values of function, meaning, and symbolism of the particular region. As a cosmological emblem of manifesting self-orientation, this external–internal or outdoor–indoor shape of the house becomes a way of materialising human existence in the tropical environment. In this specific typology, the Javanese house is generally square or rectangular in form, fronted by another semi-open space. This dual form—which can be traced from sacred to the mundane of architectural types—is a form of fusion of opposites, or a kind of local 'yin and yang', indicating stability, rationality, regularity, and visual clarity in the Nusantara architecture. Tracing back to pre-Islamic era of Hindu Buddhism belief, the *joglo* house can be seen as a symbol of the transcendent in the vertical measurement (from ground to roof form) and immanent in the horizontal measurement (from external to semi-open to internal). It not only represents the reverence traditional societies had for the sacred, or the skies, but the close rapport between individual and community, as an almost inseparable symbiotic form. The Javanese system of thought prioritises such spatial orders in organising space and phenomena rather than a temporal order (Santosa, 2000). Space and time are fundamental matters in Javanese cosmology and are essential in their relationship with matters of nature, which has rules or principles which are later referred to as natural law. The principle of causality becomes one of the basic matters in the field of the *jagad gedhe* (macrocosm, universe) and *jagad cilik* cosmology (microcosm, humankind) (Siswanto, 2005). Human life in the Javanese cultural environment is essentially based on four points of view, consisting of belief, social ties, personal expression (personality), and meaning. The Kraton and the connection with the people is a strong one. There is a genuine affection and respect for leadership amongst the people. This palace complex is the bridge between old and new and the faith that binds the cultures. There are many surrounding pavilions at the Kraton (Fig. 12.1). A green square called Alun-alun Lor or the north square is set to be the front side of the palace, with large banyan trees guarding its centre. Alun-alun Kidul or the south square is a destination renowned for its festive evening ambiance located at the palace's north–south invisible horizontal axis.

In the context of the basic Javanese house type, residents will meet with other people in an open space in front. Boundaries of the open space that block visual and physical interaction are minimised to allow for intensive relations with the outside world. The *pendhapa* is bounded only by elevated floor terraces, lines of columns, and its shade. The composition of the *joglo* house consists of a pair of rooms, namely the front/outside and back/inside (Fig. 12.2). These rooms actualise the main idea in the domestic setting, namely as a place to live and to build relationships (Santosa, 2000). In the view of the mythological beliefs of society, architectural forms are present as mythic means, as cosmological symbols of the manifestation of the fundamental type of self-orientation, supporting man's presence. The compass is based on the orientation of the four directions and one centre. Spatial concentration and figural representation at

Fig. 12.1 Surrounding pavilions at Kraton. (Source: https://www.indonesia. travel/my/en/destinations/java/yogyakarta/the-kraton.html)

the centre demonstrate that supremacy is attained by focusing on two sides of a dual traits, the exterior and interior, state and family domains, male and female, with the ruler acting as a mediator between the two worlds (Wardani, 2008). Traditionally associated with Javanese aristocrats, the *joglo* form is reserved for the palace, official residence, government estate, and the house of nobles. The word *joglo* also refers to the shape of the roof. It reflects the social and economic status of the owners of the house in the hierarchical Javanese culture. Studying Javanese houses means studying things that are invisible and give breath, placing one's soul in them, and being a part of the concrete as well the symbolic reality (Laurens, 2004).

Thus, in the complex variants that evolved from this basic form, embellished and owned by the region's local nobles, these spaces become the stage for official and ceremonial and, at times, semi-sacred activities. Public events such as meetings, dances, and ceremonial events, including the performance of traditional arts, such as dances are located in these

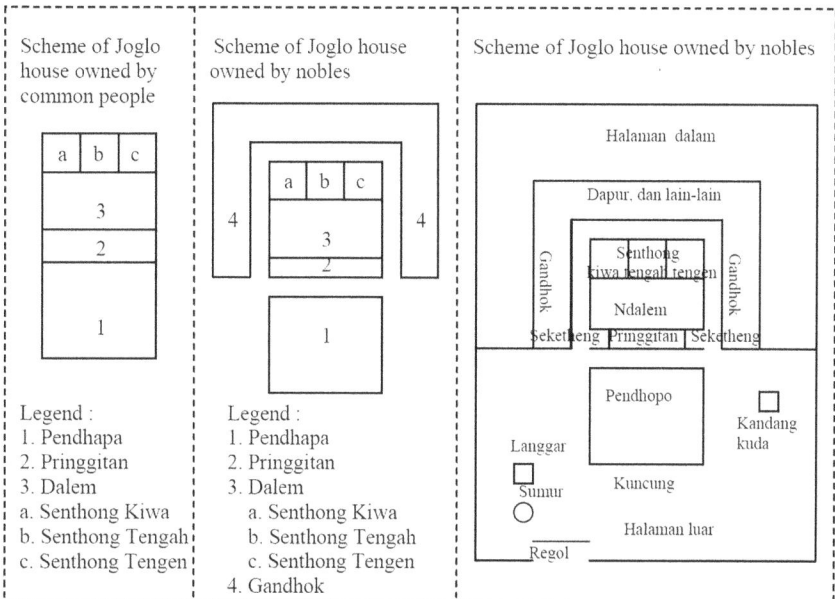

Fig. 12.2 Scheme of *joglo* house complex owned by common people and nobles. (Source: Dakung, 1981/1982: 56, 60)

shaded public spaces. The *Kraton* or the Palace of Yogyakarta is perhaps a complex variant of such a combined outdoor–indoor complex—an epitome of a form of tropicalised spatial evolvement—whose final form was essentially supposed to reflect the Javanese cosmos. In this case, the archetypal portico matured into an elegant complex of pavilions constructed based on local technology and whose physical form merged with local ancient beliefs. Within such a space, the physical and the metaphysical converged into a space that resonated with connections between God, humanity, and the natural realm.

Each feature straddles both cosmological and ecological realms and holds a special symbolic meaning related to the Javanese worldview. Architectural form reflects sky, land, and sea and reverberates through vertical and horizontal lines of Mount Merapi and the Indian Ocean. The Kraton becomes an avatar of its ecology and cosmography and not merely a physical structure. Its location is also significant and seen as being built in the centre, facing directly north towards the majestic Mount Merapi. Its south side was built facing the Indian Ocean, believed to be the abode of *Kanjeng Ratu Loro Kidul*, the Queen of the South Seas and the mystical consort of the sultan. Historically, the original and basic layout of the main building of the *Kraton* began its construction during the reign of Sultan Hamengku Buwono I in 1755–1756. The *Kraton* is used for official functions, political meetings, and as the royal residence. There is a cultural link between the compound and the people. In some ways it is almost a spiritual connection—the *Kraton* architectural form and meaning refer to an ancient and primordial form linked back to the Javanese traditional vernacular space.

Post-Islam

With the advent of Islam and its influence in the region, its impact was subtle, evolutionary, and diffusive, rather than revolutionary and invasive. Pre-Islamic forms were merely 'inflected' towards the Islamic worldview, and ceremonial spaces were transformed into more administrative and functional spaces. These palatial halls became more functionally recognised as 'audience' halls, which were not only formal public spaces but living and active spaces which play a crucial role in Malay-Nusantara civic life. They were known to be locations of community meetings, transactions such as financial and legal centres and administrative and legal spaces, which are connections with the private realm of the Malay world. These were the 'public realm' spaces that have been known to accommodate and facilitate commercial, educational, and social activities and transactions as they provide cool shaded forums and spaces. Porticoes play a key role in defining the public realm in both Western and Eastern civilisations.

The variants and permutations of such spaces, seen as a continuous volume of such shaded porticoes, within which wide colonnades merged with what is known as the *bala*i or open-air pavilions which acted as the meeting points between the 'ruler' and the ruled, particularly with distinctive staircases. For example, political administrative functions such as event court cases and trials were carried out in these spaces. An example

Fig. 12.3 (**a, b, c**) Portico variation; *Rumah Penghulu Ghani* Melaka, *Istana Kadriah* Pontianak, and *Baitul Rahmah* Perak

of how a basic residential house with an extended porch was used for administrative functions. It has a magistrate's court and meeting spaces for the leaders of the community. Such spaces are at times elevated, while spaces occupied by workers, labourers, and local sellers often occupied the ground floor spaces. The extended portico in fact contains a rich variation of morphological shapes as in Fig. 12.3.

Climatic Character of Palatial Portico Space

The *Balai Besar* of Alor Setar, Malaysia, is essentially a 'classical' type *istana* (Jahn Kassim et al. (2019), which combines an open-air pavilion-type portico and extension of the main structure to the palace with colonnades extending into a public zone and functions as a welcoming space. Originally *Balai Besar* was a wooden structure built by Sultan Muhammad Jiwa Zainal Adilin Shah (1710–1760). Spatially it is a space within an urban public space and is a palace that is accessible to the public within a palatial complex. It is sometimes known as *Balai Penghadapan* (Grand Audience Hall). Kedah was historically a state that paid tribute to Siam and thus the palace had survived several attacks from Siam and Bugis forces which had caused the building to be severely damaged. The original structure of the *Balai Besar* was based on the proportions of a Malay house with the distinctive *bumbung panjang* (oblong roof). The *Dewan Balai* are the south and north extension wings. The *Pejabat Balai*

Besar, located under *Balai Siak*, were formerly used to administrate and monitor all events in *Balai Besar*. However, during the eighteenth century, spaces at the ground floor were used as a storage area to store rice and firewood. Verandas are located adjacent to the audience hall, on its both left and right sides (Fadzidah & Mansor, 2015). Its collonaded spaces are double volume in nature, and its extensions reflect the climatic function of these extensions, which effectively shades the masonry core of the structure.

The Palace of Sultan Mansur II of Terengganu is an early 'Malay-Classical' era structure built approximately during the earliest years of Sultan Mansur II's reign from 1831 to 1837. As described by Muhammad Salleh et al. (1992), it is essentially a timber palace—now destroyed—with a deep planned palace and was built immediately after Sultan Mansur II ascended to the throne by replacing Sultan Daud as the Sultan of Terengganu. The document *Sejarah Darul Iman Hingga* 1361H= 1942M by Muhammad Saleh bin Haji Awang et al. (1992) contains a sketch of an isometric drawing of the palace, drawn by Dato' Seri Nara Wangsa (Encik Muhammad Ali bin Abdul Rahim). In layout terms, it represents the tripartite deep floor layout consisting of an elongated pavilion. In climatic terms, the depth of the *Balairung Seri* is seen as a climatic feature which shades and protects the inner *Balai* as well as the house of the royal family. The *Balairung Seri* and the inner *Balai* are separated by an internal wall that extends as an external wall at the palace yard (Figs. 12.4 and 12.5).

 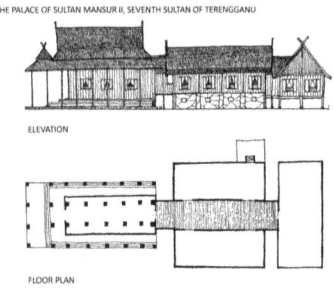

Figs. 12.4 and 12.5 Dato' Seri Nara Wangsa impression of Sultan Mansur II's palace. (Source: Sejarah Darul Iman Hingga 1361H=1942M and reconstruction of the palace of Sultan Mansur II (1833) through archival sources)

Sultan Abdul Samad's palace, Selangor, is a later Malay-Classical palace located in Langat. It was constructed in 1876, two decades before the Bandar Jugra palace was constructed. The palace has the conventional tri-cameral layout of a Malay royal Istana of the period. At the front part there was a porch and an entrance to the *balairung* or the audience hall. The *balairung* floor layout may be square in shape and was surrounded by columns that supported the roof of the space. It was enclosed by a wall made of wood stacked and assembled in a unique way, unlike other Malay royal Istana. The roof was two-tiered and covered by shingles that were most likely made of baked earth (terracotta). The other two parts of the building were the harem and dwellings of the sultan and his royal family. As described by Gullick (1975), the palace has the purest style of Malay architecture without any Western influence anywhere. According to Gullick (1975), the palace was in rich brown, red colour, most probably Chengal timber due to its durability and strength. Multiple spaces existing in the palace relate to passageways while keeping the spatial hierarchy intact, as a study of Gullick (1975) found:

> *The dwelling consists of the Sultan's house, a broad open passage, and then the women's house or harem. At the end of the above passage is the audience hall, and the front entrance to the Sultan's house is through a large porch which forms a convenient reception room… from this back passage a ladder with rungs about two feet apart, leads into the Sultan's house, and a step-ladder into the women's house.*

As applied to the tri-cameral layout, it can be concluded that the palace was divided into three main parts, the audience hall or *balairung*, the harem, and the dwellings of the royal family (Figs. 12.6 and 12.7).

Tengku Seri Akar Palace, in Kota Bahru, was built in 1886 by Almarhum Sultan Muhammad II as a wedding gift to his granddaughter, Tengku Mariam Tengku Kembang Putri. According to Nuradli Zakaria (2015), the palace was originally named Istana Tengku Puteri, or Tengku Puteri palace. It was later changed to Istana Tengku Seri Akar in 1933, because it is used as the dwelling of the eldest child of Tengku Puteri, Tengku Seri Akar Ahmad Zainal Abidin. Nuraidil Zakaria (2015) stated that Seri Akar palace was believed to be the twin of Istana Tengku Bongsu.

THE ORIGINAL PALACE OF SULTAN ABDUL SAMAD, BANDAR LANGAT, 1876

ELEVATION

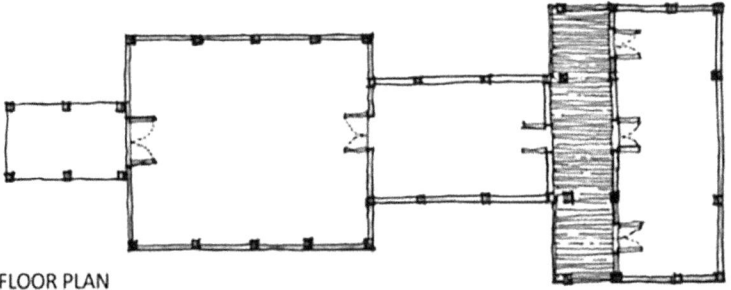

FLOOR PLAN

Figs. 12.6 and 12.7 (Source: The Bloomfield Douglas Diary Selangor 1876 and Reconstruction of Sultan Abdul Samad's original palace (1876) through archival sources)

Structurally, Tengku Seri Akar palace is mainly influenced by Western architecture. This is because it was not built on stilts, unlike the traditional Kelantan house, where the house of the people and aristocrat or nobles is differentiated by the number of stilts. If a house has 12 stilts, then it is a house of nobles or the royal family.

The tripartite floor layout existed in this palace just like other Malay royal palaces (Nuraidil Zakaria, 2015), where the front-most part is the audience hall, then the inner hall, and in the back is the sultan's and the royal families' dwelling (Figs. 12.8 and 12.9).

THE SERI AKAR PALACE, KELANTAN

ELEVATION

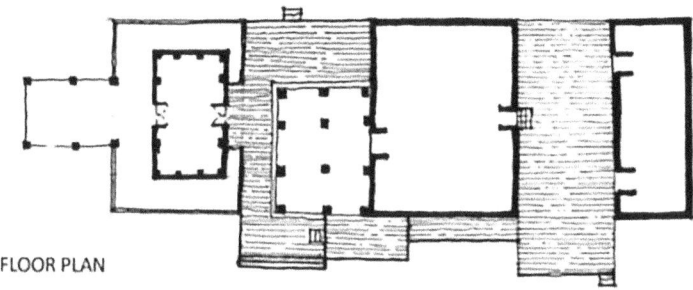

FLOOR PLAN

Figs. 12.8 and 12.9 Isometric drawing of Istana Tengku Seri Akar. (Source: http://pp-sk.blogspot.com/2015/04/siap-2-istana-tengku-sri-akar-robohnya.html   and reconstruction of elevation and floor plan of Istana Tengku Seri Akar through archival sources (by authors))

The deep plan typology is reflected in most basic terms in the elevated and all-timber form represented by the timber vernacular structures of Sulawesi and Kalimantan. In Makasar, Sulawesi, an elevated all-timber structure still survives as a palace, with the entire ground floor in columnar style, with repetitive brackets and decorative pediments. What was originally an open-air structure, characterised externally and internally by a row of striking columns (Fig. 12.10) and a simple extended covered staircase (like the Malige), had evolved into a hybrid masonry, monumental, and refined space. Yet in all cases, the space is basically for ministers, nobles, and public citizens who would traditionally sit to the left and right of the dais of the sultan. These spaces were occupied by courtiers who were individuals bearing responsibility for the royal artefacts and

a   b

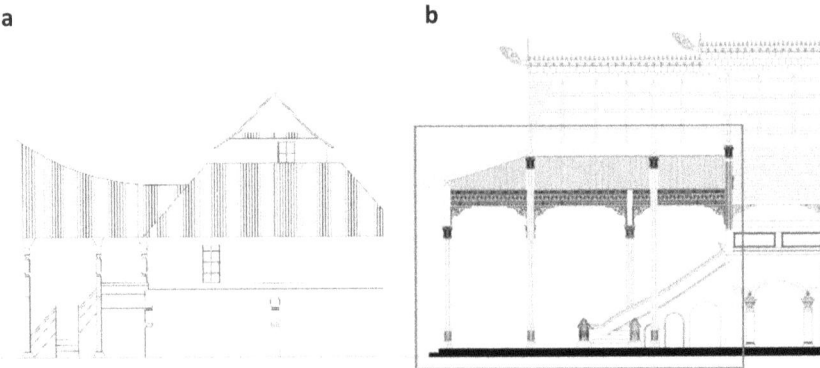

Fig. 12.10 (a) Rokan Palace and (b) *Balai Besar*, Kedah: sectional elevation showing details of open-air structures with extended 'porticoes' adorned with ornamental devices. (Source: IIUM Heritage Lab)

banners, entertaining foreign envoys, and discussing state matters with
fellow subordinates.

The 1700s Rokan Palace, surviving as an all-timber structure built by
the Minangkabau diaspora in Central Sumatera, has a similar formal
extension which covers its staircase. This (Fig. 12.10a) recall the same
language but in a more ancient, purist, and more basic and less ornamented form. Figure 12.10b is the hybrid form of *Balai Besar*, Kedah,
showing the evolution of the open-air forms and tall columns from an
all-timber vernacular expression to a hybrid, extended form of the portico.

In Kelantan's Istana Jahar, there is a similar open-air projection, built
in 1887, but with a less protruding projection, as the audience hall
appears to be pulled more into the interior. Unlike the Kedah palace, the
Jahar audience hall is partially located within the palatial interior space,
while the extended portico is used mainly for the sultan to appear to the
people in key events. After several renovations, the current frontage demonstrates the use of masonry columns and wrought iron balustrades. As
Fadzidah and Hamiruddin (2005) report, the present version of the palace was a result of successive renovations. In 1900–1905, the palace was
upgraded from a single-storey structure to a double-storey building.
Between 1905 and 1920, the frontal portico was upgraded to masonry
elements but sustained within a semi-octagonal form (Fig. 12.11).

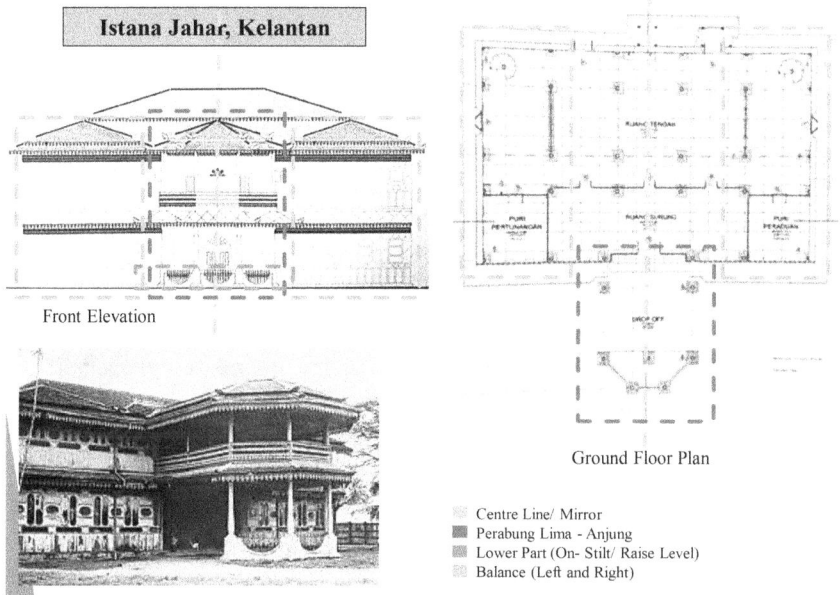

Front Elevation

Ground Floor Plan

▨ Centre Line/ Mirror
▥ Perabung Lima - Anjung
▨ Lower Part (On- Stilt/ Raise Level)
▨ Balance (Left and Right)

Fig. 12.11   Current Kelantan Jahar Palace (present time) elevation and floor plan: now a royal museum in Kota Bahru, Kelantan, showing the half 'projection' of the portico and partial masonry columns (Source: Tengku Anis et al., 2017)

Review of Typology of Layouts and Variants of 'Portico' Space

There are mainly three classifications of plan and typology observed, and the reconstruction of indigenous palaces done with references through archival sources, three typologies can be observed which can be described as follows.

The Compact Typology

This is the layout in which both public and private domains of the palatial complex are closed and physically part of one complex. The buildings such as Istana Patani, Istana Tengku Sri Akar, and Istana Lembah Kuala

Kangsar are part of this typology. Throughout the year, a gate or wall was built to separate the public and private domains (Fig. 12.12).

Examples of a type 1 palace which survive to the present day are Kadriah Palace, which is located in Kecamatan Pontianak Timur, Kota Pontianak, Kalimantan Barat, Indonesia, and Tengku Seri Akar Palace located in Kelantan.

Both palaces are categorised under the same typology, but their floor layouts are a bit different. Istana Kadriah has an elongated form, with the spatial zoning starting with the public area (entrance porch), then progressing to the semi-public space, which is the main hall of the palace. The private spaces of the palace, mainly rooms, are located at each side of the main hall.

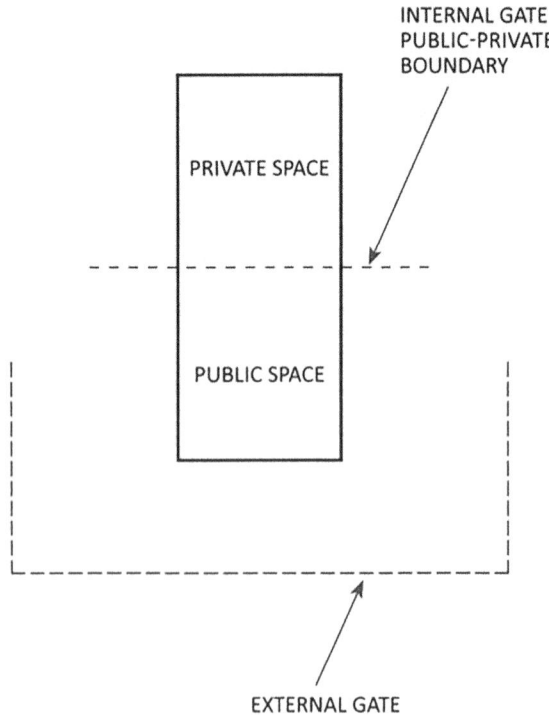

Fig. 12.12 TYPE 1: Compact form and divided by internal gate (Istana Tengku Seri Akar, Istana Tengku Bongsu)

Istana Tengku Seri Akar has an elongated floor layout, with the spatial zoning starting from the *balairung seri* as the public space, the inner *balai* as semi-public space, and the dwelling of the royal family as the private space.

The T-Shaped Typology

This refers to the typology and layout in which the frontal part of the palaces is elongated, and the back sections are arranged perpendicular to the frontal part. Istana Rokan, Istana *Balai Besar* Alor Setar, Istana Langkat of 1920s, and Istana Bandar of 1909 are the example of palaces categorised under this typology.

This typology has evolved into major architectural and urban heritage in Malaysia and Indonesia, such as *Balai Besar* Alor Setar. Various challenges and limitations arose during the study with structures that had been burnt, razed, or merely destroyed through human choice, neglect, or hazards endemic to the humid tropical context (Fig. 12.13).

Istana Rokan and Istana *Balai Besar* were categorised under type 2, which means both palaces are divided by internal separation, yet both

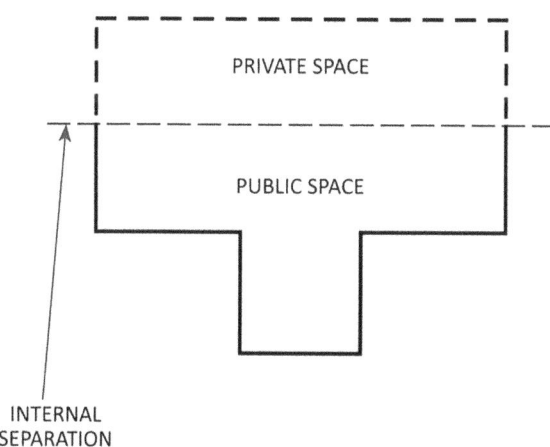

INTERNAL
SEPARATION

Fig. 12.13 TYPE 2: T-shaped and divided by internal separation (Istana Kota Wang and Istana Bandar Jugra)

palaces have floor layouts that are distinctive from one another. Istana Rokan has its *balai* at its first floor, which can lead to two semi-public spaces, which include rooms located at both sides of the building. The private space, which is the bedroom of the sultan, is located upstairs. Istana *Balai Besar* spatial zoning is kind of unique because its public space, the *balai* of the palace, is bigger compared to other palaces. From the *balai* there is a passageway leading to both the right and left sides of the building, which are believed to be private spaces for the royals.

The Split Typology

This is a typology in which the front public zone of the istana seems completely detached from the back part. This refers to palatial forms such as the famed Istana Melaka and Istana Seri Menanti, Negeri Sembilan (Fig. 12.14).

Istana Melaka and Istana Seri Menanti have largely the same floor layout. Starting from the entrance, it is a public space, until the *balai*. The right and left parts of the building house a small semi-public zone, which is an inner *balai* or discussion place for government matters. At the rear end of the building is private space, which is the dwelling of the royal family. The notion of permeability is related to both the horizontal, where there are insertions and walkways with covered pathways through buildings and blocks, and the vertical, where pocket parks and urban courtyards are integrated naturally into the fabric of the palatial complex and surroundings.

A Climatic Verification

A simulation study involving a sunpath penetration analysis based on hour-by-hour sun path of the specific location in which the collonaded model with the portico of the local palace can demonstrate its climatic performance and accuracy of the Malay portico form—the depth of the portico extension is not only aesthetic, but intuitively climatic. Its depth is a result of centuries of observation of climatic impacts and the aim of

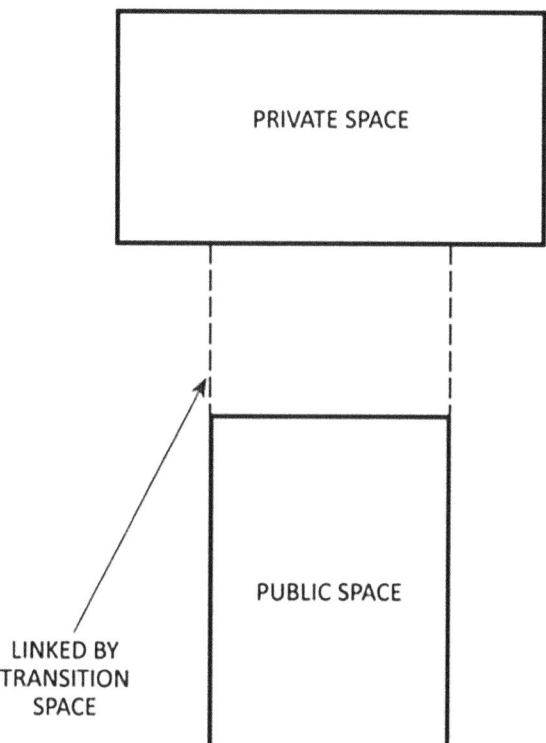

Fig. 12.14 TYPE 3: Plane two parts linked by a bridge-like structure (Istana Sultan Mansur II and Istana Istana Sultan Abdul Samad)

form in protecting and ensuring internal comfort conditions in the tropical climate. Below is the summarised result of a simulation of the sun's path and solar shading impact of the portico extension of the Istana Indragiri (Fig. 12.15) showing the effectiveness of shade according to the orientation and path of the sun.

Table 12.1 combines simplified sketches of the variations of the portico-cum-pavilion shape grammar, some of which are private spaces and others hold public functions for political administrative functions. In the Malay world the public realm occurs in semi-open spaces and extended porticoes of public buildings such as palaces and mosques; these interfacing spaces contain the shaded cool realm within which public

a   b

Fig. 12.15 (**a, b**) Istana Indragiri: elevation and photo showing depth of collonaded side portico

events are held. Social communication and interaction occur in such spaces. Hence the 5-foot typology which has so defined the heritage cities of the region is, in fact, not the vernacular type of the region, but a colonial import. The local original type is a deeper and extended portico, whose essential archetype contains a rich variation of morphological shapes while consistently acting as climatic shade to the thermal mass of internal spaces and thus providing protection for internal walls from heat absorption.

Conclusion: Remembering the Portico as a 'Space' of Appearance

Porticoes, in South East Asian traditions, were not only formal public spaces but living and active spaces which play a crucial role in civic life. From these essential typologies arise the permutations of the portico form, which appear as 'layers' and 'recesses' which protrude and recede and, at other instances, surround the main body or the core private space. The 'layered' and deep nature of these spaces not only reflects the public function but is climatically optimised to ensure their shaded impact protects the internal spaces and ensures optimal comfort conditions from the harsh tropical sun and the daily temperature cycle yet balancing the ventilative impact of tropical architecture in such a climate. The layered

Table 12.1 Hour-by-hour analysis of climatic form demonstrates how the depth of the Indragiri portico brings maximum shade to the internal core spaces during the period 2:00–4:00 pm, the hours of maximum intensity of the sun in the region

Overshadow analysis of west façade

Time	Elevation	Perspective
2:00 pm		
3:00 pm		
4:00 pm		
5:00 pm		

nature of shaded zones is not merely a projection but a series of layers which self-shaded each other and which constitute a form of tropical layerings of the public space and its promenades, a form of tropicalised public realm of that era.

These were the 'public 'realm' spaces that provide cool shaded forums and spaces. Porticoes play a key role in defining the public realm in both Western and Eastern civilisations. As Vidler (2011) summates:

> ...Porticoes would shelter the citizens from heat, rains, or snow, while paved sidewalks ... become a backdrop for civic activity. The street, planned as a building, was gradually absorbing the functions of circulation as it retained its role as a public scene.

As porticoes evolve, their functions can be described as an evolution of a form of spectacle space or 'space of appearance' in tropical Asia—a place where sociopolitical functions mingle in public life. Milner (2011) describes how, in this region, the space and the 'ruler' occupy a central position—being 'the lynchpin of the system'. Arendt's (1958) discussion in "The Space of Public Appearance" recalls how space and society form an inevitable part of governing and controlling.

Arendt likens this recurring basic type in all human civilisations which links to the perennial function of 'polis', which contains *the organization of people as it arises out of acting and speaking together*. In the case of South East Asia, they form an immeasurable aspect of the local culture. While Geertz sheds light on the nature of Negara as a theatre polity, Arendt's writings on the 'space of public appearance' refer to the crucial position and role of these public spaces, which are often formed and configured to give mankind a sense of identity and a collective platform and from which some assert political power and consciousness. Thus, Noor and Khoo (2003) explained the quality and beauty of these spaces, with carvings on walls, partition panels, windows, grilles, air vents, doors, railings, bargeboards, fascia boards, and gates meant to serve as visual indicators of social rank and status.

Marquez (2012) defines the universal role of frontage public spaces:

> In an Arendtian 'space of appearance', the common visibility of actors generates power, which is understood as the potential for collective action.

Greetz (1980) highlights the '*Negara*' in Bali's polity, which similarly harnesses the 'space of appearance' as a tool for power. He links the palatial spectacle of space to the 'theatre state', a system in which such central palatial spaces play key roles in a 'passive' system of governing. Pomp, rituals, and symbols are used, rather than war, tyranny, coercion, confrontation, or conquest. Any 'space of appearance' is temporary and fragile, and it must be continually recreated through the action and speech of individuals who have come together to undertake some common project. Their survival, public use, and weathering of pressures can be seen as a barometer of the survival of traditional societies amidst cultural destruction and pressures from modernisation and modernity. In the Asian context, the full cultural mapping of the portico, *balai*, or veranda has yet to be done, yet configurations and original space-form represent a critical issue in conservation as these spaces reflect crucial elements of identity, even cultural survival. Reflecting a genealogy of local architecture and space, in order to re-enact their evolutions, one must reconcile their changes throughout history as these are harbingers of social change. In contemporary structures, portico at the frontal space can serve as the building's foyer and entry statement. The portico can also be used as a zone of transition, connecting one area to another and bringing the public realm back together.

References

Andaya, L. (2010). *Leaves of the same tree—Trade and ethnicity in the straits of Malacca*. NUS Press.

Arendt, H. (1958). *The human condition*. University of Chicago Press.

Dakung, S. (Ed.). (1981/1982). *Arsitektur tradisional Daerah Istimewa Yogyakarta*. Departemen Pendidikan dan Kebudayaan, Proyek Inventarisasi dan Dokumentasi Kebudayaan Daerah.

Fadzidah, A., Salleh, N. H. (2005). *Measured drawings and Heritage Studies Heritage Report of Balai Besar, Alor Setar, Kedah*. Kulliyah of Architecture and Environmental Design (KAED) IIUM Heritage Center, International Islamic University Malaysia.

Fadzidah A. & Mansur I. (2015). The Genius of Tradition: Reminiscing the Balai Besar of Kedah, Malaysia., In: The Resilience of Tradition: Allusions and Abstraction of Malay Culture, Values and Forms in Contemporary Architecture and Design, Chapter 5.

Greetz, C. (1980). *Negara—The theatre state in 19th century Bali.* Princeton University Press.

Gullick, J. M. (1975). The Bloomfield Douglas diary: Selangor 1876–1882. *JMBRAS, 48,* Part 2, 10.

Idrus, Y. (1996). *Rumah traditional Negeri Sembilan: Satu Analisis Senibina Melayu* (201 ed.). Penerbit Fajar Bakti Sdn. Bhd.

Jahn Kassim, S., Nawawi, N., & Abdul Majid, N. (2017). *The resilience of tradition, Malay allusions in contemporary architecture.* Areca Publishers.

Jahn Kassim, S., Nawawi, N., Ibrahim, M., et al. (Eds.). (2019). *Modernity, nation and urban-architectural form.* Palgrave Macmillan.

Jani, H. H. M., & Hussain, M. R. M. (2014). Reclaiming the loss of the Minangkabau cultural landscape in Negeri Sembilan. *Procedia—Social and Behavioral Sciences, 153,* 317–329. https://doi.org/10.1016/j.sbspro.2014.10.065

Laurens, J. M. (2004). Arsitektur dan Perilaku Manusia, PT. *Gramedia Widiasarana Indonesia, Jakarta.*

Marquez, X. (2012). Spaces of appearance and spaces of surveillance. *Polity, 44*(1), 6–31.

Masri, M. (2012). The misconceptions of Negeri Sembilan traditional architecture. *Procedia—Social and Behavioral Sciences, 68,* 363–382. https://doi.org/10.1016/j.sbspro.2012.12.234

Masri, M., Yunus, R. M., & Ahmad, S. S. (2015). Creating cultural innovation: Towards a holistic approach in shaping a sustainable future. *Procedia—Social and Behavioral Sciences, 168,* 249–260. https://doi.org/10.1016/j.sbspro.2014.10.230

Milner, A. (2011). *The Malays.* Wiley Blackwell.

Mohamad Rasdi, M. T., Mohd-Ali, K., Syed Ariffin, S. A. I., Mursib, G., & Mohamad, R.'a. (2005). *The architectural heritage of the Malay world the traditional houses.* Penerbit UTM, Skudai, Johor Bahru. ISBN 983-52-0357-1.

Muhammad Saleh bin Haji Awang, Mohd Yusof bin Abdullah, Mohamad bin Abu Bakar, & Othman bin Ali. (1992). *Sejarah Darul Iman Hingga 1361H=1942M,* p. 138.

Noor, F. A., & Khoo, E. (2003). *Spirit of wood: The art of Malay woodcarving.* Hong Kong: Periplus Editions.

Nuraidil Zakaria. (2015). *Istana Kelantan Tersergam Sebalik Hutan Bangi: Siri Binaan Bersejarah Kelantan.* http://pp-sk.blogspot.com/2015/03/istana-kelantan-tersergam-sebalik-hutan.html

Rashid, M. S. A. (2014). *Understanding the past for a sustainable future: Cultural mapping of Malay heritage.* Paper presented at the AcE-Bs 2014 Seoul, ASEAN Conference on Environment-Behaviour Studies, Chung-Ang University, Seoul.

Santosa, R. B. (2000). *Omah: membaca makna rumah Jawa.* Yayasan Bentang Budaya.

Siswanto, J. (2005). *Orientasi Kosmologi.* Gadjah Mada University Press.

Wahab, M. H. A., Ahmad, S., Masri, M., & Hamid, A. B. A. (2014). *Malay furniture: Design function and meaning.* Paper presented at the Asia Pacific International Conference on Environment-Behaviour Studies, University of Westminster, London, UK.

Wan Ismail, W. H. (2012). Cultural determinants in the design of Bugis Houses. *Procedia—Social and Behavioral Sciences, 50,* 771–780. https://doi.org/10.1016/j.sbspro.2012.08.079

Wardani, L. K. (2008). The power of symbol at Keraton Yogyakarta.

13

In the Sanctity of Light and Shadows: The Traditional Mosques

Siti Norzaini Zainal Abidin and Harlina Md Sharif

Introduction

The distinctive character of vernacular mosques was that they were designed without domes but were instead dominated by high-pitched roof forms (Ali, 1997). The roofs were multi-tiered pyramidal formations and were common throughout Malay Peninsular Sumatra, Java, Kalimantan, Brunei, the southern Philippines, and the former kingdom of Champa in Cambodia (Ali, 1997). The roof is transformed into a focal point; it becomes part of the definition of interior space. It does not merely provide cover; rather, it defines the character of the space beneath. By splitting the roof up into a multiplicity of slopes and angles, one can shape the way

S. N. Z. Abidin (✉)
Taylor's University, Subang Jaya, Malaysia
e-mail: SitiNorzaini.ZainalAbidin@taylors.edu.my

H. M. Sharif
Department of Applied Arts & Design, Kulliyyah of Architecture and Environmental Design in IIUM, Jalan Gombak, Malaysia

© The Editor(s) (if applicable) and The Author(s), under exclusive license to Springer Nature Singapore Pte Ltd. 2023
S. Jahn Kassim et al. (eds.), *Eco-Urbanism and the South East Asian City*,
https://doi.org/10.1007/978-981-19-1637-3_13

253

light penetrates. Space remains defined by the roof bathed in semi-darkness penetrated by shafts of light and contained by walls that allow light to enter through them. As supported by Hassan and Nawawi (2014), this design element is important in tropical countries to act as a shield which protects the building from rainwater and sun rays and keeps them from getting in through the openings. Between the top and middle roof tiers are clerestory louvres that functioned to allow air flow from the stack effect and penetration of indirect natural light (Hassan & Nawawi, 2014).

As analysed by Mohd Nawayai, Denan, and Abdul Majid (2020), the traditional vernacular Nusantara Mosque largely reflects the solid effects of vernacular houses, their lifestyle, and environment. Building materials such as wood, bamboo, blocks, stone, earthenware, and *attap* are generally used in local mosques because they are effectively accessible locally. In addition, these mosques can be recognized for their multi-tiered roofs with decorated roof ridges and tiles, octagonal minarets, and square-shaped building form, as explained by Rasdi (2000).

Arbi et al. (2014) determined that the significance of roof form has been relatively pragmatic in contextualising regionalism through roof characteristics. Their analysis of form focusing on the pitch roof, which is frequently associated with the multi-tiered pyramidal roof typical of traditional timber mosques in the Malay Archipelago, includes the hip roof and gable roof commonly derived from domestic traditional architecture and the evolution of masonry type with the appearance of domes during the British colonial period (Arbi et al., 2014).

History Background of Nusantara Mosques

The Malay world, or *Dunia Melayu*, is the region that sits between the Indian Ocean and the China Sea, consisting of over 13,000 islands spreading from the northern tip of Sumatra down to Irian Jaya. At present, it is divided into six nation states: Malaysia, Singapore, Indonesia, Brunei, Philippines, and East Timor.

Traditional maritime activities relied on monsoon winds. Because of the alternate monsoon system, ships were forced to wait for the prevailing seasonal winds before continuing their voyages, which led to the formation of intermittent merchant settlements along the coast. In *Muruj al-Dhahab wa Ma'adin al-Jawhar*, the tenth-century Arab historian al-Mas'udi gave a detailed picture of a typical voyage taken by traders using the monsoon system. Ships from the Persian Gulf would usually start their journey in September or October. They would cross from Masqat to Malabar with the northeast monsoon. This journey usually took one lunar month, in which ships waited at Kulam Mali for the cyclones in the southern part of the Bay of Bengal to cease—towards the end of December. From there, the journey towards the Straits would take a month and the ships would arrive at Kalah Bar (Kedah) at the end of January.

Merchants usually spent a few weeks trading in the Straits, waiting for the southern monsoon in the China Sea. By April, when the sea is light, they will use the monsoon to get to Canton. After spending summer in Canton, the northeast monsoon took the ships back towards the Straits between October and December; they crossed the Bay of Bengal in January, from Kulam to Raysut in February or March, still using the northeasterly wind. There, they waited for the first gentle southwesterly breeze—usually in April—to get to Masqat and end their voyage at the Gulf by summer. The whole round trip typically took a year and a half (Hourani, 1963, pp. 74–75).

Structure

The mosque architecture in this region has a distinctive structural layout marked by the presence of *soko guru* (principal pillars) and supporting pillars arranged in an established pattern. The *soko guru* were usually made of massive solid wood of considerable diameters and heights, as they made up the main frame of the building structure which supported a multi-tiered roof configuration. In the absence of sufficient wood, such as in Masjid Agung Demak and Masjid Agung Cirebon Kasepuhan, smaller pieces of wood were held together with metal bands forming the central pillars. These types of pillars are known as *soko tatal* (Ashadi, 2006).

The four *soko guru* placed at the centre formed a square unit. Depending on the size of the floor plan and the height of the roof, supporting medial pillars may be required, and they were arranged at an equal distance surrounding the central square. A set of perimeter columns defines the boundary of the space, and in many mosques which have undergone extensive upgrades, these columns were not evident as the perimeter walls were replaced with cement-rendered brick walls that concealed the original structures. The structural configuration determines, and thereby restricts, the mosque's size, with the simplest form having only 4 pillars, and as the floor plan extends, the number of the pillars increases to 12, 16, 36, and 48 (Fig. 13.1). As stated by Navaee (2000), 'Mosque is the house of light on the one hand, and the light of God on the other. The structure of a mosque should place light in its heart, like the light in the heart of a Muslim.'

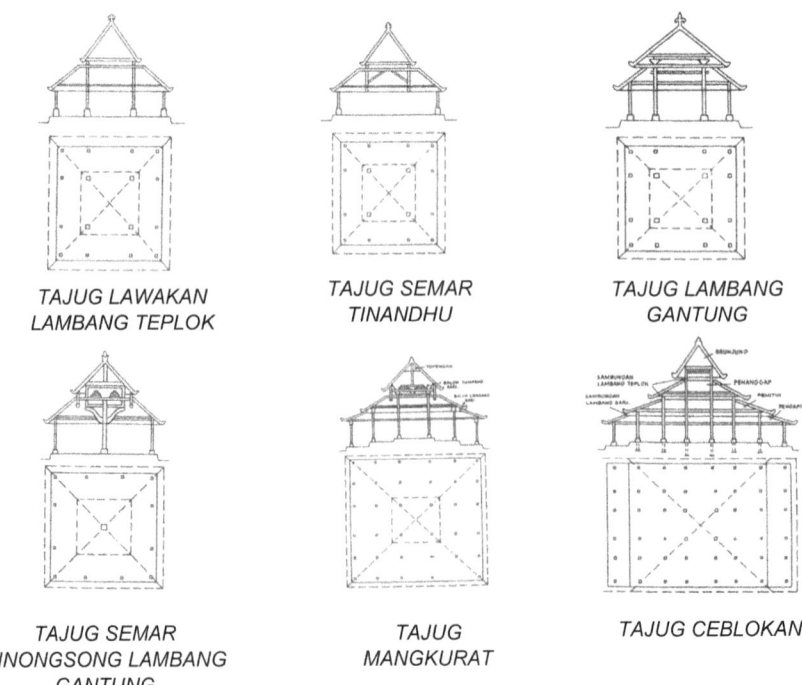

TAJUG LAWAKAN
LAMBANG TEPLOK

TAJUG SEMAR
TINANDHU

TAJUG LAMBANG
GANTUNG

TAJUG SEMAR
SINONGSONG LAMBANG
GANTUNG

TAJUG
MANGKURAT

TAJUG CEBLOKAN

Fig. 13.1 *Tajug* configuration. (Edited from Wibowo & Sukirman, 1987)

According to Said (2001), Nusantara Malay mosques in the region are relatively small compared to mosques of the Ottoman or Mughal Empire. Masjid Kampong Laut is the largest with floor area of 342 square metres, and Masjid Aur Menajung is the smallest with a floor area of 47 square metres. They accommodate congregations of 50 to 400 people. Generally, the spaces in the mosques comprise the main prayer hall, *mihrab*, attic (only in Masjid Kampong Laut), serambi (verandah), entrance hall, and ablution space. A minaret exists at Masjid Telok Manok as an extension of the roof covering the mihrab and in Masjid Kampong Laut as a 25-meter-tall structure linked by a resting space to the main prayer hall.

According to Ahmad (1999), there are two types of styles in the vernacular mosque category: the traditional and regional influences, differentiated by the design of the roof. Traditional mosques usually reflect the strong influences of traditional houses, way of life, and environment. The roof is generally a long gable roof. It is in contrast to what is seen in vernacular mosques with regional influence which can be distinguished by their two or three-tiered roofs with decorative roof ridges and clay tiles. The regional influence of mosques in Malaysia are similar to the old mosques built in many parts of Indonesia.

As observed by Rasdi (2000) there are three types of traditional mosque in Peninsular Malaysia:

1. raised timber type with three-tiered roof structure,
2. masonry type built with concrete slabs on grade with three-tiered timber roof, represented by Kampung Hulu mosque and Kampung Kling Mosque at Melaka,
3. house type with double-tiered gable roof of timber, represented by Langgar mosque of Kelantan.

Light plays an important role in Nusantara mosques, and it is articulated in traditional timber mosques to create a dynamic feeling and sense of God's presence in the religious space. Light and shadow are incorporated into the roof, which serves as an umbrella for the prayer hall. It has been shown that a natural daylight design with a light hierarchy and harmony plays a vital role in the interior environment in Majid Telok Manok Mosque, which can lead a person to reach a sense of serenity and concentration during worship activities. Light can be seen as a sculpture that gives different effects to spaces depending on how it is arranged in them. Daylight is lighting obtained from a direct sunlight source and provides the best source which comfortably matches with the human visual response (Sumarni et al., 2015).

The three-tiered pyramidal roof of Langgar Mosque in Fig. 13.2 is one of the most common features and dominant characteristics of the traditional mosque. Pyramidal roof formations were also commonly found throughout Peninsular Malaysia, Sumatra, Java, Kalimantan, Brunei, the Southern Philippines, and the former kingdom of Champa in Vietnam.

The impact from direct exposure to the low angle of sunlight is minimal, with penetration limited to the walls and ceilings. The evening's low-angle sunlight has a similar position (northwest) to the qibla orientation, where the qibla wall has limited window openings (Hassan, 2010). Fortunately, the tiered roof design provides a kind of diffused daylight through lower and upper roof window openings. While this creates a muted lighting ambience in the overall interior space; as the roof overhangs block high-angle sunlight, and the one-metre overhangs obstruct exposed direct sunlight to the prayer hall and verandah, it additionally creates more concentrated light and shadow in the prayer hall, creating a light distribution conducive to the spiritual functions of the mosque.

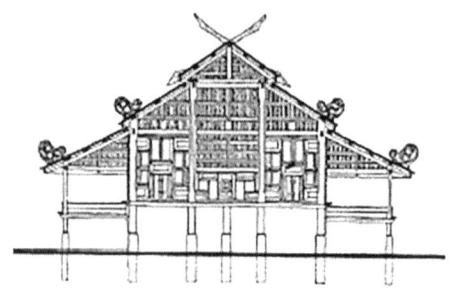

Masjid Langgar, Kota Bharu, Kelantan
Bumbung Panjang traditional house prototype employing 16
pillars construction

Fig. 13.2 Langgar Mosque, Kelantan (from Rasdi 2000)

One of the pyramidal roof types is from the Javanese mosque, which is generally two to five stories high. For example, the three-stacked roof is the most frequently found type in Java; it is used in almost all the Great (Agung) Mosques in Java built up to the nineteenth century. Another main characteristic of the Javanese mosque is its principal structure. The main structure of the Javanese mosque uses timber master columns (*saka guru*) in the centre of the main prayer hall to support the upper-hipped roof. In combination with the pyramidal stacked roof, this structure provides the tall interior space and establishes a powerful vertical axis. This strong central and vertical axiality acts as a counterpoint to the direction of qibla, providing duality in orientation in the Javanese mosque (Budi, 2004).

A generic characteristic and archetypal space is the colonnaded verandah that surrounds the main prayer halls. The verandah has been called an 'Asian tropical invention'—a shaded area separating both the inside and the outside. The verandah has a special place in local traditions and history, i.e. the colonnaded verandah-way in the Chinese shophouse and the shaded porch of the traditional rural house. The screen, brise-soleil, and louvres are also seen as part and parcel of the tropical language and design. These traditionally filter the intense light but also create shadow and shade, which result from the key characteristics of tropical design, i.e. the emphasis on roofs. As observed by Stagno (2001), this expands the relationship between tropical architecture, its roof form, and light and shadow: *It is particularly interesting to conceive architectonic space by emphasizing the way shadow is treated, rather than light, because in these latitudes it is the shadow, which unites and motivates, since intensity and excessive heat associated with external light make it uncomfortable…in this case, it is shadow that acts as the defining element in interior space. Under these circumstances it is advisable to create a design, where shadow is an integrated part of their function. This conception of space around shadow effects, has its limits defined by this play of shadow, semi-shadow and brightness, one moves from an exterior which is brightly lit to a space in shadow, and to an interior which is semi-shadow, it is a celebration of the delicate effect of shadow, highlighting this effect as one of the characteristics of tropical space.*

History and Islamisation of the Region

The Arab geographer Yaqut (d.1229) made the mosque and the *suq* the distinctive qualifiers for a place to be called a town (Grunebaum, 1959, p. 141). City centres of Islamic lands were usually recognised by their principal mosques. Ibn Battuta (d.1368/9), in his travel to China, commented on a town inhabited by Muslims where 'their *bazaars* are arranged just as they are in Islamic countries; they have mosques in it and *muezzins*' (Gibb, 1983, p. 293). Hourani (1963) included the existence of a mosque, public square, and residences of religious and commercial classes as the constituents of the urban complex defining the prominent features of a classical Islamic city.

In *Muqaddima*, Ibn Khaldun discussed the characteristics of city mosques when he stated:

> *It should be known that city mosques are of two kinds, great spacious ones which are prepared for holiday prayers, and other, minor ones which are restricted to one section of the population or one quarter of the city and which are not for the general attended prayers. Care for great mosques rests with the caliph or with those authorities, wazirs, or judges, to whom he delegates it.* (Ibn Khaldun, 2005)

In Islamic towns in the Arab-Islamic regions, the *Jami' Mosque* was always located in the middle of the classical Islamic town surrounded by the business quarters or precisely *aswaq* (markets) (EI2, *Masdjid*, p. 656). The *Dar al-Imara* or administrative centre would frequently be within its immediate vicinity. Since the mosque was a communal centre, the areas around the mosque would be occupied by *suq* of various merchandises.

In the Malay world, the major urban cities along the trade routes exhibited peculiar patterns emerging from the sultanate centres prior to the twentieth century. All the sultanate mosques found prior to the nineteenth century in these cities were built in vernacular *tajug* typology with pyramidal tiered roofs, with the exception of Masjid Agung Cirebon Kasepuhan, which employed a tiered gable roof construction. The pyramidal roof form has two to seven tiers, depending on the size of the floor that it covers. The *serambi* (verandah) forms an elemental part of its design model. It is an essential addition to the original building, in the mosque's expansion programme.

The spread of Islam in the Malay world of the 'Nusantara' has expedited the development of tiered mosque architecture in this region. At this juncture, it is interesting to quote Stagno's (2001) observation of the link between space and light in tropical architecture; however, outside of Java Island, variations to the basic model are found in mosques such as Masjid At-Taqwa Nusa Tenggara (seventeenth century) and Masjid Kampung Laut on the Malay Peninsula (eighteenth century), which were both built on stilts.

The urban landscape surrounding the ruling centre in Java, i.e. the sultan's palace, was found to be designed following the ancient pattern of pre-Islamic urban layout which had a *mandala*. *Mandala*, a Sanskrit term used in Indian manuals of government (Kulke & Rothermund, 1986, pp. 2–4), takes its physical embodiment in the royal complex layout in order to determine spatial hierarchy. It refers to the chess-like arrangement of the pre-Islamic royal city layout that could be traced in ancient Majapahit ruling centres and was found mainly in pre-seventeenth-century Javanese sultanate mosques (*Masjid Agung*). The most distinctive identifier of the presence of a *mandala* is the *alun-alun*, a large open field without any trees on it. Based on Javanese cosmography, the north is profane while the south is sacred. The *alun-alun* is the determinant, which defines the boundaries of the two zones. The western part of the *alun-alun*, where the mosque is always placed, is considered a sacred and holy site.

The Masjid Agung Demak (15c), the Masjid Agung Banten (16c), the Masjid Agung Cirebon Kasepuhan (16c), and the Masjid Agung Surakarta (19c) are all located to the west of the *alun-alun*. Outside of Java Island, Masjid At-Taqwa (17c) follows the same pattern. Other sultanate mosques do not seem to have been placed following any distinguishable patterns. Almost all of the sultanate mosques were built near the sultanate palace (*kraton*). The Masjid Agung Demak and Masjid Agung Banten palaces, although no longer extant, exist in toponyms and ruins. In Demak, the remnants of the sultanate city only survived in the form of the mosque, the public square (*alun-alun*), and surrounding village names. *Kampung Sitinggil* (*sitinggil* means high lands or places) was located to the south of the *alun-alun*, which traditionally would have been the site of the Sultan's palace; *Kauman* was traditionally the village where religious teachers (*ulema*) resided; and *Kampung Betengan* (*beteng* means fort) was probably a walled city or village (Ashadi, 2006).

Cornelis de Houtman, who led the Dutch voyage to Banten from 1595 to 1597, in his *De Eerste Schipvaart der Nederlanders Naar Oost-Indie* described in detail the layout of the city of Banten, the placement of the palace, the royal square, the mosque, the gateways, the port with its trades, the markets, the city forts, and the people's settlements. This report was equipped with sketches of Banten, its markets, and art displays (Tjandrasasmita, 2000; Mundardjito et al., 1976).

According to Guillot, the mosque, which was described by Bogaert in his seventeenth-century voyage, could not have dated earlier than 1615 as an Englishman Th. Elkington reported that it had collapsed during the night of 13–14 August that year due to lightning (Guillot, 1993, p. 95). Bogaert's description of the mosque in *Historische Reizen door d'oostersche Deelen van Asia* (Amsterdam 1711) corresponds fairly well to the existing structure of the mosque today as he explained:

> … is almost square and built with large beams that are found in abundance on Java. Its roof is in the shape of a tower… It has five roofs, one on top of another; the first and largest one covering the body of the temple; the next ones are smaller and smaller so that the last one almost comes to a point. In its centre, is raised a high [construction] which forms a real peak.

The description of the mosque's minaret, however, was not found in either Elkington's or Bogaert's account; nor did it appear in the sketches done by Cornelis de Houtman in 1595. Stavorinus was the first to mention it in *Voyage par le Cap* (1769) when he said clearly: '…there is, near the mosque, a narrow tower, but quite high, which serves the same functions as the minarets in Turkey' (Guillot, 1993, p. 96). A map held in the *Bibliotheque Nationale* in Paris, dated probably at the beginning of the 1670s, clearly shows the minaret's position near the mosque. Francois Valentijn, when passing Banten in 1694, also mentioned 'a stone tower seen from far and wide' (Guillot, 1993, p. 97). These accounts matched the widely held belief that the tower was built in 1620 by Cek Ban Cut, thereby confirming the archaeological data that the minaret was probably constructed in the first half of the seventeenth century (Mundardjito et al., 1976).

Islam arrived in the Malay world and brought with it a revolution in thinking and perspectives. With the coming of Islam, the inception of port cities, and the shift of economic activities from traditional agrarian economies to import-export of commodities, a new class of societies and new concepts of urbanism were created. The region, which had been heavily under the influence of Hindu-Buddhist cosmology, as clearly seen in the *mandala* layout of ancient cities on Java Island, now broadened its boundaries to reach out to international communities and embraced the concept of *ummah* with its orientation and focus towards one central point, which is Makkah. As Denys Lombard observed, the ancient concentric lines that were then the pattern of ancient cosmology of Javanese cities were now replaced with complex parallel networks, which then narrowed, intersected, and directed towards the ports at the coastal regions (Lombard, 2006). The basis of the ancient layout is a centre with the highest hierarchy: the *kraton* or palace, surrounded by circles with lower hierarchies, and axes. According to Purwani (2016), the most accepted Javanese cosmological layout consists of two aspects, which are hierarchical circles and axes. It is considered 'cosmological' in the sense that it represents the cosmos according to Indic cosmology.

However, the remnants of ancient cosmology were still evident in the layout of many principal mosques between the seventeenth and nineteenth centuries, especially on Java Island. The mandala arrangement still exists in principle, evident in the placements of important urban elements, such as the palace, the *alun-alun*, and the mosque. The *alun-alun* is always placed to the north of the palace, with the mosque being placed to the north-west and the residence of the *ulama* and lay people to the east. This sacred layout however was not found in regions such as the Malay Peninsula and Sumatra that received Islamic influence much earlier and with much stronger contacts than Java Island. As observed by Lombard (2006) in his review on the works of Hamzah Fansuri, Nuruddin al-Raniri, and Shamsudin, as well as *Hikayat Hang Tuah, Sedjarah Melayu*, and *Undang-undang Melaka* for example, the Islamic stimulus in the literature and the arts were found to be much stronger in the western parts of the Dunia Melayu, namely the Malay Peninsula and Sumatera. Due to the lack of archaeological artefacts and literary data, reconstructing an ancient Malay city in these regions poses serious challenges.

Daylight: The Character of the Nusantara Space

The *tajug*'s foundation is a slab-on-ground construction. However, outside of Java Island, variations to the basic model are found in mosques such as Masjid At-Taqwa Nusa Tenggara (seventeenth century) and Masjid Kampung Laut in Malay Peninsula (eighteenth century), which were both built on stilts. It has a distinctive structural layout marked by the presence of *soko guru* (principal pillars) and supporting pillars arranged in an established pattern. The *soko guru* were usually made of massive solid wood of considerable diameters and heights, as they made up the main frame of the building structure which supported a multi-tiered roof configuration. This structural configuration required the availability of huge trees, which consequently determined, at the conceptual level, the height and size of the intended mosque. In the absence of sufficient wood, such as in Masjid Agung Demak and Masjid Agung Cirebon Kasepuhan, smaller pieces of wood were held together with metal bands forming the central pillars. These types of pillars are known as *soko tatal* (Ashadi, 2006).

The consequent interplay of light and shadow in traditional mosques connotes the outcome of such structures and architectonics. Islam also emphasises pragmatic factors in enhancing serenity and comfort to its interior spaces as well as evoking emotions in worshippers. The structure of the mosque and array of columns, exposed beams, and the juxtaposition of the multi-tiered roof structure and its opening created a semi-open space while accentuating the light and shadow in the main prayer hall. The natural materials, wood carvings, and intricate details provide the mosque with a strong display of illumination of soft glowing rays of light and cast rhythmic shadows on its interior spaces. The rhythmical pattern changes with a continuous silhouette of light and shadow throughout the day that celebrates compulsory human rituals, resulting in a pleasant and calm environment for its worshippers. The intensity of the illumination creates a congregational space as well intimate moments with the Creator without compromising the adequacy of lighting for other activities. The increasing gradations of daylight and sunlight interact with architectural elements such as walls, screens, and artefacts in sacred spaces to create the dynamic animation of surfaces, solids, and structures (Abidin & Jahn Kassim, 2020).

Light and shadow mediate between materiality and spirituality, the tangible and intangible. The architecture and its elements enhance the awareness and dynamism of time. Light renders architecture a marker of time, and the interplay enhances the design, representation, and transformation of space (Simoes, 2013). According to Eco (1998), light is perceived as the common natural element in every substance, whether spiritual or material. The more an object is illuminated, the more it appears real. Light is a significant factor that exposes the characteristics, qualities, and perceptions of the interior design of a building (Hareri & Alama, 2020). In Fig. 13.3, the different times of day define the characteristic of the detailing and illustrate the interpretation of time, which signifies the notification for *salat* (prayers), which parallel worship and ritual in a day (Mohd Din et al., 2021).

In hot climatic zones, daylight is admitted through small openings or filtered through openwork transenna panels/walls (Stegers, 2008). According to El-Darwish and El-Gendy (2016), daylight should not enter from the qibla wall to prevent glare and visual discomfort for worshippers facing the qibla direction. The use of light has an essential role in creating physiological and psychological effects, as well as emphasising significant architectural elements. In addition, the quality, quantity, and colour of illumination accompanied by shadow all affect the quality and function of sacred spaces and set the mood for worship and spiritual activities (Hareri & Alama, 2020). It is therefore essential to give more attention to the lighting quality in mosques to create a sense of calm and tranquility for worshippers and users of the mosques through the design of indoor lighting.

According to Goudarzi and Saremi (2015), by using a combination of light and shadow penetrating through the clerestory windows or skylights, architects create contrast and infuse the place with spirituality. An

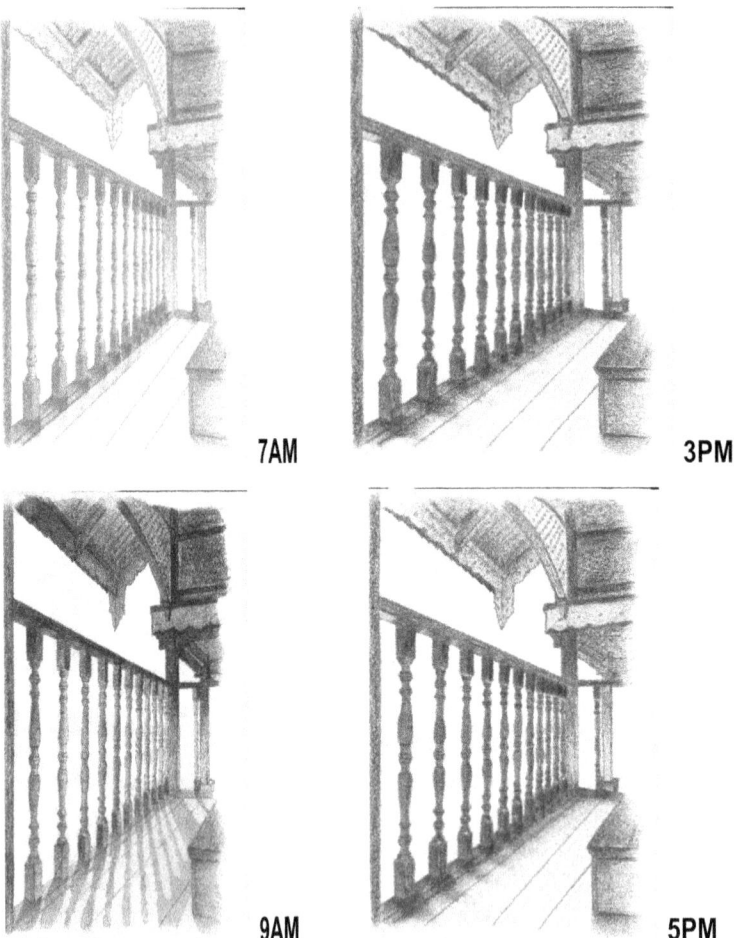

7AM   **3PM**

9AM   **5PM**

Fig. 13.3 Intensity of direct lighting defines the interpretation of time, which is a feature of traditional Malay architecture due to the interplay of shadow and distinctive architectonic elements (Mohd Din et al., 2021)

architectural space with a combination of light and shadow moves from darkness to light and provides man with a sense of movement and stability. As mentioned by Said (2001), openings permit light to illuminate the interior, which is often dark because the interior is covered by a pyramidal roof and also because of the dark hue of the timber walls and the underside of the roof (Figs. 13.4 and 13.5). The late afternoon sun may cast intricate shadows on the praying space when light passes through the carved panels. This phenomenon adds beauty to the interior setting of the mosque. At night, the scene would be reversed when light from lamps passes through the perforations casting a silhouette from the carved panels (Said, 2001).

As Zainal Abidin and Jahn Kassim (2020) explained, Almodovar-Melendo and Cabeza-Lainez (2018) described how this sequence of elements generates a typical gradation of light from the bright exterior to dark interiors, conditioning the mode of perception and residence of the space. Inside rooms, the 'void' characterised by the absence of light counterbalances with nature represented in interlocked exterior gardens by means of the technique known as shakkei or 'borrowed scenery'.

This natural scene of light and shadow (of daylight admission entering different types of tiered roof in Nusantara Mosques in Fig. 13.6) invites us to experience the mystery of emptiness, to detach ourselves from the phenomenological world, while nature becomes a catalyst to achieving

Fig. 13.4 Light penetrating through clerestory windows (selang bumbung) of the tiered roof, Masjid Kampung Hulu, Melaka (Source: Ahmad, 2015, PhD Thesis)

Fig. 13.5 Openings permit light to illuminate the interior, Peringgit Mosque Malacca (1720). (Source: Ahmad, 2015, PhD Thesis)

satori (Zainal Abidin & Jahn Kassim, 2020). Goneng (2011) in his famous reminiscence of Terengganu, Malaysia, gives a brief and succinct phenomenological description of the nature of tropical light in the vernacular context of Terengganu mosques in the earlier part of the 1900s:

> … *This is a hidden place, unknown … like most old suraus, it had an open apron, that you reached by going up a few steps of its verandah, and inside it was all dark and quiet. A shaft of light shines perhaps from a break in the roof tiles and jujube leaves strewn about, plucked from its branches by powerful winds in the night, and a shadowy mosaic of the tree canopy, painting the front porch in gloom and darkening the ground and mottling the area around the koloh with sunlight.* (Goneng, 2011)

The tiered roof demonstrated in Fig. 13.6 allows zenith passage sunlight during midday in beams (during the prayer of Zohor) that strongly create daylit spaces along the perimeter of the mosque interiors and shadow caused by direct light interspersed with dark spots, which in this case is the prayer area. In the two- and three-tiered roof typology, light

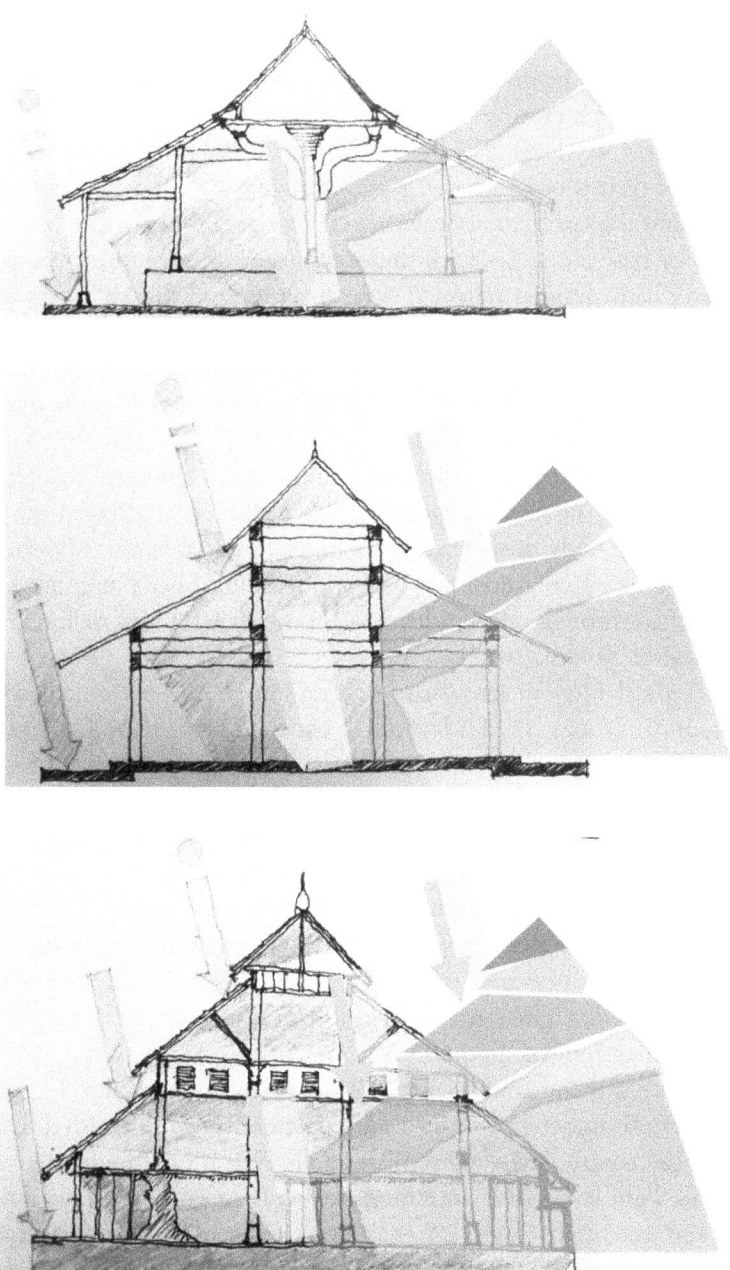

Fig. 13.6 Daylight admission entering different types of tiered roof Nusantara Mosque

enters at an angle from below and reflects off the underside of the tiered pyramid roof generating darker interiors at eye level and gradually brighter above eye level. The light and shadow interplay with the pattern of the roof beams between the gaps, overlying the surface of its interior and causing the space to appear darker. The parameter of the pyramidal tiered roof base coincides with the orientation of the summer or winter solstice, which permits reflected light to enter and diffuse to the upper part of the interior surface (Salgado, 2010). This dynamic experience changes as the sun moves, enhancing the volume, scale, and geometry of the interior space, underlining the lighting quality as well as the intensity of the shadow cast (Saraiva, 2017).

The significance of employing a combination of light and shadow may be better felt in the modern world as peace and security have been over-shadowed by a body of structure and environmental factors and the fundamental and systematic design and application of light in combination with shadow through taking advantage of the structures of such buildings (Goudarzi & Saremi, 2015).

The typical higher clerestories or skylight in the pyramidal roof of Nusantara mosques, i.e. Hidayatullah mosque studied by Latif (2021), added to the general darker interiors, causes the character of spaces in local forms to become darker, as opposed to imported typologies, such as dome types. Although this mosque type may cause greater lighting due to lower-level skylights and high reflection of the internal curvature of the domes, it loses the character of traditional mosques.

The results show that the pyramidal layered and steeper roof causes a more subdued and shared effect of light, compared to the higher and more uniform daylight caused by combined direct and reflected daylight under 'domed' roof configurations

Zainal Abidin and Abdul Latip (2015) discovered in Chap. 14, p. 194, that, generally, under a pyramidal roof, daylight levels diminish drastically towards the centre of the main prayer halls. Within the perimeter veran-dah areas, light levels were 'intermediate' between extremely low 'internal' levels and extremely 'high' external levels. Hence, in terms of daylight, locating the wide verandahs on the periphery and traditional latticed windows causes a decrease in the amount of usable daylight in the main prayer hall. It can also be seen that the illuminance levels near the windows are relatively high (compared to the mosque interiors) and fall rapidly towards the building's interior. As shown in Fig. 13.7, the light level of 30–50 lux at the window edge suddenly drops to about 10–15 lux at about 3.5 metres from the edge (building interior). In comparison to the daylighting

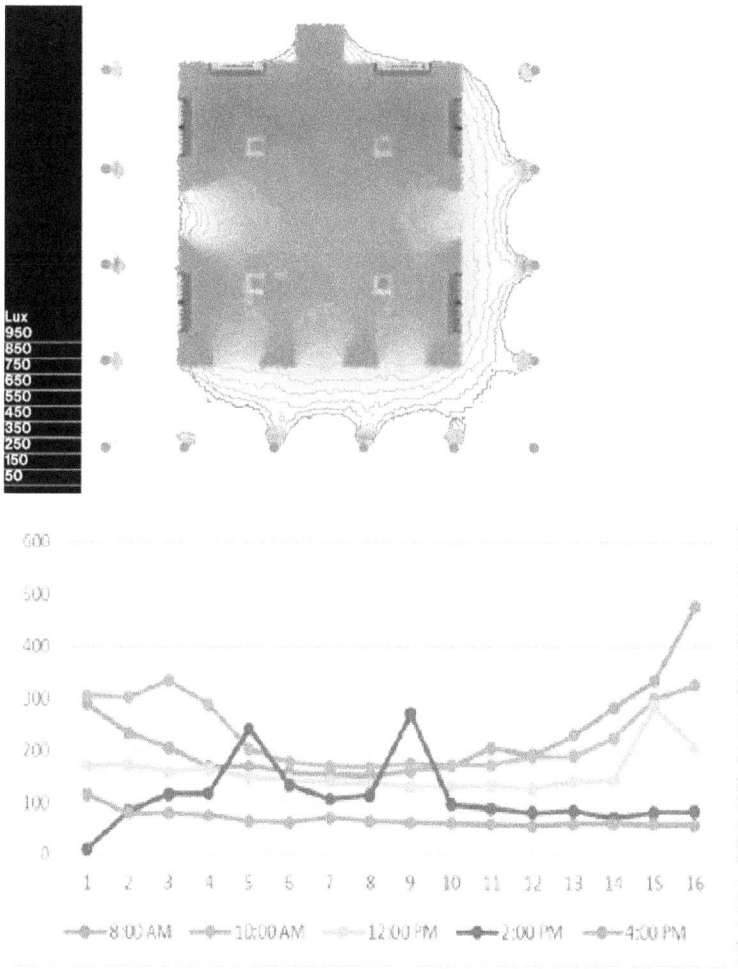

Fig. 13.7 Simulated light level (lux) at 9 am at main prayer hall under pyramidal roof structure of Kampung Hulu Mosque (Source: Zainal Abidin & Abdul Latip, 2015): measured light level (lux) at main prayer hall under dome structure during daylight hours of dome mosque type (Source: Aljofi, 2018)

performance through the dome in domed mosques studied by Aljofi (2018), the light level is higher at the central zone than near the side opening zones. The light level during the period of 1–4 pm, the period with the highest occupancy in the mosque, is between 350 and 500 lux (Fig. 13.7). Although the dome gives more light in terms of magnitude, it loses the sacred or sacrosanct nature of lighting in Nusantara mosques. The pyramidal roof form has a closer reflection of its local community, identity, lifestyle, and similarity of regional characteristics in the context of urban built environment. It also acts as a transcendental axis that connects worshipper to Creator (Latif, 2021).

Although mosques that grow in Malay and Javanese Land are conventionally without domed roofs and towers, it is not contrary to Islamic principles and rituals. Regarding the dome and tower, it is more for functional problem solving, as explained by Seyyed Hossein Nasr (1997).

Ventilation

As elaborated by Said (2001), the hot and humid tropical climate demands plenty of ventilation in buildings. Thus, craftsmen install many perforated components, such as ventilation panels (top hung) over doors and windows, perforated walls, louvred window leaves, perforated gables, and tiered roofs (similar to jack roofs) with perforated panels. Many of the ventilation panels, walls, and door leaves were carved in simple geometric patterns or with complex floral or calligraphic forms. It is particularly interesting to think of architectonic space by emphasising the way shadows are treated, rather than light, because in these latitudes, it is shadows that unite and motivate, since intensity and excessive heat associated with external light make it uncomfortable. In this case, it is the shadow that acts as the defining element in interior space. Under these circumstances, it is advisable to create a design where shadow is an integrated part of their function. Stagno (2001) elaborates on the significance of roof, space, and light in his book, which advocates responsive regionalism, allowing air flow from the stack effect and the penetration of daylight promoting values of light and shadow through the interplay of roof features.

Lighting and Carvings

Vernacular architecture is influenced by four major factors—climatic conditions, availability of building materials, craftsmanship, and references to ethnicity and local culture. Its interior is always characterised by intricate art motifs, which are either part of the window panels, fascia boards and *mimbar* (the platform furniture for the imam or the head of the religious leader), perforated, or embossed with vegetations and flower motifs. As Said (2001) explained, perforated timber boards are placed on top of doors, windows, or walls, permitting light to illuminate the interior of the building. Masjid Telok Manok has ornamental carvings (perforated walls and ventilation panels) located continuously around and above its walls, windows, and doors. The interior is generally dark because it is covered by a steeper form of roof and because of the dark hue of the timber walls and the underside of the roof (Said, 2001). The late afternoon sun may cast intricate shadows on the praying space when light passes through the carved panels. This phenomenon adds beauty to the interior sitting space of the mosque. At night, the scene is reversed when light from lamps passes through the perforations, casting a silhouette from the carved panels. Silhouettes of arabesque and geometrical forms can be clearly seen from outside, especially in the absence of light from other surrounding buildings (Said, 2001).

The unique features of the traditional mosques in Malacca are basically the square prayer hall with a three-tiered roof formation, which is supported by forty-four pillars, having four main central columns supporting the topmost pyramidal roof, columns supporting the lower middle roof, and the sides of the square space. The usage of local materials and traditional building technology and techniques also contributed to the uniqueness of the interiors of these mosques. Various local decorations have been applied to these traditional mosques, which seem to contribute to the ethnic appearance of the mosque. For example, in Kampung Hulu Mosque in Malacca, each of the windows has a grate (grille) and carved flower motifs on top. These two aspects work in general as a place of natural light in the main hall of the mosque (Ahmad & Zulkifli, 2018).

As identified by Aljofi (2018), it is also found that light penetrates through the roof that is insufficient for reading in the mosque, where most of the light depends on side windows. Fitoz and Berkin (2007) emphasised that daylight coming into the reading workplane level (six inches) should be evenly distributed during daytime prayers (12:00 pm and 3:00 pm). Sources of daylight are the roof (skylights or dormer windows) and walls (windows or full walls). Such lighting must be used with care so that glare does not reduce its usefulness by creating visual competition during religious services (Alturki et al., 2006). Further treatments could be explored to get the most out of the roof design as far as light is concerned. It is agreed by Fitoz and Berkin (2007) that spatial organisation in a mosque is directly related to daylight. Devices that regulate light could improve its distribution over the central zone of the prayer hall. Another treatment is to increase the reflectivity of the roof area around the external part of the dome. Due to mosque dimensions, side windows may not be efficient for satisfactory light. Therefore, skylight devices such as domes and a pyramidal, three-tiered roof design contribute positively to various environmental parameters.

References

Abidin, S. N. Z., & Jahn Kassim, P. S. (2020). Space, time and light-three forms of light and space-forms in Asia. *Cultural Syndrome, 2*(1), 49–58. https://doi.org/10.30998/cs.v2i1.308

Ahmad, A. A. (2015). Ruang Dalaman Masjid Melayu Tradisional Semenanjung Malaysia. PhD Thesis, Universiti Malaya, Chapter 2, pp. 55–169.

Ahmad, A.A., & Zulkifli, J. (2018), The interior design of Malaysian and Indonesian traditional mosque: Comparative studies, 3rd International Conference on Rebuilding Place (ICRP2018), 13–14 September 2018, Impiana Hotel, Ipoh, Perak, Malaysia.

Ahmad, G. (1999). The architectural styles of Masjid in Malaysia: From vernacular to modern structures in proceedings of the symposium on Masjid

Ali, K. (1997). *Architecture: Unity of the sacred and the profane, Islamic civilization in the Malay World* (pp. 254–284). Dewan Bahasa Pustaka and IRCICA.

Aljofi, E. K. (2018). The potentiality of domes on provision of daylight in mosques. *International Journal of Applied Engineering Research, 13*(7),

5103–5112 © Research India Publications. ISSN 0973-4562. http://www.ripublication.com5103

Almodovar-Melendo, J.-M., & Cabeza-Lainez, J.-M. (2018). Environmental features of Chinese architectural heritage: The standardization of form in the Pursuit of equilibrium with nature. *Sustainability, 10*(7), 2443. https://doi.org/10.3390/su10072443

Alturki, I., Schiler, M., & Boyajian, Y. (2006). Improving daylight in mosques. www.usc.edu/dept/architecture/mbs/papers/ecs/96_mosques/mosques_96.html

Arbi, E., Keumala, N., & Shah, M. (2014). Transformation of mosque architecture in Malaysia: Critical analysis of architectural history approaches. https://www.researchgate.net/publication/325809393_Transformation_of_Mosque_Architecture_in_Malaysia_Critical_Analysis_of_Architectural_History_Approaches

Ashadi. (2006). *Warisan Walisongo*. Lorong Semesta.

Budi, B. (2004). A study on the history and development of the Javanese Mosque Part 1: A review of theories on the origin of the Javanese Mosque. *Journal of Asian Architecture and Building Engineering, 3*, 189–195. https://doi.org/10.3130/jaabe.3.189

Eco, U. (1998). *Art and aesthetics in middle ages* (pp. 77–273). Can Publications.

El-Darwish, I., & El-Gendy, R. (2016). The role of fenestration in promoting daylight performance: The mosques of Alexandria since the 19th century. *Alexandria Engineering Journal, 55*(4), 3185–3193.

Fitoz, I., & Berkin, G. (2007). Space light & beliefs: The use of daylighting in churches and mosques. www.researchgate.net/publication/256715298

Gibb, H. A. R. (Ed.). (1983). *Ibn Battuta: Travels in Asia & Africa* (pp. 1325–1354). George Routledge & Sons.

Goneng, A. (2011). *A map of Trengganu*. Monsoon Books.

Goudarzi, A. R., & Saremi, H. R. (2015, June). Spiritual effect of light and shadow reflected in architectural spaces on the mitigation of man's mental pressures. *International Journal of Architecture, Engineering and Construction, 4*(2), 117–125.

Grunebaum, G. E. V. (1959). *Islam: Essays in the nature and growth of a cultural tradition*. Routledge & Kegan Paul Ltd.

Guillot, C. (1993). Banten in 1678. *Archipel, 57*(Indonesia), 89–113.

Hareri, R., & Alama, A. (2020). Lighting design in two mosque typologies in the city of Jeddah, Saudi Arabia. https://doi.org/10.2495/IHA200111

Hassan, A. S. (2010). Concept of prostration in traditional Malays mosque design to the surrounding environment with case study of Tranquerah mosque in Malacca, Malaysia. *Journal of Techno-Social, 2*(2), 1–21.

Hassan, A. S., & Nawawi, M. S. A. (2014). Malay architectural heritage on timber construction technique of the traditional Kampung Laut Old Mosque, Malaysia. *Asian Social Science, 10*(8), 230–240. https://doi.org/10.5539/ass.v10n8p230

Hourani, G. (1963). *Arab seafaring*. Beirut, Khayats.

Ibn Khaldun. (2005). *The Muqaddimah An Introduction to History* (p. 266). Paperback.

Kulke, H., & Rothermund, D. (1986). *A History of India Routledge* (Fourth Edition, pp. 2–4). Taylor & Francis Group, London and New York.

Latif, F. (2021). The architectural and interior elements as a form of cultural acculturation of Hidayatullah mosque, South Jakarta. *Cultural Arts International Journal, 1*(1), 1–11.

Lombard, D. (2006). *Kerajaan Aceh zaman Sultan Iskandar Muda 1607–136*. Kepustakaan Populer Gramedia.

Mohd Din, S., Awang, A., Jahn Kassim, S., Jalil, N., & Abdul Rahman, J. (2021). Aesthetic value of Rumah Kutai. In: Exhibition and lecture series: Malay architecture-the resilience of tradition from origins to the contemporary, 14th–28th January 2019, Museum and Gallery Tuanku Fauziah, University Sains Malaysia, Pulau Pinang. https://doi.org/10.13140/RG.2.2.32257.17766

Mohd Nawayai, S. S., Denan, Z., Abdul Majid, N. H. (2020). Façade design strategies in passive design approach for thermal comfort in Malay Vernacular Masjids: A paradigm shift. *Palarch's Journal of Archaeology of Egypt/Egyptology, 17*(9). ISSN 1567-214x.

Mundardjito, et al. (1976). *Laporan Penelitian Arkeologi Banten 1976*. Proyek Penelitian dan Penggalian Purbakala.

Nasr, S. H. (1997). *Knowledge and the sacred*. Pustaka Pelajar dan Centre of Islamic Studies (CIIS).

Navaee, K. (2000). Mosque, the icon of perfect man. Collection of articles: The conference of architecture, past, present, future (Arts University of Esfahan), 1, p. 667.

Nawawi, N. M., Jahnkassim, S., & Ibrahim, M. (2015). Dimensions of Masjid architecture: Perspectives and writings in theory and design. In Zainal Abidin and Abdul Latip (Eds.), Chapter 14, p. 194. IIUM Press.

Purwani, O. (2016). Javanese cosmological layout as a political space. *Cities*, 61. https://doi.org/10.1016/j.cities.2016.05.004

Said, I. (2001, June). Art of woodcarving in timber mosques of Peninsular Malaysia and Southern Thailand. *Journal Teknologi, Universiti Teknologi Malaysia, 34*, 45–56.

Salgado, T. G. (2010). The sunlight effect of Kukulcán pyramid or history of line. *Nexus Network Journal, 12*(1), 113. https://doi.org/10.1007/s00004-010-0019-3; published online 10 March 2010.

Saraiva, A. (2017). Between the shadow and the geometry of light: Hestnes Ferreira in continuity with Louis Kahn. KINE [SIS] TEM'17 From Nature to Architectural Matter, 173–180.

Simoes, Z. (2013), In between light and shadow: (In) visibility. Proceedings of the AIC. Conference, Association Internationale de la Couleur (AIC). 12th Congress in Newcastle upon Tyne July 8–12, Bringing Colour to Life.

Stagno, B. (2001). Tropicality. In L. Lefaivre & A. Tzonis (Eds.), *Tropical architecture: Critical regionalism in the age of globalization* (pp. 65–92, 78). : Wiley-Academy.

Stegers, R. (2008). *Sacred buildings: A design manual* (1st ed.). Birkhäuser.

Sumarni, I., Foroughmand, M., Utaberta, N., Yazid, M., Mohd Yunos, M. Y., & Ismail, N. (2015). Lighting Analysis in Mosque Architecture in Malaysia. *Advances in Environmental Biology, 9*, 452–454.

Tajuddin Rasdi, M. (2000). *The Architectural Heritage of the Malay World: The Traditional Mosque*. Johor Bahru: Universiti Teknologi Malaysia.

Tjandrasasmita, U. (2000). *Penelitian Arkeologi Islam di Indonesia Dari Masa ke Masa*. Menara Kudus.

Wibowo, H. J., Sukirman Dh, G. M. (1987). *Arsitektur Tradisional Daerah Istimewa Yogyakarta*. Yogyakarta: Departemen Pendidikan dan Kebudayaan.

Part III

14

Re-acculturising the Tropical City: From Theory to Practice

Elias Salleh, Kamariah Kamaruddin, and Shireen Jahn Kassim

Introduction

The word *acculturise* generally means to cause (a nation, tribe, or other ethnic group) to adopt the culture of another people. Though it is related to sociocultural fields, the word can be used in discourses about urbanscapes and urbanism in South East Asian cities that evolved from a historical trajectory of colonial legacies and extensive modernisation. Acculturation and 'hybridity' are often linked to its use in the fields of history and material culture, which use them to describe the

E. Salleh (✉)
Universiti Teknologi Malaysia, Skudai, Malaysia

K. Kamaruddin
International Islamic University Malaysia, Jalan Gombak, Malaysia

S. Jahn Kassim
Faculty of Architecture and Environmental Design (KAED), International Islamic University Malaysia, Jalan Gombak, Malaysia

© The Editor(s) (if applicable) and The Author(s), under exclusive license to Springer Nature Singapore Pte Ltd. 2023
S. Jahn Kassim et al. (eds.), *Eco-Urbanism and the South East Asian City*,
https://doi.org/10.1007/978-981-19-1637-3_14

amalgamation of the cultures of the colonised and coloniser. Besides acculturation, terms such as syncretism and creolisation are also used; they describe the same general evolution of intercultural amalgamation.

In his seminal book *Scenes of the Street*, Vidler observes that the theoretical solution to humankind's climate or ecological dilemma must involve viewing the urban form and architecture as a 'fusion' rather than a separation. Vidler muses:

> .... *I have interrogated the struggle for an urban architecture in the modern period, its critiques and aspirations, in the belief that understanding the historical dimensions of the debate will lead to a renewal of interest in an architecture calculated to redeem, if only partially, our 'planet of slums' and its deteriorating environment; an interest that will not simply reject 'utopia' out of hand or fall back into the complacencies of nostalgia. Written during a period in which the debates themselves were actively engaged by critics and supporters of modernism, they reflect contemporary issues as they search for their prehistory. As historical inquiries, they inevitably also engage the transformations in history writing itself since 1970, intellectual responses to the social and political conditions of postwar modernity, although its broad ethos can be derived globally. These have been defined as a range of architectural and urban design elements that reflect a certain consciousness of and consideration of the cultural and geographical identity of a region or a population.*

Thus, to 're-acculturise' carries the meaning of to unearth the underlay of local forms of ecological urbanism and to reinvigorate and integrate into within the fabric of present cities or the functions of modern life. In the post-colonial context of South East Asian nations, the trajectory and rapidity of these nations' socio-cultural evolvement and general rate of development proceed at such an accelerated rate that there is a lack of time to unearth the 'urban vernacular' and the indigenous (and thus the ecological) and, generally, more bioclimatic counterpart strategies that are interlaced with external influences and ruptures. Colonialism, and then external modernisation, causes a rupture in the natural evolutionary development of these societies, and foreign-imported forms and elements are seen as a mark of progress as physical changes of towns and cities occur at breakneck speed. Throughout these cities, the continuous impact of the urban heat island is transforming existing urban settings, with the hottest urban areas generally those having modern infrastructure, including paved areas and large buildings, without surface water or green space. The replacement of natural vegetation with paved and hardscape surfaces and buildings has created microclimates that are not conducive to the experience of traditional urban fabrics of tropical cities that once grew along the riverine and coastal regions. The origin and development of coastal or riverine urban settlements were produced by the symbiosis between climate and inhabitation. In fact, they were intuitively planned as passive cooling urban systems. These traditional urban forms and fabrics constitute passive climatic urban systems that provide outdoor thermal comfort through self-shading, low sky view factors, perhaps by the combination of built form and vegetation canopies, causing cooler prevailing temperatures and comfortable conditions. The present microclimate, which is not conducive to walking and connectivity, is an outcome of spatial effects that were caused by speculative urban pressures in recent decades and have drastically deteriorated the natural landscape, including bio-geographical corridors and, therefore, human climate comfort.

Manteghi (2016), for example, crucially highlighted that the creation of a concentrated local microclimate within urban environments is regarded as vital because urbanisation precipitates increased heat stress in hot and humid climates. Previously, urban heat island conditions in cities were recorded, but little attention was paid to the cooling effect of a city's water bodies, while the evaporative effect of water is seen as an alternative to mitigating environmental ambient temperature. Rivers are a source of coolant for the microclimate of the surrounding area. Other researchers have pointed out that evaporative cooling via water bodies or features represents the most efficient passive manner of cooling buildings or urban spaces, with the prevalence of vegetation and water bodies capable of reducing urban temperatures by 0.5 to 4.0 °C (Fig. 14.1).

The emergence of the debates on emergence of the age of the anthropocene in the light of climate change have earmarked the present century with a critical urgency to develop policies, themes and guidelines which differ from the past industrialisation age. While ecological science constitutes a basis for theoretical frameworks, guidelines, new developments to limit the destructive impacts of development, vernacular-based approaches combined with such sciences are critical in the context of South East Asia, including studies of past formations and morphologies which

Fig. 14.1 Morphological reconstruction of original vernacular urban configuration of Kota Melaka through textual and cartographical sources showing 'accretive' qualities. (Source copyright: Kamariah Kamaruddin)

contain lessons on the way forward. Vernacular patterns and formations of the past is constantly challenging as these models have either been buried under layers of development and sedimentations, or been fractured by multi-scale ruptures caused by local histories of Colonialism, erasing much of the patterns of indigenous urbanism in local regions. Yet these forms and urban elements constitute a source of language and principle critical to the formation and transformation of urban forms of cities, towns, and villages; resonating their spatial patterns at different scales. The term 'urbanism' is defined as 'a way of life characteristic of towns and cities' and defined as 'a condition of permanence'. Eco-urbanism is thus a framework or model related to the deep sustainability paradigms and principles which was once part of the histories within South East Asia's archipelago. Their river—accretion patterns (Fig. 14.1) and the centric nature of the urban core (Fig. 14.2) with its fusion of water, riparian patterns and open space greenery have made these patterns resonate with present ecological matrices that can be reconstituted into a regionalised

Fig. 14.2 A more recent and dense analysis of the later forms of urban grain in Palembang

eco-urbanist urban design framework and broad policy guidelines, reversing the deleterious effects of climatic change.

What constitutes urban design? Urban design describes the physical features that define the character or image of a street, neighbourhood, community, township or the city. The eventual character of a town or centre must be read as a whole; hence urban design is the accretion or accumulation of various elements at different scales that impinge upon the visual and sensory perceptions of urban dwellers, and consequently, affect the relationship between people and the built and natural environment. The built environment includes buildings and streets, and the natural environment includes features such as seaviews, coastlines, shorelines, roof profiles, facades and shapes, all of which must eventually be incorporated into a comprehensive framework.

To reconnect the city, the river and the people, Kuala Lumpur City Hall launched the River of Life project in 2012, and AECOM was chosen as a delivery partner through an international design competition. River of Life is one of the Malaysian government's Economic Transformation Programs, an initiative which combines high-impact projects and programmes to elevate the country to developed nation status. It is divided into three main components—river cleaning, river master-planning, pedestrianisation and landscape beautification—which cover the confluences of three city rivers, with a total area of 781 hectares and 63 hectares of water. The project is set to bring the community back to the river through a 100 per cent transformation into a vibrant waterfront with high economic and commercial value, rejuvenating the city's river and re-connecting it to the surrounding urban fabric. The project also aimed to provide a strategic framework for urban and landscape design guidelines. The guidelines ensure designs are constructed on a common baseline while promoting cohesive developments in the Klang Valley region.

Awarded second place in the Bertam architecture and development masterplan competition sponsored by NAZATTDI developers in 2016, Malaysia, Pakatan Reka led a consortium (Ranhill Bersekutu As Building Services Engineers and EAG Consulting as Sustainability consultants) to elevate sustainability into every aspect of a masterplan founded upon a concept inspired by the ecological urbanism of place. These saw a design process, inspired by an ecological survey of local tree species, which was conceptually 'deconstructed' and developed into an organic configuration, a masterplan inflected by a sweeping green corridor and imbued with the clustering centring of residences around 'green communal' seeds, evoking the traditional forms of bio-greenery which historically constituted the place. The 100-acre competitive design for Bertam Township, north of Malaysia, emerged from an extensive ecological survey of place, which led to an idea based on the local species. This was developed into a masterplan based on three green communal centres called 'seeds' which included commercial and recreational facilities, which totalled 25% (210 acre) of the site. The site is composed of recreational and open spaces and communal facilities and amenities within walking or cycling distance or reachable by public transport, along with dedicated and integrated lanes for a Bertam Road Transport (BRT) network to link the various sectors of the township and the external transportation system of the External Distributed Transport (EDT) (at the transportation hub) and monorail (at Kepala Batas). The system provides easy accessibility to public transport via an easy-to-use pedestrian and cycling network, thereby reducing dependency on fuel-operated vehicles (Fig. 14.2).

Re-acculturising Façadescapes from Archetypes

Kusno highlights a phenomenon throughout South East Asia; the rising interest in urban history as a basis of contemporary urbanism, which will evolve its cities, currently and increasingly made of 'superblocks', i.e. large urban complexes consisting of residences, offices and shops. Quality of life is also presently related to another factor—health. In new cities, these seem to be the driving force behind the growing population of young professionals that there seems to exist a critical link between health and city form. Past research suggested that the features of the built environment, such as low density, poor connectivity and lack of linkages, have been associated with decreased physical activity and an increased risk of overweight.

Meaning of Archetype

Christopher Alexander remains one of the advocates asserting the need to understand the original, and the original forms are intuitive solutions to design problems are so complex that they are best resolved by learning from '*solutions which have proved successful over an endless period of time*'. He describes these solutions as 'archetypes' or 'patterns'. Marta Pieczara in her useful ' Archetypes in contemporary architecture' asserts the same position and traces the term of archetype to the works of Philo of Alexandria, in the West [5, p. 4]. Pieczara expands the idea to a universal relevance:

> *Intended as a constantly recurring pattern or symbol that is historically grounded and shared among society, the notion of the archetype can be traced to the Platonic theory of forms, otherwise known as the theory of ideas. According to Plato, the philosophical concept of the form or idea refers to a purely intellectual model of an object, which represents its essential characteristics rather than specific details.*

Pieczara also usefully postulates:

It was not until the 20th century that the terms 'archetype' and 'collective unconscious' were presented by Carl Gustav Jung. In the framework of his psychological studies, Jung introduced the notion of archetypes intended as universal elements of the collective unconscious.

Inherited and universal, an archetype can be defined as follows:

A timeless reference of an architectural type which remains purely conceptual while having representation in various architectural projects as well as realisations in buildings, the archetypes which belong to the collective unconscious and, therefore, are intangible and purely mental. For Kahn, any architectural design starts with the form, which 'belongs to the order of thought and of the unmeasurable' [11, p. 57]. Because of this, the form differentiates one existence from another, being 'a sort of matrix, generating the meaning that is attributed to the content of the work' [10, p. 10]. It can also be defined as 'the thought of the form' [9, p. 47], which evokes the conceptual, or mental, character of archetypes. One form can have a range of individual expressions, which Kahn calls 'designs'.

Pillared and extended spaces (as in Chap. 8), punctured pavilions (as in Chap. 9) and deep portico variations (as Chap. 10) have been discussed, and these also 'constitute' the seeds and nexus of 'activated' urban life of tropical Asian sites. These archetypes can be modelled through the variations or permutations or combinations of shaded extensions, including open-air or extended porticoes, shaded squares, walkways, peristyle forms and shaded ground-floor spaces which are either separated or synthesised with enclosed private spaces and layouts. These 'archetypes' can contribute to a refreshed approach to urban-architectural streetscape and enculturated facades of a city. Yet present cities are embedded with imported and grafted forms such that the locally 'acculturated' forms had evolved into variants according to sites and places, and these variant examples of elements, space-forms, layouts, morphological studies and elevated artisanal patterns and motifs are ignored. Sociocultural meanings are lost as the fundamental layering of archetypes in spatial traditions in South East Asian history, both as a physical construct and a climatic strategy, becomes forgotten.

Lepawsky and Jubilado show that in the 'geohistories' of the street in tropical Malaysia, certain elements become crucial—for example, the shaded walkway as not only a functioning element but a heritage element, responding to the need of authenticity. The easing realisation of such public shaded spaces are crucial not only to climatic design and economic efficiency but in its ability to initiate, sustain and affect the patterns of vibrancy and 'static distribution' within tropical urban spaces. Yeang's 'Tropical Urban Regionalism' postulated a series of archetypes and models of the verandah to elevate the identity of the city based on tropical multivariate verandahs. In his seminal treatise on Kuala Lumpur as a potential 'tropical verandah city', Yeang postulated varied models and templates of potential shaded 'verandah-ways' which can be explored as urban ideations in terms of urban language of the city in the modern tropics. Although this important treatise was never realised in the context of Kuala Lumpur, its essential idea was infused into a singular award-winning project of Menara Mesiniaga, expressing triple-height sky courts that climb towers in a spiraling fashion. It was the continuous shaded zone that Yeang had envisaged as being linked to the fabric of tropical cities, manifested in an Aga Khan award-winning tower.

In his 'Tropical Verandah City', Yeang envisaged a city interspersed with a series of varied verandah and interstitial space insertions, articulations and pathways. Although inspired by the conventional traditional five footways, they are deeper and more akin to the Malay archetype of *anjung* as they are projected and 'pulled' deeper—in spaces and walkways which could basically create a richer indoor-outdoor experience in cities. These patterns of indoor to outdoor spaces were proposed as configurations of varied dimensions and which are integrated into 'open ground floors' of buildings, which would clearly distinguish the identity of the tropical city. To Yeang, the tropical city experience must be that of an emphasis of transitional spatial and 'building volumes' and interspersing climatic volumes and internal vegetated spaces between buildings.

In the tropics, urban spaces and pedestrian realms are more easily affected by the intense climate, so the experience of outdoors is governed by the daily cycle of heat and cooling. The climatic parameter and local urban morphology generate sociocultural condition and the daily cycle of economic vitality. In the tropics, shade and comfort are crucial as the years pass due to expectations and the pressures to seek the comforts of the dry and air-conditioned indoors. City dwellers are acclimatised to being ensconced in air-conditioned indoor spaces and see 'unshaded' outdoor spaces as uninviting and 'dead' in the heat of the day. Open, unobstructed space, mainly consisting of squares and streets, is desirable in a temperate climate. In tropical climates, unshaded public outdoor spaces have turned out to be unoccupied, especially under sunny conditions. Thus, intrinsic shade climatically and culturally acts as a generator of occupancy, activity and increased population distribution in the middle of the day.

Re-culturalising Urbanism: The Tropicalised 'Portico' Street

The 'portico' is a recurring pattern or archetype throughout the region, and porticoes are particularly significant in the tropics. The present five-footway shophouses are typologies which were grafted onto the local urban landscape, so their features are the outcome of multiple layering and acculturisation. The Dutch style shophouse, for example, is one of the earliest types and can only be found in Melaka. Built in the seventeenth century, these types of shophouses and townhouses are either one or two stories high with a simple façade design and limited openings on the upper floor, normally with only one centralised or, at most, two symmetrical windows. The Southern China style (1700–1800) was a modified version of the 'Chinese National' or Northern Style. The two-storey structures are built to the street edge and incorporate a sidewalk which is well entrenched in the style of the nineteenth century. Expressive gable ends adorn these rows of shophouses. Ornamentation is minimal with the upper consoles often enlarged and simply decorated with floral motifs, green glazed ceramic vents and plain pilasters. The usual orders are the Tuscan and Doric, upper-floor openings with a row incorporating features of the 'grand' classical style, with pediments, pilasters, keystones and arches. From the 1910s the use of reinforced concrete allowed for wide roof overhangs and more elaborate cantilevered concrete decoration (consoles), and this style exhibits almost exclusively a bipartite elevation with two windows. The late Eclectic style (1920–1940) features a constrained indigenous façade design with Chinese panel frescoes, which are often combined with Malay timber fretworks that fringe the cape of the roof. The Art Deco style (1930–1950) shophouse was widely used between the 1930s and 1950s. Characterised by the use of straight lines (typically three parallel), it is arranged either vertically or horizontally in conjunction with other geometric elements, creating a strong vertical or horizontal emphasis to the structure.

Residuals of Indigenous Models

The indigenous models of porticoe urbanscapes grew from local roots in the aristocratic realm. Some of these are diffused into older type 'shophouses' that characterise earlier Malay urban settlements, which were conglomerations of rows of narrower buildings with steeper roofed structures expressed by a large range of pitches. The local forms consist of steeper roofscapes with varied pitches and a multitude of lean-to walkway shade structures. These enable zones and setback routes originally consisting of zones for loading rickshaws, horse-drawn carriages and elephant stopovers. Traditionally, old routes became streets, which seem to overlap and evolved into open spaces like the *padang* or *medan* because they did not end at the edge of the open space but legibly continued into it. At the same time, the blend between the streets and such open spaces serves as a gateway to multiple types of open greenery, whether riverside or open field, where pathways blend into the natural world.

The town of Kota Bahru was the capital of the state of Kelantan which only came under English administration by 1909, i.e. the year of the Anglo Siamese treaty. The town is known for its original pattern and configuration of paths and streets which blend into a centre or heritage core. They still reflect the original layer of the Malay city which is characterised by the intimate and compact nature of the original Malay city. Its frontage street facades reflect a more indigenous form of the shophouse facade with balcony protrusions, timber weaved balustrades interspersed with lean-to shading devices. These can be seen as a 'Malay and more indigenous' urban typology of shophouses.

Hull (1976) noted how many of these large vernacular-rooted urban spaces were disregarded by colonialists in their development and infrastructure improvement plans. For example, the entire unity of the central '*padang*' was disrupted by a highway cutting through the *padang* in between the mosque and palace of Alor Setar. Traditional urban realms allow an infrastructure to be sufficiently fine-grained to allow for many choices, which generate many alternative paths by permutation. Mark C. Childs observed:

> One must see the city as: "settlements are not just the sums of their parts; their poetry and vitality comes from their collective composition—the interactions among multiple designs. Hence in studies of ancient urban forms, the fractal city can be the connection between the unified whole of this structure with its smallest part is a similar, iterative, and re-scaled. These can indicate the new conscious approach in spatial planning, i.e., towards creating a diverse sequence of spatial cells of the whole and part. The coherence between elements of this urban pattern is a reproductive and replicated process in which the iteration of elements reinforces the pattern.

An Exploration of the Aristocratic Portico as Facade Archetype

Talib and Ariffin highlight that, though a methodology of attempting to compile, categorise and characterise the vernacular bases of forms, including facades (see their study of Perak Kutai architecture), one can unearth categories of traditional typologies, whether architecture or urban spaces, that can be used to create archetypes for more climatically conscious and sustainable design. While such an analysis of form is conventionally used for Malay architecture, it will also prove useful for facadescape because it visualises the typological and morphological character of such past buildings in terms of facades and street patterns. Thus, urban designers can increase their resources with respect to local templates to inspire, evoke and guide design concepts of the city to infuse a more regional identity to tropical cities.

Urban facadescapes and urban shaded spaces can be seen as a continuum that is able to create a potentially activated urban 'fabric' and experience. Sulaiman and Shamsuddin (2001) have observed on the 'vanishing streets' in newly developed or redeveloped towns and cities—such as Malaysia. There is a need to reassess the existence of these typologies and existing promenades. By compiling, redrawing and revising documents, classifications can be attempted. These are combined with historical anecdotes of spatial experience that can be reverted and aligned with an analysis of these public zones. One recalls the typological method of Jean-Nicola-Louis Durand, a professor of architecture at *Ecole Polytechnique*, influenced by contemporary advancements in the natural sciences, by collating multiple variants of an archetype, which had evolved the use of taxonomy and descriptive geometry. Durand employed the methods of comparative taxonomy for the study of building forms where he enumerated a limited number of inventories of building elements, pilasters, walls and foundations. The result was his major work, *Recueil et parallèle des édifices de tout genre* (1801), a kind of 'typological atlas of architecture'. Using the same typological methods, a regional resource of public porticoes of the urban realm of the traditional city is remeasured, extracted and redrawn with different variations of their frontages and vernacular porticoes; (as in Chap. 12) these show the large variations and spatial differentiation of these structures throughout South East Asia.

A mapping and measurement of the public realm of these traditional complexes extracted from the seventeenth century to the 1940s palace era in the region revealed deeper projections and porticoes having three 'essential forms' or 'formal types' with their variants. It is essentially a semi-open space projecting out as a functional form of the traditional tropical verandah. These projections are from the elevational plane and some rest on columns, but in all cases the form itself is beyond the main elevation. They average around a ratio of 0.5 as seen in the width and depth as protruded or embedded into the overall form.

Potential Streetscape Interpretations of Porticoes

The following sections explore the potential of such forms in the urban density of a city formed on Malay identity, which can expand into several typological variations of layered streetscapes for the modern Malay Nusantara city with its characteristic shaded and tropicalised facadescapes:

1. Shaded recesses in the middle portico (T1)
2. Shaded recesses in the side portico (T2)

3. Shaded recesses in front and side portico (T3)
4. Opaque projections without recesses (T4)

Shaded Recesses in Middle Portico (T1)

From cases such as Baitul Rahmah and Baitul Anwar, in Bukit Chandan, Kuala Kangsar and Istana Sepahcendera, Alor Setar (Chap. 12), a streetscape with a double-storey height essentially with inserted staircases and portico projected in the mid portion within a shaded recess.

Shaded Recesses in Side Portico (T2).

From the Istana Malige forms and its variants from Sulawesi and the Melaka case studies (see Chaps. 2 and 6), models of streetscapes with a distinct shaded space and verandah that can be seen at the side of the facade

Shaded Recesses in Front and Side Portico (T3)

These include the beautiful facade character of Rumah Panglima Ghani, Melaka, which essentially is a result of a projected outdoor room to the front, which morphologically appears like a space with three projected wings. The same spatial plan is observed in a larger scale in Istana Indragiri and Balai Besar Alor Setar.

Opaque Projections Without Recesses (T4)

This particular form of streetscape includes derivations from the facades of Istana Leban Tunggal, Istana Bandar and, to some degree, Istana Jahar. In these facades, there appear to be an extension in the front, yet the overall appearance of the facade is continuous without recesses.

The layering of vernacular architecture is rich in variation: stereotomic variation ranges from a basic foundation to peristyle to half-pillared styles, and the layering of the architecture in the public realm of the

Malay world is filled with variations that can be integrated with streetscapes, whether in a more classical mode or a modern interpretation of these layers, as discussed below.

Further Streetscape Typology Permutation

Axial Typology Forms of Streetscape

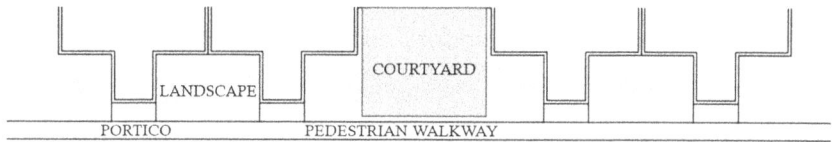

1. Building blocks are arranged in an aligned manner, whilst providing courtyard or functional spaces for each two to three blocks.
2. The entrance is enhanced through well-planned greeneries that give the sense of rejuvenation, both for the building occupants as well as pedestrians walking along the pedestrian walkway.

Binuclear Typology Facadescape

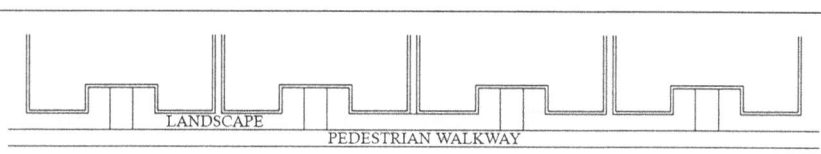

1. Commercial buildings are arranged in an aligned manner.
2. The view from both inside and outside the buildings are enhanced through landscape.

Asymmetrical Typology Streetscape

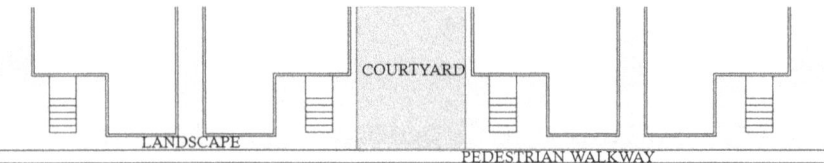

1. Buildings are arranged in mirrored and aligned manners with a court-yard every two or four blocks.
2. The area around building blocks is enhanced through greenery.

An Interpretation: Fusing Streetscape, Public Space, and Greenery as a Continuum

This character of urbanism in South East Asia, including the Malay roots of architecture and urban life, shows a spatial type that integrates outdoor space, water, trees and enclosed squares in a continuum. The shaded and semi-enclosed nature of the space is strengthened by rows of large, mature trees acting as continuous features linking one end to another. The aim is a stronger, more localised and place-linked visual structure of the streetscape with natural elements and an architectural composition that holds the urban space together, maintaining a tremendous sense of enclosure and completeness. The following images are possible interpretations and represent an exploration within a modern city framework based on the aforementioned models which evolved from the findings of earlier chapters and implies three-dimensional elements in urban space. Buildings and streetscapes are not set apart and seen individually but are part of a network of a shaded spatial continuum. These are punctuated by green nodes of pocket parks and urban patches, which are integrated naturally into the fabric of the city and which create pockets of green sanctuary or green sojourns. Under equatorial conditions, such 'pockets' can be infused with greenery and punctuation of airflow to cause cool islands within the city. Higher buildings can be located strategically to provide shade from evening sun as well as to divert the downward flow of air at increasing wind speeds from the higher levels and ventilate the more stagnant air conditions in enclosed areas on the ground level. These extended *serambi-type* spaces or semi-public or private spaces can serve as a shaded thoroughfare, extending into eating outlets and seating areas for occupants or visitors. Covered plazas and spatial extensions provide opportunities for eateries with building projections and enhanced semi-outdoor spaces that aid in allowing airflow, inducing ventilation yet providing protection from heavy rain (Fig. 14.3).

Figure 14.4 shows how such templates can be used to further generate differentiation of form, in which columnar space, the verandah trees and water bodies are fused to create models and templates in order to verify its usability to generate new forms for today's cities. The overall approach in architecture and urban design recalls the often-forgotten principle of past traditions and the crucial role of phenomenology, which in

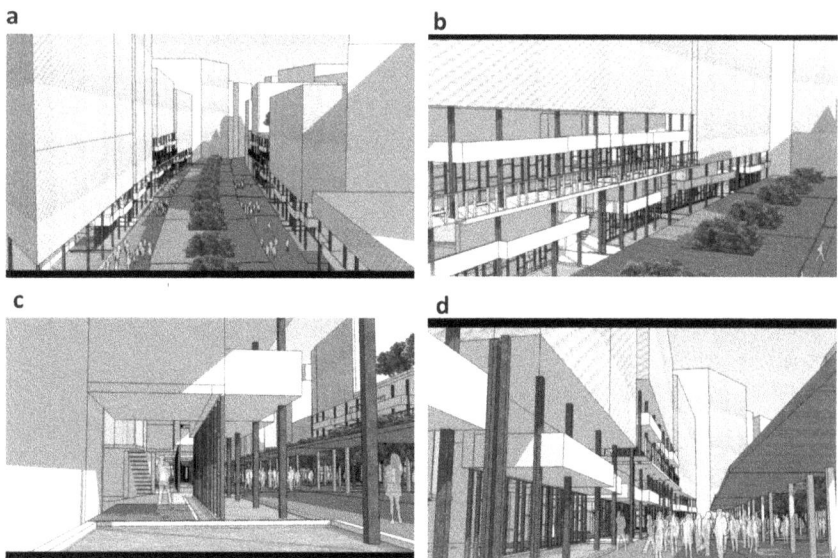

Fig. 14.3 (a–c) Explorations of possible interpretations of modern anjung in an urban core. Explorations of city facadescape integrating portico, pavillion, greenery and water-cooling infusion (combining shade, trees, water, waqf form etc.); (d) potential interpretation in a modern setting of a city in the tropics. (Source: Copyright: Mustafa Kamal Bashar)

Fig. 14.4 Facadescape with front and side portion principles in a modern city. (Source and copyright: Mustafa Kamal Bashar, IIUM)

architecture and urban features can cause and initiate the simultaneous experience, occurrence and optimisation of climatic factors and elements of environmental comfort from a natural world experience, integrating light, air and greenery. Thus, it is important in tropical architecture for roofscapes, greenery elements, gardens, pathways and gazebos to be experienced simultaneously for the impact to be felt.

Conclusions

Moshe Safdie said:

> *In order to go forward and consider the city that might be, we must look at the many visions of our cities since the beginning of massive urbanisation that marks this century.*

The climatic factor in the tropical region is a powerful driver, constantly exerting its influence on urban life forms, including the region's public spaces, urban forms and structures. By focusing on its projected portico or promenade whose character and categories can be used to generate options, an essence of the tropicality of cities within the region can be rediscovered. The templates discussed are models and ideations that arise from a more universal and 'shared' model of the tropical city, and the mapping of these elements gives a unique sense of the city of the archipelago, suggesting a certain requirement of urban guidelines such as projections and setbacks, which can be further developed.

A higher shade index and solar protection are also afforded by these models, and this necessitates a reconsideration of the morphology of shade from past to present, a richer tropical urban experience, must be re-enacted and culturally and climatically indigenised. The climatic form thus becomes part of the 'cultural' forms of expression and these have evolved from centuries of refinement and acculturation. Shade and shadow are perhaps among the most crucial characteristics of the tropical city experience, and the notion of its urban space cannot be separated from a climatically related form, yet they are optimised with respect to the cycle of daily weather and local culture. Urban space is divided between the public, the private and the transitional or semi-public. In the tropics, climatic forces evolve and affect the evolution of spatial expression and strategies of the vernacular, which gradually become 'cultural expressions' of its time and potentially part of a nation's search for a cultural identity, highlighting the critical need to reflect more regional and localised urbanism for the purpose of instilling identity in urban design policy, which is increasingly crucial for developing cities and cityscapes. Thermal comfort is one a basic physical and biological human need. The human body temperature needs to be maintained at a constant 37 ± 5 °C regardless of the prevailing ambient condition. It is important to maintain thermal conditions in buildings within acceptable limits to promote maximum human productivity and performance. The indoor thermal environment is very affected by local climate, and air movement through the building is necessary to decrease indoor discomfort due to overheating conditions in tropical climates [15]. The door thermal environment is very affected by environmental factors such as air temperature, air movement, humidity and radiation. A warm and humid climate and external air movement assist in regulating the indoor environment.

References

Hull, R. W. (1976). *African cities and towns before the European conquest*. Norton.

Manteghi, G., Lamit, H., & Dilshan Remaz, A. (2016). *The International Journal of Energy and Environmental Research, 4*(2), 7–15, May 2016___ Published by European Centre for Research Training and Development UK (www.eajournals.org)7ISSN 2055-0197(Print), ISSN 2055-0200(Online) ENVI-MET SIMULATION ON COOLING EFFECT OF MELAKA RIVER

Sulaiman, A. B., & Shamsuddin, S. (2001). The vanishing streets in the Malaysian urban scape. In P. Miao (Ed.), *Public places in Asia Pacific cities. The GeoJournal Library* (Vol. 60). Springer.

15

Marking Boundaries of Water and Land: Bridges and Gateways

Shireen Jahn Kassim, Noorhanita Abdul Majid,
Syamsul Baharin Zaibon, and Juliana Abu Bakar

This chapter discusses two boundary markers of the city in the form of gateways and bridges—which can be argued as a form of gateway—over land and water. The discussion centres around how such markers have disappeared as identities of cities in South East Asia and that these urban elements constitute a form of land-water symbolism which reflect all the

S. Jahn Kassim (✉)
International Islamic University Malaysia, Jalan Gombak, Malaysia

N. Abdul Majid
KAED International Islamic University Malaysia (IIUM),
Jalan Gombak, Malaysia

S. Baharin Zaibon
School of Creative Industry Management & Performing Arts,
Universiti Utara Malaysia (UUM), Bukit Kayu Hitam, Malaysia
e-mail: syamsulbahrin@uum.edu.my

J. Abu Bakar
Universiti Utara Malaysia (UUM), Bukit Kayu Hitam, Malaysia
e-mail: Liana@uum.edu.my

S. Jahn Kassim et al. (eds.), *Eco-Urbanism and the South East Asian City*,
https://doi.org/10.1007/978-981-19-1637-3_15

eco-urbanist elements discussed in previous chapters—mountain, roof-forms, pillared structures—but which have been drastically affected by historical events and evolution. This chapter presents changes as part of the palimpsest layering of selected cities and discusses the ecological themes in the original profiles and symbolic expressions of these urban elements.

Introduction

According to Lynch (1960, pp. 78–79) landmarks are memorable symbols and unique markers of cities. He identifies them as the key physical characteristic of place where a landmark is seen as a singularity with '*some aspect that is unique or memorable in the context*'. Lynch (1960) further referred to these urban elements as giving 'spatial prominence' and are established as landmarks which convey the essence of a community which grew from the place. Due to the fundamental role of waterways as highways, urban centres in South East Asia were formerly defined by landmarks that were structures over land and water. Due to the lack of boundaries in history either gateways and bridges became a kind of marker—over land and water—signifying thresholds to enclosed zones or a specific settlement and polity with heightened trade located at the river or seafronts.

Other landmarks include random structures of buildings and structures overlapping and layering each other, arising from and approximating multiple craggy coastal topographies of the river and coastal communities. In this region, the tropical forest and coastline present a much more inundated form of topography. Elevated structures protect settlements from the hazards of sites prone to both flooding and muddy plains. Thus, across time, the multi-layered elevations along the coast are caused by these elevated spaces, supported by beams, poles, and stilts and surmounted by a symphony of steeply pitched roofs characteristic of the tropical region. The city, as remarked by travelers, is very near the coastline, so palaces and religious structures occasionally pierce the dilating skylines.

Water Routes and Identities

The tangible and intangible heritage of a littoral city is a confluence of centuries of trade, religion, and polity. In local traditions, for example, the mouth of a river is *pangkalan* or *pengkalan* meaning 'pier', 'landing place', or 'where goods are transferred between water and land transport' is sometimes used in the *kuala* and *muara*, although such a settlement is not always located at a river mouth or confluence of rivers. Bausani, as cited by Aroujo on the nature of the habitation and settlement around the sixteenth century Melaka port, has described the port as having:

> '*at least 10,000 houses which were situated along the coast and the river of Melaka*" further added enhanced remark by Giovanni that "*the town is situated near the sea-shore and thickly strewn with houses and rooms, and it stretches for three leagues which is most beautiful to see*'.

Kuala Terengganu and Alor Setar, Malaysia and Palembang, Indonesia, resonate with the 'accretive nature of these settlements, which become cities recognised uniquely from water, from which one sees how the waterway is a life-force and the city itself is propped up on stilts so as to be resilient to the rise and fall of water levels. The skylines are varied steep pitches which extend vertically and horizontally in deep hierarchical forms seen as fragments of its total settlement ending in an orchestration of multiple skylines, resonating with the 'accretive nature' of the heritage city. Its physical structures are seen as growing from its necessity of the water and its broken-up skyline dominates the image of the city, coupled with the deep and steep fragments of its multiple rooflines. These structures with their steps and piers are repeatedly found fronting onto the river which reflects how the city and its people have a strong visual or physical connection to a river (Yassin, 2009, p. 3 cited). It is from this perspective that the gateways and bridges to a city are important urban elements that define the initial impressions of South East Asian cities.

The Symbolism of the Gateways

Gateways historically marked royal or administrative zones. Either when entering its royal zone or separating public and private zones, a gateway marks the threshold of protection, change, and privacy. The gateway almost marks different layers of the city in the form of the layers and perimeters of protective boundaries around its essentially private, semi-private, or public and public urban core. A gateway marks a change in power and hierarchy in society and the protection of its periphery and, at times, decorate a wall. Thus, gateways are entrances that can be found along a society's peripheries, and in less established polities, such protective mechanisms manifest in the form of palisades or walls around the royal enclave or zone which are pierced by the gateway entrance.

Rather than the typical hemispherical arches and semi-elliptical entrance, the profile of the localised gateway resonates with the topographical beginnings: its variations of a core tapering shape evoke the local's cosmographic outlook, i.e. the mountain. Over time this generic shape undergoes local mutation, ornamentation, and variation across the localities and regions. Thus, from the curved forms of Patani gateways to tectonic roofed forms of Western Borneo, the Malay gateway carries its own identity, yet reflects a recurring archetypal form executed in timber, masonry, or hybrid constructions (Table 15.1). The Kacapuri gate at Kuala Bahang, Kedah is a gate that marks the edge between water and land that is a fort at the river estuary. It retains the Malay image of the curved variation merged with hybrid images.

The gateway takes on the form of a multi-layer procession and entrance process. The traditions of Kelantan, steeped in the Langkasuka traditions of elaborate timber carvings, reflected histories and imageries in the histories of Patani and Thailand. In Indonesia, the gateways at times take on the direct form of mountains and the split mountains which are traditionally revered as portals to sacred powers. In Malaysia, this diffused into the idea of the sacred zone being linked to the royal family and their aristocratic families. To enter the sacred zone or royal grounds, timber gates are curved in multiple expressions yet generally resonate with the shape of a mountain. These are further added on or abstracted and are adorned with other flora-like motifs.

Table 15.1 Mountain-like profiles of gateways at Malay Nusantara cities

	Restored form of gateway	Original gateway
Alor Setar, Northern Peninsular Malaysia		
	Gate of Kacapuri, Kedah	Kacapuri Gate at Kuala Bahang before restoration.
Patani, Southern Thai		
	Gateway to royal grounds at Patani, Thailand	Sketch of entrance to Patani palace.

Patani Threshold

One of the northernmost frontiers of the Malay region was Patani, an earlier legacy of Langkasuka. Its entry gate to its traditional royal zone has a simply tripartite curved and graceful gateway, evoking a mound. This recalls how the morphology of mountains in the Malay psyche is a conception seen not only as an abode of heavens but as a transition to it, reserved for kings or their dynasty. The profile of the mountain is seen in many variations, from austere to ornate, surmounting, or adorning a portal. While it simply surmounts a gateway to a royal enclosure, its resonance of the mountain form is seen as embodying a threshold into the sacred. Other motifs are then added to this generic form to symbolize this transition.

Such layering and its imageries find their genesis in the histories of the Malay city, from Aceh and Patani in the north to Johor and Banten in the south. The palatial realm of the Penyengat Island, Riau region, the last sanctuary of the Malay kings of the Melaka line, has mound-like adornments of its peripheral columns with a curving mountain-like motif in metal overhead. Other complexes of these regions, such as the Sambas (Fig. 15.1) and Kadriah complex, are essentially buildings with the fundamental public to private layers or zoning, between which are pathways and gates. The ambassador, Sui, who visited Kelantan, then known as Kerajaan Tanah Merah, in the year 607 Masihi (according to Hijri calendar) wrote about and documented the capital city of Chin-Tu, Kota Seng-chih, or Kota Singa, which had three layers of the gateway with a '*gunongan*' (mountain) shape or arch ornamented by flora motifs and golden bells.

Fig. 15.1 A drawing of Songkhla Gateway, 1905

Songkhla's gateway (Fig. 15.1) recalls how was the seat of an old Malay kingdom. The Chinese historian/traveller Wei Pu Chiu situates the famed Langkasuka to include regions to the south of Songkhla. Its history as a centre of international maritime trade, in particular with Quanzhou in China influence can be seen in the decorative patterns of the Chinese forms and details in this gateway. In earlier times (200–1400 CE), the city of Songkhla had historically formed the northern extremity of the Malay Kingdom of Langkasuka. The city-state then succeeded as the Sultanate of Singgora took power, and later the city became a tributary of Nakhon Si Thammarat. The city suffered damage during several attempts to gain independence. The gateway expression and profile reflect the growth of Songkhla between 1775 and 1912, with the local and external powers combined to consolidate its development into an important port city on the gulf coast. The influence of Chinese traders is also evident in the details of the gateway that is still standing in the city.

The Gateway of Songkhla today that is situated in the Chinatown of downtown Songkhla still retains its original features which had adopted the tapering curve resonating mountain forms that are evident in the Malay gateways. Still adorned with Chinese details, the distinct 'curved mountains' flanking the sides have distinct Malay features as found in the gates of Patani, Kadriah, and Kedah.

Gateways of West Borneo Kingdoms

The traditional gateways of the royal cities of West Borneo which were set up and built around the seventeenth and eighteenth centuries recall their specific profile and style unique to the region. These profiles range from timber to hybrid and consist of combinations that set them apart from other cultures and are devoid of any external influence. Their form and construction can be described as hybrid. Profile-wise, they depart from the usual mountain reference and have a slight iconic edge to those of Peninsular Malaysia, yet they incorporate timber structures with masonry sides of the entrance, in curved half-mound profiles which still recall the notion of the mound. Though theirs is simple and less ornate, they recall their parallels in the facades of Italian architecture which typically have volutes that frame the gateway. In the gateway for Sultanate Sambas (Fig. 15.1) and its royal enclave, its entrance gateway combines a pavilion-like timber structure with a locally linked pitched roof and a base that reflects the mound-like curvatures that can be linked to the regional form and character in the eighteenth century. Such hybrid forms and profiles can be found in Pontianak too and are repeatedly used throughout the region to frame the entryway.

Bridges as Gateways over Water

Bridges were a form of gateway over water—rivers and estuaries—and as a connector between royal, administrative, and mercantile and commercial zones. The nearness and availability of water enable the buildings, bridges, and urban spaces to be permeable to the cooler atmosphere, thus bridges become an accumulator and unifier of commercial markets that grew over water and the boundaries of water and land. Bridges of the Malay world are represented by several Malay words: *jambatan, titi, gertak, limban,* and *pelimban,* depending on their size and functions. It can inherently be a symbol of communication and union between two distinct realms. Salamak and Fross (2016) suggested that bridges are often seen as indicators of progress in technical innovation and imply economic potential.

The bridges' role is vital in city planning as a connector with architectural and cultural significance on the two sides of the Melaka River. In their original form and construction, it is known to have had a wooden roof that characterises the perished Melaka bridge's identity. Iconographic bridges are known in old Malay cities, yet many of these have perished with time or historical incidents. The original Melaka bridge was burnt to the ground by the Portuguese, hence by mapping surviving contemporaneous bridges in nearby tropical maritime cities, the image of the Melaka bridge re-emerges and can be formed. Thus, the bridge is rebuilt from past conceptions and observations which see the water as part of the land.

Hybridity in city forms captures the extreme contrasts or resources and social hierarchies in societies. As Birnas and Mirka (2016) assert,

hybridity is a word often used concerning cultural or artistic mixture, and usu-
ally associated with post-colonial cultural theories. Hybridity may be considered
an analogue to ambiguity, multivalence, fusion, and interbreeding. One recalls
the character of hybridity when reminiscing structures that can mediate between
elements very different from each other.

The bridge recalls the above quoted terms multivalent, ambiguous forms 'mediating structures', a term with deeper resonance, especially in past urban spaces and territorial-geographical systems. Such hybridity in the South East Asian region may take the form of traditional pergolas or trellises in historical gardens. They may be reinterpreted in contemporary forms, mingling industrial relics, pathways, and new elements such as pedestrian bridges.

Historians and colonial writers described the original Melaka bridge as 'heavy wooden', which could explain why it was destroyed when burnt. The wooden part may have been the upper main section of the bridge. De Jong and Van Kick (1960) describe how a traveller had portrayed the bridge:

…Besides these requisites for the wedding, he kept 8,000 pieces of artillery in
the city. For as it extended like a turban for a distance of one league along the
coast, was entirely built of wood, and lacked walls and moats (being defended
solely by its men, as is customary for larger settlements), he had provided it with
this great number of pieces of artillery to be placed all along the coast if any
armada was to appear.

The eastern part of the town is called Ilher, and the other, the western, Upi; they were inhabited by two Javanese, great in wealth and business, with large families, who, not being able to dwell in the city proper, chose to live below on their own. In between there runs a river like a salt-water estuary, which well within the city receives some freshwater from the swamps and marshes of the interior. Near where this river joins the sea there was a very large bridge of heavy wood, which connected the city with the royal quarters, adjoining Ilher, where his mosque of stone and plaster were situated, surrounded by some dwellings of the highest nobility.

During the fifteenth century during the Sultanate, the mouth of the river was described as 'continuously dragged by a crowd of public slaves, this allowed larger vessels, like those arriving from Bengal and Coromandel, to enter its mouth. These ships brought textiles and rice needed for local consumption. (De Jong & Van Kick, 1960)

Giovanni da Empoli's description of Melaka closely resembles that of other travellers. The writings by the Portuguese chronicler Fernão Lopes de Castanheda also describe the bridge as wooden. They were visitors who, writing many years after Melaka's seizure, seems to have accessed a lost report prepared by an anonymous eyewitness:

This city of Melaka lies on the coast of a great kingdom called Siam located at the mouth of a small river that flows into the sea in a small bay. It lies in two degrees to the north, and has a very good harbor at that time, this city had a length as [the distance] from Xabregas to the monastery of Bethlehem, but [it was] narrow [in width]: it would have about thirty thousand houses.

The river divides it into two parts: the passage from one to another is by a wooden bridge, as most of the houses are, especially in the seaside, and others are very noble houses [made of] stone and lime. The palaces of the king are over a hill in the southern part of the city, and in it is his Great Mosque and live all the noblemen. And to the northern bank, where the city is wider than in any other part...

The wooden bridge described by Castanheda would be the bridge before the year 1511 because, at that time, the mosques and the palace are still in place. Another vital record was the book of Ma Huan (1433) *Yíngyá shènglǎn* (The Overall Survey of the Ocean's Shores) about the countries visited by him throughout the Ming treasure voyages led by Admiral Cheng Ho (Zheng He). Ma Huan stated that:

The Melaka River flows in front of the palace before emptying into the sea. The timber bridge is the central marketplace of the city and there are more than twenty pavilions built on the bridge to accommodate the trade of various goods.
—Yingya Shenlan, Ma Huan

Another translation by Mills (1970) stated:

There is one large river whose water flows past the front of the king's residence to enter the sea; over the river, the king has constructed a wooden bridge, on which are built more than twenty bridge pavilions, (and) all trading in every article takes place on this (bridge).
—Mills (1970)

Figures 15.2 and 15.3 are Portuguese illustrations of Melaka circa 1509–1512 and 1630. Both showed the bridge as a completely wooden structure with a roof. The image by Ferdinand Magellan is more elaborate among the two, offering a longer bridge with two separate roofs. The sides were semi-open, emphasizing the railings. The Spanish colonials drew a similar drawing in 1665. The drawing showed a timber bridge with a roof with openings on the sides.

Nevertheless, the bridge was depicted as a combination of masonry and timber by some visual records during the colonial period. A Portuguese drawing suggested that a timber bridge was constructed on a

Fig. 15.2 Gateway to the Royal zone, Sultanate of Riau Lingga, Pulau Penyengat, Indonesia

Fig. 15.3 An old photo taken in 1904 showing the masonry construction of Gerbang Kota Tengah

masonry base. The base was built from a series of tall masonry columns that connect to tall staircases on each side of the banks.

A second map drawn in 1635 showed the bridge was continuous from masonry walls marking the banks of the estuary. The masonry walls were distinctly represented by reddish colour compared to the wooden palisades encircling the city of Melaka. The combination of construction techniques and materials was a possible method of continuing the masonry walls used for the fort. Since there were no visual records of the physical components of the Melaka bridge, the drawings from Portuguese and Dutch artists suggest certain characteristics of the original bridge. The drawings show the bridge's reconstructed version after the Portuguese seizure in 1511, which appears to be a simple timber bridge with a roof. During the conquest of Melaka, the conquering army had burnt and torn down the original bridge, mosque, and palace within the city.

Contemporaneous Examples from Surrounding Regions

These covered timber bridges are found throughout maritime South East Asia during the fifteenth century and a bridge description in 1433 resembles many bridges in Vietnam with a semi-open wooden structure with roofs. The covered bridge of Thay Pagoda, Vietnam, for example, is a simple timber bridge resting on a masonry arch wall, which suggests some drawings recorded by colonists.

Nevertheless, the wooden bridge of Hoi An, with masonry expression and timber construction of the Hoi Nan bridge, suggests a resemblance. However, it differs from the detailed aesthetics of the Melaka bridge but nevertheless forms a gateway on the river. One recalls the medieval city of Hoi An, a relic of an ancient commercial port of the sixteenth to the nineteenth centuries in Vietnam. Hoi An (Quang Nam) was once a busy commercial port connected to various other ports in the world. This fact has similarities to Melaka, which was an entrepot in the fourteenth to fifteenth centuries. According to historical documents, during the seventeenth and eighteenth centuries, the city bustled with boats and people. The book *Phu Bien Tap Luc* by Le Quy Don, a famous Vietnamese scientist in the eighteenth century, describes a similar scene of medieval maritime centres: '*all the goods are here; hundreds of big cargo ships cannot transport them all at the same time*'. During this period, Hoi An was an urban centre with an international commercial port that flourished in South East Asia and became an essential economic base of the Nguyen lords, kings of the Nguyen dynasty in Cochin. The interior of the bridge supports the function of the bridge as a link for the movement of people and commerce.

Closer to Melaka, Sumatera has Minangkabau traditions which exhibit the notable architecture of a covered timber bridge, recorded at Alahan Panjang, Sumatera. Figure 15.2 refers to such a covered bridge typology in the Malay world typologies. The bridge was built from timber and adorned with carvings that are also a gateway to the opposite side of the river. It has a roof design that resembles the roof of *Rumah Gadang*, which is a prevailing style in Tanah Minang, Sumatera Barat. It also has seating alongside the railings. The simple structure resembled the prevalent traditional *gonjong* roof design of the area, a simple pitch roof with a distinct curve upwards at the ends (Fig. 15.3).

Recalling Alahan Panjang, the Melaka bridge's details would be similar and reflect the same typology in structure with a width used for commercial activities. The Tapan Han Bridge in Bangkok (Fig. 15.3) is another covered bridge, with a tiered form of roof, which resonates with the characteristic fragmented form discussed as an architectural character of South East Asian architecture that represents its essentially climatic form. The form further suggests how a bridge was seen as a structure for occupation, not merely for crossings; and in historical writings it has two distinct layers, the original layer featuring a traditional bridge as the original bridge was burnt by the invading Portuguese, and then the sublayer built by the Dutch in a revision of the Melaka bridge. The colonial rendition differs markedly from the traditional covered bridges of the Asian region.

The colonial rendition of bridges recalls similar colonial stylisations of gateways such as the Gerbang Kacapuri and Gerbang Inggeris (English Gate) located at the mouth of the Kedah River at Kuala Bahang or Kuala Kedah. The two gates are part of the red brick fort which remains and can be seen to this day. The fort was built during the reign of Sultan Abdullah Mukarram Shah when he ascended the throne of the Kedah State Government in 1760, with the aim of defending the State of Kedah from Siamese military attacks at that time. Construction work began in 1771 and was completed in 1780 with the help of skilled masons imported from India whose first task was to make bricks. The mortar for the walls is said to be a mixture of sand, egg whites, and honey. The fort covers an area of 2 acres, and the Kacapuri Gate (as shown in Table 15.1) was the first built on the north side facing a stream known as Alor Melaka. On the side facing the sea and the river, two layers of walls were built and the space between them was filled with earth. When the State of Kedah received the British Adviser, the city was used as its administrative centre, and a new gateway was built, the Gerbang Inggeris. While the Kacapuri Gateway was the first built and retained Malay features of the curved *gunungan*, the Gerbang Inggeris is an imported feature with arches and keystones that resemble English architecture.

Eclectic-Islamic and Colonial-Era Influences

By the early 1900s, external stylistic influences were evident as a result of the increasing cosmopolitanism of the gateway identity. Pulau Penyengat, the lady bastion of the Riau Johor Sultanate, reflects a gateway (Fig. 15.5) that has the typically dominant masonry archway yet whose form is made into a hierarchy, being narrower at the top. The gateway is a combined eclectic design between Islamic and colonial-era influences. The gateway to the Masjid Raya Sultan Riau (Fig. 15.4) also uniquely reflects the Malay tapering form but one which evolved into an eclectic form—the typical pointed Islamic forms of the Middle East.

Fig. 15.4   Original decorative finials of old gateway representing insignia of sultanate which resemble the curved 'Islamic' forms of the Aceh Stone

The gateways of Kedah inherited the eclectic-Islamic and colonial-era influences. The royal seat of Kedah was relocated to Alor Setar by the Kedah monarch in 1735, and forts and gateways were part of the built environment established as part of the royal realm and defence of Alor Setar and the littoral port of Kuala Bahang. There are three significant gateways in Alor Setar: Gerbang Kota Tengah, in the city centre and Gerbang Kacapuri and the Inggeris Gate in Kuala Bahang (rename to Kuala Kedah).

The Gerbang Kota Tengah (Centre City Gateway shown in Fig. 15.5) is located in the city centre. The gate was part of the urban core surrounded by the royal administrative buildings, mosques, and residences. The masonry gateway marks the entrance to the walled grounds for the royal palace. Gerbang Kota Tengah is a unique gate that has combined elements of regional, Islamic, and colonial architectural details. It has compartmented roofs with pediments and curved roofs which exude traces of Malay *gunungan* or mountain features. The curved elements can

Fig. 15.5   A covered bridge in West Sumatera, Indonesia (1877–1879). https://cdn0. enacademic.com/pictures/enwiki/67/COLLECTIE_TROPENMUSEUM_Overdekte_ brug_over_de_rivier_Gumanti_bij_Alahanandjang_TMnr_60003071.jpg

be seen in many other gateways of the Malay world, as discussed earlier. It is claimed by many that the design features of the gateway are linked to the Merong Mahawangsa legacy from the Old Kedah kingdom. The finials on the sides also resemble the Aceh stones, but also with disputed origins (Fig. 15.6). Some historians believe that the design associated with the Aceh stones was also originally a feature from the Old Kedah civilisation, but this remains unverified. The Aceh stones are also used as grave markers for many sultans and royal families of Kedah. The gateway has arches and column features which seem to be an eclectic interpretation of borrowed motifs.

As Gospodini (2001) asserts: *Historical urban cores representing long living survivals from the past constitute counter structures to the ephemerality of fashions, products, values, etc., which according to Dietvorst and Ashworth is rooted in the growing of events in time (acceleration of history) characterising the era of new modernity* (see Ashworth & Dietvorst, 1995, p. 3). Urban elements were historically and irrevocably changed due to their

Fig. 15.6 Tapan Han Bridge, Bangkok circa 1890 with characteristic of the traditional covered bridge. (Source: Vorbild Rialto-Brücke (Venedig): Chronik Thailands. Bangkok, Postkarte, um 1890. http://www.payer.de/thailandchronik/chronik1890.htm

histories of colonisation, creating a multifaceted typological and morphological layering of urban elements and typologies within their morphological core. Within these cities, what constitutes a definition of their urban identity requires a relook at definitions of these layers and the continuous reframing of thresholds of cultural change. Configurations, forms, and types may range from original vernacular–indigenous to early modern configurations and stylisations in typologies, which have undergone multiple changes, across somewhat compressed eras of their urbanscapes. The gateways and the bridges can be looked at as different or similar identities according to the perspectives and interpretations of the viewers. The two urban elements established the genius loci of South East Asian cities. The analyses presented here reveal the symbolic significance of the gateways and bridges as key urban markers, landmarks, or elements, their tangible and intangible heritage, combined with eco-urbanist profiles and urban rituals. A historical pre-colonial urban core analysis uncovers the strategic potentials and ability to integrate both sustainable and urban regeneration and validates how a more layered view of constructed urban patterns and infrastructure can assist urban planners and policymakers in developing and reconstructing place-making, and a sense of place in cities.

References

Abdul, T. A. Q. B. R., & Nawawi, N. M. (2021). Architectural Regionalism During the Neo-Classical Era: Classifying the Architectural "Hybrid" Stylistic Forms. *Cultural Syndrome, 3*(1), 46–82.

Ashworth, G. J., & Dietvorst, A. G. J. (1995). Tourism and spatial transformations; implications for policy and planning.

Bocarro, A. (1635). View of the colonial Portuguese fortress. *Urban Geographies: Cities, Places, Regions.* Retrieved April 1, 2016, from http://urbangeographies.tumblr.com/post/95996920902/malacca-melaka-malaysia-view-of-the-colonial

Couling, N. (2014). Spaces and flows: An international journal of urban and extra urban studies. *Spaces and Flows, 4*, 76.

De Jong, P. D. J., & Van Wijk, H. L. A. (1960). The Malacca Sultanate. *Journal of Southeast Asian History, 1*(2), 20–29.

Gospodini, A. (2001). Urban design, urban space morphology, urban tourism: an emerging new paradigm concerning their relationship. *European Planning Studies, 9*(7), 925–934.

Hybridity in Landscape Architecture-WB. informal-brandmark-inverse. (n.d.). Retrieved July 8, 2022, from https://soa.utexas.edu/courses/spring-2021/hybriditylandscape-architecture-wb#:~:text=Hybridity%20may%20be%20considered%20an,an%20architectural%20structure%2C%20a%20building

Lynch, K. (1960). The image of the city, (p. 208). MIT Press: Cambridge MA.

Mills, J. V. G. (1970). *Ma Huan Ying-Yai Shenglan-The overall survey of Ocean's Shores* (Feng Ch'eng Chun, Trans. from Chinese and text ed.). Hakluyt Society.

Salamak, M., & Fross, K. (2016). Bridges in urban planning and architectural culture. Proceedia Engineering 161, 207–212.

Timur, U. P. (2013). Urban waterfront regenerations. In Advances in landscape architecture. IntechOpen.

Yassin, A. B. M., Eves, C., & McDonagh, J. (2009). Waterfront development for residential property in Malaysia. In Proceedings from the PRRES conference 2009—The 15th annual conference of the Pacific Rim Real Estate Society. University of Technology Sydney.

16

Ecology, Structure and the Regalia: Framing the Evolving Language of Malay Architecture

Tengku Anis Qarihah Raja Abdul Kadir,
Puteri Mayang Bahjah Zaharin,
and Shireen Jahn Kassim

Past Discourses on the Malay- Nusantara language of public architecture had generally focused upon its evolving timber elements, construction and expressions. Its abstractions into the modern context are less commonly discussed, yet questions always remain on the conceptions, including generic definitions, terms and methodology in separating structure, non-structural elements, and ornamentation within a theoretical framework of language of architecture based on its history within South East

T. A. Qarihah Raja Abdul Kadir • P. M. B. Zaharin
Centre of Studies Architecture, College of Built Environment,
Universiti Teknologi MARA (UiTM), Shah Alam, Malaysia
e-mail: tengku.anis@uitm.edu.my; bahjah@uitm.edu.my

S. Jahn Kassim (✉)
International Islamic University Malaysia, Jalan Gombak, Malaysia

© The Editor(s) (if applicable) and The Author(s), under exclusive license to Springer
Nature Singapore Pte Ltd. 2023
S. Jahn Kassim et al. (eds.), *Eco-Urbanism and the South East Asian City*,
https://doi.org/10.1007/978-981-19-1637-3_16

Asia. The problem arises when discussing, generalising and theorising language which arise from constructions, and the gap between discourses in timber and masonry construction and expressions.. Using Gottfried Semper's four elements of architecture as an armature, this chapter uses such fundamental frameworks to develop a classification of architectural language based on the vernacular evolvements across time, and which divides such evolvements into essentially four elemental groups. Semper's four elements are seen as parts of the evolution of a local fundamental style, which is universally linked to the vernacular, in which formal elements of architectural expression arise from vernacular elements of construction and language, which undergo 'petrification'; thus sustaining the basic expression, although material and technology may have evolved. These help and contribute in resolving a gap and polar binary between the language of the 'modern' and the traditional timber-based vernacular architectonics of the region.

Introduction

To preserve cultural and climatic elements of language and localised forms despite evolutions and drastic changes in material and technology throughout centuries, there must be a universal armature that affords a thought process and continuity between local vernacular forms and modern forms; despite the changes in material and technology. Any discussion of the language of the modern vernacular for tropical South East Asia must be able to be traced to a root form, which is predominantly timber, but which is able to associate changes in construction with similarities in language and grammar, despite changes in its earlier (primarily timber- based) expressions and later stages of its evolvement, including masonry and metallic construction and ornamental elements. Semper's theory of 'four elements of architecture' provides a way of discussing and 'theorising' the evolving language arising from construction and from building structure.

The *Four Elements of Architecture*[1] is a book by the German architect Gottfried Semper, a theorist who practiced, taught, and published in the mid-1800s. He spent more than a decade completing it. Translated by Harry Frances Malgrave,[2] the book outlines a theory of architecture and architectural style which is founded upon the notion of the inherent and natural tendencies of indigenous societies to petrify their primitive forms. Semper's fundamental argument, which asserts how in every society there is a natural tendency of indigenous societies to petrify their forms, i.e. they translate timber language into masonry expressions, as discussed in these more complex 'cosmopolitan' versions of the vernacular. In many cases, their grammar and decorative elements survive and prevail as they evolve with the advent of new construction and production technologies. Semper's book[3] caused ripples and controversies in its time because it inverted the order of the architectural design process, the philosophy and central argument of the 'structure' being the defining aesthetic principles of form. As Lukito[4] suggests:

> *It inverted the order of the structure-ornament hierarchy with the structure now becoming a kind of temporary scaffolding.*

Earlier, it was Semper's idea and framework of the primeval '*primitive hut*'[5] that was given a framework to assert an anthropological view on the fundamentals of architectural language which resonates and aligns with the natural evolution of vernacular societies.

---

[1] Semper, Gottfried. *The Four Elements of Architecture and Other Writings*. Trans. Harry F. Mallgrave and Wolfgang Herrmann (Cambridge, 1989). ISBN 0-521-35475-7.

Semper, Gottfried. Style in the Technical and Tectonic Arts; or, Practical Aesthetics. Trans. Harry F. Mallgrave (Santa Monica, 2004). ISBN 0-89236-597-8.

[2] Ibid., 1989.

[3] Gottfried Semper, 1962. Style in the Technical and Tectonic Arts, Or, Practical Aesthetics, translated into English by Getty Publications, 2004.

[4] Yulia Nurliani Lukito, *Exhibiting Modernity and Indonesian Vernacular Architecture: Hybrid Architecture at Pasar Gambir of Batavia*, the 1931 Paris International Colonial Exhibition and Taman Mini Indonesia Indah, Springer, 16 Oct 2015 page 47.

[5] Mlagrave, Harry, "Gottfried Semper: In Search of Architecture." Journal of Architectural Education, 38(4), pp. 33–34.

Semper uses the idea of the '*Caribbean hut*' as a universal and primordial idea to represent the basic house or unit of architecture, the primal and simplest unit. The '*Caribbean hut*' (Fig. 16.1) is simply seen as an idealisation, a fundamental beginning and essence of the architectural act within which one can find '*all the elements of antique architecture in their pure and most original form: the hearth as the Centre Point, raised earth as a terrace surrounded by posts, the column-supported roof, and the mat enclosure as a spatial termination or wall*'. The primary argument of Semper's thesis is that the beginnings of architectural style generally gravitate around these primordial '*four elements*', which recur even across changes and mutations in material, technology, and stylisation. Asquith and Vellinga (2006) and Watkin (2000) similarly observe and mention '*petrification*' as a natural evolution of all societies. They observe how the Greek classical temple recalls the elements of earlier primordial structures in timber. Semper (1962) argues that given the right resource and conditions, indigenous societies will eventually evolve and, in so doing, petrify and mutate their traditional structures and artefacts into similar or abstracted forms as they form more advanced societies. He argues that the primitive hut has essentially four fundamental elements or '*principles*' that recur across time and are reflected in their evolution from their base material to masonry counterparts or complex interpretations.

Malay Architectural Language and Variation of 'Four Elements'

Attempts to culturally map the continuum of Malay expression into contemporary architecture will begin with timber expressions, yet key elements of language evolved into masonry and eventually petrified into public domains and frontages of architecture. There has been a tendency to characterise and describe Malay style as merely essentially an expression of the protective roof, yet on closer inspection there is a fundamental set of grammar rules that has survived across all permutations and petrifications (Table 16.1).

Table 16.1 Petrification observed in vernacular palaces of Aceh and Perak

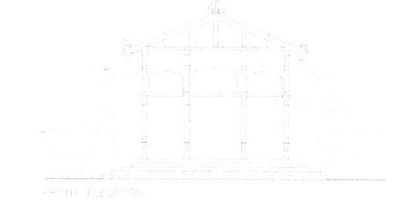

Rumah Aceh reflects elevated nature of its central zone known as the 'female' zone and its four-pillar structure; its front elevation and ornamentation are an evolvement of what was earlier its 'side' elevations

The Istana Aceh, 1860s, initially built during the reign of Sultan Iskandar Muda, reflects the four-pillar principle and style and a 'masonry' evolution of the elevation 'middle' zone of the Rumah Aceh.
(Source: authors drawing)

Vernacular Kenangan palace of Perak[a], shown here in its renovated version, an epitome of the heightened aesthetic style of the Kutai vernacular of Perak featuring the 'weaving' technique prevalent in the region. A feature of the Perak aristocratic style is the ground floor balustrade, which tends to encircle the ground floor zone.

The 'petrified' version of the ground floor encircled vernacular here seen at the side elevation of the Istana Hulu, Kuala Kangsar, a palace built by Captain Maurice Alexander of the PWD in Kuala Kangsar with vetting by the reigning Sultan Idris of the time. It was known that the sultan would send back drawings to the British colonial office to protest certain elements and insist on Malay elements.

[a]The final renovation of the Kenangan Palace was done in the 1920s. However, it was constructed earlier and was much earlier known as Istana Lembah, or the Palace of the Valley. Yet it is suspected to be part of an even earlier palace which can be traced back to the Istana Sri Sayong of the 1600s in the original palace of Sayong, built by the sons of the sultan of Melaka, who exiled and then rebuilt their dynasties in Perak. See discussion in https://sembangkuala.wordpress.com/2011/10/23/a-quandary-part-2-an-istana-in-kuala-kangsar-c-1927/

In the context of Indonesia, Lukito (2015) referred to Semper when she observed that a distinctive hybrid vernacular style of the Indonesian style when evolved into the form and language of Pasar Gambir, a stylised pavilion design by local designers funded by the Dutch during the 1930s. He described this particular pavilion as significant in representing a certain stylistic trend or strand during that era, where petrification occurred as the culmination of a growing interest in hybrid vernacular architecture during the 1920s in Indonesia. The Dutch employed local Indonesian designers who started to study, collect, and use Indies vernacular architecture. Dutch architect Hendrik P. Berlage visited the Indies in 1923 and in 1931 published a book titled *My Indies Voyage*, in which he promoted the Indies vernacular architecture. Amongst others who link the Indonesian hybrid vernacular pavilion of Pasar Gambir of Indonesia not only to an appropriation of the indigenous vernacular language but to, essentially, aesthetic tendencies that consistently sought a modernisation of the vernacular while imitating and evoking it at the same time, Lukito (2015) writes as follows:

> … *The unique construction of Pasar Gambir could be related to the idea of woven fabric proposed by the 19th century German architect and theorist Gottfried Semper. The woven fabric was essentially patterned and ornamental. He saw textiles as a manifestation of man's desire to beautify by designing and decorating, i.e., the cultural role of the decorated wall. As embellishment reflects culture.*

Evolvement of Vernacular into Four Essential Elements

Falling back on Semper, Kawamukai (2000) summarised the usefulness of his theories as the region attempts to derive a language or style suited to the modern yet rooted to the vernacular: 'After this new theory, he searched toward the "beginnings" *of architecture to grasp at 'four elements' (hearth, mound, enclosure, and roof). He tried to describe architectural histories in terms of modifications of the four elements, because he thought that relations of the four elements could not be fixed, rather that each element could metamorphose independently according to conditions of racial characteristics, climates, topographies, etc.*' Akos[6] further expands on the significance of Semper's theory: '*That would be a potential interpretation of Gottfried Semper's theory of Stoffwechsel (material transformation), which explains the ability of materials to undergo change by considering the products of human téchne*' (Akos, 2017).

Recall Semper's link of the '*four*' elements found in all forms of indigenous architecture and which arise from the abilities and skills in the traditional crafts of all ancient societies. He argues that in each society, the fundamental element of architecture boils down to 'four elements':

- hearth—metallurgy, ceramics;
- roof—carpentry;
- enclosure—textile, weaving; and
- mound—earthwork

In one of his main works, *Style in the Technical and Tectonic Arts*, or *Practical Aesthetics*, Semper proposed how architectural style has arisen, and thus can arise, from the anthropological beginnings of architecture. In his earlier book published in 1851, Semper emphasises that, for him, the Caribbean hut was '*not a figment of the imagination*' but '*a highly realistic example of a wooden structure taken from ethnology*' and that he would place '*before the reader the equivalent of the Vitruvian primitive hut in all its details*'.

The relevance of this to South East Asian architecture in general and Malay architecture in particular is, as Akos mentions, with reference to Semper's writings on how he saw the timber style '*... as a formal language which corresponds with the characteristics of wood but which, after several metamorphoses, can develop into "stone style"*'.

Though the vernacular is known as '*architecture without architects*',[7] Nusantara architecture is a naturally evolving architecture, arising from

---

[6] Moravánszky, Ákos. 2017, Metamorphism: Material Change in Architecture. Basel/Berlin/Boston: Walter de Gruyter GmbH, 2017.

[7] Despite the terms' being used interchangeably, there is a subtle difference between the term 'indigenous' and 'vernacular' and how it is used in architectural discourse. The term indigenous refers to traditional architecture built by traditional means and resources and thus frequently relates to tribe and locality, where vernacular refers to a larger dimension and can encompass present time and stylistic principles, such as the 'critical vernacular', a principle coined to represent abstract vernacular in modern buildings.

the conditions and constraints of place and site in the region. It generally encompasses forms and styles that reflect the age-old traditions of local timber artisanship, the materials prevalent locally, and the enduring character of place. As communities evolved, these skills were refined as seen as the epitome of place. The craftsmen worked for the wealthiest figure in the community. The people who identify themselves as ethnic Malays are found not only throughout the peninsula of West Malaysia but also in coastal East Malaysia, Brunei, southern Thailand, parts of Sumatra, Java, the Riau Islands and Kalimantan in Indonesia, southern Philippines, and even as far as Colombo, Sri Lanka, and Cape Town, South Africa, the 'Chams' in Cambodia, and Vietnam. The *Sejarah Melayu* (also known as the Malay Annals), a seventeenth-century text on the history of the Malays, says that for almost 2000 years, the non-stop traffic between India and the archipelago, as well as with China, Champa, and Cambodia, provided a plethora of cultural influences through trade, culture, and inter-marriages.

The Malay house—the genesis—is an indigenous tropical architecture reflecting not only the geography and climate, but the artisanal and aesthetic skills of the Malays.[8] Many have written on it (including Chap. 10), and despite its many variations and ethnic localisation, due to influences such as Bugis, Riau, Patani, Java Acheh, and Minangkabau,[9] and these styles[10] reflect these influences yet share common traits of the same character of Malay architectural principles. As discussed by Nasir

---

[8] A definition of the Malays has been discussed by various ethnographers, historians, and cultural theorists, including Reid (2004). Understanding Melayu (Malay) as a Source of Diverse Modern Identities. In Journal of Southeast Asian Studies, 32(3), 295–313; Milner, A. C. (1982). The Malays. United Kingdom: Nielsen Book Data; and Andaya, Leonard, 2010. Leaves of the Same Tree—Trade and Ethnicity in the Straits of Malacca. NUS Press. Singapore.

[9] Bahauddin, A,, Hardono, S., Abdullah, A., & Maliki, N. Z. The Minangkabau house: Architectural and cultural elements. WIT Transactions on Ecology and the Environment, 2012, 165, 15–25. https://doi.org/10.2495/ARC120021

[10] Hosseini, E., Mursib, G., Nafida, R., & Shahedi, B. Malay Vernacular Architecture: Mirror of The Past, Lessons For The Future Malay Vernacular Architecture: Mirror of the Past, Lessons for the Future (November 2016)

(1997),[11] Ibrahim (2013),[12] Tahir et al. (2002), and Wan Ismail (2005),[13] the vernacular house form is the primal form, a 'natural growth' amidst its local topography, climate, ecology, and geography, i.e. the prevalent hot, humid climate alongside a jungle-infested inhospitable ecology; both house and palace style revolve around an elevated form, wide openings, and layered yet wide protective roofs, and a linear-like arrangement of spaces emerge from its tropical environment. Construction-wise, Sabrizaa and Sufian (2008) divides the language which expresses structure and which separates a set of grammar rules between 'structure' and '*ornamentation*'. All in all, Hilton (1983)[14] describes the essential character of the Malay house construction and which focuses on modularity and efficiency:

> … *The common features of the great variety of Malay/Indonesian houses, together with the Japanese house* [Engel, 1964, p. 47], *is a mode of construction, the post-lintel, completely contrasting with the stud-wall. Strong corner posts are connected by extended horizontals that support the floors and form the lintels of any doors or windows. Doors and windows can be large without affecting the strength of the structure, and walls can be of the lightest construction since they are non-load-bearing. Diagonal bracing is replaced by strong wedged mortises which impose dimensions on the members which, coupled with requirements for optimum spans, creates a functional and elegant framing.*

Wong (1982) highlights a strong link between the style of the house and the style of palaces; both exhibit full-height windows, decorative wall, wallboards, decorative eaves, and finials, and ventilation panels are expressed in a variety of decorative motifs that reflect the local climate.

---

[11] Nasir, Abdul Halim, Wan Teh, W. H. *Warisan Seni Bina Melayu* (First). Bangi: Universiti Kebangsaan Malaysia.1997b

[12] Tahir,M.M.,Usman,I.M.S.,Ani,aI.C.H.E.,Surat,M.,Abdullah,N.aG.,&Nor,M.F.I.Reinventing the traditional Malay architecture: creating a socially sustainable and responsive community in Malaysia through the introduction of the raised floor innovation (Part 1). Energy, Environment, Ecosystems, Development and Landscape Architecture, 2002. Pages 278–284.

[13] Wan Ismail, W. H. (2005). Houses in Malaysia; Fusion of The East and The West (First Edit). Skudai, Johor: Universiti Teknologi Malaysia.

[14] ROGER N. HILTON, Defining the Malay house. Journal of the Malaysian Branch of the Royal Asiatic Society, Vol. 65, No. 1 (262) (1992), pp. 39–70. Published by: Malaysian Branch of the Royal Asiatic Society.

Variants and interpretations may vary from state to state and from region to region. Amoroso (2014)[15] asserts that as Malay society underwent tumultuous changes during colonisation by the British, both houses and palaces gradually became cosmopolitan in their expression, the simple serambi and anjung. The Kutai house evolved into refinements reflected in higher forms in an aristocratic house and into higher aesthetic style (Table 16.1). The serambi is a covered but open outdoor portico in which the host or owner of the house sits with guests and relaxes and enjoys the evening and night air. As it evolved, it became hybridised and its stylisation, at times, adopted external language such as syncretic elements. Throughout its evolution, spatial extensions to the left and right parts of the house are seen running from the main core spaces, but the main space is distinguished by its generous extension and its boundary of columns or pole positions which define each corner. The primal shape is a symbol of the habit of culture, evolved through centuries of typologies, functions, and climatic characteristics.

Walls

Semper *'articulated for the first time the four elementary motives underlying the making of architectural expression or style form'*. He says:

> *Architectural motives develop in a quasi-evolutionary manner. Meaning there were civilisations which develop artistic tradition in one material then later this was evolved or mutated or enhanced into another material. For example, tapestries into coloured tiles. Or wall panels. Which emulated in character the older textile style.*

Semper describes how

> *Enclosures (walls) were said to have their origins in weaving. Just as fences and pens were woven sticks, the most basic form of a spatial divider still seen in use in parts of the world today is the fabric screen. Only when additional func-*

---

[15] Amaroso, Donna J., 2014. Traditionalism and the Ascendancy of the Malay Ruling Class in Malaya, National University of Singapore Press.

tional requirements are placed on the enclosure (such as structural weight-bearing needs) does the materiality of the wall change to something beyond fabric

The wall is the first of the four elements and relates to textiles. Enclosures (walls) were said to have their origins in weaving. Just as fences and pens were woven sticks, the most basic form of a spatial divider still seen in use in parts of the world today is the fabric screen. The archetypical Perak's Kutai house is characterised as a pattern of weaving wall in which the local palm leaves are woven and layered. The Kenangan Palace of Kuala Kangsar is a heightened version of the technique, in which the motif of a flower is used as the basic pattern of the weave. Later, craftsmen also formed or represented fabric patterns using other materials. Subsequently, the weaved wall appears as appropriations of this essential vernacular fundamental element or strategy in language. In the chequered patterns of wooden walls, in which within the Nusantara tradition is at times called *janda berhias*, as in Kelantan's architecture,[16] such traditional patterns can be read as eventually evolving into more geometric patterns. For example, in Figure 16.6 (Istana Jahar), its facade walls can be read as representing an evolution of such 'weaved patterns' expressed in newer materials and thus, one can argue that the different forms of *weaving* had, by the end of the 1800s, found their cosmopolitan and 'modern' evolved expressions, or version in such 'geometricised panels'. Chequered variations of the 'weaved' wall in patterned walling can be found in terms of a fusion of timber craftsmanship and carpentry found in certain Malay states in the Nusantara. A 'weaved' pattern traditionally expressed in a series of wood-carved panels in the palaces and houses found predominantly in the eastern states of the Malaysian Peninsula, can be argued as evolving into the composite geometricised panels of the late 1800s and later, to the glass and steel weaved pattern of the highrise building in Malaysia's capital, Putrajaya, as seen in the 4G 11 tower (see Jahn Kassim et al., 2017).

---

[16] Ibid., Ab. Aziz Shuaib, 2013.

The Plinth or Mound

Semper (1820) additionally has distinguished the critical elements of architectural language, and defined them as the 'plinth' and the 'wall', which he has associated with the tectonic, primarily with lightweight, linear components. The simplest Malay house has a simple plinth in the form of consisting of a masonry pads (or in Malay terms, the *lapik tiang*). Jahn Kassim et al. (2019) highlight how these masonry elements can be classified into five categories, from the simple block to the full masonry style. The masonry block can be related to what Frampton (2008) has termed as the stereotomic mass, seen as an extension of earth, to provide the earthbound base for the rest of the building and to ascend from the earth-base. The stereotomic element is in its simplest version, a brick or masonry pad, yet later it can be argued as evolving into masonry columns and walls and became more closely associated with creating sculptural form and volume.

What is crucial in Semper's theory is how it suggests towards the transition between elements that are essentially the tectonic part of architecture to those which essentially arise from the stereotomic . It is the combinations or the contrast afforded by these light-weight elements and heavy construction that create the expressive potentials of the language of architecture local to the region. It is the combination of the tectonic and stereochromic that creates the perceived *heaviness and lightness* of architectural language or style. Recalling how Semper usefully generalises the meaning and expressions of the '*tectonic*' as essentially … *the product of human artistic skill, not with its utilitarian aspect but solely with that part that reveals a conscious attempt by the artisan to express cosmic laws and cosmic order when moulding the material.*

By the 'stereotomic' Semper means that the development of a form of language of architectural expression is a variation of a form of earthwork formed out of the repetitious stacking of heavyweight units.

Plinth Base and Full Column Type

The Semperian 'plinth' can thus be used in reading the language and the language of local architecture can be read as having evolved into full-height masonry columns and half-column full moulded base. This can be seen in the palatial frontage of Istana Lima Laras in Batu Bara, Sumatera, built in 1912. The palace has a symmetrical structure in which a wide open-air portico extends from left and right and continuing to the back for more private zones. Similarly, in the Istana Jahar (Fig. 16.1), similar to the Lima Laras, both cases demonstrate how a combination of masonry structural columns and striated columns can rise as pillars and pedestals to the full height of the ground floor level. The timber-based vernacular language which it had originated from, can be described and read as having 'partially mutated' into 'hybrid' expression with stereotomic masonry elements while still retaining key elements and proportions of the local archetype.

A further evolvement that can be argued as eventually forming a sub-style in which the ground floor expressed in full masonry stereotomic style, such as the beautiful but decimated Istana Langkat, and the Rumah Dato Biji Sura had evolved into a full masonry and earthbound form of architectural expression. From an earlier archetype of lightweight 'stacked' structure, the language evolved into a combination of 'moulded' ground floor base and a light -weight timber structure upon it. In this full masonry style of the ground floor, the openings seem to be carved out of

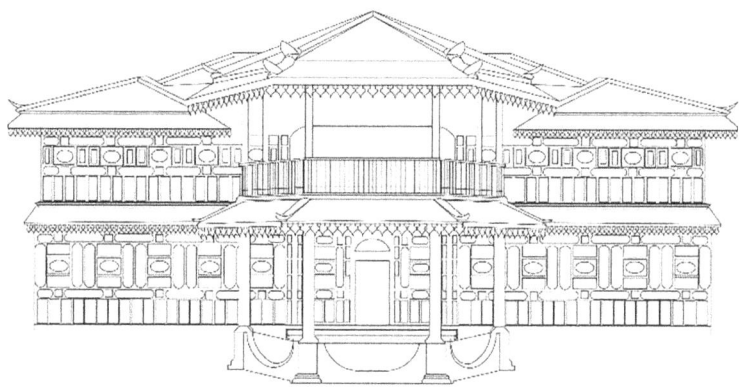

Fig. 16.1 Istana Jahar, present version of 1855. Facades represent evolving forms of 'weaved' patterns—traditionally in full timber—but later expressed in glass and timber composites in a Kelantan palace

an essentially thick mass or masonry and is then combined with timber floor above. Rumah Tok Menteri (early 1900s) can also be argued as a variant of this evolving style. This basically combine a moulded masonry ground floor while the upper floor is in full timber vernacular, depicting the key elements of the tropical vernacular, i.e. conventional large, shuttered windows, an open-air colonnaded ground floor, and the typical 'bumbung *panjang*' typology of roof.

In the Balai Besar, Alor Setar (originally constructed in the 1700s but renovated in the 1800s), and Istana Indragiri (constructed in the later half of the 1800s), the idea of the earthbound mound can be seen in the evolving nature of form which transposes itself into a central masonry core and surrounded by a series of slender columns. The Balai Besar or Royal Audience Hall of Alor Setar, Malaysia, similarly, in its original form was a timber palace attached to a private palace and this extension was basically a space within a space, and in its present form, it consists of a series of columns (some made from cast-iron) surrounding a central masonry core. Its ornaments and decorative elements reflect expressions of Malay-Siamese synthesis, with some absorption of colonial influences, but still retaining the essence of Malay form, fusing timber, masonry, and the technology of cast iron.

Istana Bandar (Jugra, built in the late 1800s) and the Hulu palace (Kuala Kangsar) can be argued as a language of full petrification, with key defining elements which still capture and recall the essences of the vernacular or original Malay style. Columns are now pilasters, and the entire mass of form no longer projects a tectonic character, and its tectonic elements can be read as almost fused into the mass. Completed in 1903, the Istana Hulu was built for the reigning Sultan Idris Mursyidul Azam Syah and was sited atop Bukit Chandan Hill. Neoclassical pilasters and cornices have been mixed the Malay form yet one can still argued that parts of the building still retain the Malay vernacular in its rear half of the building, including its roof, fascia board, and finial elements.

History of Traditional Malay Roof

The earliest form of traditional Malay houses originates before the era of colonisation. The houses were built by the indigenous ethnic Malay to accommodate their basic needs. The architectural forms were influenced by the living culture, tradition, and the tropical climate and incorporate basic design principles that respond to the natural surroundings. The houses were built on stilts with floors raised as high as 8 feet above the ground for protection against dampness, flood, and wild animals and for added ventilation. Each house is equipped with stairs that connect the ground to the *serambi* (porch or verandah), which serves as an intersection to the main entrance of the house. The interior of the house is partitioned to create separation between the internal spaces and for fire protection. The roof is one of the primary key features of the Malay traditional house. The typical roof structure consists of a sloped roof supported by timber posts and beam structures and fitted with ornaments on the edges of the roof. The roof form comprises several types and differs according to the shape and pitch of the roof and the interior segments of the house that it covers.

Bumbung Panjang or *long roof* or *gable roof* is the oldest traditional roof form that existed before the colonial influence (Lim, 1991). Built by the indigenous ethnic Malay in the early years, it is widely used in the West Coast of Peninsular Malaysia, although this roof form can also be found in parts of the East Coast. *Bumbung Panjang* comes in various shapes and characteristics, which differ in each Malay state. However, the general features consist of a long central ridge that runs through the length of the building with a high and steep inverted 'V' sloped roof, supported by *tunjuk langit* or kingpost. Its simple roof form allows easy construction among the indigenous community and provides good ventilation through its high-pitched roof that creates a deep attic or *loteng* and placement of ornamented grilles, called *tebar layar*, at the gable ends.

Bumbung panjang comes in three different variations: *Lipat Pandan*, *Lipat Kajang*, and *Atap Layar* (Abdul Malik, 2012) [Fig. 16.2]. The inverted 'V' shaped sloped roof is steeper in *Lipat Pandan* as compared to *Lipat Kajang*. *Atap Layar* consists of an added roof that provides an

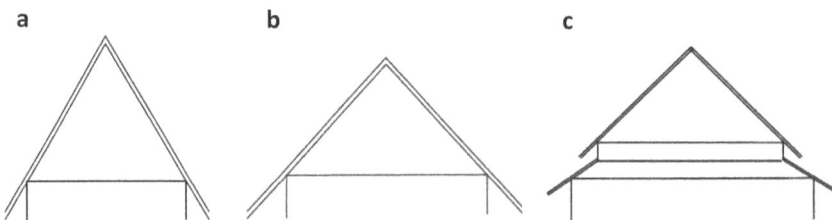

Fig. 16.2 (a) *Atap Lipat Pandan*, (b) *Atap Lipat Kajang*, (c) *Atap Layar*. (Source: Author)

extension to the inverted 'V-shaped roof. Apart from ventilation, the high steep-sloped roof helps in providing an efficient rainwater surface run-off. *Lobang Chermin* or skylight is often inserted at the sloped roof for natural light penetration. Most of the earlier *rumah bumbung panjang* used *atap nipah* as the roof cover due to its good thermal insulating properties. However, this has been modified with the use of clay tiles (senggora) and *atap belian* in present-day constructions (Sheppard, 1969; Nasir, 1996).

Some Bumbung Panjang roofs are decorated with ornamental elements, such as the wooden gable fascia board known as *Pemeles*. The *tebar layar* is designed with decorative elements which are commonly found in floral or geometric patterns. *Rumah Bujang* and *Rumah Tiang Dua Belas* or *Rumah Serambi* are some examples of the earliest type of traditional Malay houses that apply the *bumbung panjang* roof form. These houses are commonly found in Terengganu and Kelantan. The significant difference between *Rumah Bujang* and *Rumah Tiang Dua Belas* is the number of pillars that support the house underneath, called *Tiang*. The size of *Rumah Bujang* is smaller and narrower, with six supporting pillars. *Rumah Tiang Dua Belas* consists of 12 supporting pillars. These additional pillars provide a floor extension to the house, known as *serambi* or verandah. There are two types of *Rumah Tiang Dua Belas*. The unroofed verandah is known as *Lambor*, while *Selasar* consists of an extended roof from the main roof that acts as a shelter for the verandah. The roof for the *Rumah Bujang* and *Rumah Tiang Dua Belas* are fitted with gable edges and ornamented gable screens called *Tebar Layar*. In Kelantan, the *Tebar Layar* is commonly known as *Tubang Layar* and is usually decorated in *Daun Tar* or the arenga palm tree leaf motif. In addition, some of the *Rumah Bujang* and *Rumah Tiang Dua Belas* are designed with a shallow horizontal gable platform located at the base of the gable ends known as *Lantai Alang Buang or Undan-Undan* (Fig. 16.3). This platform is designed to store unused brass household utensils (Sheppard, 1969).

Unlike *Bumbung Panjang*, *Bumbung Limas*, *Bumbung Potong Perak*, and *Bumbung Atap Meru* are not considered an indigenous roof forms (Wan Ismail, 2005). *Bumbung Limas* or the hip roof has five ridges that are sloped on every side. The roof style reflects the neighbouring and colonial house influences. The word *limas* is believed to derive from the Malay word *lima*, which resembles the five roof ridges (Nasir, 1996). The roof structure consists of a central roof ridge with four roof ridges and ridge coverings that descend on every side to cover the four corners of the

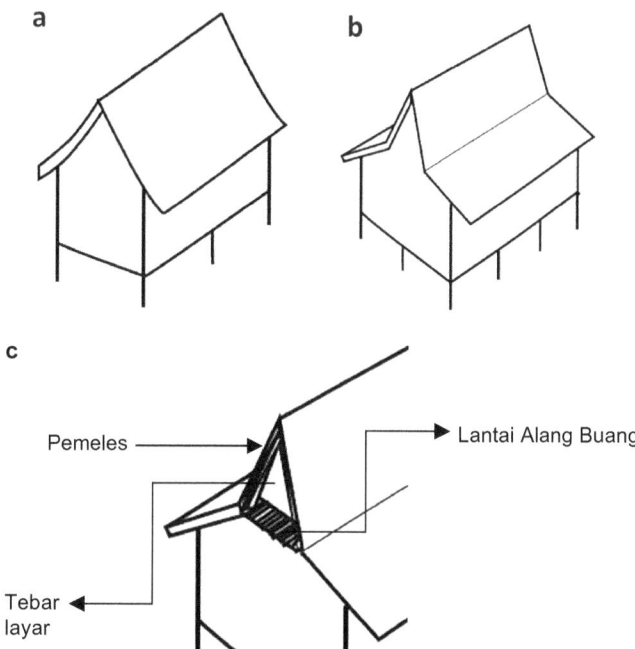

Fig. 16.3 (a) *Bumbung Panjang* roof form in *Rumah Bujang*, (b) *Bumbung Panjang* roof form in *Rumah Tiang Dua Belas*, (c) *Bumbung panjang* roof form with *Pemeles, Tebar Layar* and *Lantai Alang Buang*. (Source: Author)

house. The pitch of the sloped roof is shallower as compared to *Bumbung Panjang*. *Bumbung Limas* has no gable ends, *tebar layar*, or decorative ornamentation at the gable peak. The roof form was initially designed to be useful, practical, easy to construct, and inexpensive rather than attractive.

Bumbung Panjang and *Bumbung Limas* have undergone a series of modifications. The *Bumbung Potong Perak*, also known as *Bumbung Potong Belanda*, *Limas Potong Perak*, or the *gable hip roof*, is an example of roof form that combines the characteristics of *Bumbung Panjang* and *Bumbung Limas*. This roof form is designed with a central roof ridge that runs through the length of the house. At the end of the central roof ridge lies a shallow gable with a narrow sloping roof at the base of the gable that extends out in *bumbung limas* shape to cover the four corners of the building. The narrow sloping roof replaces the *Lantai Alang Buang*. Like *Bumbung Panjang*, the roof is fitted with *Tebar Layar* for added ventilation into the internal spaces of the house. In addition, the *Bumbung Potong Perak* roof form is elaborated with decorative elements such as *Buah Buton or Tunjuk Langit, Ande-Ande, Pemeles*, and *Kepala Cicak* that highlights the tradition, culture, economic status, and nobility of the local community (Fig. 16.4).

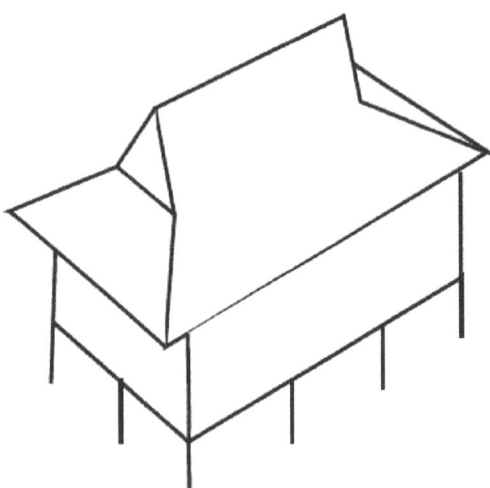

Fig. 16.4 *Bumbung Potong Perak* roof form. (Source: Author)

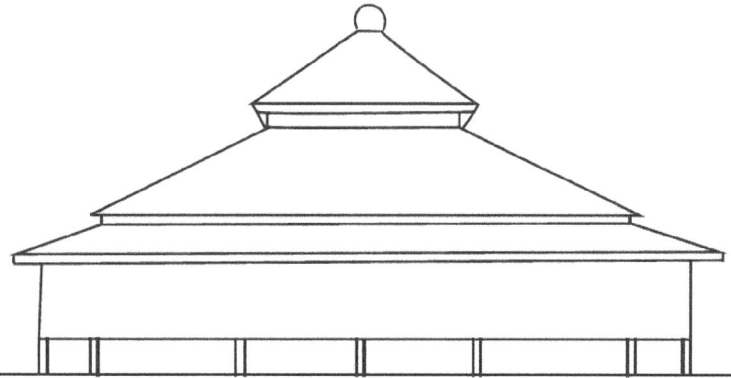

Fig. 16.5 *Bumbung Atap Meru* roof form. (Source: Author)

Bumbung Atap Meru consists of a tiered pyramidal roof. Its tiered shaped roof provides a higher headroom for better ventilation. This type of roof form is seldom seen in Malay houses and is mostly used in traditional mosque designs (Fig. 16.5).

Roof Decorative Elements of Traditional Malay House

Decorative elements form part of the non-structural components that highlight the aesthetic value of a traditional Malay house. These elements are crafted on roof, wall, window, and door by skilled and artistic craftsmen and reflect the identity and socioculture of the local community. In addition, some components or ornamentations hold deeper philosophical and sacred meanings. The early development of ornamentations is believed to be influenced by the Hindu culture but was later guided by Islamic principles (Hussin et al., 2017). The decorative elements are commonly crafted on wood, with metal, clay, and concrete mixes becoming popular later. The ornamentation designs are influenced by natural forms such as floral or plant motifs, including leaf, stalk, flower, fruit, and tendrils or geometrically shaped patterns (Shuaib et al., 2013), with some in fauna motifs. Table 16.2 lists the decorative roof elements, descriptions, and general application at *Bumbung Panjang, Bumbung Limas, Bumbung*

Table 16.2 Roof decorative elements in traditional Malay roof (Source: Author)

Roof decorative element	Description	Function and value
Tunjuk Langit	Also known as *buah buton* in Kelantan and *buah gutung* in Terengganu, *tunjuk langit* is designed in an upright position at the tip of a gable end and hip or pyramidal roof. It comes in two significant shapes. The straight vertical shape or *jenis batang* or rod is commonly used in *Bumbung Panjang* and *Bumbung Potong Perak* roof forms. The round shape or *jenis bulat* is commonly applied at the middle and top of the *Bumbung Limas* and *Bumbung Atap Meru*.	Mainly used for aesthetic value. In Kelantan, the *buah buton* is believed to be influenced by the traditional houses in Cambodia (Sheppard, 1969). It symbolises protection against evil spirits.
Tebar layar	Also known as *singap*, *tebar layar* is a triangle carved panel placed at gable ends. *Tebar layar* can be found in *Bumbung Panjang* and *Bumbung Potong Perak* roof forms.	*Tebar layar* functions as a barrier to the roof space. Some are designed with ornamented grilles for natural lighting and ventilation.
Pemeles	Also known as *pemeleh* or *peles*, it consists of decorative timber panels constructed as gable fascia boards. The design varies according to state with a curved and pointed top in houses in Kelantan and Terengganu. *Pemeles* can be found in *Bumbung Panjang* and *Bumbung Potong Perak* roof forms.	*Pemeles* functions as a gable fascia board. The decorative elements provide aesthetic value to a house.
Lantai Alang Buang	Also known as *Undan-Undan*, *Lantai Alang Buang* is a carved shallow horizontal gable platform constructed at the base of the gable ends. *Lantai Alang Buang* is commonly found in *Bumbung Panjang* roof forms.	It serves as a horizontal platform to store unused brass household utensils.

Material	Image/location at roof
Carved timber in the early years with present-day using concrete mix.	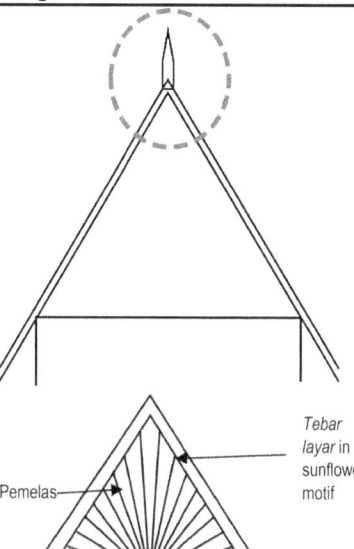
Carved timber planks or louvres.	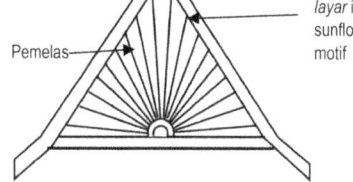
Carved timber panels.	
Horizontal carved timber panels.	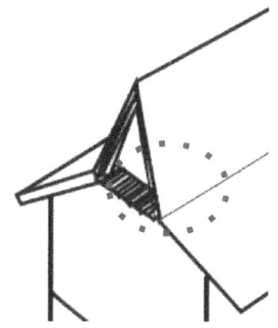

(*continued*)

Table 16.2 (continued)

Roof decorative element	Description	Function and value
Sulur Bayung	*Sulur bayung* is a decorative element in tapered protruded carvings on top of four corners of hip and pyramidal roofs. The initial design motif was influenced by the shoots of climbing or creeping plants. *Sulur Bayung* is commonly found in *Bumbung Potong Perak*, *Bumbung Limas*, and *Bumbung Atap Meru* roof forms.	It is mainly used for aesthetic value. The *sulur bayung* motif symbolises the relationship between humans and god.
Sisik Niaga	Based on a fauna motif, *Sisik Niaga* is carved along roof ridges and is commonly found in *Bumbung Potong Perak*, *Bumbung Limas*, and *Bumbung Atap Meru* roof forms.	It is mainly used for aesthetic value. The *sisik niaga* motif symbolises strength and power.
Ande-Ande	Also known as *papan manis*, ande-ande serves as a decorative fascia board at roof eaves and is commonly found in *Bumbung Potong Perak*, *Bumbung Limas*, and *Bumbung Atap Meru* roof forms.	Apart from aesthetic value through its ornamentation, *ande-ande* provides additional coverage for timber rafters and prevents moisture from entering the roof.
Kepala Cicak	*Kepala Cicak* is a protruded decorative element located at four corners of *papan manis* (decorative fascia board) and is commonly found in *Bumbung Potong Perak* roof form.	*Kepala Cicak* functions as a fascia board. The decorative elements provide aesthetic value to a house. The *kepala cicak* motif symbolises strength, courage and protection against evil spirits and bad omens.
Tiang Gantung	*Tiang Gantung* is a hanging column mounted internally at the bottom of a gable peak. It is commonly constructed in traditional houses in Negeri Sembilan.	It is mainly used for aesthetic value. It symbolises power and is believed to bring a bad omen if it falls.

Material	Image/location at roof
It is usually constructed using ceramic or cement plaster.	*Sulur bayung* motif
It is usually constructed using ceramic or cement plaster.	*Sisik niaga* decorative element on roof (Source: Rashid et al., 2021)
Horizontal decorative or carved timber.	
Carved timber.	*Kepala cicak* motif
Carved wood mounted on a roof, 60 to 100 cm in size.	

Potong Perak, and *Bumbung Meru* (Shuaib et al., 2013; M S Ab Rashid et al., 2019, Rashid et al., 2021).

Though an enclosure protects and encloses the space the hearth, the roof further encloses and protects against weather. The roof is an assembly that has remained relatively stable throughout the history of architecture. Though modern methods are more sophisticated, and materials have changed, the essential idea of a roof remains strong. Even in pavilions, where enclosure is not necessarily important, the roof is expressed as a main element.

The Hearth—A South East Asian interpretation

However, it is in the interpretation of the hearth that the contentions arise. Though the first three elements of Semper's theories—wall mound and roof—can directly and physically be interpreted and linked with the fundamental elemental blocks of Malay Nusantara architecture as these are commonly seen as its essential style, the 'hearth' has no direct parallel in the tropical heritage. Yet it is fundamental to the idea of architectural expression, as says Semper:

> *The hearth is the germ, the embryo, of all social institutions. The first sign of gathering of settlement and rest after long wanderings and the hardship of the chase, is still the set of the fire and the lighting of the crackling flame…* (p. 198)

In his book *Frame and Generic Space*, Bernard Leupen (2006) insightfully draws a parallel with respect to this principle of the *hearth*, suggesting that, though Semper refers to heat sources and the modern parallel of integrated *building services*, the *hearth* in Semper's fundamental model can also be linked to the recurring heart of architecture, which refers to any symbolic 'centre', whether of a house or building. Extrapolating and reinterpreting this idea in the South East Asian climate, in which there was no major archetypal tradition of hearth due to climate, it has traditions of metallurgy mainly in symbol and artefacts. Hence, this idea of symbols that signify the centre is crucial to the nature of local societies as they are perennially drawn towards a centre of sacredness—primarily their leaders and their traditions. The centrality of these domains to the longevity of society had produced and evolved multiple sacred objects and artefacts expressed in metallurgy—reflecting universally mankind's perennial quest for immortality and protection. One recalls the timber architecture's associated cult practices of burying metal objects—such as coins—within the bases of central columns for protection or imbuing the soko guru or main superstructure of a house with certain objects based on the local underlying belief of protection and longevity. In a more sacred expression, roofs in traditional South East Asian architecture are not mere protective and climatic devices, but are adorned with metallic embellishments, from the ridge metal adornment of the Melaka palace to the sixteenth-century three-dimensional 'selembayung' ornament of palaces seen in Istana Hulu and the combined selembayung and cross kris shape in Balai Besar Kedah. In Malay culture, for example, the act of imbuing structures with sacred strength derived from metallurgical traditions is observed as expressed in the recurring *lipat kijang* forms—a double kris cross forms reflecting the sacred strength of the Malay royal or warrior regalia.

Cogan and the Kris: Symbols of 'Strength'

The cogan or the ceremonial fan and the 'kris' are both fundamentally made from metallurgy and ironwork. The cogan is regalia for the installations of monarchs and depicts a leaf-like fan with a Malay inscription in Arabic script (known as Jawi). It is regarded as part of the inheritance/*pusaka* of the Malay sacred lines of the sultan. Its '*leaf*' or mountain-like shape evokes the symbolism of the *kayon* or *gunungan* and at times is believed to allude to the pointed shape of the ubiquitous betel leaf/sireh. The particular *cogan* in the Riau tradition is the golden fan used in the installation of the sultan. Based on the *adat istiadat diraja* (royal custom), the consent of the holder of the *cogan* (royal regalia) of Johor-Riau, the installation of a new sultan was only valid if it took place with the regalia. The regalia was fundamental to the installation of the sultan; it was a symbol of power, legitimacy, and the sovereignty of the state.

The kris, on the other hand, represents a Malay traditional weapon that symbolises its culture, and thus its the epitome of Malay strength and protection. The Riau variation of the kris is one of the few key artefacts in the royal regalia, of which two have been preserved. As the kris is a symbol of power in the Malay Archipelago, it has been used as part of ceremonial traditions and which can be divided into three parts; one that the wavy blade/billah (kelok), the hilt/hulu, and the sheath/sarung. The kris has morphed from a weapon and evolved into a social status symbol, and it is found in Indonesia and is indigenous to Malaysia, Thailand, Brunei, Singapore, and the Philippines, where it is known as *kalis* with variants existing as a sword rather than a dagger. The kris is believed to possess an essence, presence, or magical powers, and the kris's distinctive character is in its blade-patterning achieved by alternating iron and nickelous iron (*pamor*). The Riau *kris* design demonstrates the close link between the Riau Lingga sultanate and the Bugis princes and closely follows the Bugis models.

Both regalia type forms appear as evolvements of ornamentations, particularly on the roofs of Malay palatial structures (Fig. 16.6). The crossed kris or keris *bersilang* represents not only sacredness but also protection and strength, appearing on frontages and gateways. These crossed finials were also believed to be in the head of the Famosa Melaka stone gateway or archway. The crossed kris inscription was believed to be later erased and superseded by a gun weapon symbol. To the present day, its symbolism is reflected in the *lipat kijang*, which essentially evolved from a double cross of two kris and the mountain is reflected in gateways and ornamental dressings of the roof. Examples are the Balai Besar, Kedah, in which on the ground floor columns are shaped like *Kayu berlurah Buah gelugor* are divided into 16 facets and decorated with *Bunga sulor paku* on the top of them. Capitols of the columns on the upper floor are decorated with the Malay *sailor paku* motif consisting of a single motif shoot of fern. Eight pieces of the fern motif carved from wood are secured to the plain capitol with two nails each and possibly *damar* glue as well, following the octagonal cross section of the column. The brackets are essentially based on a triangular form, which are fused with local floral patterns. Other than that, it incorporates three layers of the *awan larat*.

Fig. 16.6 Elements of 'regalia' morphed into language—the Balai Besar, Kedah. (Adapted from source: IIUM heritage lab collection 2005)

Conclusion

The development of architectural style in a society is a combination of forces in its sociocultural history. Through the use of cases from a specific region, the Malay region, the evolution of this change could be charted and gaps in its evolution could be suggested and if so, a new stylistic position could be charted. A key point by Semper (1852) is '*the realisation that architecture everywhere had borrowed its types from pre-architectural conditions of human settlement*'. He goes on to say, "*Four indigenous arts would continue to influence architectural production in later stages of development where they were raised to the status of symbols or emblems. Central to the evolvement of civilisation, a concrete theory of style arises from an examination of the material technical and ideal preconditions of style.*"

The hybrid language evolved still recalls the roots of the local style and archetype—tracing back to the vernacular house form that encapsulates a language of pure topicality and a 'natural ecological extension and growth' of the tropical region's culture, topography, climate, ecology, and geography. The layered forms of roof, with wide openings, layered spaces, wide protective roofs, and linear-like arrangement of functions, are replete with variations, and even the pitched form, its latest branch before giving way to colonial influence, resonates with the ubiquitous *rumah bumbong panjang* or *rumah limas*, with embellishments on its fascia boards and on its finials and ridges. These 'modernised' or 'hybridised' forms are responses to the dynamics of modernity of a changing world and public realm. The stylistic grammar and rules should be further semantically described and identified in order to contribute to a new language of urbanisation amidst the alarming loss of character in Asian cities. This Classical Malay architectural style can be expressed in modern materials and thus contribute to the emergence of a new language of urban architecture.

Endnotes

Semper, G. (1989). *The four elements of architecture and other writings* (H. F. Mallgrave and W. Herrmann, Trans.). Cambridge. ISBN 0-521-35475-7.

Semper, G. (2004). *Style in the technical and tectonic arts; or, practical aesthetics* (H. F. Mallgrave, Trans.). Santa Monica. ISBN 0-89236-597-8 Ibid., 1989.

Semper, G. (1962). *Style in the technical and tectonic arts, or, practical aesthetics.* Translated into English by Getty Publications, 2004

Lukito, Y. N. (2015, October 16). *Exhibiting modernity and Indonesian vernacular architecture: Hybrid architecture at Pasar Gambir of Batavia, the 1931 Paris international colonial exhibition and Taman Mini Indonesia Indah* (p. 47). Springer.

Mlagrave, Harry. 2014. Gottfried Semper: In Search of Architecture." Journal of Architectural Education, 38(4), pp. 33–34.

Lindsay Asquith, Marcel Vellinga. (2006, March 10). *Vernacular architecture in the 21st century: Theory, education and practice.* Taylor & Francis

Kawamukai, M. (2000). A study on the four elements of architecture, *65* (538), 235–242

Masato Kawamukai. A study of Gottfried Semper's science, industry and art. Journal of Architecture and Planning (Transactions of AIJ). 2004, Vol.69, No.583, p.165.

Moravánszky, Ákos. 2017, Metamorphism: Material change in architecture. Basel/Berlin/Boston: Walter de Gruyter GmbH.

Reid, A. (2004). Understanding Melayu (Malay) as a source of diverse modern identities. Journal of Southeast Asian Studies, 32(3), 295–313

Milner, A. C. (1982). The Malays. United Kingdom: Nielsen Book Data.

Andaya, Leonard, 2010. Leaves of the same tree—Trade and ethnicity in the straits of Malacca. NUS Press. Singapore.

Bahauddin, A,, Hardono, S., Abdullah, A., & Maliki, N. Z. The Minangkabau house: Architectural and cultural elements. WIT Transactions on Ecology and the Environment, 2012, 165, 15–25. https://doi.org/10.2495/ARC120021

Hosseini, E., Mursib, G., Nafida, R., & Shahedi, B. (2016, November). Malay vernacular architecture: Mirror of the past, lessons for the future Malay vernacular architecture: Mirror of the past, lessons for the future. In *The proceedings of 8th SEATUC symposium 4–5 March 2014 Universiti Teknologi Malaysia at Johor, Malaysia.*

Nasir, Abdul Halim, Wan Teh, W. H. Warisan Seni Bina Melayu (First). Bangi: Universiti Kebangsaan Malaysia.1997

Tahir, M. M., Usman, I. M. S., Ani, a I. C. H. E., Surat, M., Abdullah, N. a G., & Nor, M. F. I. (2002). Reinventing the traditional Malay architecture: creating a socially sustainable and responsive community in Malaysia through the introduction of the raised floor innovation (Part 1). *Energy, Environment, Ecosystems, Development and Landscape Architecture*, 278–284.

Wan Ismail, W. H. (2005). Houses in Malaysia; fusion of the east and the west (1st edn). Skudai, Johor: Universiti Teknologi Malaysia.

Mohd Sabrizaa, A. R., & Sufian, C. A. (2008). The traditional Malay architecture: Between aesthetics and symbolism. In *Proceedings of Seminar on intellectual property and heritage issues in built environment*

Hilton, R. N. (1992). Defining the Malay house. *Journal of the Malaysian Branch of the Royal Asiatic Society*, 65 (1), 262, pp. 39–70. Published by: Malaysian Branch of the Royal Asiatic Society.

Wong, S. (1982). *Timber architecture and styles in Malaysia* (PhD thesis), University of Western Syndey, Australia.

Amaroso, Donna J., 2014. Traditionalism and the ascendancy of the Malay ruling class in Malaya, National University of Singapore Press.

Norwina, M. N., & Noor Hanita, A. M. (2011). *In search of the origins of the Malay-Muslim architectural heritage through Masjid built form: Malay vernacular architecture: Traditional and contemporary expressions.* ISBN 978-967-418-057-7, 40–39.

Shuaib, A., & Enoch, O. F. (2013). Application of Kelantan traditional aesthetic values into the architecture of contemporary homes. (Demetri Porphyrios, 1982) Arts and Design Studies, 6 (15). www.iiste.org, ISSN 2224-6061, ISSN 2225-059X (Online).

Mohamad Rasdi, M. T., Mohd. Ali, K., Syed Ariffin, S. A. I., Mursib, G., and Mohamad, R. (2005). *The architectural heritage of the Malay World the traditional houses.* Penerbit Universiti Teknology Malaysia. ISBN 983-52-0357-1.

Jahnkassim, Shireen, Abdul Majid, Noor Hanita, Nawawi, N. (2017b). The resilience of tradition. Areca Books

Jahn Kassim, Majid, Mohd Sharif and tengku Anis. (2019, May). The Hybrid Aeshetics of the Malay vernacular. *International Journal of Recent Technology and Enginerring.*

Semper describe' ceramics as a type of material, rather than any specific material "..The general properties. Is their plasticity and malleability. All… products made from them are therefore ' the type originally made from soft paste'

Demetri Porphyrios, A. P. (1982). Classicism is not a style, Volume 52. Michigan: Architectural Design.

Thoenes, B. E. (2003). Architectural theory: from the Renaissance to the present: Thames and Hudson 2003.

Deupi, Victor, Transformations in Classical architecture, 2019. OROEditions. His discussion of how the classical is also found in vernacular societies and their constructions is particularly evident in the introductory pages of this book and represent a pathway forward to highlight a new language of the vernacular which can be consistently and universally applied across all vernacular societies.

Frampton, Kenneth and John Cava, *Studies in Tectonic culture*. Thames and Hudson, 2000.

Utusan Headquarters. (2018). Malaysian Architecture.

References

Abdul Malik, H. (2012). *Arsitektur Tradisional Melayu Kepulauan Riau*. Lembaga Adat Melayu Kabupaten Natuna Provinsi Kepulauan Riau.

Akos, M. (2017). *Metamorphism: Material Change in Architecture*, Birkhauser.

Amaroso, Donna J. (2014). *Traditionalism and the Ascendancy of the Malay Ruling Class in Malaya*. National University of Singapore Press.

Asquith, L., & Vellinga, M.. (2006, March 10). *Vernacular architecture in the 21st century: Theory, education and practice*. Taylor & Francis.

Hilton, Roger N. (1983). *Defining The Malay House*, Journal of the Malaysian Branch of the Royal Asiatic Society, Vol. 65, No. 1 (262) (1992), pp. 39–70.

Hussin, H., Baba, Z. & Hassan, A. (2017). The philosophy in the creation of traditional Malay carving motifs in Peninsula Malaysia. *Geografia: Malaysian journal of society and space, 8*.

Ibrahim, W. S. H. W. (2013). Identiti Seni Bina Melayu Dalam Era Globalisasi, 1–21.

Ismail, W. H. (2005). *Houses in Malaysia; Fusion of The East and The West* (First Edit). Skudai, Johor: Universiti Teknologi Malaysia.

Jahnkassim, Puteri Shireen, Abdul Majid, Noor Hanita, Nawawi, N. (2017). *The Resilience of Tradition; Malay Allusions in Contemporary Architecture* (First). Penang: Areca Books.

Jahn Kassim, S., Abdul Majid, N., & Abdul Latip, N. S, (2019). *Themes of Classicality in Malay architectural language*, Jurnal Melayu, Dewan Bahasa and Pustaka, vol 1.

Kawamukai, M. (2000). A study on the four elements of architecture. *Journal of Architecture and Planning (Transactions of AIJ)*, *65*(538), 235–242.

Kawamukai, M. (2004). A study of Gottfried Semper's science, industry and art. *Journal of Architecture and Planning (Transactions of AIJ)*, *69*(583), 165.

Leupen, B. (2006). *Frame and generic Space*, 010 Publishers, 2006, 1–254.

Lim, J. Y. (1991). *The Malay House: Rediscovering Malaysia's Indigenous Shelter System*. Penang: Institut Masyarakat.

Lukito, Y. N. (2015). Colonial Exhibition and a Laboratory of Modernity: Hybrid Architecture at Batavia's Pasar Gambir. *Indonesia 100*, 77–103. doi:10.1353/ind.2015.0014.

Mlagrave, H. (2014). Gottfried Semper: In search of architecture. *Journal of Architectural Education, 38*(4), 33–34.

M S Ab Rashid *et al* 2019 *IOP Conf. Ser.: Earth Environ. Sci.* 385 012022

Nasir, A. H. (1996). *The Traditional Malay House*. Shah Alam: Penerbit Fajar Bakti.

Nasir, Abdul Halim, & Wan Teh, W. H. (1997). *Warisan Seni Bina Melayu* (First). Bangi: Universiti Kebangsaan Malaysia.

Lukito, Y.N. (2015). Colonial Exhibition and a Laboratory of Modernity: Hybrid Architecture at Batavia's Pasar Gambir. Indonesia 100, 77–103. doi:10.1353/ind.2015.0014.

Rashid, sabrizaa et al. Architectural characteristics of malay traditional houses through decorative elements: a comparisan between perak limas' house (plh) and johor limas' house (jlh). Malaysian journal of sustainable environment, [s.I], v. 8, n. 3, p. 87–102, mar. 2021. ISSN 0128-326X.

Semper, G. (1820). *The Four Elements of Architecture and other writings*. Cambridge University Press.

Semper, G. (1962). *Style in the technical and tectonic arts, or, practical aesthetics*. Translated into English by Getty Publications, 2004.

Sheppard, M. (1969). Traditional Malay House Forms in Terengganu and Kelantan. *Journal of the Malaysian Branch of the Royal Asiatic Society, Vol. 42, No. 2 (216)*, pg 1-9.

Shuaib, A. A., & Enoch, O. F. (2013). Application of Kelantan traditional aesthetic values into the architecture of contemporary homes. *Arts and Design Studies, 6*(15), 15–25.

Tahir, M. M., Usman, I. M. S., Ani, a I. C. H. E., Surat, M., Abdullah, N. a G., & Nor, M. F. I. (2002). *Reinventing the traditional Malay architecture: creating a socially sustainable and responsive community in Malaysia through the introduction of the raised floor innovation* (Part 1). Energy, Environment, Ecosystems, Development and Landscape Architecture, 278–284.

Watkin, D. (2000). *Karl Frederich Schinkel. In A history of western architecture* (3rd ed.). London: Laurence King Publishing.

Wong, W. (1995). *Timber Structures in Malaysian Architecture and Buildings*, (March), 305.

17

Tracing Water-Land Architectural Symbolisms of the Malay Nusantara

Ismail Jasmani, Shireen Jahn Kassim, and Zumahiran Kamaruddin

The resonances of the archipelago's climatic and topographical environment are found in the imageries contained within its urban iconographic elements and architectural ornaments. These include references and metaphorical images of elements of climate (such as clouds), waves, water, fauna, and flora of the region. This chapter attempts to unify the themes of Malay artefacts and architecture as representing the common dualistic themes of land and water reflected in architecture and urbanism, whether in vernacular techniques and patterns (such as weaved walks and

I. Jasmani
International Islamic University Malaysia, Jalan Gombak, Malaysia

S. Jahn Kassim (✉)
Faculty of Architecture and Environmental Design (KAED), International Islamic University Malaysia, Jalan Gombak, Malaysia

Z. Kamaruddin
Department of Applied Arts and Design, Kulliyyah of Architecture and Environmental Design, International Islamic University Malaysia, Jalan Gombak, Malaysia

© The Editor(s) (if applicable) and The Author(s), under exclusive license to Springer Nature Singapore Pte Ltd. 2023
S. Jahn Kassim et al. (eds.), *Eco-Urbanism and the South East Asian City*,
https://doi.org/10.1007/978-981-19-1637-3_17

chequered panels) related to wave-like patterns or artistic curved motifs recalling cloud and vegetal forms. A water-land duality theme permeates South East Asian monuments and structures, and such recurring simultaneous themes of water, land, and flora-fauna 'landforms' are evoked in flora and fauna, and sky-earth patterns. The chapter weaves the underlying ecological themes of South East Asian motifs reflected as eco-patterns of South East Asian architectural ornamentation.

Introduction

Macfarlane (2015) asserts that natural landmarks and a region's topography, landscape, and ecosystem effects on the region's cultural forms leave a powerful imprint on its language due to the power of its landscape which has 'invisible' content. Symbols are inspired by histories, imaginative shapes, natural forms, and cultural visions and have become *place language*. Tropical and maritime ecology in South East Asia are similar, powerful drivers of architectural expressions. They are known to inspire forms and a repertoire of motifs from which builders, carvers, and craftsmen reconcile their need to embellish built forms with the equal need for meaning in their environment. In peninsular and inland South East Asia, for example, decoration in the form of filigrees and reliefs are common ornamentations, and in the traditional architecture of the maritime era, these are mostly carved in wood (which was abundant) and some in masonry and metalwork. Architecturally, these are expressed in joints, intersections, columns, railings, balconies, and in the openwork running between columns of a variety of traditional typologies and buildings, including palaces, mansions, and mosques and are essentially motifs of underlying ecological concepts and themes, which were, at times synthesised with geometrical forms and patterns.

In the Malay-Nusantara context, its traditional architecture, for example, frequently depict carved components with complete patterns that are extracted and abstracted from ecological elements, and these constructional components are largely found with a variety of compositional elements including plant and vegetation elements, primarily flowers, flower buds, leaves, fruits, and stems, which are often combined and composed in a harmonious arrangement. These elements are depicted in gentle curvatures and flows from a center source, often termed as *ibu* (literally translated as *mother*), which are verbally expressed as a source of growth. Plant seeds, flowers, and flower vases are common, central motifs that represent *ibu*. Calligraphy, and plant leaves were generally used as different types of combined elements as central motifs. This implies that central motifs are found in a variety of shapes including the sources of growth. Seeds, flowers, and flower vases are depicted as revealed sources and they were popular and commonly portrayed as *ibu*. Plant elements were vital in every floral design of a complete pattern, and they are constituents of the complete composition. In short, the craftsmen who carved components with broad ranges of *awan larat* (carving design in meandering form) design were capable of further enrichment by departing from the monothematic selection of plant elements and decorating panels with a wide variety of plant parts. This mode of embellishment creates a sense of unity in diversity. This has been the mutual mode of expression for carvings from Peninsular Malaysia.

In regions such as Borneo, Thailand, and Bali, ornamentations using the themes of local fauna and animals was part of the local ornamental practice, with mythical figures incorporated into the architectural decorative expressions of the vernaculars, including in the architectural traditions of Borneo. However, in the other traditionally Islamic regions of the Nusantara, while there is a predominance of vegetal and geometric elements, there are, occasionally, motifs of animal figures used, such as an expression of the local cuckoo bird in the Balai Besar palace (originally built in the late 1700s and renovated in the late 1800s) of Kedah. These motifs had been found located above the doorframe, and at times, are found flanking the *astaka*, with butterfly motifs adorning the ends of beams above the verandas of certain sections of the palace and found again, in the local mansions. The acts of carving and moulding represent essentially a process of interpretation and continuous reiteration, by the local artisans who were completely engrossed in refining their traditions. Hence as they refine and reiterate, they gain inspiration from ecology and nature, as they observe and abstract from elements from their surrounding ecosystem and environment such as particular plant and animal motifs. These components can be argued as eventually being extracted and categorized into three types of architectural elements, i.e. according to structure, component non-structural element, and surface decoration. The perforated wall panels for example, are often, non-structural elements and which can be found in the form of a variety of fascia boards, barge boards, and door leaves, and ventilation panels over doors or windows. They are not only decorative in their physical form, but in their climatic effects as at different times of the day, they cast intricate shadows on the floor, adding beauty to the interior and to the experience of time and climate within the interior spaces. Thus, carved components of timber buildings and architecture were not only physical expressions, but climatic tools and methods to cast particular environmental effects which allow an appreciation of the outdoors indoors. They have both functional and aesthetic purposes. Even elements such as the perforated panels allow both light and ventilation and view of the surrounding ecosystems as it afford the occupants an appreciation of context of lush tropical vegetation and a rich profusion of floral life which are part and parcel of traditional architecture of the region. These are captured and immortalised in visual form and in visual rhythms. within the architecture.

Depictions of floral elements such as the leaf, stalk, flower, fruit, and tendrils are common in these traditional works but they are never static but are reworked and varied according to site, place, and cultural peculiarities. The variety of leaves depicted and incorporated for example, ranges from the two-part broken leaves to three-edged leaves. The three-part leaf of the Malay *petola* leaf, for example, is a kind of climbing plant, such as the edible gourds, the *peria* or the bitter gourd plant. The stalk is typically used as the backbone of the carving structure and this is then balanced with the organic forms of flowers, leaves, and tendrils. Plants are typically depicted in the recognisable curved silhouette of the stalk and are traditionally linked to Malay Nusantara expression in local decorative patterns.

Carvings and their decoration exude feelings of concentration, persistent attachment to traditions, and a general depth of high appreciation of art. Floral motifs, for example, are ubiquitous, usually derived from local flowers, and beautification is accomplished according to the creative imagination of the craftsmen. Moreover, the geometrical motif is mainly from spiritual beliefs and religious values. If the motif is in the form of calligraphy, it represents an Islamic influence and represents the artistic and poetic talents and predispositions of the locals. The Malay *awan larat*, for example, is a term originating from the word *awan* and *larat*. The word *awan* means cloud and *larat* means continuously and laboriously moving, meaning the 'moving cloud' motif, which has become much loved to many craftsmen. The word *larat* at times has been seen as being linked to the movement of 'creeping and spreading'; thus *awan larat* means a spread-out pattern. It is an almost sacred pattern in Malay classical carvings, and there are essentially two categories of *awan larat*: originally Malay *awan larat* and Javanese *awan larat*. The original Malay *awan larat* consists of a huge floral pattern and is typically composed in a wavy-like pattern which are extended in a distance starting from a point, getting longer and wider, with its stem coiling softly, and with the typical leaf folded. In this motif. the source (*punca/ ibu*) is based on a half-ring consisting of eight leaves executed in a natural formation connected by a fine tracery of stems until it covers the typical whole decorative panel.

1. The Ketam Guri Motif

The Ketam guri motif is synonymous with the profusions and convolutions of the ecological leaves and tendrils. The batik industry and the textile arts have evolved this pattern from its essential form into variants of motifs and patterns. The plant itself has anti-diabetic, anti-bacterial, and anti-fungal medicinal capabilities and essences. The resulting patterns are curved and convoluted due to the curved nature of the plant. The *Ketam guri* motif is typically depicted as a central flower surrounded by curved leaves and foliage. This recalls another popular motif in the Malay world, which is the *Sulur Kacang Laut* motif, which is essentially a form of convoluted tendrils derived from the *Sulor Kacang* plant. The motif itself depicts a kind of natural and silent movement, representing the process of growth in natural plants. In the motif below, the panel itself is composed with a balance and symmetry, and the *bunga sulur kacang laut* itself is presented as the central motif carved moving upwards, having emerged from the flowerpot. The twirling leaves flow within the semi-circular panel, and they curl downward depicting a movement of the leaves that suggests the process of growth, and these are repeated and then positioned on the left- and right-hand sides of a ventilation panel (17.3). To woodcarvers, this represents the ever-present power and presence of the Creator (Kamaruddin, 2011).

2. The Kerikal Motif

The Kerikal is a wide flat flange, with a plain cavetto descending into a traditional flat shallow bowl, with intricate floral patterns consisting of the blooming of beautiful locally found flowers. The Malaysian version has similarities to the motif of scrolling foliate on the *Parang Betinon* or *Klewang* on the silver inlaid from Sumatera, Indonesia, most probably Palembang in the mid-nineteenth century. The ceremonial silver-inlaid *Klewang* is at times, fully pierced finely on the silver blade. The third motif is almost the same as those found on the oval dulang silver-alloy with emblem motif found widely in Riau-Lingga. It is said that this Bunga *Kerawang* is the basis of the curvatures of the local stylistic styles of foliate found on refined crafted silver trays with the finely chiseled motif.

3. Teruntum Motif

The Teruntum motif itself is derived from the term *Teruntum-tuntum*, which means to grow again and again. It also means 'to always bloom and be vibrant'. The pattern of the Teruntum resembles a jasmine flower along with the sari-sari proverbial jasmine flower.

4. Bunga Langkasuka

The Bunga Langkasuka is popularly found in Terengganu and Kelantan and are found as exquisite carvings in structures built as early as the seventeenth to nineteenth centuries. For example, a wooden panel can consist of motifs of the Daun *Ketumbit* on a central floral motif with the *Daun Langkasuka* surrounding it. Both are medicinal plants. A motif can evolve into a braided figure-of-eight pattern *of Daun Dewa (Langkasuka)* and *Daun Ketumbit*. Langkasuka was known as a kingdom founded early in the second century AD, and it was the first Malay kingdom located in the neighbourhood of modern Patani. The Langkasuka motif was known as a spiral motif and this motif was inspired by the process of growth in nature. It has been also related to the origins from the earlier Ayuthaya kingdom of Siam and the Majapahit kingdom. Basically, the motif depicts the intertwining of the *Daun ketumbit* (Leucas Lavandulifolia), a flowering plant with small white flowers which have nutritional and medicinal value.

The Langkasuka motif is inspired by the process of growth in nature (Rosnawati, 2005) and is found in the various Malay expressions of artisanal traditions, used in their rituals and customs. This particular Langkasuka motif or Kelopak Dewa is known to symbolize natural energies that the Malays typically associated with the eco-system such as the natural types of soil, water, and the different directions of the local wind. This motif is carved using the technique of semi-piercing forms, like those which the artistic forms are carved with relief, such as architectural carving on cengal wood. The leaf-shaped motif can even be linked to graceful finger-type gestures of the movement of Malay martial arts of self-defence known as *Silat*.

5. Bunga Raya Motif

The *Bunga Raya* or hibiscus is prevalent and continuously found in both Malay modern and traditional arts and crafts. The *Bunga Raya*, declared Malaysia's national flower in the late 1950s, is used time and time, not only to represent the Malay cultural identity, but the national identity. By the end of 1958, the Malaysian Ministry of Agriculture suggested seven flowers to be designated the national flower. Amongst these flowers were *bunga kenanga*, hibiscus, jasmine, lotus, the local rose, bunga *cempaka*, and *bunga tanjung*.

6. The Nago Besaung Motif

The Nago Besaung motif is of Nusantara origin and is typically, amongst others found as a Songket pattern featuring a *Nago Besaung* motif with a rose pattern in the middle. The *Nago Besaung* motif was believed to originate from the Songket patterns of the history of traditional Palembang. The *Nago Besaung*—also known as *Naga Bertarung*—motif is named as such as the heads of the dragons face each other. The dragon motifs often symbolise the element of power and status due to the intricate details and the use of gold threads commonly found in the pattern. Because of how the heads of dragons confront each other, this motif is conventionally used by, and associated with, royalty. *Songket* was believed to have started a rich maritime trading empire based in Sumatera.

The Parang Rusak Barung motif (often abbreviated *Parang rusak*) originated from Sunan Paku Buwana III in 1769 and was at the time instructed to be only used by the King of Kasunanan of Surakarta Hadiningrat (Hidajat, 2004). There are at least two versions of the origin of this motif. The first version states that this motif was created by Raden Panji of the Kingdom of Kediri in East Java in the eleventh century. The second version states that this motif was created by the Sultan Agung of Mataram in Central Java. What was generally accepted is that the motif of *Parang rusak* is one of the sacred motifs conventionally worn by the kings of *Mataram*.

7. The Bunga Ketumbit Motif

The Bunga Ketumbit motif is traditionally inspired by an herbaceous plant called *bunga ketumbit* (*ageratum conyzoides*) and has a long history of traditional medicinal uses such as healing of illnesses such as the healing of wounds and minor illness such as the sore throat. The motif been continuously imitated and abstracted by Malay craftsmen throughout eras and regions. Traditionally, this motif was used and owned by high-ranking members of society and royalty. Because of this, these talented and highly skilled craftsmen which continuously evolve these patterns were usually designated as 'royal artists'.

8. The Bakawali Motif

The Bakawali or *Ephyllum oxypetalum* is known as a traditional medicinal plant. The preference of the plant motif is based on the specialty of the plant, including the medicinal uses, the essence of its attraction in terms of ecological traits, taste, and scent. The ornamental value is clearly related to the design motif where it contains floral design elements including flowers, leaves, branches, flower buds, and stems, and hence the motifs are used in traditional houses in a decorative function and for natural ventilation. It creates a sense of welcome to the vistor, and enhances the wall as a facade of the enclosed space inside such traditional houses.

9. Kepala Cicak Motif

The Kepala Cicak motif is known to have been influential from the days of the Sultanate of Demak in the fifteenth century, which is the third oldest kingdom in the Nusantara and fourth in South East Asia. The *Kepala cicak* motif is known to be found, amongst others, in the corners of traditional Malay house roofs in the form of the tumpu *kasau or papan cantik*. The lizard symbol is not only used in old, traditional Malay architecture and is found frequently in the Malay pantun, e.g. *cicak disana disini, cicak sarang bergulung rotan, adik disana saya disini, macam burung sahut-sahutan,* in *'perumpamaan',* in *cicak berak kapur,* and in children's songs

In South East Asia, the rich ecosystem has become the repertoire of carvers and craftsmen, and by the era of the advent of Islam, there is even more focus on the natural forms of flora, as Islam discourages imitation and expressions of aqua and terraforms in architecture. Yet a common

Fig. 17.1 Sample of a symmetrically carved wooden panel with tendrils of convoluted patterns of local ecology

theme and archetypal pattern is the duality or mix between water (including vapour and clouds) and land.

The Makara—A Water-Land Symbol of Pre-Islam

A recurring motif or image appearing across South East Asia architecture and artistic artefacts is the *makara* image. The *makara* appears and emerges time and time again across the width and breadth of form and spaces of traditional and monumental complexes, structures, building components, and artefacts of the local arts, including artisanal works and traditions. In Sanskrit, the word *makara* itself means 'water-monster' or 'sea dragon'. In Hindu mythology, a *makara* was known as essentially a sea creature that serves as a vehicle (vahana) for Ganga, the river goddess, and the sea god, Varuna. In later eras, makaras were typically depicted as half mammal, half fish with an aquatic hind portion and a terrestrial head, such as that of an elephant.

Initially appearing on the forefront of boat prows which were sharply upturned at both ends, with a *makara*-like figure at the prow, the makara is believed to represent a protective means in the ancient world from the hazards of tropical seas and forests. The form of the *makara* itself is significant, and the *makaras*, although initially emerging from a crocodile form, were typically depicted as half mammal, half fish with an aquatic hind portion and a terrestrial head, such as that of an elephant (Fig. 17.2).

Makara in Traditional Architecture

Makara-like creatures (Figs. 17.3 and 17.4) were generally found to adorn South East Asian architectural entrances and gateways and are traditionally seen as the guardians of these thresholds and entryways. The image is, amongst others, found in the lower portions of entrances, staircases, gateways, basic pots, water sprouts, and carvings in structures and even weapons and pottery in areas ranging from India to South East Asia.

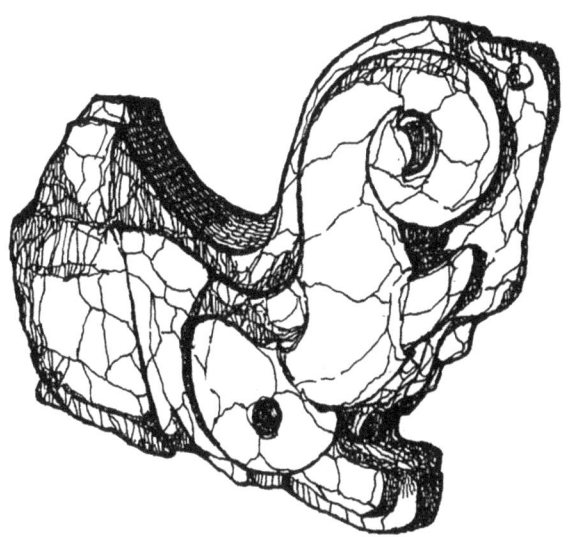

Fig. 17.2 A stone-based *makara form of unknown origin found as part of archi-tectural ornamentation* displayed in the Ethnology Museum, Malacca, Malaysia

Fig. 17.3 *A Makara* Statue above Doorways, of a traditional monument in Cambodia

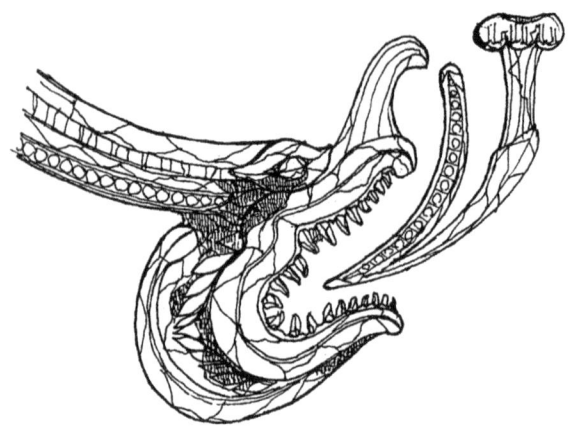

Fig. 17.4 Makara Engraving at the Arch of Ananda Phaya Scales. (Temple, Bagan, Myanmar)

In South East Asia's most ancient civilisation, the Lembah Bujang, archae-ologists from Penang uncovered a stone *makara* which was found in archaeological digs along with a site near the River Mas tributaries, which is the location at which many of the temple structures within Kedah's Bujang Valley were found. The *makara* found in Sungai (River) Mas was essentially a hybrid form carved with refined carving and from granite and was ornamented with fauna forms and motifs such as an elephant trunk, a bull's horn, and a crocodile mouth. A similar *makara* form was found in Melaka by the British forces during a time in which they were digging for structures on the hill overlooking the mouth of the River Melaka. It was found near the present St-Paul Church, originally the site of the original palace of the fourteenth- and fifteenth-century Melaka sultanate. The British placed the *makara* on display as they did the other motifs and plaques found along this wall. Yet the findings of this granite-based *makara* in Malacca, which are currently on display in the Ethnology Museum in the former Dutch Stadthuys building, suggest that there was even an earlier layer of structure there. In this relic, the *makara* form itself was a creature combining a fish and a mammal, and the Malacca relic displayed the tail of a fish and the head and trunk of an elephant, although its weathering had somewhat obscured the tail.

In both the Bujang Valley and Melaka sites, the *makara* relic had a similar wide-open mouth, similar in form and morphology to the Katmandu and sumatera *makara*. The main characteristic and embellishment of the *makara* spout are the so-called foliage motif, which appears like the elongated tail of the mythical creature. In other sites, the chimeric crowding of different species onto one main crocodile-like generic 'makara' form is characteristic of later stages of the *makara* and particularly found in complexes across East Asia. In several complexes and cases, one sees instances of form whereby from the open jaws of the *makara* emerges a cow or a bull. Known as a mythological symbol that originates from India, basically, the *makara* is a variation in images that depicts a hybrid creature formed from a juxtaposition of several creatures that resemble the crocodile.

Formal Evolution Across Time

Ranasinghe (1991) characterises how, over time, the fearsome qualities of the *makara* seem to rise to a crescendo and translated onto ominous ornamentations in architecture, particularly as guardians to entrance. For example, the *makara* at times adorns the upper level of gateways and is known as the *makara torana*. Commenting on the primordial significance of the *makara, torana*, Ranjith Fernando opines:

> *The makara torana represents the janua coeli or Gate of Heaven in sacred art; it marks the entrance to the niche, or cave of the world* which is the dwelling place of Divinity. In Sinhalese Buddhist art, it frames the entrance to the inner sanctum wherein is found the image of Divinity (the Buddha or Bôdhisattva) and even in relatively modern temples the darkness of this inner sanctum conveys the idea of the 'cave of the world'.*

Elena Semeka (2000) reports that the most ancient form of *makara* was shaped like a fish. The body of this fish-like *makara* is elongated with two snouts and its jaw resembling sharp teeth. However, it is the crocodile-type *makara* motif that is most prevalent and most widely known. It has an elongated body covered in scales. The body ends with a twist and the front resembles a twisted nose trunk. Ranasinghe (1991) aptly summarises the *makara* as essentially a hybrid or chimeric aquatic creature. There is a third type, which has closely resembled elephants, with a protruding and upturned nose and trunk and ending like a crocodile, with architects in Thailand and Cambodia pointing out how the *naga* imagery was essentially part of the same water-based traditions in iconography as the *makara*.

The word *naga* itself comes from Sanskrit and its pronunciation differs in the various Tai dialects where it is found. For example, the pronunciations *ngan, ngua, nam ngu ak-ngu*, and *nam ngum* can be found in Thailand and Laos (Ngaosrivathana & Ngaosrivathana, 2009). *Nagas* are depicted in a variety of forms in architecture, such as the water *naga* in Ahom, the crocodile among the Shan, and others which have been recalled in present times and amongst ornamentations reflected as design themes in modern constructions and the making of spaces. Past researchers have asserted that the persistence of the *makara* can be linked to the traditional universal motif of the *naga*, and in some parts of East Asia and South East Asia, there is a gradual merging of the two images in multiple iconographies. Basically, these lands with their many rivers, islands, and long coastal stretches gave rise to several 'water civilisations'—civilisations that flourished because of their location near a prominent water body, where images and visuals of both *naga* and *makara* predominate.

Resonating with the South East Asian Subconscious

The duality of flora, fauna land, and water and resonances of nature are part of the South East Asian subconscious as they evolve from era to era. Sumet Jumsai observed in Thai cultural symbols (published in Thai in 1982), the essence of Asia's maritime history is reflected in architectural-urban symbols and formal attributes of the 'nautical' nature of the indigenous to the region. Similar diffusions are traced to typologies that recall the river-sea-tropical jungle realm of the climate and context and how the spiritual uncertainties of this specific region had translated into the residual imageries of sea and land.

They essentially and universally embody the contrasts between humanity and wilderness. The tropical context, climate, and geography are an idyllic environment with a land full of contrasts and underlying currents and dangers. Cosmologically, they represent the contrasts found in South East Asia, an idyllic region yet full of the perennial ideal struggle between humanity and the encroaching and immediate danger of nature and its forces, creatures, and elements. All in all, it serves as a beacon, a pointer to the nature of the South East Asian archipelago's identity in terms of surface patterns and ornamentations. The chimeric juxtaposition of land and sea has made it a particular symbol of the character of South East Asian geography and terrain, thus breeding visual cultures and, thus, architecture and urban symbols replete with water and land references.

References

Hidajat, R. (2004). Kajian Strukturalisme-Simbolik Mitos Jawa Pada Motif Batik Berunsur Alam. *Bahasa dan Seni, 32*(2), 289–303.

Kamaruddin, Z, (2011). Compositional variations of Awan Larat in traditional Malay wood carving: Diversity and unity in the expression. IIUM Press, International Islamic University Malaysia, First Edition, 2011 ISBN: 978-967-418-030-0

Macfarlane, R. (2015). *Landmarks*. Penguin.

Ngaosrivathana, M., & Ngaosrivathana, P. (2009). *The enduring sacred landscape of the Naga*. Mekong Press.

Ranasinghe, L. (1991). The evolution and significance of the Makara Torana. *Journal of the Royal Asiatic Society of Sri Lanka, 36*, 132–145.

Rosnawati, O. (2005, June). Seni ukir Melayu: Asal usul dan perubahan rupa dan jiwa (Malay art of woodcarving: Derivation and transformation of form and content). In Proceeding of International Seminar The Spirit and Form in Malay Design.

Semeka-Pankratov, E. (1984). The meaning of the term makara in light of comparative mythology.

18

Vernacular Typography as Reflections of the Nusantara: Cultural Inflections in Street Vendor Signages

Agung Zainal Muttakin Raden
and Muhammad Iqbal Qeis

Vernacular typography is an expression that grows and develops in every urban community based on local wisdom. In Jakarta, the capital city of Indonesia, vernacular typography can be found fashioning the city, from signage for restaurants to the stalls used by street food vendors. A photographic survey is used to document the use of vernacular typography in restaurants and street food vendors around Jakarta. The vernacular typography has created a distinct brand identity that helped fashion Jakarta's identity as a melting pot of various ethnicities and cultures. The brand identity displays a form of distinct ethnic characteristics incorporated into the letters, creating an identity inflection of Nusantara culture to the otherwise rigid roman typefaces often shown in bold and placed in a landscape layout with centre or justified text alignment. This identity inflection has transformed Jakarta into a museum of typefaces rich with cultural and local expression.

A. Z. M. Raden (✉) • M. I. Qeis
Universitas Indraprasta PGRI, Jakarta, Indonesia

S. Jahn Kassim et al. (eds.), *Eco-Urbanism and the South East Asian City*,
https://doi.org/10.1007/978-981-19-1637-3_18

Nusantara Cultural Identity

Rich and diverse cultural expression is one of Indonesia's identities, and the archipelago is rich with numerous ethnicities, languages, arts, and traditions. However, this diversity in cultural expression faced a long history of colonialisation, internal democratic transition, and the threat of global competition. Cultural expression, both tangible and intangible forms, has been eroded in recent years. Nevertheless, alongside the cultural erosion that is happening, globalised interactions also add to the richness of local culture through the process of cultural transformation (Yeganeh, 2020). The open nature of cultural transformation means that the change will inevitably happen whether naturally or forced through economic interactions or policies. With a millennium of history as a hub for trade and sea routes, the archipelagic region of Indonesia always faced challenges regarding the transformation of culture, language, and identity arising from the interactions between locals and foreigners during maritime trade and travel (Lauder & Lauder, 2016). Laden with this sense of fragility and vulnerability, Nusantara cultural identity is influenced by the concept of acculturation as a result of developing an inward-looking concept to adapt to the challenges when coming into contact with another culture.

Acculturation is one of the most important processes in developing Nusantara cultural identity as a hub for maritime trade and travel where a culture from outside is accepted and then assimilated into its own culture, creating an adaptable form of expression without losing the identity and personality of the original culture. Globalisation represents the compression of the world and the intensification of worldwide relationships. Its influence is significant for economic, political, cultural, and social facets of global culture (Mawhood, 2014). Globalisation, which brings with itself various facets of material culture reflecting different lifestyles, is very influential in the lives of the younger generation. Although shared among numerous identities, one crucial value that can be observed as the local wisdom of the people living in the Nusantara archipelago is rooted in the concept of eco-urbanism.

Eco-Urbanism in Nusantara Archipelago

The culture of the people of the Nusantara archipelago has been founded on a particular philosophy of life that seeks continuous harmony with the universe. The Minangkabau, for example, embody the philosophy of *"alam takambang jadi guru"* (nature as a teacher), reflecting a continuous need for humans to learn from nature. Nature teaches humans to survive. The people of the Minangkabau people have studied their environment since the time of their ancestors and are familiar with nature and the ecosystem (Kurniasih et al., 2017).

The shape of the Gadang House, a house unique to the people of Minangkabau, resembles a buffalo horn, arising from an ethos often associated with *Tambo Minangkabau Alam*. The story tells of a buffalo fighting match between the Javanese and the people of Minangkabau. At the end of the story, the buffalo from Minangkabau won the match, so the term *minang* means winning, and *kabau* means buffalo (Franzia et al., 2015). The traditional house is decorated with ornaments related to nature, such as *kaluak paku*, which is the curved tip of the fern (Pteridophyta), shoots of bamboos, and *siriah gadang*, which is a large piper beetle. In addition to the Minang community, the Javanese are also familiar with terms related to nature, one of which is '*Kena iwake aja nganti buthek banyune*', meaning that to achieve the goal, it does not have to be destructive to nature.

Evolution of Design in Nusantara Archipelago

Design as a cultural artefact gives meaning and value. Cultural preservation in design aims to maintain the values of treasured local wisdom. Designers and artists should pay attention to three important things when creating something out of traditional objects: preservation, revitalisation, and transformation (Nugraha, 2018, p. 237). Preservation has the aim of protecting the original tradition from change. Preservation involves keeping an object from destruction and seeing to it that the object is not irredeemably altered or changed (Bjorneberg, 2016).

Revitalisation aims to bring back traditional practices in contemporary society. Transformation aims to reinvent an old form of tradition so that it fits into and suits contemporary lifestyles (Nugraha, 2018, p. 237).

The existence of Hindu-Buddhist religion in the Nusantara archipelago and its way of life can be observed from the overwhelming legacy of temples scattered across several areas in Indonesia. The epics of Ramayana and Mahabharata are adapted to the local Indonesian contexts, which were adopted and mixed from the original Indian stories. The arrival of Islam in Indonesia then brought changes in the fields of design and architecture, thereby changing society and its way of living. The designs on the tombs in Trowulan and Tralaya are evidence of a fusion of Islam and Hinduism. This tomb is located on a Hindu-Buddhist heritage site. The stones mark the burial of Muslims; however, they are dated to the Indian Śaka (ś) era rather than the Islamic Anno Hijrae and use Old Javanese rather than Arabic numerals (Ricklefs, 2001, p. 5). In the field of architecture, the synthesis of Islam and Hinduism can be seen in the architectural design of the Great Mosque of Mataram Kotagede Yogyakarta.

The Great Mosque of Mataram Kota Gede Yogyakarta in Fig. 18.1 is a synthesis of Islamic and Hindu-Buddhist culture. This mosque consists of a courtyard, a fence, and a tomb. A Paduraksa-shaped gate still stands at the entrance to the main building of the mosque. Paduraksa is a connecting access gate between areas in a special building complex. The top of the gate is decorated with kala ornaments, namely a giant face with bulging eyes, a wide nose, and an open mouth.

Fig. 18.1 The Great Mosque of Mataram Kotagede Yogyakarta and Paduraksa Gate. (Source: Author)

As seventeenth-century colonialism entered Indonesia, the culture brought by the Dutch was introduced as a form of the then modern and advanced European culture. Indigenous people were taught that a European culture was a form of high culture. The Dutch adopted the local culture so that their European teachings could be well received by the indigenous people. The presence of colonialism is the cause of the inhibition of the synthesis of Javanese-Islamic culture. The synthesis between indigenous and colonial cultures can be seen in the design of the Bangsal Prabayaksa at the Kanoman Keraton Cirebon. Bangsal Prabayaksa has wall ornaments in the form of ceramics from Europe which, since its installation to the present, has never been repaired.

The historic evolution of design in the Nusantara archipelago reflects the ethos of eco-urbanism, which is an underlayer, which was in turn influenced by Indonesia's multicultural maritime history. The existence of the spice route affected the growth of ports, which were the centre of Indonesian trade at that time. International trade along sea routes began to flourish in Java from around the tenth century. This spurred the growth of ports along the coast, which were capable of handling international trade, and those on river estuaries, which handled regional trade (Lauder & Lauder, 2016).

This maritime history influences the expression when local people migrate and choose the formation of street vendors to face the modernisation of the city while maintaining its local cultural roots. Street vendors are an alternative street economy that is friendly to the community. Street vendors are not only appreciated for their unique taste, comfort, and affordability but also contribute to the country's economy, the persistence of the community's cultural and social heritage, as well as the potential to maintain and improve the nutritional status of the population (Hill et al., 2019).

The representation of local wisdom through the formation of street vendor stalls shows an independent economic power. The use of typography on street vendors serves as local visual culture and performs an issue of interest between authority and power orientation that creatively becomes a new cultural identity. The dynamics of migrant life in the informal sector also come out in the phenomenon of visual culture that the migrant develops. The visual culture developed by the migrant helped in settling their cultural identity in the ever growing metropolis. It has been proven to be an intention of the urban population that migrates from a remote area (Damayanti, 2016). As typography played an important role in the design work, from the use of traditional scripts in *prasasti* or stone epitaph placed as a landmark in the Hindu-Buddhist kingdom to the application of typography on street vendors in the modern era, it is apparent that we need to observe the role of typography in conveying the essence of Nusantara cultural identity.

Typography in Nusantara Archipelago

The function of typography is very important in the development of visual communication design. Typography can be applied in the fields of architecture, interior, environment, and other fields. Danton Sihombing argues that the works that appear always to represent the spirit of the times from the actions of a graphic designer in responding to every need for visual communication through the dimensions and disciplines contained in typography (Sihombing, 2015, p. 16). In the Bauhaus era, a text consisting of content and purpose should be able to dictate the design. That means the graphic design created must represent the content of the text. Typography must be able to mediate between the content of the message and the reader who receives the message (Jury, 2006, p. 8). Typography is the art of selecting and arranging the layout of letters and typefaces for printing and reproduction purposes (Maharsi, 2013, p. 2).

The development of typography in the Nusantara archipelago was influenced by writing traditions and scripts originating from India. These scripts developed throughout the archipelago and then mixed with local cultures such as the Old Javanese script (kawi) which developed in the Java region to Bali (Balinese script), Old Sundanese, Khad Lampung, Batak script in the Batak region, Lontara script in Bugis, Incung script in Kerinci, and Pégon which is an Arabic script adapted to the Javanese or Sundanese dialect (known as the Jawi script in Sumatra and the Serang script in Sulawesi). These scripts would later be shelved and changed to Latin scripts influenced by the colonial era. However, the traditional scripts can still be found in inscriptions and ancient manuscripts stored in several libraries, museums, and even preserved by the experts in the community.

Fig. 18.2 Panji Tales Story Collection National Library Indonesia. (Source: By author)

Figure 18.2 shows one of the pieces of evidence of the archipelago's writing tradition that continues to grow. Here, the pages show not only text but also wayang illustrations as content highlights. This book tells a story that developed in the archipelago, albeit with various versions. The typesetting and layout were good and structured, making it easy to follow.

Figure 18.3 shows the influence of wayang images which were still maintained even though the use of traditional scripts had been changed to Latin script. However, the Latin script was modified to create a distinct style while the illustrations still followed the visual styling found in ancient manuscripts. The styling of the Latin script to express a distinct locality, resulting in a non-standard typeface as an expression of the local community, is called vernacular typography (Murtono, 2014).

Vernacular Typography

In the field of typography, the term vernacular is known for the art of typography that is done spontaneously. The term vernacular first appeared in the field of architecture. The everyday language through which a group, community, or region communicates is vernacular. It is a recurrent aspect

Fig. 18.3   Vernacular Batik Label. (Source: By author)

within graphic design as designers draw on the vernacular by incorporating 'found' items, such as street signs, and borrowing low-culture forms
of communication, such as slang (Ambrose & Paul, 2009, p. 69).
Vernacular typography is shown as a representation of emotion and
expression which is growing in society. Vernacular typography (some also
refer to it as ethnic alphabets) found on various writings, pictures, and
signs in the local environment could become a cultural asset of a country
(Raden & Qeis, 2017).

Naomi Haswanto in her dissertation said that vernacular typography
referred to the system and visual style of letters created by design methods
using locally available resources. Typographic vernaculars are produced to
meet local needs and circumstances and are used by urban people in their
daily lives (Haswanto, 2011, p. 71). Haswanto highlights vernacular
typography found in the informal sector in the city of Bandung by mapping letters or typography types in formal typographic classifications
such as serif letters, sans serif letters, square hooked letters (slab serif),
ornamental, and concatenated fonts. In another study, Haswanto argued
that although most of these ethnic alphabets are often ignored because of
their 'old' and traditional look, they create a uniqueness which more or

less will become a local genius in Indonesia (Haswanto, 2013). Local genius refers to what humans know, how they behave and what strategies they develop to sustain their existence where they live (Ruastiti, 2011). Vernacular typography creates a typeface that took inspiration from society's daily activities. This typeface reflects the expression of traditions and familiar and distinctive causes in society since the typeface creation process started from local values (Murtono, 2014, p. 115).

Vernacular typography can be a reflection of identity as innately these represent certain feelings or emotions. The choice of a typeface in vernacular works makes the work unique and easily recognisable. Vernacular typography as identity relates to local traditions and is the product of an urban society that has an artistic spirit. This expression produces typographical works that vary according to the spontaneity of the maker. Vernacular typography is not primarily thought to be read or to transmit a message, but rather to be seen as expressing cultural identity and belonging and to mark territory (Järlehed, 2015).

Vernacular Typography in Signage

Signs in a city are very important as pointers and information providers. Signage is part of the graphic-design environment. Signage should serve as an information provider and not only as decoration in a city. Signage and other visual wayfinding cues can help the people navigate their environment when there's no one around to ask (Calori & Vanden-Eynden, 2015, p. 7). Vernacular signage sometimes escapes road users. A pedestrian who casually reads a sign made for hours or days pays little attention to the technicalities of its manufacture (Hao, 2018, p. 6).

The current development of typefaces used for signage is very diverse. However, we can still find vernacular typography in some signage in several cities. Typography in signage has a relationship with the linguistic landscape. Linguistic landscapes are around us all the time and we can see language signs on the streets, inside shops, on government buildings, banks, schools, etc. The highest density of signs can be found in urban centers, in the main shopping streets and commercial areas (Gorter & Cenoz, 2017, p. 234). Typography in signage has contributed to defining information and naming specific locations, directions, or identities. This means that typography in signage can be said to be landscape typography. The typographic landscape is the landscape formed by a subset of graphic elements in the urban environment: characters that form words, dates, and other messages composed of letters and numbers (Silva Gouveia et al., 2009).

Vernacular typography in the signage of street vendors forms an understanding of cultural expression in a multicultural community. Various types of letterforms and font styles are present in street vendors' signs. Letterforms play a very important role when representing a visual work. The placement and selection of letters are strategic factors in conveying the message. Street vendors use letterforms as signs in their shops, influenced by the visual culture and local wisdom of their origin. The influence can be in the form of colour, ideology, myth, and way of life.

To further understand how typography as an element in a design is crucial to communicate local wisdom in the design in Nusantara archipelago, especially in Jakarta as an urban area, this study observed the use of vernacular typography in street vendors across Jakarta which embodies the philosophy of living in harmony with nature. In 2018, based on the initiative funded by the Jakarta government, the urban economy has flourished and seen a resurgence as more than 170,000 street vendors were operating in the Jakarta area (Hadi, 2018). The two common street vendors that were scattered across Jakarta are a vendor from West Sumatra and a vendor from East Java.

Street Vendors from West Sumatra

West Sumatra is one of the regions in Indonesia with a matrilineal system. Life in the core areas was defined by a matrilineal way of life. This means that certain kinship groups follow the female descent of a mother. The woman's brother is responsible for her children rather than her husband (Stark, 2013). The Minangkabau ethnic group of West Sumatra has a tradition of migrating outside the region of West Sumatra, which is known as *merantau*. *Merantau* means the movement of Minangkabau people from West Sumatra to other regions in Indonesia, or other countries (Franzia, 2017). The basic culture of Minangkabau is tradition. Aside from their philosophy which shows their attunement to nature, they also are a very religious people. One of the famous Minangkabau proverbs is *Adat Basandi Syarak, Syarak Basandi Kitabullah*, meaning that the Minangkabau tradition is based on religion (Islam) and the religion is based on the Qur'an. Their unique identities can be seen applied in their attire, wedding ceremonies, and traditional houses.

Sate Padang is one of the typical dishes of West Sumatra. It is sold from a typical cart and at Padang restaurants. This West Sumatran cuisine is famous for its distinctive aroma and spices, making this special culinary delicatessen able to transcend geographical boundaries. Sate Padang represents one of the general characteristics of traditional Minangkabau dishes, which are an important part of Indonesian gastronomy (Sani et al., 2016). Sate Padang has a variety of flavors based on the region such as the Sate Padang typical of Bukit Tinggi, Payakumbuh, Pariaman, and other areas in the West Sumatra region (Fig. 18.4).

Besides Sate Padang, there are several other culinary delights, such as rendang, beef jerky (dendeng), eggs, snapper head curries (*gulai kepala kakap*), green chili sauce, jackfruit vegetables, and other special dishes. This food menu is usually available at Padang restaurants. *Rendang* is commonly made with beef (especially tenderloin) with a special sauce containing a high amount of coconut milk (Nurmufida et al., 2017). In addition to rendang, dendeng is also a dish that requires special

Fig. 18.4 Sate Padang street vendors. (Source: Author)

Fig. 18.5 Padang Restaurant. (Source: Author)

techniques in cooking. Meat that has been seasoned with spices before cooking must be *batokok* (*batokok* means being pounded) so that it becomes flat and then dried in the sun; once it dries, it is fried over low heat with a lot of oil until it is submerged (Mardatillah, 2020).

The typography used in Sate Padang carts and Padang restaurants is vernacular in style. Some of the letterforms were created spontaneously, and some imitated Latin fonts. Each letterform is made by painting or cutting parts of the letters and then pasting them on glass for easy viewing (Fig. 18.5).

The tradition of *merantau* and proverbs are applied in every business run by the Minangkabau community. The characteristics of Minangkabau ethnicity can be seen in the architectural forms of houses, shops, and carts for trading. The characteristic of gonjong always looks good on house roofs, fences, and signage in shops. The form of the *bagonjong* is the main icon in the food stall logo, modified from *rumah gadang* or *rangkiang*. It gives a symbolic representation of Minangkabau culture and tradition, apart from the commercial needs of the logo (Franzia et al., 2015).

The shape of the gonjong is represented in the food stall as an identity. The name uses a specific characteristic of typography, which is also often modified to the form of the roof. The colours give the identity of the food stall, and the typography enhances the characteristic of Minangkabau culture and identity. The logo gives the cultural identity of Minangkabau other than a commercial representation of the food stall (Franzia et al., 2015).

Figure 18.6 shows the application of *gonjong* on the signage. The history of printing that developed in Bukittinggi, West Sumatra, made the Minang people close to modern typography. Vernacular artists combined spontaneously created letters and Latin fonts that were printed and then traced.

Table 18.1 shows the vernacular and Latin font commonly used to make signage. Vernacular letterforms in Sate Padang text use serif with modifications at the bottom of the terminal made downwards. The idea for this vernacular design comes from the letters Caslon and Baskerville, both of which are transitional in style.

Transitional is a term often used to describe the design of certain printing types. transitional describes a letterform that shares features with both the old-face letter and the modern letter. To explore the relationships among these three terms, it will be useful to analyze exemplary typefaces for each application (Eliason, 2015).

Fig. 18.6 Application of *Gonjong* as signage. (Source: Author)

Table 18.1 Vernacular and Latin Font

	Vernakular—with cutting stiker
SATE PADANG	Baskerville Bold
SATE PADANG	Big Caslon
SATE PADANG	Brim Narrow Half Extrude Outline
SATE PADANG	Brim Narrow Half Extrude

Source: Author

Table 18.2 Vernacular and Latin Font

	Vernakular—Old Style with cutting stiker
TAKANA JUO	Cooper

Source: Author

In addition to the identity of the *gonjong*, colour characterises the Minangkabau ethnic identity. The colour used to colour the text of *Takana Juo* is red with a yellow shadow. Acculturation of Chinese culture in the Minangkabau region has an influence on the visual works presented. The dominance of red, yellow and gold gives the impression of a cheerful, luxurious, noble, warm. These colours are not only present in the profane area but are also present in the sacred area (Table 18.2).

Street Vendors from East Java

East Java is the largest region in Java Island. The people of East Java, especially the city of Lamongan, have strong ties to tradition and philosophy. Historically, people's lives were known to be very religious because they maintained their ancestral heritage (Arifrahara, 2020). The myth that develops in the Lamongan community divides the two culinary areas. The north-east area produces culinary soups or water elements such as coffee shops, Soto, and other water-based dishes. The south-west region produces dry food or no sauce, such as Pecel Lele, Pecel Ayam, Tempe Penyet, and seafood. Aside from this division in culinary production, the people of East Java follow the spirit of *bondo nekat*, which means having a strong will (literally means recklessness). As the second most populous province in Indonesia, the people of East Java are always eager to migrate outside of the region, leaving East Java to find work in urban areas.

The typical cuisine of East Java often adorns cities in Indonesia. The famous dishes that are often found in urban areas include Soto Lamongan and Pecel Lele (catfish). Soto is one of Indonesia's culinary categories that includes soupy dishes made from meat or vegetable broth and contains shredded meat or chicken, vermicelli, and bean sprouts, among other ingredients (Yudhistira & Fatmawati, 2020). One of the famous types of Soto is Soto Lamongan. Soto Lamongan is a specific kind of Soto from Lamongan, East Java, and has spread to many other regions (Wijana, 2018).

Besides Soto, Lamongan is famous for its dishes made from catfish called Pecel Lele. Pecel Lele is a dish consisting of fried catfish served with traditional chili sauce, tofu or tempeh, and warm rice. The two dishes are sold separately, although both are typical foods from the same region. These two culinary delights adorn the corners of the city at night, from main roads to narrow streets.

The tents for Soto and Pecel Lele look lively, as seen in Fig. 18.7. The letters used are the sans serif type, or letters without hooks, and the serif types with slight modifications and improvisations by vernacular artists. Sans serif refers to type without serifs and very low to uniform thick-to-thin stroke contrast (Cullen, 2012, p. 42). This letter appeared around 1816 which was introduced by William Caslon.

Sans serif types are far more often seen in display roles, though, as headings and titles and in advertising (Felici, 2012, p. 73). Sans serif fonts are also known as Grotesque. The Helvetica-like model is named Akzidenz Grotesque. These were some of the first styles to be cut in stone, and they have had periodic returns to popularity due to their simplicity, as well as their somewhat industrial look (Strizver, 2013, p. 44). The following table shows the Lamongan tent stalls using serif and sans serif fonts (Table 18.3).

A serif is a small finishing detail at the start and end of strokes (Cullen, 2012, p. 42) (Table 18.4). Serif means a hook. This hook is the part that connects the stroke and the end of the terminal. This is a large category of typefaces with one common denominator: all have serifs. Simply put, serifs can be described as extensions, protrusions, or, more elegantly, finishing strokes extending from the ends of a character (Strizver, 2013,

Fig. 18.7 Pecel Lele and Soto Lamongan. (Source: Author)

p. 42). The serif typeface is inspired by Italian handwriting called Lettera Antica. Serifs are classified as old-style, transitional, modern, and slab. Serif construction consists of (1) reflective and transitive, (2) bilateral and monolateral, and (3) abrupt and adnate. Variants in serif include cupped, hairline, rounded, slab, and wedge. In the typographic literature, serifs are generally believed to have a significant impact on readability (Arditi & Cho, 2005).

Artworks displayed are roosters and catfish, and for seafood the images that appear are shrimp, squid, and clams. Lamongan society believes that catfish have philosophical values, namely animals that are resistant in

Table 18.3 Sans Serif

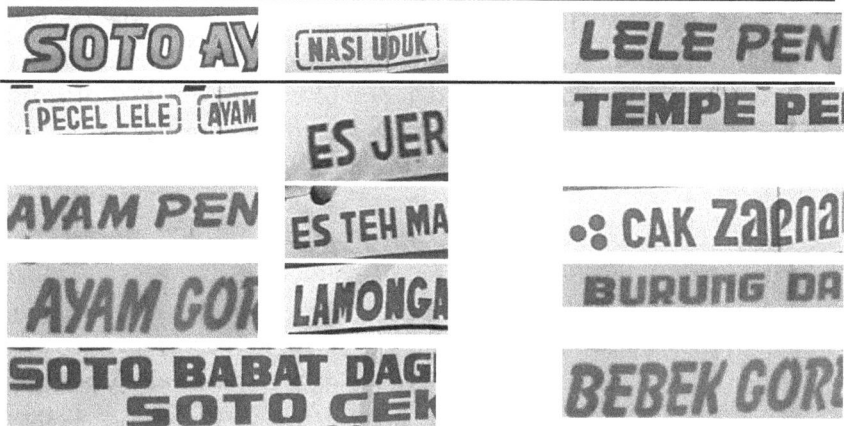

Source: Author

Table 18.4 Serif

Source: Author

various conditions, tough, and unyielding. The rooster generally symbolises strength and courage so that its form can be considered a manifestation of the spirit of Lamongan merchants overseas. The philosophy of the rooster is strong, tough, and flowing sustenance. With the display of roosters in the Soto tents and Pecel Lele or Pecel Ayam, the owners believe that the business they run will be strong in facing competition and the sustenance that always flows.

Conclusion

The inclusion of Roman letters in the colonial period became an identity that filled the architectural spaces of the building. Colonialisation introduced Roman letters and replaced native Indonesian characters such as Sanskrit and other ancient scripts. However, the regional identity is still trying to be maintained even though the ancient letters are no longer used.

The preservation of local identity is enhanced through the incorporation of iconic material elements from the original culture with Roman letters brought by the colonialists and the creation of vernacular typography that reflects the distinctive culture and identity of the archipelago. The impact of this growth non-formal economy sector such as the culinary field, in particular street vendors.

The formation of street vendors such as tents and carts is an effort to preserve nature because carts and tents do not require natural reconstruction so the landscaping of the vegetation is not disturbed, in contrast to the formation of restaurants or buildings that changed the landscape and vegetation in a city. The establishment of restaurants will mobilise people to move from one area to another, while the formation of carts and tents did the opposite as they are the one moving towards the community so that consumption distribution becomes more effective. Hence, the formation of tents and carts is rooted in the local wisdom with the concept of eco-urbanism at its heart.

The uniqueness of street vendors in applying typography is spontaneous. The selection and arrangement of the letters used by vernacular artists are based on visual experience inspired by the region of origin. The selection and arrangement of typefaces used by vernacular artists are based on a visual experience inspired by the region of origin as well as the fonts used by modern shops.

The typefaces that are applied to Soto tents and Pecel Lele vendors are arranged symmetrically and asymmetrically. Some tents display the owner's name for branding purposes. The menu list dominates in this type of culinary tent. This is very practical so that customers know what menus are available. Lamongan cuisine has a tradition that has been passed down from generation to generation. The menu can represent coming from the north-east or west-south Lamongan region. This is what is still maintained today so that even though they come from the same area, they have their own uniqueness. The uniqueness of the traditional house of West Sumatra manifests in the form of distinctive typography, which is shaped like a gonjong. The simplification of the shape of the traditional house which has very complex ornaments becomes an identity that is easily recognisable in society.

The identity of the archipelago, namely unity in diversity, combines all local identities. This makes local identity no longer primary, but only an accent in the expression of national identity (identity inflection). The pattern of identity inflection is presented by street vendors and recognised by the state. This acknowledgement is not in the form of a policy but rather adopts the same pattern of inflection. Meanwhile, not only traditional ornaments can be included, but also modern landmarks that have been firmly attached as local identities can take part in identity inflection through the formula: Roman letters + regional elements = expression of identity.

Figure 18.8 shows Latin script plus regional elements, namely the stylised form of Kembang Goyang as an inflection of Jakarta identity which is expressed through the Jakarta 494th anniversary logo with the title *Jakarta Bangkit*. This theme is to signify the revival of the economy, social conditions, and sustainable development in Jakarta. The application of vernacular typography carried out by street vendors eventually became an urban expression that settled in Nusantara society. This becomes a kind of guideline in expressing their local identity without deviating from the agreed rules of unity in diversity.

Fig. 18.8   Jakarta's 496th anniversary logo. (Source: Author)

The examples above show that the Indonesian people have an inward-looking concept in which they maintain their identity by searching for existing material elements and then reflecting them in material form to make them easier to accept. This also shows that visual culture is an important tool in maintaining the identity of the archipelago because, through visuals, the people of the archipelago are able to explore their local cultural values.

References

Ambrose, G., & Paul, H. (2009). *The fundamentals of graphic design*. Ava Publishing SV.

Arditi, A., & Cho, J. (2005). Serifs and font legibility. *Vision Research, 45*(23), 2926–2933. https://doi.org/10.1016/j.visres.2005.06.013

Arifrahara, G. (2020). Visual Communication Morphology Study in Stall Banner of Street. *Vendors in Lamongan, 391*, 75–79. https://doi.org/10.2991/assehr.k.200108.017

Bjorneberg, B. (2016). Renovation, restoration, preservation, conservation. Retrieved December 5, 2020, from https://www.conservation-design.com/renovation-restoration-preservation-conservation

Calori, C., & Vanden-Eynden, D. (2015). *Signage and wayfinding design*. John Wiley & Sons, Inc. https://doi.org/10.1002/9781119174615

Cullen, K. (2012). *Design Elements Typography Fundamentals a Graphic Style Manual for understanding how typography affecs design*. Rockport Publishers.

Damayanti, M. N. (2016). The vernacular typography of street vendors: Migrant cultural identity in Surabaya. *The International Journal of Visual Design, 10*(4), 17–28. https://doi.org/10.18848/2325-1581/CGP/v10i04/17-28

Eliason, C. (2015). 'Transitional' typefaces: The history of a typefounding classification. *Design Issues, 31*(4), 30–43. http://www.jstor.org/stable/43830429

Felici, J. (2012). *The complete manual of typography: A guide to setting perfect type* (R. Gulick, ed.). Adobe Press.

Franzia, E. (2017). Cultural wisdom of Minangkabau ethnic community for local—Global virtual identity. *Mediterranean Journal of Social Sciences, 8*(1), 325–329. https://doi.org/10.5901/mjss.2017.v8n1p325

Franzia, E., Piliang, Y. A., & Saidi, A. I. (2015). Rumah Gadang as a symbolic representation of Minangkabau ethnic identity. *International Journal of Social Science and Humanity, 5*(1), 44–49. https://doi.org/10.7763/IJSSH.2015.V5.419

Gorter, D., & Cenoz, J. (2017). Linguistic landscape and multilingualism. In J. Cenoz, D. Gorter, & S. May (Eds.), *Language Awareness and Multilingualism* (pp. 233–245). Springer International Publishing. https://doi.org/10.1007/978-3-319-02240-6

Hadi, F. (2018). Jumlah PKL Naik Drastis, Kepala Dinas Koperasi UMKM dan Perdagangan Klaim Program OK OCE Sukses. https://wartakota.tribunnews.com/2018/07/04/jumlah-pkl-naik-drastis-kepala-dinas-koperasi-umkm-dan-perdagangan-klaim-program-ok-oce-sukses

Hao, T. Z. (2018). *Jalan-Jalan typography #1: Towards vernacular typography*. Hrf Type Design.

Haswanto, N. (2011). *Fenomena Tipografi Vernakular Masyarakat Sektor Informal Perkotaan Sebagai Ekspresi Budaya Masyarakat Urban Kota Bandung*. Institut Teknologi Bandung.

Haswanto, N. (2013). The local genius typography as a source of idea for Latin-based typeface design in visual communication today. *ITB Journal of Visual Art and Design, 4*(2), 155–161. https://doi.org/10.5614/itbj.vad.2013.4.2.7

Hill, J., Mchiza, Z., Puoane, T., & Steyn, N. P. (2019). The development of an evidence-based street food vending model within a socioecological framework: A guide for African countries. *PLoS One, 14*(10), e0223535. https://doi.org/10.1371/journal.pone.0223535

Järlehed, J. (2015). Ideological framing of vernacular type choices in the Galician and Basque semiotic landscape. *Social Semiotics, 25*(2), 165–199. https://doi.org/10.1080/10350330.2015.1010316

Jury, D. (2006). *What is typography (first)*. PageOne.

Kurniasih, U., Rahman, A. R., & Sari, S. M. (2017). The meaning of Merantau (Wandering) in Petatah-Petitih (Proverb) of Minangkabau. *Journal of Higher Education & Research Society: A Refereed International, 5*(2), 528–537. https://herso.org/vol-v-issue-2-october-2017/

Lauder, M. R., & Lauder, A. F. (2016). Maritime Indonesia and the Archipelagic Outlook; Some reflections from a multidisciplinary perspective on old port cities in Java. *Wacana, 17*(1), 97. https://doi.org/10.17510/wacana.v17i1.428

Maharsi, I. (2013). *Tipografi Tiap Font Memiliki Nyawa dan Arti*. CAPS.

Mardatillah, A. (2020). The enterprise culture heritage of Minangkabau cuisine, West Sumatra of Indonesia as a source of sustainable competitive advantage. *Journal of Ethnic Foods, 7*(1), 34. https://doi.org/10.1186/s42779-020-00059-z

Mawhood, K. (2014). *The effect of globalisation on typographic practice.* University of Reading. http://typefacedesign.net/wp-content/uploads/2016/01/Mawhood-Katy.pdf

Murtono, T. (2014). Penguatan Citra Merek Batik Dengan Tipografi Vernacular. *Acintya, 6*(2), 114–125. https://jurnal.isi-ska.ac.id/index.php/acintya/article/viewFile/215/215

Nugraha, A. (2018). Transforming tradition in Indonesia. In S. Walker, M. Evans, T. Cassidy, A. T. Holroyd, & J. Jung (Eds.), *Design roots* (1st ed., pp. 168–182). Bloomsbury Publishing Plc. https://doi.org/10.5040/9781474241823.ch-015

Nurmufida, M., Wangrimen, G. H., Reinalta, R., & Leonardi, K. (2017). Rendang: The treasure of Minangkabau. *Journal of Ethnic Foods, 4*(4), 232–235. https://doi.org/10.1016/j.jef.2017.10.005

Raden, A. Z., & Qeis, M. I. (2017). Typography and local culture how local values influence Batik label design in Yogyakarta and Surakarta. https://doaj.org/article/8d40a4b345da40b2bd59f49eeecca87f

Ricklefs, M. C. (2001). *A history of modern Indonesia since c.1200 (third).* Palgrave Macmillan.

Ruastiti, Ni Made. (2011). The concept of local genius in Balinese performing arts. *MUDRA Journal of Art and Culture, 26*(3), 241–245.

Sani, M. R., Alia, M. N., & Riyadi, D. (2016). Sate Padang Sumatera Barat Sebagai Gastronomi Unggulan di Indonesia. *Gastronomy Tourism, 3*(1), 274–282. http://ejournal.upi.edu/index.php/gastur/article/view/3640/2594

Sihombing, D. (2015). *Tipografi dalam Desain Grafis (Revisi).* Gramedia Pustaka Utama.

Silva Gouveia, A. P., Lena Farias, P., & Souza Gatto, P. (2009). Letters and cities: Reading the urban environment with the help of perception theories. *Visual Communication, 8*(3), 339–348. https://doi.org/10.1177/1470357209106474

Stark, A. (2013). The matrilineal system of the Minangkabau and its persistence throughout history: A structural perspective. *Southeast Asia: A Multidisciplinary Journal, 13*(1), 1–13.

Strizver, I. (2013). *Type Rules: The designer's guide to professional typography.* John Wiley & Sons.

Wijana, I. D. P. (2018). Semantic relations of soto headed attributive noun phrases in Indonesian. *International Journal of Languages, Literature and Linguistics, 4*(4), 251–255. https://doi.org/10.18178/IJLLL.2018.4.4.182

Yeganeh, H. (2020). Salient cultural transformations in the age of globalization: Implications for business and management. *International Journal of Sociology and Social Policy, 40*(7/8), 695–712. https://doi.org/10.1108/IJSSP-02-2020-0030

Yudhistira, B., & Fatmawati, A. (2020). Diversity of Indonesian soto. *Journal of Ethnic Foods, 7*(1), 27. https://doi.org/10.1186/s42779-020-00067-z

19

Epilogue: Sustainability, 'Sejahtera' and the South East Asian Continuum

Dzulkifli Abdul Razak

Eco-urbanism, derived from a term that denotes a rising movement or the ideation of ecological urbanism, is a new approach to cities. Mostafavi and Doherty (2016), of the Harvard School of Design, treat eco-urbanism as a critical theory and design praxis that can propel the twenty-first century onwards based on the premise that *"… an ecological approach is urgently needed both as a remedial device for the contemporary city and an organizing principle for new cities."* In her *'Ecological Urbanism: The Nature of the City',* Hagan (2014) highlighted a similar role, defined by a convergence of 'culture' and 'nature', to reconstitute a new urbanism, particularly the need to depart from the technological focus of the 1990s and the present day. In a movement towards redefining urban design and architectural praxis in a diachronic partnership with the natural world, the role of cultural inflections, sociocultural ethos and bioclimatic mimicry is crucial. In an era of climate change, urbanisation and ecology must be melded with culture in order to reinstate the role of ecology and

D. A. Razak (✉)
International Islamic University Malaysia, Jalan Gombak, Malaysia

site-specific design within the city. Hagan (2014) reiterates that the eco-logical narrative and its 'embryonic modes of practice' must be fused with 'the narratives of urbanism and its older, deeply embedded modes of practice'. This combined ethos of the melding of art and science has implications for cities and will impact their metabolic as well as social and formal dimensions, and Hagan explores the extent to which environmental engineering and natural systems design can and should become drivers for the remaking of cities in the twenty-first century.

Eco-Urbanist Cities of South East Asian Memory

It is the archipelagic nature of South East Asian cities, which historically evolved along the littoral region near seas or river coasts. These cities are of varied scales, layered upon the urban *negeri* (or maritime) based settlements, which made their historical and traditional forms and patterns close to that of the local ecology. Following the gradual disappearance of the *nagara* ceremonial centres and civilisations by the thirteenth to fourteenth centuries, Miksic (2018) described the parallel rise of 'heterogenetic' cities, i.e. centres of settlements which tend to be located at junctions of trade routes and whose morphologies and layouts have been perceived as disorderly, dense and organic. Yet as this book suggests, on closer study, they contain common shared patterns, themes and theories which can be brought into an overall framework of sustainable urbanism which arises as a perfect fit with their context.

Miksic (2018) asserts that classic South East Asian languages had no word for *city*. Complex settlement patterns did exist, but Seasian employed different factors in classifying settlements. The word *nagara* in Sanskrit, according to Miksic (2018), carries two meanings. Combining traditions in both present-day Malaysia and Indonesia, it originally and primordially referred to either a temple with a ground plan which has square ends or a royal capital. The term was sometimes spelled *nagari*, which, according to Munoz (2006), implies the presence of a palace, a *pura* or *puri*. Both come from the Vedic word *pur*, meaning 'rampart' or 'fort'. With reference to Java, Stutterheim defined the walled palace complex as a *puri* and referred to the inner palace where the ruler lived. For example, the fourteenth-century Java poem "Desavarnana" uses both *pura* and *puri* interchangeably. The word *nagara* is defined in most Sanskrit-English dictionaries as 'town'. In Seasia, the word evolved into many local variants. The *nagara* in fourteenth-century Java meant a walled palace complex and its immediate surroundings, as in Cambodia. A fourteenth-century Javanese court text suggests that this was a criterion for defining a *nagara*: 'What is called the *nagara*? All where one can go out (of his compound) without passing through paddy fields.' In Indonesia, especially in the Desavarnani, in a fourteenth-century poem about the capital of Majapahit, *nagara* referred to compounds of the ruler or other nobles, usually walled, and others where relatives and high officials lived. People who lived in the *nagara* of Majapahit included artisans, possibly wage-earners independent of patrons, thus forming a kind of floating population. *Nagara* is contrasted with *desa* or *pradesa*, meaning a non-urban district and with *thani*, peasants' cultivated land or rural settlement.

The Concept of Sejahtera

Interestingly, the concept of *sejahtera* (Dzulkifli, 2018, 2020) is predicated on the same, yet slightly different, theoretical and operational premise. *Sejahtera* comes from the Malay language and carries a positive connotation of abundance, happiness, prosperity, peace and tranquility. It is a multi-layered concept that conveys a deeper meaning than any single word can convey. As such, it has no equivalence in other languages, nor can it be accurately translated into different languages owing to its close cultural embeddedness and nuances in the local tradition. Likewise, the Japanese word *ikigai* has a special meaning, as does *ubuntu* for Africans or *lagom* for Swedes. They are indigenous terms that convey culturally laden values that act as an innate compass to direct them to a balanced way of life. *Lagom* means 'just the right amount'—i.e. adequate, or enough as a guiding principle to a sustainable lifestyle. *Ikigai*, a sense of purpose representing value, well-being and moderate living. *Ubuntu* refers to "humanity" and is translated as 'I am because we are'. In essence, it is a word that represents 'the middle way' in navigating and nurturing life in a sustainable way embracing all humans. These terms are not limited to the regional or national dimensions because they speak of the interconnectedness of people. The concept they embody is far superior because it involves real life and real people interacting in the real world.

With this development, the philosophy and concept of *sejahtera* created a historic milestone given its vision of 'co-existence' and alignment with 'collaborative relationships' located in a US$20 million eco-park on a 200,000 square metre natural location in the Municipality of Tongyeong, in the southern part of the Republic of Korea (Dzulkifli et al., 2018). In this connection, the concept has evolved into a regional and international concept with the establishment in 2011 of the Sejahtera Centre and Sejahtera Forest in the southern part of the Republic of Korea. The forest is particularly meaningful not only because it is next to a national park, but more so because it is also a 'living laboratory' that embellishes 'the unique traditional culture of the Asia-Pacific region with an emphasis on coexistence'. Indeed, this is well summed up by the vision of the Sejahtera Project: *"Coexistence between human beings, man and nature, present and future generations."* There is no doubt that the bold initiative of 'collaborative relationship' rooted in the deeper meaning and philosophy of *sejahtera* will enlighten future generations. As stressed by UNESCO (2014), 'Sustainable development cannot be achieved by technological solutions, political regulation or financial instruments alone. We need to change the way we think and act. This requires quality education and learning for sustainable development at all levels and in all social contexts.' In this case, it naturally blends in the vision of 'coexistence' between humans and nature in a balanced way. The Sejahtera Project also comprises an eco-park and a creative research and teaching centre. Recognized by the United Nations University in Tokyo, it became the UN Regional Centre of Expertise on Education for Sustainable Development. Within it, not only are policies crafted, but participants and members learn to live in a total *sejahtera* community and continuum—practicing total walkability, living in a total recycling loop, with zero-plastic waste, celebrating only biodegradable consumables, a responsible approach to consumerism and a responsible eco-footprint, yet representing the minimum expectations of an urban way of life, but founded and predicated upon a value-structure and foundation of zero harm to the environment. A parallel citizen-based initiative to organically grow a Sejahtera Leadership Initiative (SLI) based on the SPICES model (see Fig. 19.1) complements regional and international organisations, including universities, and leverages its participation beyond Malaysia in a leadership position.

SPICES describes the positive attitudes and understanding of sustainability issues with respect to the use of resources, conservation of the environment and the maintenance of balance and harmony that goes beyond the 3Ps (people, planet and profit) of sustainability. Periodic reinforcement of the internalisation process as part of the 'learning by doing' towards sustainability ensures the success of the strategy. Without doubt, 'relationship' (or co-existence) is an important concept in making *sejahtera* work, taking the cultural context and nuances into account. Collaborative relationship in particular embraces compassion, empathy and the uncompromising spirit of oneness transcending differences and bitterness, bringing about much needed close relationships, co-existence and interdependency.

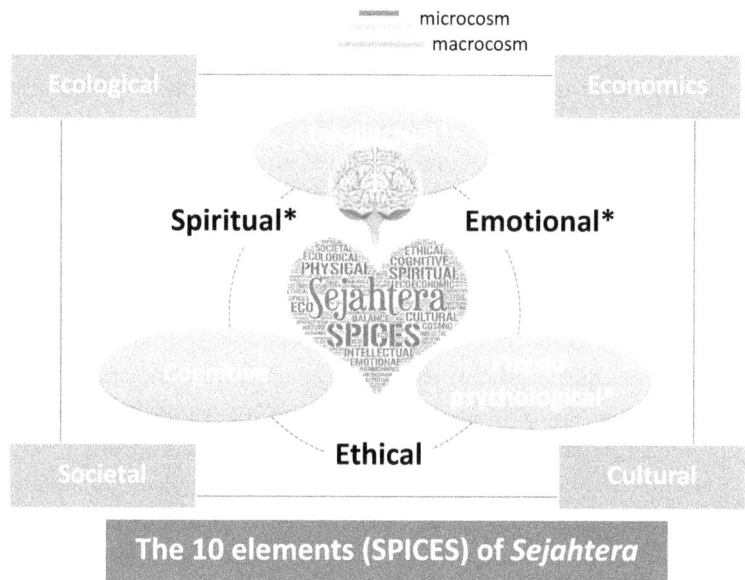

Fig. 19.1   SPICES Model

The ultimate character of a town or centre must be read as a whole, so urban design is the accretion or accumulation of various elements—at different scales—that impinge upon the visual and sensory perceptions of urban dwellers and, consequently, affect relationships between people and the built and natural environment. The past heritage of this region and its built environment include buildings and streets, and the natural environment includes features such as sea views, coastlines, shorelines, roof profiles, facades and shapes—all of which have evolved in a natural unfolding, with some surviving and others being decimated. It is time these values, themes and praxes be incorporated into present planning and urban design policies, which are lacking in this region, due to our extensive orientation as a result of historical colonisation. For it to be comprehensive and thus present a local framework, its terminology must reverberate into citywide urban design recommendations, which are highly necessary to ensure that the built environment continues to contribute the qualities that essentially differentiate a sustainable city.

The concept of *sejahtera* recalls a network of human communities and a conurbation of the past, within which smaller communities are linked into a large thriving metropolis. These types of network can again be reframed in the present and future, as the virtual and the physical become layers within the future city that need to come together—virtually and physically—as a community acting in the best interest of the environment and for the future. The fabric of the future city must again evoke the values of the traditional continuum, yet embodying universal, multicultural modern values and efficiencies of the future. Spirituality, in the ethos of a city embodying *sejahtera*, does not overlook the spiritual or the soul; it eschews the dualistic ways of modern outlooks but still considers important the need to understand in comprehensive manners and methods the technological and empirical concepts of modernisation. *Sejahtera* transcends eco-urbanism ideas of the present for it combines the innate human need for basic values and spirituality. Thus, buildings, symbols and structures go beyond mere function and must recall such needs as those which in traditional times were expressed in ornamental creations and symbolic embellishment, which constitute the perennial search for values and the connection with the human soul. In the past, the palace and the mosque were traditionally built and yet historically expressed in such terms; in modern life, this must again be reconstructed and recelebrated.

Traditionally, the past city and future *sejahtera* communities celebrate the centre as an inversion of today's cities; their centres were, and should be, green lungs and green centres, free from pollution and urban heat, with spaces for walking, cycling and being in the shade. Key structures and public spaces are designed as conduits of health, as they were, and should be located in proximity and close to each other. Historically, South East Asian cities grew at littoral locations, benefiting from sea and river breezes. In the public spaces of today, water is crucial, and it not only cools but is physically and psychologically soothing, a means of overcoming rising mental stress in cities. These should be how they once were built, spaces which have constant connections with nature, looking onto and into the existing ecology and trees, bordering water bodies, lakes and rivers. Historically in South East Asia, these were the locations of the accumulations and accretions of trading stalls, structures and associated commercial spaces including links with nearby colonnaded public promenades and aristocratic structures. More than merely a port and a fort, the Kota Melaka, both a city and a state at the same time, grew from a maritime point strategically located midway between 'the turn of two monsoonal winds' and at the mouth of a large navigational river and deltaic plain, allowing ships to easily navigate and birth. Both river and hill became a natural defensive tool bordering the 'royal' site; cooled by orchards and breezes, its axially organized and green core opened into a multicultural commercial area, linked by visual pathways of a direct administrative apparatus and support structures. Similarly, the more structured, more axial character of cities such as the original old cities of Kota Bahru, Kelantan, Kuala Terengganu and Pontianak, Kalimantan, located inland along the banks of rivers and coastlines and once surrounded by rice-producing land, had been planned axially to face the river to the west and towards the direction of the, surrounded by *kerabat* houses to the north, the *masjid* with *madrasah* on its side and *padang* in front of it, and to the north the *pondok* and the local population.

Historically, the city's public realm had always included spaces along the water's edge from the river and the *padang* finger out north and south into pathways shaded by trees and bounded by fences and interfacing typologies. Its urban public realm occupies the open spaces that link the district components, and the water's edge was originally dotted by large trees to provide shade. Historically, and generally, the urban realm incorporates greenery to a high level, allowing the continuous experience of shade and shaded comfort amidst the tropical yet salubrious experience from permeable spaces to walkways. For example, tree-lined pathways allow the experience of dappled tropical light, but within the comfort conditions required in outdoor tropical scenarios. Rivers and streams are major components of the city's identity, so a given terrain creates a variety of views to, from and, in some instances, between significant resources. Such conditions demand that several aspects occur simultaneously, i.e. proximity to water, coolness in hill valleys, constant shade and overhanging greenery. This is because it is necessary to have simultaneous impacts of visual, thermal and optical factors from the surroundings to enable all parameters linked to comfort to conflate with the social, spiritual, physical and environmental elements of the surroundings to prompt visitors to remark on such conditions. The tropics are a region with a very intense climate; though shade is needed, the experience itself must combine rain, sun and light, with the experience of coolness in order to create variation. These were described vividly by many travelers of the past era and they contain experiences of elements of air, water and light, including monsoonal storms and breaking sunlight.

As Professor Ahmad Murad Merican aptly highlighted in his keynote speech at Universiti Sains Malaysia (USM's) exhibition of Malay architecture (2018), these underlying values can also be encapsulated by the word *budi* in the Malay language. *Budi* is both in its seed and nexus, in the vernacular house forms, and it can be translated into urban and city form. The *kampong* is the essence, the physical embodiment of *budi*. It is architectural and expressive yet naturally grew from the ecology of the region. This seed of *budi* was further expanded, elevated and evolved into the symbolic and monumental structures in past cities. *Sejahtera* is framed in the indigenous concept of *hati budi* and *akal budi*, which resonates closely with the scientific idea of 'heart-brain' discovered recently. This at once makes Sejahtera Leadership unique in its understanding and approach to leadership (namely *kepemimpinan*). Thus, *sejahtera* is not easily rendered into other languages because of its comprehensive and multi-layered meaning and nuances. It underscores that indigenous knowledge and wisdom have had their own uniqueness, strength and relevance for the local community over the years. Although it is often translated as 'well-being' or even 'prosperity', its inherent meaning is much more than that. In fact, it is 'beyond well-being'. It is human-centric in that it spans the macrocosmic–microcosmic nexus. It is macrocosmic because it relates humans to the external environment—nature and fellow beings, including other species. It is microcosmic because it embraces the 'self' and the inner (esoteric) dimensions, including spiritual consciousness.

The urban form, founded upon a *budi* or goodness or a 'service' to the environment, is much akin to a form of ruralised city design, which has disappeared, where visitors, dwellers and travelers could not differentiate the boundaries between nature and development. These forms must again reflect the crafted nature of past urban design and is presently conspicuously absent in newly planned cities. These heritage-based associated urban forms represent highly sustainable entities and may even be said to recall a form of bio-urbanist 'urban vernacular' whose forms are a total conflation of nature, symbol and function and whose roots stem from the symbolic fusion of human-and-nature as a model or type.

Conclusion

The advent of the age of the Anthropocene (as attested by Bonneuil [2016]) has instigated and propelled debates across the world on the urgent need for a drastic revamping of developmental and design paradigms and frameworks. These and earlier efforts and ideas have initiated movements, such as green urbanism, eco-cities and, more recently, bio-urbanism and bio-philia, which recall past convergences between man and nature. Proponents of the bioregionalist position have studied the sustainable characteristics, yet these must be localized and a return to a study of the forms of the past, and the climatic forms and the vernacular should consolidate into a more ecological and yet indigenised perspective and themes needed for the new developments. 'Eco-urbanism' is a deep sustainability paradigm that recalls the ecologically elevated city patterns of the past, and one could argue that these have shown the same eco-urbanist consistency across the scales of development, i.e. throughout a study of planning, architecture and ornamentation. *Sejahtera* is a local concept with similar shared themes and character that form an ecological matrix with typo-morphologies that can enhance present urban centres and guide future development. These quasi-urban sites recall the notion of the tropical principles that can be traced back to ancient local cosmography and present principles of ecological development. It is argued that the outcome of this book can be reconstituted into a tropicalised and bio-urbanist design framework and broad guidelines that may contribute to reversing the deleterious effects of rampant development. Eco-urbanism reflects a regionalised model with a bio-mimesis type of urban core and urban form—thus highlighting themes of ecological design that can return the city and urban life to a highly sustainable entity combining both nature and development and, thus, reconciling man and nature and the essential role of heritage cities of the past in the quest and agenda for future sustainability.

References

Bonneuil, C. (2016). *The shock of the Anthropocene: The earth, history and us.* Verso Books.

Hagan, S. (2014). *Ecological urbanism: the nature of the city.* Routledge.

Hans-Dieter Evers, Rüdiger Korf. (2000). *Southeast Asian Urbanism: The Meaning and Power of Social Space.* LIT Verlag Münster.

Miksic, J. (2018). Khao Sam Kaeo: An Early Port-City between the Indian Ocean and the South China Sea ed. by Berenice Bellina. Journal of the Malaysian Branch of the Royal Asiatic Society, 91(2), 155-159.

Mostafavi, M., & Doherty, G. (Eds.). (2016). *Ecological urbanism.* Zurich: Lars Müller.

Munoz, P. M. (2006). *Early kingdoms of the Indonesian Archipelago and the Malay Peninsula.* Didier Millet, Csi.

Razak, D. A. (2020). *Essay On Sejahtera: Concept, Principle and Practice.* IIUM PRESS.

Razak, D. A., Khaw, N. R., Baharom, Z., Mutalib, M. A., & Salleh, H. M. (2018). Decolonising the Paradigm of Sustainable Development through the Traditional Concept of Sejahtera. In *Academia and Communities–Engaging for Change: Learning contributions of Regional Centres of Expertise on Education for Sustainable Development* (pp. 209–219). Tokyo: United Nations University–Institute for the Advanced Study of Sustainability.

UNESCO. (2014). Global action programme on education for sustainable development.

Index[1]

---

[1] Note: Page numbers followed by 'n' refer to notes.